As Told at The Explorers Club

VOLUME I: THE EXPLORERS CLUB CLASSICS SERIES

As Told at The Explorers Club

MORE THAN FIFTY
GRIPPING TALES OF ADVENTURE

Edited and with an Introduction by George Plimpton

THE LYONS PRESS
Guilford, Connecticut
AN IMPRINT OF THE GLOBE PEQUOT PRESS

The Lyons Press is an imprint of The Globe Pequot Press

Designed by Casey Shain

ISBN 1-59228-035-8

10 9 8 7 6 5 4 3 2

Library of Congress Cataloging-in-Publication Data is available on file.

Acknowledgments

As Told at The Explorers Club is the first volume in the Classic Series under The Explorers Club imprint. Published on the eve of our Centennial Year, this collection of stories and articles selected from our past publications is a tribute to tales told around the long table and to the spirit of exploration.

Support and inspiration for establishing the imprint came from the President of The Explorers Club, Richard Wiese, and from Jay Cassell and Tony Lyons of The Lyons Press. Thanks also go to Clare Flemming, Curator of Research Collections, for providing access to the records in her care, and to Janet Baldwin, former Librarian and Curator of Collections, who suggested reprinting our own stories for this inaugural edition.

Club members who were essential to this endeavor are George Plimpton who took time from his own writing to give professional guidance, George Gowen, Catherine Nixon Cooke, and Gary Hermalyn.

Lindley Kirksey
Explorers Club Imprint

Dedication

As Told At The Explorers Club is dedicated to our founding fathers who in 1904 had the foresight to form The Explorers Club.

Frank M. Chapman
Curator of Birds and Mammals, American Museum of Natural History

Caspar Whitney
Author; Editor, *Outing Magazine*; War Correspondent [Spanish-American], *Harpers Weekly*

Marshall H. Saville
Professor of American Archaeology, Columbia University; Curator of Archaeology, American Museum of Natural History

Hershel C. Parker
Professor of Physics, Columbia University; mountaineer; author; founding member of the American Alpine Club

David L. Brainard
U.S. Army Lieut.-Colonel: Sioux, Bannock, & Nez Perce Campaigns; Survivor, Lady Franklin Bay Expedition (1881–84); in 1882 claimed furthest north at 83 degrees, 24 minutes, 30 seconds north latitude

Henry Collins Walsh
Journalist; historian; explorer of Central America and Greenland; founding member of the Arctic Club of America

Frederick A. Cook
Surgeon and ethnologist to the first Peary Expedition; leader of the SS *Miranda* Expedition (1894); surgeon on the *Belgica* Expedition [with Amundsen, first ship to overwinter in the Antarctic, 1897–98]

Richard C. Wiese
President of The Explorers Club
June 17, 2003

Contents

Foreword

This volume is comprised of true-life stories by members of The Explorers Club, surely the preeminent organization of its kind. The contents have been selected from three previously published works. The first (1931) was titled *Told at The Explorers Club*, with the subtitle "True Tales of Modern Exploration." The second volume (1936) was titled *Explorers Club Tales*, with a somewhat longer subtitle, "True Stories of Exploration, Research and Adventure as Told at The Explorers Club by Men of Daring and Achievement." The third volume (1941) did not require a subtitle since its title was thought to be all-inclusive: *Through Hell and High Water*. A fourth volume was planned but was becalmed because of World War II and never published. Contents from it appear here, as well as selections from *The Explorers Journal*, whose first number appeared in 1921.

The present volume goes back to the subtitle tradition: "More than Fifty Gripping Tales of Adventure." (There are actually fifty-one). In a sense it is odd that there are any at all. An oft-quoted sentiment states that explorers would much prefer their expeditions to be free of anything that might constitute an "adventure." Vilhjalmur Stefansson, a former president of the Explorers, remarked upon it quite candidly: "Adventures are a mark of incompetence." Andre Gide once mourned, "The drawback to a journey that has been too well-planned is that it does not leave enough room for adventure." One of the stories in this collection (by Roy Chapman Andrews, also a past president of the Club) starts off, "I am averse to writing about adventures, for I dislike them. They interfere with work and disrupt carefully laid plans."

Fortunately, as we know from Robert Burns's "To a Mouse": "The best laid schemes o'mice and men /Gang aft a-glay;/ An 'eave us naught but grief an pain,/ For promis'd joy."

In what follows, the range of catastrophes is considerable: two airplane crashes, one of them Charles Lindbergh's, forced to bail out somewhere over the midwest; there are tales of serious troubles at sea, among them Leonard Outhwaite's "Biscay Gales" and Edward Weyer's "Compass that Talked"; Horace Ashton writes about being lost inside the earth, and Warren King Morehead's story is titled simply enough, "Buried Alive." Catastrophe is flirted with in Jean-Marc Boivin's "Hang-Gliding on K-2," Glenn Porzak on climbing Mt. Everest, and in Curtis and Kathleen Saville's accounts of rowing across the Atlantic and the Pacific Oceans. There are thrilling rescues— Burt M. McConnell's "Rescued from the Death Trap of the Arctic"—even tips on how to survive while awaiting rescue: Stefansson explains that to sleep in the snow, long thought to be fatal, is not, and poses the question, is it all right to eat snow? Answer: yes.

As would be predictable with exploration, confrontations with animals often occur—Anthony Fiala with bears, Mervyn Cowie with lions, Herbert F. Schwarz with an army of ants; and in a lovely turnabout, C. Suydam Cutting writes not about hunting cheetah but hunting with them—cheetahs belonging to a 300-pound maharajah who keeps pet lions, tigers, and sloth bears.

There are chapters that are scientific in nature: on the okapi, the king cobra. Historical: on Hannibal's elephants, on Sitting Bull's death. Controversial: Amundsen on Stefansson, Stefansson on Amundsen. Speculative: Was there cannibalism amongst the survivors of Sir John Franklin's expedition? Does the Yeti exist? Thomas Baker Slick thinks it does.

All this, and, as the advertisers say, much more.

Readers will note that the stories from *Through Hell and High Water* are prefaced by introductory remarks from the book's editor, very much as if someone sitting at what is referred to in the Club's histories as "The Long Table" had leaned forward to still the general conversation and called upon a member with an interesting story to tell.

A word about the Club itself and its "Long Table": On May 28, 1904, fifty men well-known in exploration circles met at a dinner at the Aldine Association and decided to organize a club with its object to unite explorers in the bonds of good fellowship and to promote the work of exploration. The initiation fee to join this worthy cause was ten dollars, five dollars for non-residents, and the annual dues were twenty dollars for residents and just five for non-residents. Despite these come-hitherly low sums, the membership was small, meetings irregular and sparsely attended, largely because the Club did not have its own quarters. This was rectified in 1912 when the Club took over an empty loft at 345 Amsterdam Avenue. Here the social activity increased to such a degree that in 1922 the Club purchased a townhouse at 47 West 76th. In 1928, both solvent and popular, the Club leased an eight-story building, hoping to pay off the investment by renting out five stories of bedrooms. The membership turned out to be better explorers than landlords; the lease was terminated, and the Club moved twice more, finally settling into a building at 10 West 72nd opposite the Dakota House.

The Club there has been described as having a distinctive smell one detected on coming through the front door—"a savour of carpets and camels and musk . . . a beguiling pungent aroma, not too pervading . . . "

Every afternoon at four o'clock members on hand in the clubhouse sat around an oaken table in the lounge where tea, coffee, and light refreshments were served without charge. Because the Club's social activity centered there—where members told their stories, compared notes, and planned future expeditions—the table became known as the "Long Table of Fellowship." One felicitous phrase states that "around the Long Table one hears the names Shanghai, London, Rio de Janeiro and Lima but only as stopovers on the way to Tatsienlu, Kuressaare, the Matto Grosso or Machu Pichu."

For many years the dean at the Long Table was Dr. Franklin P. Lynch, known mainly for his explorations in the Congo. He presided not only over those seated at the table but also over a "toast-making machine" which apparently failed him on many occasions, indeed so often that a kind of identification code among Explorers Club members meeting in the field was to refer to Dr. Lynch's burnt toast.

Also at the Long Table was a Scotsman named Seamus (Gaelic for James), The Chief of Clannfhearghuis of Stra-chur, known simply (and for obvious reason) as The Chief. Outfitted in his country's military uniform—tartan, sporran, dirk, and so forth—and carrying a silver-headed cane, he was

a familiar figure at Club proceedings. In conversation he was fond of inter-
spersing appropriate sayings or snatches of verse in Gaelic which he would
then translate into English. I would think this a somewhat annoying trait
frankly, to be easing through a tale of misfortune in the Congo, say, at the
Long Table, and have the chief suddenly offer a comment in Gaelic, even
if quickly translated into English. But he was beloved apparently, and much
admired.

I have seen a photograph of the Long Table, four gentlemen sitting
rather stiffly at it, as if told not to budge by a photographer. Against the wall
behind them is the great curve of an elephant tusk, various animal heads and
Club flags. No sign of Francis Lynch's famous "toast-making machine." In
the foreground is a little four-wheeled trolley carrying a box from which rises
a bare tree with an African gray parrot perched on a branch. Legend has it
that the parrot greeted a number of members by name.

In 1965 the Club moved yet again, to its present quarters at 46 East 70th,
the former townhouse of the coats and threads magnate Stephen C. Clark.
These days the passing on of stories and so on, continuing the tradition of the
Long Table, often takes place on the occasional Thursday evenings when a
lecture is scheduled. The members meet in the Library on the second floor,
one end of which is graced by a large oil painting depicting the moment on
Sunday, June 22, 1884, when Lt. A.W. Greely's party was rescued by men from
the U.S.S. *Thetis* and U.S.S. *Bear*. Under it is an Elizabethan oaken table that
on lecture nights is covered with a white table cloth upon which rest the in-
gredients to loosen the members' tongues and give rise to what Mark Twain
used to refer to as "stretchers"—flights of imagination that push a story to the
edge of belief and sometimes beyond. Alas, a gray parrot perched on its
portable cage is not on the premises but there is a stuffed polar bear the members pass on the way across the hall to the lecture in the Clark ballroom with
its massive walk-in fireplace. The Clark's considerable art collection that
hung on its walls (I have been told there was a Picasso in the Club's eleva-
tor) was given away, half of it to the Metropolitan, the other to Yale
University. Now the walls display Explorers Club memorabilia, in particular

the framed flags carried on notable expeditions by Explorers Club members—Roy Chapman Andrews' trip to the Gobi desert in 1925, Thor Heyerdahl's voyage on the *Kon-Tiki* in 1947, as well as flags carried on the Space Crafts *Apollo* 8 and 15.

The two rooms on the second floor not only hold pictorial evidence of what the membership has done in the past, but surely they provide a "Long Table" atmosphere conducive to throat-clearing and the start of a tale of adventure. In the old days listeners at the Long Table would call out at the end of a story, "It's a crying shame that isn't written down."

Here they have been . . .

George Plimpton
August 7, 2003
New York City, New York

PART ONE

Africa

The Ghosts of Ngulia

BY MERVYN COWIE

D o you believe in ghosts? Well, I don't either, but I have to admit that certain things happen in most unexpected ways, and forever defy any logical explanation. Some years ago I had a long tussle with ghosts and I eventually had to accept defeat. It all started and finished with lions. Let me tell you how it developed.

Three of us—Ken Beaton, Tabs Taberer, and myself—planned to find a new route from Amboseli to the Tsavo River in Kenya—not a great distance, but difficult because of the extremely friable nature of the volcanic soil, and frequent barriers caused by lava flows. We set off from Amboseli in a truck, with enough food and water for a week, intending to pitch our tents at various places along the way, and explore a possible road alignment on foot. Ken and Tabs were old-time hunters before they joined me in the National Parks Service, so among the three of us we had a good working knowledge of big game and bush lore. We were supported by three very experienced African Rangers.

The going was rough and slow. At many places we had to build make-shift causeways to get the truck across the gulleys. It was stiflingly hot and huge black storm clouds gathered to the East. We pressed on, making only about five miles in an hour, until we all felt it was time to camp for the night. The heavy clouds closed in around us with the astonishing speed of a tropical thunderstorm, leaving only enough time to gather in a good supply of fire wood. We huddled inside the truck and watched the deluge and the water surging down the valleys.

It was almost dark when the rain stopped. We tried to move the truck to higher ground, where it would be better for pitching tents, but this proved to be hopeless. The wheels dug deeply into the soft mud and in a few yards the truck was well and truly stuck.

We were tired and had run out of daylight, so we put our camp beds on an outcrop of rock, near the truck, and hoped that it would not rain again during the night. Two of the Rangers, wisely perhaps, bedded down on top of the tents and equipment inside the truck; while the third—the driver—chose to sleep on the seat in the cab.

After a welcome mug of hot soup, we settled in for what we hoped would be a peaceful night. We were glad to have the dry logs, collected before the storm, to make a good fire, ostensibly to keep marauding lions away, but also for good cheer. A camp without a fire is eerie and lifeless.

We had all tucked in and some stars were glistening to the East—a good sign for a fair night. There was no moon. The air was clean and cool after the rain, moving gently through the trees, with the scent of acacia flowers and damp soil. I thought then, as I have many times before, how impressive the silence of the African night is—broken only by the sound of crickets, and the metallic "chink-chink" of the frogs, and the soothing little "purr" of a Scops owl.

I had already dozed off when something startled me. There was no sound. Even the crickets and frogs were silent, but I had a sinister feeling. I felt that some ominous ogre was moving into the camp. I tried to dismiss these thoughts as nonsense. A bit tired after a long day, I told myself to shut up and get to sleep.

As I peeped across at the flickering fire I distinctly saw a form moving through the shadows, just beyond the fringe of light—then another, and another. I sat up, hardly daring to admit that a cold shiver was running up and down my back.

The forms drew nearer, and in a way, I was relieved to see that they were lions and not ogres. I watched as they closed in towards the fire. Obviously curious and surprised to find people sleeping out in the open, I thought. Lions are much more aggressive at night than in daylight, and so I was not unduly concerned. But then they moved in between our beds and the fire. This was alarming. Lions in this district were known to be fierce but not man-eaters. I didn't like their attitude. They were getting uncomfortably near our beds.

I gave a shout to wake Ken and Tabs, and the leading lioness snarled and came closer. By now we could clearly see that there were seven, all apparently lionesses, although two were large enough to be maneless males—a curious feature which is not unusual in the lions of Tsavo.

The situation had now become dangerous. All the usual deterrents such as fire and noise had absolutely no effect. Ken, who was also alarmed, gave a tremendous shout. This was a signal to the nearest lionesses to crouch down, ready for a spring. Tabs looked round behind him to see another stalking him from about twenty feet.

The Rangers in the truck, who were peeping out through an opening in the tarpaulin, shouted warnings to us. The driver in the cab put on the headlights. Although the lions were not directly in the beam the extra light helped us to see better and to realize that we were about to be deliberately attacked by seven determined lions.

Tabs grabbed his rifle and fired a shot over the head of the stalking lioness. I fired a shot over the leading lioness on my side, and we both fired more shots, still determined not to shoot at one of these animals. It was our fundamental duty to protect them but it seemed a strange back-to-front ideal, when we needed all the protection we could get from the lions. But not one of us was yet convinced that these lions would actually spring and carry us off. In later years I realized how wrong we had been.

The first few shots made the lions jump back, but not without some sinister growls and snarls. Ken had left his gun in the truck, but Tabs and I went on firing. The noise of these big guns, in the silence of the night, was terrific. The huge booms echoed miles across the valley, and up towards Kilimanjaro, the snow-capped summit of which could be seen silhouetted against the stars. This was too much for the lions, and they reluctantly retreated, but not far. We could still see their pale forms moving about on the fringe of the firelight.

After some pointed comments about lions in general, especially this pride of seven, which appeared to behave like their ancestors, the famous Man-Eaters of Tsavo, we decided to retreat into the back of the truck. This

offered some protection, with its high sides and canvas cover. Moving ourselves, and our blankets, within easy range of these aggressive lions, however,
presented a problem. We knew that activity and sudden movement might
easily provoke the lions to attack.

We worked out a plan where one of us would move the bedding while
the other two kept guard with the rifles. Sure enough, the movement enticed
the lions to go down into a stalking position and creep towards us. More
shots, some hitting just near the leading lions, kept them at bay until we were
all huddled in the truck. It was stuffy, and there was not much room for five
of us on top of the tents, but it was preferable to being out on a camp bed, a
few feet from seven snarling lions.

We had stoked the fire with the few pieces of dry wood that remained,
and we watched to see what the lions would do. They lost no time in moving
right up to the truck, and even sniffing at the tailboard. I heard them padding
round and round until finally they gave up and silence returned—except for
some manly snores from Tabs and one of the Rangers. I concluded that there
must be at least two kinds of lions: those that are afraid of people and a fire
in a camp, and those that are not. We all agreed that we had never encountered such determined lions, and we had to accept that we had been in a
mighty risky situation. In the bright light of a lovely sunrise, it seemed that
the horrors of the night had been a bad nightmare, but the footprints were
there, all around our beds, to tell the story of what had happened, and what
might have happened.

It took most of the morning to get the truck out of the mud and move it
onto harder ground. By late afternoon we had not progressed more than a
mere ten miles, having had to make many detours to avoid soft hollows of volcanic ash, now looking like thick gravy. We camped on hard ground; this
time putting up a tent for shelter, in case of more rain. The night was cool
and silent and we all turned in early.

Again I sensed the same sinister feeling of something untoward. The
flaps of the tent were open and I had quite a good field of vision, past the fire
and towards a ridge of lava rocks. We had taken various precautions, in case

of more lion trouble, although not one of us believed we would see the same lions again, as it was about ten miles from our previous camp, and much more, if they followed our wheel tracks.

But they were there—the same seven lions, creeping towards us and snarling. What the hell. I shook Ken and Tabs to wake them, and said "Here we go again." Ken let out some pretty pointed remarks about lions and all kinds of ungrateful wild animals. Tabs was even more outspoken, while he was feeling for his rifle next to his bed. I said something about them being the same seven lions and shouted for the truck headlights to be put on. The lights were well aimed and Ken agreed that they were the same lions, with the two larger ones that could be males. We both whispered our utter astonishment that these lions had followed us so far and so quickly.

Tabs checked that his gun was loaded, and stood up to start firing. He peered past the fire and said, "Where are they?" I looked and Ken looked, and there was nothing to be seen. Nothing stirred. We all remained silent for what seemed a long time, but there were no lions. Tabs then told us what he thought of bastards who have silly dreams. Ken and I assured him that we were properly awake, sober, and relatively intelligent people, but we had to admit that there were no lions. They had vanished.

We all went out of the tent and had a thorough look around. There was nothing to be seen or heard. Tabs scorned us all the more. I appealed to the three Rangers in the truck. Two confirmed that they had clearly seen the lions, that they were the same seven, and were aggressive. The third Ranger, who was in the cab, and who had switched on the headlights when Ken and I clearly identified the lions, said he had not seen anything. Putting on the lights established that he was awake and watching when we were looking at the lions, and yet he was adamant that nothing was there. And so the score was that four of us had seen the lions well enough to count and identify them, while the other two said we had been dreaming—sheer imagination.

We watched and we argued. Ken and I were so certain of every detail, leading up to the moment when we identified the lions as being the same frightening seven that tried to molest us the night before, that Tabs eventually accepted that we were right. Strange, we all said, how quickly they all vanished, and we debated long into the night why they had been suddenly scared away. The crickets chirped, and a hyaena wailed mournfully in the far distance. I lay awake filled with ponderous thoughts, trying to work out events which could not be explained.

In the bright light of a golden sunrise we carefully inspected the damp ground. *There were no footprints,* not even within a radius of two hundred yards from the camp! Tabs treated our observations of the night with utter scorn and contempt. Ken, the two Rangers, and I were still absolutely certain we had seen the lions, but we had to admit there were no footprints. Where we had seen them creeping forward, snarling, and switching their tails, was on soft, wet, volcanic soil—impossible even for a caterpillar to cross it without leaving a mark.

The arguments this way and that reached absolute deadlock, but nobody would alter their convictions; four one way and two against. The old Ranger who had been in the cab of the truck said quite calmly, "You will never find anyone who will agree about these lions, because they are '*Shaitani,*' they are of the Devil, they are the reincarnation of seven witches who were burned to death in a baobab tree." We at once asked the obvious question: "Were they the same lions at our first camp?" The old man solemnly and calmly just said, "Yes." But what about the footprints? He said, "They sometimes leave tracks, and sometimes kill people, and sometimes they don't."

We were more confounded. Ken and I spent a lot of time working out precise angles from our tent, and trying to see if by some chance the lions were on rocky ground where they would leave no tracks, but this was not possible. The ground was soft, or at least muddy, for several hundred yards and our own footprints stood out like craters on the moon.

To this day I can offer no sane explanation of these adventures with the seven lions but you will have to concede that the Ranger's interpretation becomes more convincing when I tell you about the Ghosts of Ngulia, which forms the next part of my story.

∙ ∙ ∙

As the plans took shape for the development of the Tsavo National Park, Kenya's largest big-game sanctuary of over 8,000 square miles, roads had to be made, boundaries had to be demarcated, and accommodation for visitors had to be provided. What was the use of establishing and protecting this wonderful wildlife paradise if nobody could see it? And so a small lodge was constructed at Ngulia, in a fascinating fold of the Ngulia mountains and the usual haunt of many wild animals.

Tabs had the job of getting six cottages built, as well as water supplies and roads of access organized. It was the first lodge of its kind in the East African National Parks, and was initially well accepted and very popular—until the ghosts took control.

The first indication of something unnatural was a report given to me personally by a very sensible, matter-of-fact English woman—a farmer's wife. She told me that she had been staying at Ngulia with her family and enjoying the scenery and the animals. Her husband and nine-year-old boy occupied one cottage while she and their daughter, aged eleven, used another cottage, some forty feet away.

During the night she was roused by the noise of a door creaking. She sat up and was surprised to see the front door open, and in the cold light of a half moon, a low slinking form swaying in the doorway. She was not really frightened, as she construed that the form was the low branch of a tree, moved by a gentle breeze. She was puzzled, however, as to why the door should have blown open, having been properly closed and bolted when they went to bed. She closed it again; but before bolting it, she opened it slowly, and then quickly, to see if it made a creaking noise but there was not a sound. Moreover, she noted that there were no trees or bushes near the door. The time was midnight.

In the morning the family discussed the events of the night, and the "men" of the party dismissed the creaking door and the slinking form as so much nonsense. The girls were far from satisfied, and had misgivings about another disturbed night. It was therefore arranged that the two parts of the family would exchange cottages, the men asserting that they could deal with any intruders, ghostly or otherwise, come hell or high water!

Just before midnight, the father was wakened by a creaking noise, like old ships' timbers, and the door slowly opened. There in the doorway was the low form of something swaying in the shadowy moonlight. He grabbed a flashlight and, upon giving a shout, he was startled to see a lion rear up on its hind legs and disappear. He recalled with absolute certainty that the door had been securely bolted when they went to bed. A little feeling of shame, for ridiculing his wife's report of the previous night, entered his confused and frightened thoughts. His son was terrified. This second encounter was too much for these people. It broke their nerve and they packed up and returned to their farm.

Tabs thought that the frame of the door was loose and with a hard push, he found that sure enough the door, although locked, would open. Tests, however, failed to open the door, but Tabs maintained that a really heavy thrust could do it. The frame and the hinges were all duly reinforced and we hoped peace would return to Ngulia.

Nothing happened for some weeks. Then there was real trouble. A lion broke into the servants' quarters of the lodge, seized a laborer by the head and dragged him away. A general alarm was raised and the entire lodge panicked. They set up such a hullabaloo that the lion dropped his victim and made off into the night. The unfortunate laborer was taken to the hospital, a hundred miles away, and after some months recovered.

The incident caused a crisis at Ngulia. The servants demanded to be taken back to their homes, and all the reservations at the lodge were cancelled. Tabs tracked the lion back from the lodge and was surprised to come upon seven lions, which tallied exactly with the seven we had encountered over a year before, all maneless, but two larger than the others. Even Tabs began to feel that his convictions were being challenged. The old Ranger's stories of the seven witches, who were now lions, had been vigorously revived by the events of recent weeks. He thought that the man-eater he had been tracking was clearly one of the seven.

We conferred and decided that this lion must be shot: since once a lion takes to eating humans there can be no reprieve. This lion, anyway, was probably a direct descendant of the Man-Eaters of Tsavo, the maneless lions that defied the construction of a railway from Mombasa to Nairobi at the end of the last century. They inflicted a reign of terror for nearly six months, and during that time devoured twenty-eight Indian coolies and scores of unfortunate African natives. The man-eaters were eventually dispatched by Colonel Patterson, but only after terrible ordeals. The mounted skins of these animals are displayed in the Field Museum in Chicago.

Tabs sat up for two nights, waiting for the man-eater to return. Just at midnight, during the second night the lion glided into full view, under a flood light operated by a car battery. One telling shot with his .470 rifle, and the lion was dead. The servants rejoiced, confidence returned, and we all thought the Ghosts of Ngulia were finished forever. The lodge reopened to visitors and everyone said the creaking door stories were just bally hoo.

All was well for some three months when suddenly the whole situation cascaded into the previously familiar realms of horror, fear, and conjecture. A man, sleeping alone in one of the cottages, was wakened by a slight noise and an uncanny feeling. He felt the warm breath of a large animal breathing over his face. In extreme terror he pulled the bedding over his head and yelled out desperately. In pulling up the blankets, his hand hit something warm and hairy. There was a crashing noise, thuds and a growl, and then silence. He was scared, very scared, but he slowly stretched out for a flashlight and saw that the spare bed next to him had been tipped over. The door was open. The time was midnight. He spent the rest of the night locked in his bathroom with a lamp burning.

Back came all the beliefs about the lodge being haunted, and nothing made any sense. Reports of such adventures are usually exaggerated and distorted, but in this case, the pattern of the incidents was consistent. People were frightened and it seemed that nothing could allay their fears. Tabs and I decided that the remaining six lions must be destroyed. There was enough evidence to establish that there had been seven lions and the man-eater was evidently one of them. Each time a cottage door was opened, the same lions were found in the immediate vicinity. We did not believe the old Ranger's story about the witches in the baobab tree, but we accepted that the remaining lions were very likely to be or to become man-eaters.

Then, one day, the water tank fell over for no apparent reason. One of the cottages went up in flames. It was not occupied. Weird reports came in from all kinds of people who had previously been to the lodge and were afraid of being ridiculed until the Ghosts of Ngulia became a general conversation topic. The old Ranger smiled and said you can't withstand the curses of a witch-doctor, but we decided these lions were to blame.

We set traps, and put out poisoned baits but nothing happened, although footprints showed that the lions had prowled around them. Tabs decided to rig up his floodlight arrangement and sit up for the lions, together with two Rangers, each armed with a heavy rifle and ensconced inside a barricaded truck. After some time, they heard a rustle in the grass, and Tabs put on the floodlight. There were the angry-looking lions, or more correctly, five lionesses and two larger lions that could be males. There was absolutely no doubt that there were seven—not six. It was near midnight. They snarled, and crouched, just as they had done near our camp beds, and Tabs whispered to shoot—each man taking aim at a different animal.

In order to get a better aim one of the Rangers moved and inadvertently kicked the clip from the terminal on the battery which provided electricity for the lights. The arena was plunged into darkness, intense darkness, because of the contrast with the lighted scene. Tabs quickly grasped the clip and restored it to the battery terminal.

There were no lions. Nothing stirred. They had vanished in a matter of not more than five seconds. Even the spotlight on the truck, shone around 360 degrees, revealed no sign, no eyes. Nothing moved. Tabs looked long and hard at a large baobab tree just a few yards away. He wondered about the old Ranger's story.

We conferred for weeks while the buildings stood stark and empty. Termites began to take their toll. There was no way out, the Ghosts of Ngulia had proved too powerful, and so I ordered the destruction of the lodge. The cottages were torn down and the site restored to its pristine state—all except the new water tank which remained standing like an epitaph, a memorial to the seven witches of the baobab, who would never die.

— PREVIOUSLY UNPUBLISHED

The Lady and the Coelacanth: Remembering the Zoological Discovery of the Century

BY J. RICHARD GREENWELL

On February 15, 1989, I arrived in East London, a town on the south Cape coast of South Africa. It was my first visit to that country. What took me there was a woman. A very special woman. Her name is Marjorie Courtenay-Latimer, and exactly 50 years before she had made a discovery which was to rock the scientific world; indeed, all the ichthyology and vertebrate paleontology textbooks had to be rewritten. For what she discovered was the coelacanth (pronounced *see-la-canth*), a form of fish believed extinct since the Cretaceous, the time of the dinosaurs, over 60 million years ago. Her find is considered today the zoological discovery of the century.

It was a routine day on December 22, 1938. Miss Courtenay-Latimer was working on a fossil reptile display at the East London Museum, where she was the curator. She was also the head of every department, as she was the only employee the small museum had. East London was a sleepy town in those days, far removed from the problems of the world. In Europe, Hitler's takeover of Austria and dismemberment of Czechoslovakia—and the prospect of war—seemed light years away.

The other key player in the events of that day was Hendrik Goosen (pronounced *hoysen*), the captain of the *Nerine*, an Irvin and Johnson fishing trawler. The *Nerine* was returning to East London with a haul of fish, but Captain Goosen decided to first sail to the mouth of the Chalumna River to lower the nets one more time. That's where interesting marine specimens could be found, and he often tried to bring in things for both the Museum and the Aquarium. Little did he realize at the time how zoological history would be changed by his chance decision.

One of the fish brought up in the nets was a peculiar, blue specimen that neither he nor the deckhands had ever seen before. His first thought was to keep it alive for the Aquarium, but he then realized that he would have to break the partition in his tank to make the 5-foot-long fish fit into it. "Let it die," he said. "We'll give it to the Museum instead." After docking, Captain Goosen asked a clerk in the office to phone Miss Courtenay-Latimer and tell her that there was a pile of specimens she might be interested in. After that, he took off on a month's leave, quite oblivious to the profound discovery for which he was responsible.

The clerk called Miss Courtenay-Latimer at 9:45 A.M. She thanked him, but continued working on the fossil display, mulling over whether it was worth going down to the dock. She was used to these calls. Every few weeks, her friend Captain Goosen—or somebody else at Irvin and Johnson—would call to let her know that there were some new specimens for her; sometimes there was something interesting, sometimes there wasn't. After some initial hesitation, she decided that, since it was Christmas, she should at least go down and give everyone her season's greetings.

She phoned the taxi company, but a different driver—by name of Harrolds—showed up this time. He drove her and Enoch, her young Xhosa assistant, down to the dock. She first stopped by the office, and then boarded the *Nerine*. After running through the pile of specimens, she decided that there really wasn't anything worth saving. But then she noticed a strange, blue fin sticking up from beneath the pile of fish, starfish, and seaweeds. She uncovered what she later was to describe as "a beautiful fish . . . it looked like a beautiful china ornament."

Unable to identify it, but certain that it was something very rare, she and Enoch carried it to the waiting taxi. Harrolds at first would not let her put it in the boot (trunk), but she won the argument, and finally got the specimen to the Museum. She went through all her natural history books, but found nothing that even resembled it. What could it be? After a while, Dr. J.

Bruce-Bays, the Museum Board Chairman, stopped in. "It's just a rock cod!" he exclaimed.

Undaunted, Miss Courtenay-Latimer placed the specimen on a hand-cart and, with Enoch, pushed it all the way down to the hospital morgue. Surely they would help her by freezing it so it could be preserved? The man at the morgue, Mr. E. Evans, was a very tall man, and he drew himself up to an enormous height, peered down at young Courtenay-Latimer, and exclaimed: "No, no, no, no, most definitely not. No stinking fishes in the morgue!" She then took the fish—again by handcart, walking through the heat of South Africa's early summer—to the Cold Storage Commission. Surely they would help? The man at the cold storage—curiously called Andrew Latimer but no relative—again answered negatively: "I won't have any stinking fishes in the cold storage!" Now, one has to remember that in the male-dominated South Africa of the 1930s, women and their opinions were not regarded with particular esteem; and it so happened that our heroine was only a 32-year-old "slip of a girl." What would *she* know?

By now she felt "like a deflated balloon," and in desperation decided to take the specimen to a Scotsman named Robert Center, who did taxidermy for the Museum. Mr. Center agreed to help. They bound the fish in formalin-soaked sheeting, and placed it in his cold room. Later that day, certain the fish was some archaic and possibly very valuable form, Miss Courtenay-Latimer wrote to her friend J.L.B. Smith. She included a rough drawing of the fish, asking if he could identify it. Smith, chemistry professor at Rhodes University in Grahamstown, had over the years developed a part-time interest in fishes into serious ichthyological research. He was later to become South Africa's leading ichthyologist.

It so happened that Smith was on Christmas leave at his cottage in Knysna with his new wife, Margaret. The letter was forwarded to him at Knysna, but did not reach him till early January. By then, Mr. Center had gutted the fish in order to mount it, and all the soft, internal tissues had been discarded. When Smith got the letter, he stared at the drawing in disbelief. "A bomb seemed to burst in my brain," he later wrote. Smith realized that the fish had to be a coelacanth form. But how could that be? It was impossible! It would be like finding a living dinosaur! Such things never really happen, except in fiction. Without a telephone, and with piles of chemistry exams to grade, Smith agonized over what to do. If it wasn't a coelacanth—and how could it be?—he would make a complete fool of himself. If it was, then he had better prepare himself for the storm which would surely follow—and he had better get those exams graded first!

All through January and into February Smith and Courtenay-Latimer exchanged letters, cables, and phone calls (Smith was able to use the phone in a grocery store). The 350-mile trip to East London was not such an easy thing as it may seem today. The roads were unpaved then, and heavy rains often turned a one-day drive into a three-day horrendous adventure. It was a long, agonizing period for both of them, but finally, on February 16, 1939, Smith arrived at the East London Museum. Trembling with excitement, he inspected the mounted fish. There could no longer be any doubt. It was a coelacanth, known previously only from fossils. This was, then, a true "living fossil." He turned to Miss Courtenay-Latimer and said: "Lass, this discovery will be on the lips of every scientist in the world." And so it was.

News of the find spread across the front pages of the world's leading news-papers. At first, of course, many zoologists and paleontologists were incredu-lous, particularly those in North America and Britain. Who is this J.L.B. Smith anyway? He isn't even an ichthyologist. The fish should be sent to the British Museum—they'd know what it is! Eventually, these negativists piped down, and Smith described the species, in *Nature*, as *Latimeria Chalumnae* (after the names of the discoverer and the river). But, still, distraught over the loss of the specimen's internal organs—which could have told physiologists and evolutionists so much—Smith sought complete vindication. And the best way to do that was to find a second, complete specimen.

Smith was convinced that the fish had been a stray which had probably been swept down to South Africa by the Mozambique current. He thought that the place to look, therefore, was probably up north. With the outbreak of World War II, the coelacanth was rapidly forgotten. It also interrupted Smith's plans, but after the war his search continued. By now, he had abandoned chemistry altogether, spending all his time on fishes. In the course of his collecting expeditions, he distributed trilingual coelacanth "wanted" posters in villages up and down the eastern coast of South Africa and Mozambique.

Finally, after a 14-year search, on December 24, 1952 (again at Christmastime!), a cable arrived from fisherman Eric Hunt, on the Comoro Islands—between Madagascar and the African mainland—then a French colony. A second coelacanth had been caught—Smith had been right about the location. However, if he didn't go quickly, the French authorities would confiscate the specimen. But Smith was unable to get there. Those islands had no regular airline service, and all the officials who could help him at the University and in the National Science Council were on Christmas leave. In desperation, Smith sought the help of the Prime Minister, Dr. Malan, who immediately put a South African Air Force DC-3 transport aircraft at his disposal.

The crew, which had been pulled from Christmas leave for a "special mission," were stunned when Smith, once airborne, informed them that their job was to pick up "a dead fish." But, once they heard the details, they soon warmed up to the enterprise. Smith whisked his second coelacanth out of the Comoros, returning in triumph to Cape Town, to the waiting Prime Minister, and to full scientific vindication. The drama, like a fairy tale, had come to a sudden, sweeping, and happy climax.

In 1956, Smith related the entire story, at least from his own perspective, in his book *Old Fourlegs*. The title was taken from his belief that the coelacanth's strange, limb-like fins were used for walking on the sea-bottom, a hypothesis only recently disproven. It turned out, of course, that Comoran fishermen had known the fish all along. The fish that paleontology said had been extinct for tens of millions of years was known to them as *kombessa*.

Following the 1952 find, the French closed off the Comoros—the fish's only known habitat—to other nationalities, and essentially took over coelacanth research. Smith became increasingly obsessed with fishes. Every hour not spent doing research on fishes was time wasted; thus, he declined most social invitations. He died in 1968, but his work was carried on by his wife, Mary Margaret, through the new J.L.B. Smith Institute of Ichthyology. She herself became an ichthyologist of world renown, and died in 1987.

And so, 50 years went by. During that period, Hitler took Europe and lost it, Britain gave up her Empire, America put men on the Moon, and Richard Nixon came and went (twice, actually). And what became of Marjorie Courtenay-Latimer? She retired in 1973, after serving as curator of the East London Museum for 42 years. Now 82, she tries to live quietly in her cozy home in East London. But perhaps "quietly" is not the right word. With a bubbly, goodnatured personality, Marge, as she is known to her friends, is always on the go. The natural world was her *whole* world when she was young, and although that "slip of a girl" has added a few extra pounds in the intervening half century, she is still, in her early 80s, that same bouncy naturalist, Marjorie Courtenay-Latimer.

Miss Courtenay-Latimer is an Honorary Member of the International Society of Cryptozoology (ISC), of which I am secretary. Thus, on December 22, 1988, the 50th anniversary of that historical phone call and her saving of the specimen, I decided to call her with my congratulations. I caught her at the Museum in the midst of anniversary festivities, and she had to keep the mayor waiting to speak to me. Thrilled that somebody was actually calling from America, she invited me to visit her. This I already had in mind, and I flew to South Africa a few weeks later. I had planned my visit so that I would be with her at the Museum on February 16, 1989, 50 years to the day that J.L.B. Smith arrived and verified her discovery.

But there is a humorous side to our first meeting, on the 15th. I first called her to confirm the hour of my visit, but, just before I arrived at her home, a young student rang her doorbell. Knowing me only by name, and thinking it was me, she let him in. "I hope you had a good flight," she said, wondering how such a young, scruffy character was to lecture at the East London Museum the following day. "A good flight?" answered the student as he took some archaeological artifacts out of a sack. He had dug them up in the desert, and wanted her opinion. "Oh my," she said, inspecting them with interest. "And you brought these all the way from Arizona to show them to me?" "Arizona?" answered the incredulous youth. "No, I dug them up here, in the Cape Province." "But I thought you had just flown in?" Fortunately, at that point, the doorbell rang again, and my own arrival cleared up the mess.

I spent a pleasant, relaxed day with Marge, and she told me the whole story, from beginning to end. I picked and probed for every minute detail, and taped it all (interested EC members may obtain a complete transcript from ISC, P.O. Box 43070, Tucson, AZ 85733, USA). She spoke of those early pre-coelacanth days in the 1930s, of how she built up the Museum, and of how she met and got to know Smith. She told me of her disappointments and frustrations trying to save the specimen, and the distorted versions published many times since. "For many years," she said, "I thought, why? Why didn't I chuck it overboard and be finished with it?" But, of course, she never would have. Another frustration was that, in her eyes, Captain Goosen had never really been recognized for his part in the find. "I always felt," she told me, "that without Captain Goosen there never would have been a coelacanth."

That evening, I was privileged in having Marge take me to visit Captain Goosen and his wife at their home, and we all had dinner together. Captain Goosen, now 84, is a modest and down-to-earth Afrikaner of gentle temperament. Although he had a twinkle in his eye, there was no fancy talk or deep philosophy here. How did he feel about the coelacanth 50 years later? "Oh, not much. It was marvelous catching it, but . . ." (As I write these lines, in January of 1990, I have just received word from Marge that Captain Goosen died on January 5. A quiet and decent gentleman, Captain Goosen survived his coelacanth by exactly 51 years.)

The next day, Marge and Nancy Tietz, the new director of the Museum, took me down to the dock—the only river port in South Africa—and showed me where Captain Goosen used to bring in the *Nerine*. Marge was able to pinpoint the exact spot. Except for the Irvin and Johnson buildings, which are now gone, she said it was pretty much the same. Afterwards, Miss Tietz suggested trying to find the house of the taxidermist, Mr. Center. I was surprised to learn that Marge had not been back in all those 50 years. But she

found the house, and stood in wonder, remembering her trials of half a century before. "It looks exactly as it used to," she said. We knocked on the door,
and a middle-aged woman opened it and looked at us curiously. "Excuse
me," said Marge, "do you know of the Centers, who used to live here in the
1930s?" "Oh no," answered the woman, "we've only been here for 12 years."
"Oh, well, thank you," said Marge, as she turned to leave. "Just a minute," I
interjected. "Aren't you going to tell this lady why we are here?" "Oh, she
won't be interested," answered Marge. I turned to the woman in the doorway
and asked: "Have you heard of the coelacanth?" "Yes, of course," she
answered, "the fish." "Have you heard of Miss Courtenay-Latimer?" I persisted. "Yes, of course," she answered, with increasing puzzlement showing
on her face. "Well, this is Miss Courtenay-Latimer," I told her with great
delight, "and the reason we are here is that this is where she brought the fish
50 years ago, to your house."

We talked for another minute or two. I don't remember the poor lady
saying much. But I do remember her still standing there in the doorway as
we drove away, with a look of utter bewilderment on her face. I often wonder
what she later told her relatives and friends.

We then went to the old museum building, now converted into a technical college, and Marge showed us around, remembering what was here
and there 50 years before. This, of course, was February 16, the day J.L.B. had
arrived at that very building. And even almost the right time. As she saw her
old haunts, I could tell that many memories of times past were surfacing in
her mind. I am sure that it was an emotional moment for her, and I was glad
I was there to share it with her.

Soon afterwards, we went to the new Museum building across the
street, where we met Captain and Mrs. Goosen, and had lunch with the
staff. Then came the visit to the Coelacanth Hall, and—there it was! The
original coelacanth; the first one from that fateful day, the zoological type
specimen. It sits proudly in the middle of the hall, surrounded by displays
and memorabilia. I insisted on some photos, and I took one with Marge and
Captain Goosen standing next to their historical find. After I had given my

lecture, and the others had left, I had a chance to return to the Coelacanth Hall. It was just the two of us. We spent the rest of the afternoon together, Old Fourlegs and me, and it eyed me continuously as I photographed it and studied all the displays.

Later in the week, I went to Grahamstown—about a two-hour drive—to visit the J.L.B. Smith Institute of Ichthyology. I was extended every courtesy (including a key to the building!) by the new director, Mike Bruton. The Institute, now an independent, government-funded entity, still has close ties to Rhodes University. With over 400,000 specimens in its collection, it is probably the largest ichthyology research institute in the world. Although most of the Institute's research activities involve other species, the coelacanth, of course, holds a very special place in the hearts of the staff. In the lobby is a permanent coelacanth exhibit, the highlight being the second (Comoros) specimen acquired by J.L.B. in 1952. One senses right away that, while the atmosphere at the East London Museum revolves around Marge and the first coelacanth, the atmosphere at the Smith Institute revolves around J.L.B. and the second coelacanth.

In the lecture hall, where I also spoke, a temporary 50th anniversary exhibit had been set up, and I spent many an hour reading historical coelacanth-related documents and correspondence which had been dug out of the archives for the occasion. Also, raised on a wooden platform, were many of J.L.B.'s personal effects: fishing rods, specimen bottles, log-books, microscopes, and the like. J.L.B. is revered at the Institute (I heard that, if one is very quiet, his shadow may sometimes be seen passing by). Being able to hold and feel some of his personal effects added a new dimension to my visit, a dimension which cannot, of course, be gained by just reading the accounts of this brilliant, eccentric individual.

In a way, the story of the coelacanth, besides being scientifically important, represents the perfect human drama. The old fish, the sea captain, the young naturalist, the desperate professor, the prime minister, the Air Force crew, and the impossibility of it all becoming possible. I doubt if any novel or movie script could fully capture the personalities of the individuals or the dynamics of the story. Sometimes, for some reason, Fate moves all the pieces to the right places, and that is precisely what happened in South Africa a half-century ago.

What did finding a living coelacanth mean for science? These forms, belonging to an order of lobe-finned fishes known as the Crossopterygii, and the extinct (or presumed extinct!) rhipidistian fishes, were thought to be in the lineage that eventually evolved into all land vertebrates—known as tetrapods—from amphibians to mammals, including humans. Thus, in a sense, the coelacanth could be called our oldest living relative. It has often been thought of as a "missing link," which is actually a misleading Victorian term.

In any case, the coelacanth, with very little anatomical change since the Upper Devonian, about 400 million years ago, is certainly the oldest verte-brate form known to exist today.

More recently, some specialists have attempted to revise this "missing link" scenario, proposing that coelacanths share an ancestry with the lineage which eventually gave rise to the lungfishes and the tetrapods. Thus, although still very ancient and marvelous, it would no longer represent a tran-sitional form—or "missing link"—from fish to amphibian. To most people, such technicalities are irrelevant. The coelacanth, to them, represents a won-derful thing in a humdrum world. I myself am continually amazed at how many people know about it, even when they don't remember any details, or even know how to pronounce the name properly. It simply represents a piece of magic in an increasingly technological world.

Fossil coelacanths have been known for about 150 years, but none of the fossil species—there are about 70 species in 27 genera and four families—reaches 2 feet in length, while the living genus, *Latimeria* reaches 6 feet. The most recent coelacanth known to science—until December 1938, that is—was the genus *Macropoma*, which disappeared from the fossil record about 80 million years ago.

To find live specimens of such an ancient form—true "living fossils"—was of tremendous benefit to ichthyologists. They have been able to study its biology and physiology in a way that was not thought possible before the discovery, for fossils tell one very little about internal structures. Most of the fish's skeleton is composed of cartilage, and the spine is simply represented by an oil-filled notochord. Its internal organs are both archaic and modern, perfectly suited, apparently, for its cryptic mode of life.

However, *Latimeria* is still very much of a mystery, partly due to the fact that no specimens have yet survived captivity for more than a few hours. They live hundreds of feet below, and some form of stress kills them at the surface. Various attempts have been made, or proposed, to keep specimens alive for public display and study (including a project backed by The Explorers Club and directed by Jerry Hamlin). It was only recently that Hans Fricke, a German ichthyologist, filmed—for the first time—the species in its own habitat, by descending in a submersible. Fricke, Bruton, and Canadian ichthyologist Eugene Balon have also recently formed the Coelacanth Conservation Council, partly out of concern for the fish's survival. There are now about 200 known specimens, and, instead of being the casual by-catch it used to be, the fish is now targeted by Comoran fishermen. As they are in great demand by museums, aquariums, and private collectors, a specimen can bring in a tidy sum.

The population is not thought to be very large, and it may be the only population in existence (although there are hints of other populations elsewhere). Tragically, then, the continual demand for the fish could result in its eventual extinction. That phone call of December 22, 1938, as magnificent as the discovery was, could inadvertently have also set into motion its death sentence. Thus would end a story which began 400 million years ago, when the world was much younger, and the dinosaurs hadn't even been thought of, much less humans. South Africa, of course, has no control over what conservation measures Comoran authorities may or may not take. But Professor Bruton, who represents the next link in the chain initiated by Smith, is working hard with his colleagues to save the species. And I believe it will be saved.

As for Marjorie Courtenay-Latimer, the 50th anniversary has given her pause to look back over her life. "It's been a really *happy* life," she told me.

"And the coelacanth was part of that, and always something very, very special. With all the troubles and worries that I had, it was always there as one of my real treasures."

Would she now do it any differently? "No, never," she answered. "If I came back to earth again I would do just what I did before, including the struggle for the coelacanth. I mean, it was really a hard struggle to save the thing, but I would do it again. Call it a woman's intuition. It's wonderful to know that that intuition, or call it what you may, is recognized 50 years later. It's been great fun."

As for me, I shall always cherish my coelacanth visit, and the people I met and the stories I heard. I didn't go into forests or swamps this time. But it was a real trip of exploration, a trip through time and history, the kind which sometimes gives one cause to marvel at the wonder of it all. Before I left the Coelacanth Hall, I took one last, long look at Old Fourlegs. Then I turned and walked out into the bright sunshine of East London.

—THE EXPLORERS JOURNAL, FALL 1990

J. Richard Greenwell is originally from Southwest Surrey, England. After a six-year stint in Peru, he joined the University of Arizona arid lands program in 1974. Since 1982, he has been Secretary of the International Society of Cryptozoology, in Tucson, Arizona and has conducted zoological and crypto-zoological fieldwork in Mexico, China, New Guinea, and the Congo. His primary interest is terrestrial mammalogy. He has also published a book, Animals Without Heritage, *by Harper & Row in 1991.*

Martin and Osa Johnson: Exploration Was Their Way of Life

BY KENHELM W. STOTT, JR.

The year 1921 was to be a turning point in the saga of Martin and Osa Johnson. The location was the New York headquarters of The Explorers Club. Martin lit a cigar as he listened intently and with growing enthusiasm to an older member of the club.

"East African game herds are going the way of the American bison," Carl Akeley explained. Akeley was a multifaceted genius—the father of today's taxidermy techniques, sculptor, wildlife photographer, and inventor. As he talked with Martin, his plans for a two-tiered African Hall in the American Museum of Natural History were well underway. Miniatures of each diorama had already been created and the African Hall, completed after Akeley's death in 1926, remains the most spectacular display of its kind in the world. Depicting scenes from all parts of Africa, it is dominated by an elephant group in the center of the hall.

"African wildlife is already diminishing," Carl explained. "Someone must record the land and its animals photographically, and you and Osa are ideally suited for the task."

Despite the fact that the Johnsons had just returned from a two-year marathon expedition during which they had made three films (one in the New Hebrides, another in Borneo, and a third in Malaya, Ceylon, and southern India), they followed Akeley's advice and sailed from New York for Mombasa in October 1921.

Their first African trip was largely a matter of trial and error. With two Ford camera-cars and the primitive photographic gear of the times, they first filmed the game of Kenya's Athi and Kapiti Plains, next the Ithanga Hills, then the Mara triangle, which is a part of the Serengeti ecosystem and still refuge to vast numbers of hoofed mammals and their predators. They then headed north to film the fauna of the deserts of what was then the Northern Frontier District.

At two sites in particular—one is now known as Buffalo Springs and the other has recently been gazetted as a national reserve, Shaba—they obtained a brilliant series of stills and movies of reticulated giraffe, Grevy's zebra and beisa oryx. With funds running low, they pushed further north over ancient slave and game trails to the 4,700-foot-high, forested Mount Marsabit, which was said to be inhabited by some of the largest surviving 'tuskers.' Reports proved accurate and other forms of both forest and desert creatures were also plentiful.

One crystal-clear morning the Johnsons hacked their way through the forest to find themselves standing on the precipice of a crater, at the bottom of which sparkled a cobalt lake. The dense forest about them, the lake below, and bleak deserts extending beyond for hundreds of miles in every direction, provided an awesome spectacle.

"Oh, Martin, it's paradise," Osa observed emotionally. Previously referred to as Gof Sokorete Dika by locals and as Crater Lake to the few outsiders who had viewed it, it was to become known to thousands of Americans and Europeans as Lake Paradise. Even most maps of today, if they indicate its existence at all, still list it as Lake Paradise or Paradise Lake.

When they returned to America, Carl Akeley wrote in *Natural History* Magazine, "Mr. and Mrs. Martin Johnson . . . gave to the world a photographic record of African game that was of greater interest and beauty than any that had been brought out of Africa before." High praise from Caesar was heady stuff. The American public reacted with enthusiasm to their film *Trailing Wild Animals in Africa* and Martin's book *Camera Trails in Africa*.

On December 1, 1923, they sailed again from New York for Africa, but this time with the finest in photographic equipment and automotive gear. Funds from their first African film and book were substantially augmented by the American Museum of Natural History, George Eastman, and Willys-Knight.

Their immediate goal was to return to Lake Paradise for an extended stay. This time they established a permanent camp, the foundations of which still exist. In addition to comfortable living and dining quarters, they constructed a village for their staff, extensive vegetable gardens, a guest house, and a photo lab in which Martin could develop both stills and hundreds of feet of motion picture film.

During the three and a half year Lake Paradise expedition they made several extensive excursions, one to the Ndoto Mountains near Lake Turkana (Rudolf), and another to Tanzania's Serengeti Plains, where they joined forces with Carl and Mary Jobe Akeley, who were in Africa collecting specimens for the still-incomplete African Hall. Together the Johnsons and the Akeleys photographed the famed lions of the Seronera, whose descendants still lure scientists and tourists to the area.

The Johnsons returned to Lake Paradise while the Akeleys surged westward to the Virunga Volcanoes to gather material for a mountain gorilla diorama. There Carl, who had been unwell for several months, died in 1926 and was buried on the saddle between Mount Mikeno and Mount Karisimbi. The Johnsons returned to America in May 1927 with superlative photographic material, the best of which appeared in their *Into The Blue*. Martin's book *Safari* became an overnight best seller (and years later Osa was to write of the expedition as *Four Years in Paradise*).

By mid-December of the same year, the Johnsons were on their way back to Africa, this time with George Eastman as a companion. They left their ship at Alexandria and ascended the Nile by train and riverboat to Rejaf in the southern Sudan. Heading southwest, they filmed northern white rhinos, then moved into the Ituri Forest, in what was then the Belgian Congo, to photograph pygmies. Still traveling with Eastman, they crossed Lake Mobutu (Albert), hired a launch and sailed up the Victoria Nile for their first view of what were then called Murchison Falls.

Upon reaching Nairobi, they parted company with Mr. Eastman and proceeded to purchase what was to be the only home they ever owned, a lovely two-story building surrounded by lawns and gardens in the residential Muthaiga suburb.

In March of 1928 they returned to the Serengeti to spend seven months filming lions, the most detailed photographic study anyone had made of the great cats. The stills and motion pictures resulting from that safari have yet to be surpassed. They were nothing short of superb and serve to underscore Martin's brilliance as a photographer. While the films lacked color, they consisted of extreme close-ups depicting lions, not as savage beasts, but as great, friendly creatures with a strong sense of territoriality and family unity.

In March 1929, Martin published *Lion* and released the commercial film *Simba*. Later in the year the Johnsons produced a second film, *Across the World with Mr. and Mrs. Martin Johnson*. Comprised of excerpts of all preceding expeditions, it was accompanied by a 'voice-over' narration. Their first experience with 'talkies,' it was released in 1930. Long before it reached the screen, however, the Johnsons were back in Africa with sound equipment and engaged in one of their most difficult assignments—filming sound pictures of mountain gorillas on the Virunga Volcanoes.

They had left New York on November 15, 1929. Upon reaching Nairobi, they had their fleet of cars shipped west by train across Uganda. The 'long rains' had begun in Kenya, making travel by road (such as they were) difficult. At Butiaba, they once again hired a launch, photographed and recorded the roaring waters of Murchison Falls as well as a classic series of hippopotamus close-ups that established a photographic tradition that has since become a cliché in African wildlife films—a shot of one yawning hippo after another, the overall effectiveness reaching almost hypnotic proportions. Then it was on to the Ituri Forest to film pygmies again, this time recording their songs as well. A classic shot reveals Osa placing a record on a phonograph and singing and dancing while accompanying a popular song of the day—one by one the pygmies recover from their initial surprise and join Osa as she dances.

By August 30, 1929, Martin and Osa had accumulated more than sufficient pygmy footage. Driving southeast, they reached the base of Mount Mikeno. Hiring an army of porters, they climbed to the site of Carl Akeley's grave, which was situated at an altitude of approximately 10,500 feet with the peak of Mikeno soaring to more than 14,000 feet on one side and Karasimbi, nearly 15,000 feet, on the other.

They found gorillas abundant in the region, hearing their roars, other vocalizations, and chest-thumpings, but catching only brief glimpses of the great black shadows as they moved through dense hagenia or bamboo forests. When first they met a large 'saddle-backed' male face to face, Osa was to describe the encounter: "All of our big game adventures are as nothing to the thrills I've had today." Her reaction was similar to that of virtually every other wildlife observer upon meeting that first wild gorilla.

Glimpsing gorillas was not, however, photographing gorillas. The Johnsons succeeded in catching an occasional shot, but never the quality of film portraits that the public had come to expect of them. Though legally protected, the gorillas had not yet begun to lose their fear of mankind (as they were to do in later years during the studies of Schaller and Fossey).

Reports of a plethora of gorillas near Alimbongo in the mountains west of Lake Edward encouraged them to change locales. A road running through the hills parallel to the lake provided easier access to varied types of forest and rendered moving cumbersome sound equipment less difficult. Photographic results improved enormously and their new site provided an entirely unexpected bonus. One morning while moving through the forest on foot, they unintentionally marched into a spread-out troop of feeding gorillas.

While most members moved in one direction, two young animals playing off to one side ran in the opposite direction. In desperation, they climbed a tall tree. The Johnson crew immediately began clearing the area around the tree of all vegetation. Once that goal had been achieved, they set about chopping down the tree. As it fell, the Johnsons and their staff ran in with heavy nets and captured both animals, who were stunned by the fall but unharmed.

Unlike the tiny infant gorillas that had previously been captured by trappers (whose inhumane technique involved shooting a mother gorilla to obtain her suckling child), each of these gorillas weighed more than a hundred pounds and was judged to be in excess of four years of age. They were placed in the fence-backed truck that had been the Johnsons' mobile bedroom and were driven back to Nairobi along with an infant gorilla the Johnsons had bought from natives along the roadside. Although manual examination of two heavily furred, one hundred pound plus gorillas was impossible, their behavior caused the Johnsons to believe that they were a pair—male and female.

Until that time, gorillas had seldom survived captivity for any great period. But Mbongo and Ngagi, as they were called, offered a rare opportunity for scientific observation and perhaps for procreation. Snowball, the infant gorilla, was placed in the National Zoo, a subsidiary of the Smithsonian Institution, Washington, D.C. Mbongo and Ngagi were sent to the San Diego Zoo, which had already acquired a reputation for rearing and breeding delicate primates.

In time, it became evident that the San Diego gorillas were not a pair, but both males. They lived to become fully adult 'saddle-backs' and were the object of many observational studies. Their capture, as well as the footage of other wild gorillas, of pygmies, of hippopotami and Murchison Falls, was recorded in *Congorilla*, released in 1932 as was a book of the same title.

Later in the same year, Martin asked Osa, "How'd you like to learn to fly, honey?" Mrs. Johnson was more than surprised since Martin had long expressed an aversion to flying. "You'd better," he continued, "because I've just bought two airplanes."

On January 23, 1933, Martin, Osa, their crew of technicians, and two amphibious Sikorskys were off-loaded at Cape Town. After a two-week delay, both planes took off on a zigzag course for Nairobi, 4,400 air miles away. Landing fields were few and navigational ground equipment nonexistent, but somehow the two planes (using lakes, wherever possible, for their landing strips) arrived at Wilson's Airdrome in Nairobi. The larger, two-engined plane bore zebra stripes and had been christened 'Osa's Ark.' The smaller, single-engined Sikorsky had giraffe markings and bore the name 'The Spirit of Africa.' Two years later, the latter craft was to be renamed 'The Spirit of Africa and Borneo,' since the Johnsons' last expedition was to take them back to the Kinabatangan River in British North Borneo.

Once the two planes had reached Nairobi, Martin and Osa, both of whom were now accomplished pilots, and their crews, began an 18-month air-safari that was to carry them 60,000 air miles over East and Central Africa. Within the area, only a few emergency fields existed. Elsewhere Johnson crews went first by truck to hack fields from the wilderness and store supplies of fuel.

Traveling by air provided mobility that provided many advantages. Some flights involved no more than a couple of hours and carried them over terrain that had required as much as a month of trekking during the early days of Model T, ox cart, foot, and camel safaris.

The number of firsts the Johnsons chalked up on the aerial safari is beyond count. They flew over Mount Kenya's 17,000-foot peaks and photographed them from above for the first time. Lack of pressurization prevented them from flying over Kibo, the higher (19,340 feet) of Kilimanjaro's two peaks, but they easily crossed Mawenzi, the lower. They filmed the 'Sea of Jade' (Lake Rudolph as it was then, and now Turkana) and filmed the crater lake of Central Island. On this excursion they made the first sound films of that vanishing tribe, the Elmolo, as well as the more numerous Turkana. Other highlights included films of seemingly endless herds of elephants in Kenya's Lorian Swamp, the wildebeest migration as it surged across the Serengeti, and a plane packed with pygmies who enjoyed flying but were not overly impressed with such a mode of transportation.

On the ground, they used their planes as blinds. Near Seronera, one sequence depicts an indignant Osa as she whacks an overly curious lion over the head with a bag of flour. They flew to Garissa on the Tana River to meet Trubee Davison of the American Museum and The Explorers Club and white hunter Al Klein collecting specimens for the late Carl Akeley's nearly completed African Hall.

After 18 months, Osa became seriously ill and it became necessary to fly her to Europe following the Nile from Juba to Cairo, then along the Mediterranean to Tunis. Once across the sea, they passed over Italy and France and finally landed in London, where Osa received sufficient medical attention to enable the Johnson party and its two planes to board the S.S. *Manhattan* at Southampton.

When they returned to the States, Martin published *Over African Jungles* and edited two films, *Baboona* for commercial release and a second to accompany their cross-country lecture tour.

Unnoticed, an era had come to an end—the Johnsons' 14-year relationship with Africa was over. During that period they had provided the documentation of East and Central Africa and its fauna, tribes, and landscapes far beyond the fondest hopes of Carl Akeley so many years before. They had made Nairobi more familiar to most Americans than Wichita. They had revealed to the world that East Africa was not a land of danger and disease but one of the loveliest regions on earth. Martin and Osa Johnson had become international heroes to two generations, their names synonymous with adventure in Est Africa. But they were never to see it again together.

— *THE EXPLORERS JOURNAL*, SEPTEMBER 1980

Kenhelm W. Stott, Jr. is the author of the following articles on wildlife that appeared in past issues of The Explorers Journal: "Siamangs of the Malay Peninsula," *June 1977;* "Search for the Duber Dibhuded," *March 1978;* "The Wary Bongo," *March 1979; and* "The Beira," *March 1980, co-authored with C. Jackson Selsor. His book, from which the present article was abridged by the author to include only the African expeditions, is now in its third edition. The book includes 140 photographs from all of the Johnson expeditions—three to the South Seas, two to Borneo and five to Africa. Copies are available from the Martin and Osa Johnson Safari Museum Press, Chanute, Kansas.*

Memories of the Last Crusade

BY LOWELL THOMAS

Almost two decades have elapsed since the experience I am about to relate, but with each passing year I find that it stands out as the most unforgettable in all my memories.

When we took off from the aerodrome at Heliopolis one afternoon in the autumn of 1917, I little knew what a dramatic, historic spectacle I was to witness. We had heard several reports in Cairo about the Palestine campaign, but they were all vague, technical, military, laconic. There was a rumor that Allenby was advancing, that a mysterious chap named Lawrence and his Arabs were bewildering and hamstringing the Turkish armies. Though there were no definite advices, yet the impression had gained ground that something exciting was about to happen. That is why I contrived to wangle a passage in a British battle plane on that date. At the controls was Major A. J. Evans, hero of numerous brilliant escapes from the enemy.

The aerodrome from which we took off was in the heart of the Land of Goshen, where Joseph settled his aged father and brethren. ("And thou shalt dwell in the land of Goshen, and thou shalt be near unto me, thou and thy children and thy children's children, and thy flocks, and thy herds, and all that thou hast: And there will I nourish thee.") Into that same land of Goshen, "even unto Gibeon," the victorious General Joshua had swept with fire and sword. And across that region Joseph and Mary with their Holy Babe had fled from the sadistic superstitions of Herod. To be sure Goshen is not mentioned by Saint Matthew, the only evangelist who narrated the flight into Egypt. But as Joseph was without the funds to buy a passage from Jaffa to Alexandria or across the Gulf of Hermopolis, the assumption is inevitable. So on either hand as we flew was ground steeped in history, the sacred history of three great religions.

35

With a few loops above the Pyramids, a flip of our tail in the face of the Sphinx, off we zoomed across the Suez Canal and over the sand dunes of Sinai's mystical desert. To our left shimmered and gleamed the blue waters of the Mediterranean. Far to the south, almost lost in the heat haze, loomed portentously the dim outline of the grim mountain where Moses, amid flashes of lightning and awful thunderclaps, received the tablets of stone that established the imperishable foundation of a code of criminal, civil, and religious laws which now govern the relations of human beings over some four-fifths of the earth's surface.

Presently we were traveling as the crow flies over the wilderness crossed by Moses and his Twelve Tribes. But I was not going as Moses did, on foot or camelback. Like his successor Elijah, I was wafted in a flaming chariot. And, instead of taking forty years for the journey, I made it in less than four hours. Leaving the dried-out bed of old Lake Serbonis on our left, we boomed across the plains of Philistia, that once fair, highly cultured and prosperous land. And so we swung off into the hills of Ancient Judea.

Thrill upon thrill registered through my eyes into my brain. Under our wings, at one moment, was Bethlehem, the sacred place of the Nativity, today virtually a suburb of Jerusalem. A few miles to the east was the silver sheet of saline water that all the world knows as the Dead Sea. Then Jericho, the city whose capture by Joshua still has the military experts guessing. And the Valley of the Jordan, the river which shares with the Ganges a reputation for waters of healing properties.

It was just at sunset that I caught my first glimpse of the Holy City, the most romantic spot on earth, the place sacred alike to Christian, Mohammedan, and Jew, the site of the Holy Sepulcher, the goal of all the wars between the Crescent and the Cross. Aloof and waterless, surely some mystic power must have preserved it through forty centuries of vicissitudes. And here was the thrill of thrills: Allenby's army had just captured that focus of the world's tragedy, romance, and history. The place which had defied the great Coeur de Lion, which the brutal, destructive Turks had held in the face of the objections of the entire civilized world, had come once more under the dominion of a Christian power. The successors of "Richard Yea-and-Nay" had accomplished, after seven centuries, the task which broke that lion heart.

Evans flew us about one thousand feet above the most sacred of this earth's hills, the Mount of Olives. On one slope I could easily make out that mystical Garden of Gethsemane where the Savior spoke those deathless words: "Father, if thou be willing, remove this cup from me: nevertheless, not my will, but thine, be done." The Garden whose name has become a synonym for acute spiritual agony in all languages. With such thoughts, Evans and I crossed the Valley of Kedron and found ourselves directly above Jerusalem. Just beneath our right wing was a building with a beautifully proportioned dome. It was the Mosque of Omar, with its matchless mosaics, erected on the site of the old Tabernacle of King David, the Holy of Holies, King Solomon's Temple. Thus I had my first sight of Ancient Jerusalem in the most modern way possible. From aloft I first saw the tower of David, the Walls of Jerusalem, the Holy Sepulcher. It seemed indeed that we were looking down upon Eternity.

Evans landed on the old Turkish aerodrome outside Bethlehem and there we passed most of the night. But just before dawn a car of the Royal Flying Corps took me around the outer wall of Jerusalem to the foot of the Mount of Olives. Thence I went on foot up the holy mountain, as some millions of other pilgrims have walked it for almost two thousand years. The dawn broke just as I reached the summit. As the first rays of the Judean morning sun touched the walls and domes, spires, and minarets of Jerusalem with fingers of gold, there I stood, alone, looking down upon a magic city.

As I gazed upon its panorama I could not help reflecting upon the more amazing panorama of Jerusalem's history, a history longer than that of Rome, more tragic than that of Athens. Babylon is gone, Nineveh is no more, Thebes and Memphis a mass of glamorous ruins. But Jerusalem today is alive, full of vitality, the center of the thoughts of hundreds of millions.

The first mention of the place, I believe, was in the Tell el-Amarna letters dug up not so long ago in the ruins of Thebes. These were official communications to an Egyptian Pharaoh from one of his vassals in Asia Minor.

From them we learn that, some time between 1400 and 1300 B.C., the king of a Palestinian city called Urusalim was complaining to his overlord about the raids of certain wild desert tribes. Probably this appeal for help referred to the Judean campaigns of Joshua, who was making desperate efforts to include the kingdom of the Jebusites in the network of his conquests. Though he defeated Adonizedek, king of Jerusalem, at the battle of Gibeon, took him prisoner, and generously hanged his captive, Joshua never was able to take the city. Almost impregnable in the midst of its stony, waterless hills, it resisted all the onslaughts of the children of Judah until a man, greater even than Joshua, a great soldier who was also one of the world's great poets, came to rule over Israel. In all probability it was about the year 1049 B.C. that the stronghold of the Jebusites fell before the shock troops and the generalship of King David.

If you stand atop the Mount of Olives, your mind inevitably wanders to Jerusalem's most glorious days when David's poetical but cynical son Solomon was building there his splendid temple and magnificently playing host to the Queen of Sheba, having made his capital famed throughout Asia Minor for its power and riches. After that brief, brilliant epoch, we see the era of Jerusalem's decline, the secession of the Ten Tribes. Civil war sweeps the land, treachery and intertribal politics. The Assyrian sweeps down like a wolf on the fold. Unhappy Judea becomes the bloody cockpit of that part of the world, a helpless buffer state between the power of Egypt and the ambitions of the great Mesopotamian conquerors. So our memory sees that unhappy period ending with Jerusalem crushed and desolate, her people ravished from their homes, twice carried into captivity, their proud temple, the Holy of Holies, destroyed.

Could any ordinary city, any ordinary people have survived such disasters? What must have been the emotions of the 5,000 odd of the Beni-Israel, whom Cyrus the great Persian allowed to return to the home of their fathers? Their leader, Sheshbazzar, was a man of the blood royal, a lineal descendant of King David. Hilaire Belloc tells us that it took them from April until August to make the long trek along the banks of the Euphrates. "When the exiles got back to the old territory of Judah and Benjamin they found it half deserted and more than half wild. Even in Hebron the Arabs were established; to the north, where had been the kingdom of Israel, the very mixed blood of the Samaritans. . . . In the neighborhood of the Holy City itself (by this time more than half in ruins) there were brigands and wild beasts." Under the benevolent (or indifferent) suzerainty of the Persian satrap of Damascus, Jerusalem revives. Through calamity, captivity and exile, the followers of Sheshbazzar and Zerubbabel had preserved two things—the spiritual consciousness that they were the Chosen People and the Torah, the Law. And so we see Ezra as Governor of Jerusalem and rebuilding the temple, his successor, Nehemiah, completing the great wall.

Fewer than a hundred years are to elapse before the might of Persia crashes on the banks of the Issus. The Jews have a new overlord, the precocious, ambitious Macedonian genius. One year later they have a chance to see this fearsome Alexander when he visits Jerusalem.

Indeed they had reason to fear him. Whether out of gratitude to the memory of the friendly Persian kings or sheer stubbornness, they had declined to transfer their allegiance to the conqueror. In his eyes they were an unimportant but turbulent lot to be punished for their impudence. But as he approached the city, the spectacle of Jaddua, the High Priest, in his sacred robes of hyacinth and gold, appealed to the superstitious temperament of the Macedonian who thought he himself was a god. At the sight of the High Priest, followed by a train of lesser priests and dignitaries in white raiment, Alexander's wrath melted, he sank to his knee and kissed the sacred inscription on the miter.

And so down through the centuries stretched before my eyes the panorama of Jerusalem's conquerors—Ptolemy Lagi, Seleucus, Ptolemy Philopator, Antiochus the Great, and Antiochus Epiphanes who profaned the temple, the gallant Judas Maccabeus who purified it, Pompey, Herod, Titus who once more destroyed the Temple, the legions of Hadrian who razed the city and drove plows over the sacred ground where once had stood the city of David and Solomon and where Christ had gone to his death. Surely, the ruthless victors must have thought, this time, Jerusalem is no more.

But the Roman Empire was to learn what other conquerors learned before and since: "No one attacks Israel with impunity." Dispersed once more by Rome's legions, the Jews gradually returned. Incredible as it would have sounded to Hadrian, Jerusalem was rebuilt and, with the Christianization of the empire, it became a Christian city.

The centuries rolled on; once again Zion was stormed, this time by Chosroes the Persian who took Christian prisoners by the myriads and sold them into slavery. (The Holy City was a forbidden place to Jews under the Christian Empire.) Chosroes also took away the True Cross, which was recovered by the Emperor Heraclius, who restored the Holy Land to Christendom.

Thus again Jerusalem flourished in glory, a city whose name was sacred through a large portion of the civilized world. But a still worse scourge was at hand. Islam, in the person of the fierce Caliph Omar, swept over the land. "No one attacks Israel with impunity." Decadence overtook the Arab conquerors of Palestine. Their comparatively mild rule was followed by a far more fearful calamity.

In the Eleventh Century appeared the Seljuk Turks, a race of indomitable fighters. Arab civilization collapsed, to be followed by a regime that could hardly be described as a civilization at all. For the Turk, whether Seljuk or Ottoman, never contributed anything but death and degradation, created nothing but destruction and corruption. So we see the heroic but futile pageant of the Crusades: Godfrey de Bouillon, Tancred the Norman, Saint Louis of France, Richard of the Lion Heart and—Saladin the Magnificent. With the death of Saint Louis upon the hill of Carthage, the last Crusade ends. For 640 years Jerusalem is in the hands of the power justly characterized as "the Unspeakable Turk."

So what a glorious spectacle spread itself under my eyes on that morning in the Fall of 1917! Incredible as it seemed, the Fifth and last Crusade was victorious. Aided by the Sons of the Desert under the mysterious Lawrence, Sir Edmund Allenby had advanced solidly and irresistibly to the gates of Jerusalem. He had approached with the utmost care. He might have driven the Turko-German garrison out from a distance with bombing planes and artillery. But he did not turn so much as a single cannon on the Holy City, lest his shells might fall on the sacred Wailing Wall of the Jews, on the Church of the Holy Sepulcher or the Mosque of Omar, which Moslems regard as the third holiest place in the world. So, forcing the Germans and Turks back on either side of the town, he fought his way eastward through the Judean hills. Von Falkenhausen beat a hasty retreat. Seven centuries of Turkish misrule had come to an end. Zion again was in the hands of the Christian.

An amusing incident followed. On the morning of the tenth the British were encamped in the Judean hills a few miles away from the city. One of Allenby's divisions was the Sixtieth, Cockneys to a man. An officer dispatched a company cook and a Tommy to forage for eggs. Cockneys are notoriously unable to find their way anywhere except about London. So it wasn't long before those two were hopelessly lost. They found themselves on a broad high-way. Around the bend on a hill they saw a great walled city, glittering with domes and minarets. Though they didn't know it, what they saw was Jerusalem.

As they approached this strange place a party emerged from the western gate. One man carried a white flag; another, riding a horse, wore on his head a red fez. The latter turned out to be the Arab Mayor of Jerusalem. Falkenhausen had withdrawn during the night, so the Mayor was coming out to make his official surrender of Jerusalem to Allenby. As he approached the two Tommies he made a grandiloquent, flowery speech to fit the occasion. After it was, some-what haltingly, interpreted to the bewildered Tommies, the cook replied:

"But we don't want the 'Oly City, Guv'nor. What we wants is heggs for our horficers."

To the Mayor this was incredible. He insisted upon turning over the keys to the two men. So it happened that, after virtually thirteen centuries of Mohammedan rule, the place that Richard Coeur de Lion failed to capture was turned over to a Cockney cook. But that wasn't all.

The Tommies reported to their commanding officer, a major. He, burst-ing with pride, conveyed the news to his brigadier, General Watson. Naturally every general officer in Allenby's army was willing to give his right arm for the honor of accepting the surrender of the holiest city on earth. General Watson promptly decided that he would proceed to Jerusalem at once for that purpose. Thereupon the Major, taking the cook along as a guide, hurried to the city, found the Mayor and arranged for the whole thing to be done all over again.

The entire population of Zion was out in full fig to greet the General and his shining staff. Flags flew, crowds cheered, flowers were strewn, the Mayor repeated his eloquent speech, and Jerusalem was formally surrendered into the hands of Brigadier General Watson. The latter then officially notified his divisional commander, Major General Sir John Shea. He, an Irishman and a devout Catholic, was not going to let any Protestant so-and-so put one over on him. So he sent back word that he would arrive on the following day to accept the surrender of Jerusalem.

That made it necessary for Brigadier General Watson to jump on his horse, ride to the city and arrange with the bewildered Mayor to repeat the ceremony a third time. Once more the crowds were out, flags flying, cheering, singing, speeches. But this time it was noticeable that the enthusiasm and spontaneity of the affair were growing a trifle thin. There was a weary tone in the Mayor's voice as he droned through his oration once more. Thus for the third time was Jerusalem surrendered.

Sir John Shea sent word to Allenby of what he had done. Back came a reply by courier that he, the Commander in Chief himself, would arrive shortly to accept the surrender of Jerusalem. This time General Shea had to rush to Jerusalem and arrange for a return performance.

Allenby arrived in state, horse, foot, artillery, and a long string of staff cars full of Brass Hats. Then he made a superb gesture. Instead of staging a triumphal entrance, he walked into the Holy City on foot through the old Jaffa Gate—as Allenby put it, "where One had walked before." Again the crowds were out, again the flags fluttered, again the Mayor made his speech. And so Jerusalem was surrendered for the fourth time, as the enthusiasm of the multitude and the eloquence of His Honor descended to plumb zero.

A month later the Mayor of Jerusalem died of pneumonia. The legend now current in Zion is that he died of exposure, the consequence of having to make that speech of surrender so often.

I passed many days in Jerusalem. Of course the capture of the Holy City had made a profound sensation the world over, but particularly throughout the British Empire. It earned for Sir Edmund Allenby the rank of Field Marshal and the title of Viscount Allenby of Megiddo and Armageddon. Several other honors were handed out. King George V was unable to come to Palestine in person, but he sent his aged uncle, H.R.H. the Duke of Connaught, to hold the investiture of the decorations. One of the men to be thus honored was absent, somewhere out in the Arabian desert. Though he had played a vital part in the campaign, only a few members of Allenby's staff knew his name.

About the time of the Duke's arrival, I was strolling through one of the winding streets of Jerusalem. As I passed a group of Arabs, one in particular arrested my attention. Though arrayed in a most striking Arab costume, he was beardless and a blond. Now the Arabs don't consider a man full grown unless he has a beard. They swear by their beards. And I knew there was no such creature as a blond Arab. So I made up my mind to find out all I could about that phenomenon.

I went to the office of the Governor of Jerusalem in an old palace outside the Damascus gate. The British incumbent of the office of Pontius Pilate was Colonel Ronald Storrs. To him I expressed my reportorial curiosity about the blond Arab. Colonel Storrs stood up, opened a door and through it I looked into another room and saw the beardless chap in full Sherifian panoply, sitting at a table and reading a work on archaeology.

"Let me introduce you to Colonel Lawrence," said Storrs and added, "the uncrowned king of Arabia."

The beardless blond Arab smiled shyly. He had just slipped through the Turkish lines in disguise, at Allenby's orders, to receive his decoration from the hands of the Duke of Connaught. That chance meeting with T. E. Lawrence on the Street of the Christians in Jerusalem was to start me off on ten years of wandering up and down the face of the earth. I had a long series of conversations with him. He helped me to obtain Allenby's consent to my joining him and his Arab fighters far to the south, in the Hedjaz. And thus it was that I was able to bring back the first account of the Revolt in the Desert, the first story to reach the ears of the world of the almost incredible adventures of Lawrence of Arabia.

Another bit of comedy connected with the event came to light later. Allenby issued an order that no troops should enter Jerusalem until a military police system had been established. This grieved the soul of my friend Colonel Barney Todd of the Tenth Australian Light Horse. He said to himself: "By all the laws of luck in war, we're sure to be shifted somewhere else before our turn comes to enter the city. So we'll miss the sight of our lives." So, in flagrant disobedience of orders, he dismounted his regiment and took them into Jerusalem. The first place they visited was the American Colony store.

This had been established by a Chicago lawyer and his wife. Several years before this lawyer had given up his practice, wound up his affairs in Chicago and, with a party of devout friends, had come to the Holy Land. The idea was to await the fulfilment of ancient prophecy, the second coming of the Lord. When it became apparent that the Lord was postponing his second advent indefinitely, the lawyer and his wife, to occupy their time, established the American Colony store.

There Colonel Barney Todd and his Anzacs made their first call. The Colonel proceeded to buy up all the picture post cards in the place. He then addressed them to all the rulers of the earth he could think of. One went to the King of England, another to the Prime Minister of Australia, another to the President of the United States, and to all the Sultans of Asia whose names he could recall. On each of those cards was the legend: "Have just captured Jerusalem. Yours truly, Barney Todd."

Stout fighters, those Australians, ideal shock troops, magnificent horsemen, rollicking, robust fellows. But their respect for military discipline, or perhaps I should say military etiquette, was nil. They came from the mines and sheep stations of Australia, where one man's as good as another, and a damn' sight better.

An English major of my acquaintance was anxious to find the so-called Wells of Moses. He asked an Australian soldier, a private, to direct him. The private didn't know the way but at that moment he espied his captain. "Hey, you!" shouted the private to the captain: "come here and tell this English bloke how to get to the Wells of Moses."

To the English major's amazement, the captain meekly obeyed. The Englishman asked the private how on earth he got away with such effrontery.

"Well," replied the Anzac, "when this war broke out, a lot of us chaps who own stations volunteered, joined up as privates. It wasn't until later that officers' training camps were established. So it happened that some of the chaps who used to work for us went to the training camps and became our officers. That bloke used to ride boundary for me, and when it come to orders, when I'm around, it's *me* who gives them."

The Australians were not only lusty fighters but accomplished robbers. I mean that in the polite sense of the term—thieves of the better sort. When an army is in enemy territory, it is the men who can steal food for themselves and fodder for their horses most proficiently who last longest.

Each night before the Australians of the Tenth Light Horse went into action, their padre would call them together and give them a historical description of the terrain where they were to fight on the following day. For instance, if it was the Vale of Ajalon, he would tell them about the battle fought there by Joshua and how he commanded the sun and moon to stand still. If it was Hebron, he would discourse about the Cave of Machpelah, where Abraham and Sarah, Isaac and Rebecca, Jacob and Rachel are buried.

The night before the capture of Bethlehem the padre repeated the oft-told tale of the first Christmas Eve. He related how, nineteen hundred and seventeen Christmases ago, the Angel of the Lord appeared and announced that a Savior had been born in the city of David and gave the glad tidings to the shepherds who watched their flocks. Whereupon one of the troopers from the back blocks of Queensland spoke up and said:

"Yes, Padre, and they'd better watch their flocks *tomorrow* night!"

—*EXPLORERS CLUB TALES* (1936)

Lowell Thomas was familiar to all through his voice, daily giving out vital news and pertinent comment over the radio. Author, lecturer, and historian; he was attached to the Belgian, French, Italian, Serbian, American, British, and Arabian armies, in turn; an observer with Hedjaz forces, historian of the Palestine Campaign and Arabian revolution, also the German revolution. He uncovered the romantic career of Lawrence of Arabia to the world. He hobnobbed with kings, pashas, sheiks, and native princes, in India, Malaya, Upper Burmah, and Central Asia.

There *Is* Such An Animal

BY PATRICK PUTNAM

Introduction by Seyward S. Cramer, Editor, *Through Hell and High Water*, 1941

There was quite a stir a few years ago when the Readers' Digest published an article about a dude ranch in Africa. We had just begun to get used to the idea of having such "ranches" in all parts of the United States—there was one only about forty miles away from New York. Somehow the idea of a dude ranch in Africa seemed out of place—Africa was supposed to be a vast place of dense forest, full of wild, man-eating animals, and almost entirely populated with fierce, black savages.

Much of that impression had been the fault of wild stories and inadequate textbooks in our public schools. As a matter of fact, I have know few people who have lived in Africa that did not have a desire to live there the rest of their lives. They most generally term it a paradise—and it must be from some of the tales.

Pat Putnam was the owner of the dude ranch, and it is not a ranch in the sense of our Western conception of the term. Africa is a large place and the white settlers few and far between after one leaves the cities. Pat rather fell in love with this particular spot in the Ituri Forest and built his home there and included several guesthouses within the compound. Both he and his wife were friendly souls and they enjoyed the company. Those guesthouses were occupied much of the time—by friends, acquaintances, and tourists who happened to be passing on the highway that passed close by.

Soon the Putnam place became well known and people flocked here. It was an ideal spot for vacationing, loafing, writing, all sorts of things. Within the houses you had all the comforts of civilization yet a five-minute walk took you into the heart of the forest; primeval forest, if you will.

Don't get the idea that Pat was an innkeeper. That was just incidental. You might say that it was a hobby. It wasn't his principal hobby either, because that was his interest in the okapi. Tell us something about that, Pat.

I don't mean to say that okapis are my lifework but they are certainly a part of it. Some of you chase after stamps or coins or bronzes and devote much of your spare time to this hobby. The only difference is that my okapi is just a little bit harder to find, and if I do get one that is alive I have to take care of it and feed it.

To many of you, okapi is probably little more than a name. The foolish build-up publicity about the animal has led people to expect a shocking, unbelievable, gigantic dinosaur come to life again. There is one up at the Bronx Zoo—it is the only one in America today—and I would suggest that you go up there and see it. You will find it about as big as a donkey, though its high forequarters and long neck make it seem much taller.

The Dictionnaire Larousse, with true Gallic clarity and inaccuracy, gives one of those little dictionary pictures of an okapi, and then describes it as a rare animal, a cross between a zebra and an antelope. Well, I must say that it *looks* like a cross between a zebra and an antelope, but it just isn't. Zoologists say that it is a cousin to the giraffe, a sort of forest giraffe which didn't get along quite as far on the road to absurdity as its grasslands cousin did; the okapi has an extremely long neck. Instead of being spotted, its coat is of a dark-red color, and it is the broad, sharply contrasting horizontal white stripes that would remind you of a zebra. Its hoofs, of course, are cloven, and its footprint, except to the practiced eye of the native, looks very much like the hoofprint of a forest buffalo.

Like most forest animals, the okapi has large ears that are round in shape, upright and mobile—it can turn them forward, sideways, and nearly backwards. Unfortunately, there are pictures of drawings and even some museum settings which place the animal out in grasslands. This is absurd—almost as absurd as it would be to place an Ituri Forest pygmy in an Eskimo igloo. The okapi is a forest animal and would have nothing to eat if it ever wandered out onto the grasslands.

But to pick up the Dictionnaire Larousse again. Few dictionaries with any claim to accuracy have carried on the "cross between zebra and antelope" fallacy but they all continue to call it "rare."

"Why, isn't it a rare animal?" I am asked. "Do you really see many of them?"

No, I see them damned seldom, perhaps five times in ten years, and I do an awful lot of tramping through their forest. But you, sir, do you see many rats in New York?

Obviously, an alert, shy animal that is not often seen by noisy, blundering purblind white men is not, *ipso facto*, a rare animal. "Rarely seen" is in no way synonymous with "rare." I have seen solemn sentences in solemn books such as "the total number of okapi estimated to exist in the world is not over 300." My guess—and you'll have to take my word for it that I know more about them than any other *muzungu*—is that there are about fifteen thousand of them in existence. The odd thing about the matter, and what does in a way make them rare, is the fact that they are found only in the Ituri Forest, and nowhere else in the world. Now, the Ituri Forest blends imperceptibly into the rest of the great West African Forest, extending al the way up to Liberia, and it is one of the multitudinous mysteries of nature that the okapi should not exist throughout the whole area. In that whole extent of forest there are all the kinds of leaves that they like to eat, thousands of the clear sand-bedded streams where they like to spread their forelegs and drink, the moist, moderately warm atmosphere in which they thrive, even the leopards and Negroes that like to eat them. Why, all of us who ponder such questions ask ourselves, does the okapi not spread throughout the whole of the great West African tropical rain forest?

The answer is the simplest in the world: "I don't know." But the fact remains that the Ituri Forest in the Belgian Congo is the only place where they are found. They are strictly protected and, so far as the white man is concerned, the prohibition against killing them is rigidly enforced. There is much truth to my saying that it is much easier to get an okapi than to get a permit to get an okapi.

Not so for the natives—the Negroes and pygmies in their vast forest ranges. Back in 1928 I was in the Makere country. From the forest came a call. The natives with me in the hunting camp answered, and ran down toward the stream. I followed, and we met a man carrying the tail of some animal. There was rapid happy talk in Makere in which I caught the word Nyama—it means both animal and meat.

"Yes," said the hunter, "I'm going to our village with the tail; then they'll know I've really got one in my trap, and the woman will come out to cut it up and carry it in."

Of course, I went along. He led the way for several miles—through the forest, over knolls, along level stretches of leafy ground, down across stream and swamp, and up again to dry ground along the winding game path—before we came near to the nyama. Then around a turn in the path, and there it was, big, dark red, stretched dead on its side, with broad white stripes on its hind legs.

"Yes," I thought, "that's what it is." I was astonished and delighted, for I had heard of this "very rare animal" but never hoped to be lucky enough to see one. The sharp knifes had already slashed through the skin before I could think twice or speak once. Too late to save the skin. "Cut off the meat," I said, "but don't cut through the bones. Save them for me. I want them. I'll give you francs."

"White men are crazy," they probably thought, "but it's better to do as they want." At any rate, they didn't cut through the bones, and soon the meat was all in baskets, and the women started off with them slung on tumplines over their foreheads. The men reluctantly tied the bones together, and onto poles so that two could carry them, but the skull they didn't pack. "Bring the skull," I said. "No," they answered, "it's bad luck to take the skull back to the village. If we did, Nangala would never get another one." But francs talked, and the skull came with us. Some of the francs went to the medicine man, I suppose, to make an antidotal charm.

That was my first trip to the Congo. Milt Katz and Fred Wulsin, our boss, had gone on toward Lake Chad and I was left on my own. All my collections were ethnographical—knives, spears, baskets, stools—and the lot went to Peabody, the anthropological wing of Harvard Museum. In unpacking the stuff, Dr. Hooton came upon the old bones and said: "What the devil had Putnam sent us this young elephant for?"

So they lugged it across the court to the zoological wing. It was spring, and Dr. Barbour was sitting on the steps smoking a cigarette. "Tom," they shouted, "do you want some elephant bones?" He lifted his ponderous frame, and glanced at the bones. "Elephant, hell!" he said. "That's an okapi."

I think he was glad to get it, but I asked him never officially to acknowledge it, because I knew the laws against killing, capturing, or being in possession of the skin or bones of an okapi, and I didn't want to be arrested when I went back to the Congo. There is a statute of limitations, however, and "now it can be told."

My next spell in the Congo was working for the Congo Red Cross, and I didn't have much time even to think of okapi. But when I started building my place at the Epulu, I thought of trying to capture some. I knew the government wouldn't let me capture them for myself, but I got permission to "save any that were caught by natives, and keep them on my place, the okapis to remain the property of the Government." Capturing and keeping them would be an expense, but I was glad to accept these terms, both for the fun that it would be if I succeeded and for the attraction some okapis in my back yard would be to tourists.

All excited, I called my men, and said, "You've all got traps out in the forest, I know. Next time an okapi falls into somebody's pit, don't kill it, but come and tell me, and I'll pay you 300 francs for it alive. If I hear that any one of you has caught an okapi in his pit, and instead of telling me, has killed and eaten it, I will report him to the District Commissioner for killing an okapi, which you know right well is against the law.

The days went by, and the weeks. So-and-so came in and said he'd seen okapi tracks right near his pit, but he'd gone around it. Yes, a big one. Would he be likely to come back again? Well, maybe. *Maneno ya mungu*—affair of God. I didn't leave my place often, and my chauffeur Ngimo was a great trapper, with plenty of time to trap, for it was beneath his dignity as a chauffeur to do much of anything around the place except drive a car. He was a good fellow, but rather quarrelsome with the other men, being of the Bobua tribe, and perhaps because he smoked too much *banghi*.

I went out to look at Ngimo's pits, and the other men's. Clever simple traps they are, too. In some well-trodden game trail they dig a pit, about six feet long, six feet deep, and three wide. Reeds are laid across the top two or three inches apart, and on top of these are skillfully scattered dead leaves from the forest floor, so that the covering of the pit is indistinguishable from the forest floor.

Well, their pits seemed to be all right, and well tended. Tending consists mainly in going out after a rain to replace the leaves that have been washed from the cover into the pit. One day I was walking along, enjoying the forest which I so love to wander in—just as I like to walk along Fifth Avenue and look at the shop windows, and occasionally looking up to the skyscrapers—when *pht!*—there was nothing below me, and then *plump!* There I was inside looking out, or rather on the bottom of the pit looking up. I was not hurt a particle, for I had had no time to brace and stiffen myself. With my sheath knife I cut a step in one wall and was out in a jiffy.

That was the first time, and in following years, when I had official permission to go all out after okapi and had pits all through the forests, many's the time I have been so trapped. Fortunately for me, it's not the custom of the tribes around my place to stick sharpened stakes in the bottom of a pitfall.

I heard a story once, though, of an unfortunate native who fell into a pit into which a wild boar had already fallen. Naturally in those narrow quarters the wild boar made short work of him.

When I did start trapping, Ngimo must have prepared the right kind of medicine, for one fine day he rushed up and said there was an okapi in his pit. Immeasurably excited, I called the workmen and their wives together, and we all went out with machetes, axes, and shovels. Sure enough, there was a real okapi in the pit, and he seemed in fine shape. It is amazing that these heavy animals don't break a leg or two when they fall so far onto a hard clay or gravel bottom, but my own experience proved that when you're not prepared you don't get hurt.

I told my people to start building a wattle fence, but it was evident that spearing the okapi would be much more in conformity to their taste and habit. Then we carefully shoveled earth back into the pit, and soon the okapi gave a lunge and was out and butting into our wattle fence. Our enclosure was none too strong, for I soon learned that the okapi is a powerful butter, and with his hind legs gives kicks like cannon shots. At one corner of the corral we built a thatch roof, half of it inside the corral, to protect the okapi from the torrential afternoon rains of the season, and half outside the corral for me to sleep under.

Of course, I wouldn't leave my pride and joy. Mary, my wife, came out and had a look at her, and named her Maude, and then went back to set our carpenter to building a crate. During the first night we heard a leopard coughing pretty close, but he never did get up the necessary courage to come in for the good okapi meat he could smell.

News soon came from Mary that the carrying crate was finished. So I walked home to test it—the pit was only about a mile from our house. The crate had no top, but it had a solid floor, and, made of heavy mahogany, was a frightfully cumbersome thing. Judging that about eight women would weigh as much as Maude, we put them all in the crate; laughing, they were carried around our workman's village, while the twenty-odd carriers and the villagers cheered.

It seemed to be all right, so we took it out to the pit, soon lured poor Maude into it with some tempting leaves, and started to carry her into the village, where we had prepared an enclosure. A carrier would slip now and then, the crate would lurch, and Maude thrashed around. It was a tough job, and we were all relieved, and pleased to get her home. Maude backed out of the crate. She seemed all right, and ate well.

When the weekly mail truck passed the next day, I sent a proud telegram to the Governor General. But the next week I had to send a less proud one: "The okapi died." In the autopsy, I found she had a badly broken lower jaw, which she must have cracked on the sharp edge of the crate when she jumped around during her trip.

Well, Maude was the first of many okapis that we caught. She had stood about a week of captivity. The next one, Mutu Moya (Man Alone) lasted four weeks, and probably died of starvation. I kept him out in a corral near the pit in which he was caught, and I think that the guardians I left with him spent far more time feeding themselves and resting than collecting forest leaves for Man Alone.

Finally one lasted for months, and then suddenly sickened, and died a day or two later. The autopsy showed thousands of intestinal worms. That is the secret of what kills okapis in most cases. Like the human hookworm, the eggs are in the droppings; the larvae hatch out, penetrate through the skin of the feet, and then circuitously work their way to the intestines. Almost surgical cleanliness of the corral fixed this trouble, and finally I did have flourishing okapis in my back yard.

Tourists flocked to see them, and many took pictures with amateur movie cameras. A few professional motion-picture expeditions turned up. Amateur or professional, they were nearly all insistent that I put lots of greenery around the fence, and I have had the amusement back here in America of seeing one movie after another showing proudly "the first movie ever made of a wild okapi in its native haunts." Of course, none of them were of free okapi, and my back yard was "its native haunts." No one has yet made a movie of free okapis, and of still photographs I believe only one is genuine. A Central European traveler, a Hungarian, I think, was driving along the main road one day a few miles from my place, when he had the extraordinary luck of seeing an okapi cross the road ahead of him and the extraordinary skill to get a photograph of it. He has not had the publicity he deserves for his picture, which I believe is unique.

Once years ago, when the automobile road was brand-new and the okapis had not yet learned what a dangerous place it was for them, with natives with spears walking along and white men with guns in cars and trucks, I was riding along on a horse. Several hundred feet behind me one of my men was on foot, carrying my gun and camera. Riding to the top of a hill, I saw an okapi a little ahead of me happily feeding on some leaves by the roadside and quite unaware of my presence. I slipped off my horse, and made frantic signals to my man. Of course, I didn't dare shout to him. I wanted my camera, but he wanted meat, so he carefully put down the camera and tiptoed up with the gun. I exploded. The scolding didn't faze my man, but the okapi didn't like such a display of temper and crashed off into the forest. I wish I hadn't missed the only chance I ever had to photograph an uncaptured okapi.

No, a movie of a wild, free okapi would be a prize. You would have to be lucky enough to meet one on the road in the daytime, and that gets less and less likely. Photography in its true native haunts, the forest where it is always twilight, is mighty close to impossible.

The last time I saw one of my okapis was in Hollywood last spring. Strange things do happen, and I found myself working for Metro-Goldwyn-Mayer on a bigger and better Tarzan picture. They planned to send a crew out to the Congo, and leading that crew around would have been my job. The war came along and canceled all that. While we were still working on it, I was looking through all the four Tarzan pictures that M-G-M has made; halfway through *Tarzan Finds a Son* there across the screen walked my okapi in my back yard, the fence well screened by bushes. It was a ten- or fifteen-second shot, and I found that M-G-M had paid $2,000 for it. That's another shot I wish I hadn't missed.

With all those okapis out in the forest, and only one in America, something will probably be done. And I want to be mixed up in it. New York is a hard place for me to leave and I'll surely tarry at some of the hot spots in the African part of this war, such hot spots that I won't let my present wife, Emilie Baca, come with me, although she grew to like that jungle home of mine.

But if you ask me "Do you want to go back?" there can be only one answer—an emphatic "Yes!" To me, that forest on the Epulu River in the Ituri is pretty much of a paradise.

To begin with it was nothing but river and forest. Gradually, with a score or so of natives who did the dirty work for $2 apiece a month, and with the help of my first wife, the late Mary Linder, to make it beautiful—for she had been a landscape architect—we got enough of the giant trees cut down to make room for building, sawed them up into beams and planks for framework and doors, and collected phrynium leaves for thatching, so that a house, then houses, slowly grew. And there was a garden to clear and plant and tend and a road to be cut from the main road through the forest to our place, and two bridges to be built on that short road—so full of streams is the Ituri. Plenty, in fact, to keep busy, not to speak of the medical work I kept on doing for my old patients, the Negroes and pygmies.

But okapis are a fascinating hobby, and if I found time for it in those days, I'll probably be at it again. Drop in on me sometime, and we'll tramp the forest together and learn about okapi. Perhaps you'll like what I call real living.

—THROUGH HELL AND HIGH WATER (1941)

Witchcraft Among the Zulus

BY CARL VON HOFFMAN

T
hough long acquainted with white men, and influenced in countless ways by civilization, the Zulu still clings to his belief in the supernatural powers of witches and witch doctors, who play a large part in the life of Zululand.

One who has lived with these folk can understand the spell of their spirit world. The semitropical sun throws bright highlights and casts deep shadows. The distant vistas are filled with mirages. There is the danger of snakes and lurking beasts, and the spell cast by mystifying nights. The effect of all this is so strong that even the white man may find it difficult at times to keep his balance.

It is a perfect setting for the native with his world of spirits, good and evil—a world largely controlled by hovering ancestors and adverse spirits. The closeness of primitive existence to nature gives a supernatural meaning to almost every detail of life. Any elephant or lion may be an embodied spirit, while the venomous snake is regarded as a reincarnated ancestor, to be worshiped and protected as such. Even the shadows cast at night by trees conjure up to the native mind a world of treacherous spirits seeking to destroy him. Thus his main occupation is the appeasement of his ancestral and other spirits. Disease, misfortune, and death are attributed to them, and to those who invoke such spirits by witchcraft.

In Zulu the word *Abatakati* means witch, and the word *Ungoma* signifies a witch doctor, but to the native mind there is a world of difference between them. The witch doctor functions as a distinguished member of the community, the witch as an outlaw. Both deal in the occult, but the witch invokes evil spirits for his designs, while the witch doctor drives them away.

The role of the witch doctor is that of guardian against witches and evil spirits. He tells the villagers how to fulfill their destiny, and he cures by driving the malignant spirit out of the sick body. He divines the cause of people's troubles and smells out forbidden deeds. As a dealer in the occult he can bring good or bad luck, or death. From the white man's viewpoint he is also a sinister power who brings about ritual murder, but to the native he remains an oracle whose findings and omens are almost infallible.

The witch invokes adverse spirits and deals in black magic. He deals in things evil, and he casts spells which bring misfortune, disease, and death. A witch will come in handy when a native wants protection or revenge, but he is also a dispenser of charms, and as such carries on a lively, if underhand, trade with the natives. He sells them advice, medicines, and love potions, and tells fortunes. But any dealings with the witch are somewhat risky, since a person otherwise innocent may fall under the spell of the witch and may become suspected of practicing witchcraft himself. The natives may laugh at the witch when he comes in to the kraal to tell fortunes, but they go in awe and even fear when they seek him out for some hidden purpose. The witch for his part plies his trade under cover of darkness, for detection may mean his end.

There are all sorts of witches of both sexes, but practically all fall into two main categories—the professional and the casual. When a Zulu speaks of a witch, he is thinking of a professional witch, of a person who spends his time in black magic and those services can be had at a price. This person may live openly as a typical native, occupied with the usual daily village routine. There is the usual family life, although in the case of the male witch there may be more wives because he can afford to buy more. Sometimes a reputed witch had to be pointed out to me, since he couldn't be picked out of a crowd, but more often he stood out by his eccentric hairdress or by the extra number of ornaments tied about his body. Other witches are recluses, living apart from the villagers, often pretending poverty or posing as beggars. The witch belongs to no guild such as that of the witch doctors, but the craft is usually handed down as a family tradition.

The casual witch is a common event. He may be any person accused through malice or hearsay, or a person who has committed an act of witchcraft for some personal reason. Every Zulu man, woman, or child lives in constant fear of being accused of witchcraft. Anything that deviates from the normal routine of life is attributed to evil spirits or witchcraft, and the native constantly goes about with the words witch and bewitched on his mind, although he is very reluctant to utter the words. But the words come out too often, and tragedy follows.

Typical of what goes on continually is the case of an old woman in the Impangei district. At the white trader's post where I spent the night I heard that the natives up the hill were out in the bush looking for a witch. The next day I got the details. Two old women had been quarreling over some tobacco, and afterward the aggrieved one was heard to mutter something about the other being an old witch. Some time later she took sick with a cold and let it be known she had been bewitched. When asked who had bewitched her, she accused the other woman. The sick woman died, probably of pneumonia, but to the natives all evidence pointed to witchcraft. The accused woman, knowing what was in store for her, cleared out into the bush. Had she remained, she would have been tried before a witch doctor and probably put to death. That she ran away was sufficient proof to the natives that she was guilty. As for the old woman, death was more or less certain, whether at the hands of the natives or by prowling beasts of the bush.

The professional witch operates in devious ways. Much of this is through suggestion, with a great play on local superstitions. If a Zulu, on awakening, finds something smeared on his neck, he knows that a witch has marked him for death. More common is the placing of sticks, fetishes, or medicines in the doorway of a marked man. In such cases fear and brooding by the victim often lead to death. He may run to the witch doctor, who may help him with potions that ward off the evil influence, or may divine the guilty witch and in that way put a stop to the influence. The fear of being possessed makes the native suspicious of any unusual act.

On one of my early trips to Zululand I entertained a chief with the usual conjuring tricks, and among other things I made a coin disappear and then produced it again from off the bare leg of a native. The effect was quite unexpected. The native was frightened and grave doubts were raised among the rest as to whether he was bewitched and his soul enslaved by an evil force. It took some explanation to reassure them that the white man's magic could not affect a Zulu. Once assured, the native asked for the coin, since it had come from his leg and therefore must be his.

It is through potions that the professional witch does most of his work. Potions are used for almost everything—to attract, protect, bring luck, and kill. Poisoning is a well-developed art in Zululand, as throughout Africa, and the venom comes from herbs, leaves, and snakes. Each witch is supposed to have his own secret formulas. Poisoning is common, but its fatal consequences are invariably attributed to the evil spell invoked by some witch. The fear of the evil spell is especially noticeable at meals. No food is served without assuring the guest that no evil spell or poison has been placed in the food. For the chief there is always the tester who tastes first of everything served. In drinking from the common beer pot, the chief, and each guest in turn, drinks only after the tester has taken a few gulps before them. There are also legendary poisons, some of which may produce effects by power of suggestion. A common sight, when a leopard has been shot, is to see the natives pluck out the whiskers of the animal. Leopard whiskers are both feared as an evil potion and treasured as a medicine. When put into food, they are supposed to produce nausea and death, but when mixed with the flesh of the animal, the result is a healthful dish which produces great courage.

Tricks and deceptions of various sorts are also resorted to by the professional witch. Ventriloquism is a well-developed art among Zulu witches, and is sometimes worked in conjunction with silhouettes. In one instance I know of, a shadow having the outlines of some wild beast, with moving jaws, fell across a kraal, and a voice was heard calling. The natives rushed out of their huts to see a shadow trying to swallow a cow, and heard a voice demanding that the best cow be driven off to a ravine and left there for a hungry spirit. The natives sometimes obey such a voice, but on this occasion they lit fires and stood guard against the evil spirit. The next morning they called on the witch doctor that he might divine whether it was an evil spirit or a witch. As usual, the witch doctor knew that it was not *Amadhlozi*, a spirit, but a witch throwing a silhouette by moonlight, probably from a near-by tree, or that it might even be the shadow of a tree swaying in the wind and made use of by a witch. As usual, he knew who the witch was, but still went through the process of smelling out the guilty one.

The tactics of the professional witch are also attributed at one time or another to the casual witch. A native may have his cow go dry, and, having dreamt that a certain person had evil designs on his cattle, he thereupon accuses that person of having bewitched his cow. The accused person may not even deny it, since he may feel he has no control over his soul while asleep, and so lets the witch doctor divine the "truth," after perhaps presenting him with a goat as a present. If guilty, he may have to replace the cow, and a stigma falls on him which makes his future hazardous.

A man may also function as a casual witch if, for instance, he makes use of a love charm without first making some sacrifice, such as slaughtering a goat for his ancestral spirits. There was the incident of the native who had gone hunting with a love charm and had managed to bring back a buck. Later, a friend died, and it was rumored that this had been caused by the hunter failing to make the necessary sacrifice.

The casual witch may even be accused of stealing souls and thus be put in the class of a professional witch. The Zulu buries his dead within the kraal, near his huts, for fear that the bodies may be dug up by witches. It is firmly believed that witches resurrect corpses stolen from graves, shrink them into dwarfs, and use them as their agents. The enslaved soul thus becomes an instrument of evil under the command of a witch. On one occasion a hyena was driven off while digging up a fresh grave. No one could convince the natives that this was not a witch who had taken the form of a hyena seeking to enslave another soul.

Some witches have acquired great reputations and are in demand throughout Zululand. It may even be said that the witch becomes immune to punishment in proportion to his reputation. Eminent witches are called by rival chiefs to throw spells over their enemies, and may even be secretly attached to a chief's staff, although they are outlawed by the white man. The chief himself, however, is careful not to be openly associated with witches, or in any way thought of as practicing witchcraft.

When I was with Selimano Zulu, paramount chief, I entertained him with my usual bag of tricks, including that of the color-changing handker-chief. For the native this meant witchcraft, but I assured the chief it was merely a mechanical trick. On offering it to him as a gift he accepted it but seemed annoyed at not being able to make use of it. He explained that, if he performed the trick before his people, they would suspect him of witchcraft, which was unbecoming a chief, whereas, if he let his people in on the trick, he would lose face for having divulged it. But the average chief will make use of avowed supernatural powers, falling short of witchcraft, to maintain his prestige. I watched a chief demonstrate before his people with a double-bar-rel shotgun. A native was lined up a few yards distant, and the chief, after placing a charmed necklace around his neck, leveled off and shot point-blank at him. The man walked off scared out of his wits, but unharmed, and the chief explained that he had protected the fellow from harm, even from the white man's bullets. A sheep was then produced and tied to a stake at about the same distance. When the chief blazed away again the sheep fell dead with a huge wound in its body. The sheep had not been immunized from harm by the chief. The natives, of course, never realized that the shot from the first shell had been removed, but attributed the miracle to the chief's power of protecting his people.

The influence of witchcraft on the native mind, and the role played by the witch doctor, were vividly demonstrated to me when I was staying with the Changane-Zulu tribe in the low veldt along the Sabi River.

At this time I had a native skinner, by name Ngzimba, who was in the habit of disappearing at night, although there were no villages near the camp.

I soon learned that he was spending the time at the river bank, waiting for elephants to come down to drink in the hope that he could pick up some elephant dung. In moving camp, he piled a bag on to the truck, and, since it smelled bad, I asked for an explanation. He then confessed to the elephant dung. Some weeks later he came into camp with a bundle of giraffe ribs under his arms. As the skinner, he was able to collect other bits, such as lion fat, all of which he piled on the truck. It turned out that this was destined for a witch in return for a love potion.

When we made camp at the Sabi River, Ngzimba disappeared for days. We learned that he was courting a girl in a near-by village, the daughter of my native hunter, Bones. This man had refused to let his daughter marry Ngzimba, since the latter could not produce the *Lobola*, that is, the price of thirteen cows, for the girl. Elopement would have meant theft, with the father taking revenge on Ngzimba's relatives while Ngzimba was fleeing Zululand. The alternative was witchcraft, not in a serious way but sufficient to make the girl infatuated with him. When the opportunity offered itself, he made use of his love potion by rubbing it on the girl's arm and then telling her that she was now in his power and that when the moon rose she would be drawn to his kraal or else be made to dash about braying like a zebra.

I learned of this later, after I had seen the father of the girl consulting a witch disguised as a fortune teller. In a squatting position, constantly clapping his hands, he kept repeating that his daughter was bewitched while the witch kept mumbling the name of Ngzimba. When the performance was over, I asked Bones what it meant, and he said that his daughter was bewitched, that she was running about braying like a zebra. Going out of the kraal, we saw a group of native women running after a girl along the edge of a precipice. They fortunately caught her in time, and when we reached the point, I saw that the girl was mad. She was dragged back to the kraal, shrieking and actually braying, and I was told that this had been going on for days.

I heard no more of the matter for some days, but the mysterious silence of the natives, including my own men, made me suspect that something was up. Where before they had laughed about the love potion affair as a good joke, they now merely shrugged their shoulders when asked for news. On my next trip to the village, I finally discovered what was going on. The path crossed a ravine, but on this occasion my men tried to make a detour on the pretext that the stream was no longer fordable. Since it was the dry season, it was obvious that the stream had not risen since I last crossed it. I finally got the real reason out of one of the men. A great witch doctor had come into the country and was about to drive all evil spirits from the people, and he had chosen that very ravine for the spot where he would drown these evil spirits.

It turned out that the witch doctor was Lucas M'Zungu, a great Voodoo doctor, a combination of witch and witch doctor with a smattering of the white man's religion. I approached the place with caution in the hope of watching the performance unobserved. The Voodoo practice, as any witch-craft, was forbidden by the white man's law, and my appearance would prob-ably have disrupted things. But I was soon discovered, and so proceeded to assure the doctor that he need have no fear, since I was not a government official. After some hesitation, the man came forward and, in Zulu, with a few English words thrown in, said that he was about to drown some spirits. There were three pots near by, with fires beneath, and some of the women were pouring water into them. The Voodoo doctor, dressed in a black robe, stood there holding a Bible in Zulu script, and mumbling incantations. The patients now came forward, stripped to the waist, to be anointed by the Voodoo doctor with lion fat, and among them was the girl who had been bewitched by Ngzimba, muttering to herself but no longer raving. Each of the patients was then told to kneel and drink from the can of water placed before him, while the doctor kept up his incantations. The hot water was served in gallon cans, which formed part of the Voodoo equipment, and the patient was not allowed to stop drinking until the can was emptied, as oth-erwise the magic would lose its force. As soon as one can was emptied by a patient he would be given another, urged on by being told that the more magic he consumed the more certain was the cure. Some were able to fin-ish the second gallon, and all were plainly bloated and apparently in great discomfort.

When all drinking had ceased, the doctor showed them how to insert their fingers in their mouths as far back as possible, with the result that much vomiting started. To those struggling, the doctor shouted that the evil spirit was fighting within them, that it was trying to stay in their stomachs, and must be driven out by throwing it up.

After ridding themselves of the water, the patients got up and walked away with smiling faces, for now they were unwitched. The raving girl was among the cured. When the Voodoo doctor, M'Zungu, left the ravine, his safari contained goats, cows, and sheep that had been paid him for the cure. I later learned from the girl's father that among these were four cows that Ngzimba had owned but which had been seized by the chief's order. Furthermore, Ngzimba had apparently cleared out for good. Had he remained he would, no doubt, have found his standing in the community very sadly impaired.

— EXPLORERS CLUB TALES (1936)

Carl von Hoffman knew his Africa, which he trailed from Cairo to the Cape, as he who reads may know. As lecturer and author, his study of wild races inspired as well as educated. He spoke and wrote, displaying many hard-won pictures, from Formosa to Madagascar, and his listeners and readers were unfailingly entertained and convinced, with his fellow-explorers, that Carl von Hoffman "knew his stuff."

PART TWO

Alaska

A Day I Should Have Stayed in Bed

BY ROBERT C. REEVE

J oe Jacobs, the old fight promoter, had a name for the week of July 4,
1943. "Those were seven days I should have stayed in bed."

It started on a flight to McGrath with my old Boeing 80A. That was
quite an airplane. It had three engines, three tails and four wings and
would pack eleven thousand pounds. For ballast I was carrying four
spools of one inch cable. Just as I hit Rainy Pass I heard a shot like a cannon
emanating from my starboard engine. Looking back, I saw that the number
one cylinder had popped off and taken a section of the leading edge of the
wing along with it. The connecting rod was battering the engine case to
destruction, but that wasn't a big problem. There just wasn't anything to do
about it. The real urgency was to get back to Anchorage before the wing
vibrated loose and sailed off.

When I arrived over Cook Inlet half an hour later, I knew I would never
make Merrill Field in the turbulent air. Searching for a roost among the
creeks and stumps on the mud tide flats, I eventually spotted a clear spot
about 500 feet long and down the plane came to a halt still in one piece. The
landing was rough, but not too bad. I radioed my friend, Art Woodley, to
come and get us; we were soon back at Merrill Field—all in good shape
except that I had only two good engines, and no spares.

That situation was easily solved. A well-known construction company
had surreptitiously high-graded one of my old engines and I had been quietly watching them rebuild it before claiming it. They had just completed
it. I produced my bill of sale and I was back in business after a violent hassle
of objections to which they were obviously entitled under the circumstances.

Firing up my old Fairchild FC2W2 the next day, I ferried a load of timbers to the Boeing and constructed a scaffold to remove the damaged engine.
To get the new engine into the Fairchild, I had to remove the cylinders and
refit them on the power case after installation. Blocking the master rod
securely in position, I depended on both skill and luck to keep it from slipping on my final installation of the master rod cylinder. Any old mechanic
has already guessed what happened. The rod slipped and I had to remove
every cylinder and start over again, another two days delay.

Well, after five days I was finally ready to go. Fortunately, a stiff wind
came up and I made it off and over to Merrill with my heavy load.

There a new assignment awaited me under my wartime contract with
the Alaska Communications System. A rush radar installation was needed at
Amchitka in connection with the proposed air and sea invasion of Kiska,
then occupied by the Japanese. In a matter of hours I was headed for the
Aleutians.

Everything went fine until I was ten minutes out of Cold Bay and the
field went zero zero. Now, there is nothing unusual about this condition
on the Bering Sea except for one thing. It was eleven o'clock at night and
I only had an hour's remaining fuel; and at eleven o'clock it doesn't stay
light in the Aleutians as it does farther north. It was pitch dark. By this time
the whole peninsula had fogged in and I was cruising around on top at
1,000 feet.

Well, "Mister," I thought to myself, "you are in a nice kettle of fish. In
fact, you are in just about the most unenviable and worst fix in which any
flyer ever found himself. Pitch dark, roosting on top of 1,000 feet of dense fog,
field closed, no place to go, and not more than 25 minutes of fuel remaining."
Just about my only out was to crash land the plane on the lower slopes of
Pavlov Volcano some fifty miles away.

But I knew that I could never make it with my remaining fuel. Racking
my brain for another out I suddenly recalled a phenomena I had observed
several times previously while cruising on top of the fog banks. Wherever the
cold glacier streams from the mountains flowed into the Bering Sea there was

always a thin rift about the confluence caused by the difference in the dew point and temperature of the different waters.

To find one of these rifts and let down and ditch in the Bering was my only out; and I had to find one but fast. Leaning the mixture controls of the engines to conserve fuel we headed on a course that would place us in a favorable area to locate one of these rifts.

Twenty minutes later my starboard engine quit with a startling cough. That meant I had about four minutes to go before the others quit, out of fuel.

I had my luck. Right below me I could barely discern the thinnest suspicion of a rift. Wheeling the plane around and lining up the rift I made the fastest, steepest let-down I ever experienced.

In about 30 seconds, although it seemed like 30 hours, I knew I was going to make it. Through the murky darkness and drifting fog banks I could discern the phosphorescent glint of the Bering surf just ahead. It was the greatest sight of a lifetime.

Chopping the throttles we ditched with a crash and with wheels down at that—the gear was not retractable. We had made it!

Polling my six radar specialist passengers for injuries, I found they were ambulatory, as fortunately the cargo had not broken loose. Roping them together, I got them safely to the shore. When the tide ebbed in a few hours I was able to salvage the aircraft radio and storage battery. Soon I had contact with the Cold Bay Army base and gave them our approximate position near Cape Leontovich.

I also salvaged several quarts of Tom Burns whiskey belonging to one of the passengers. After a number of toasts to our good fortune, we lay down in the sand to await the morning.

Dozing off, I suddenly awoke with a feeling of a strange presence. Sure enough, a huge brown bear was sniffing at my feet. Not altogether sure but that this apparition was nothing more than a phantasmagoria induced by shock and fuel oil, I watched the bear pass down the line of sleeping soldiers. On reaching the last man he gave a sudden snort and woof, and rapidly evaporated in the mist. Later investigation disclosed that an empty Tom Burns bottle was lying in the vicinity, which no doubt gave evidence to the bear that a number of panthers were in the vicinity and he obviously wanted no truck with them.

When daylight came we found some driftwood and started a fire. Soon airplanes were heard overhead and within minutes our breakfast came, raining down through the fog bank. My pals in the 54th Troop Carrier Squadron had sighted the smoke coming on top of the fog and hit the target. Radio contacts disclosed that a Coast Guard PBy would land when the fog dispersed and take the injured to the Dutch Harbor hospital. A search rescue crash vessel would salvage the radar and plane crew that night. Soon the injured were evacuated and we had the radar back in Cold Bay to continue to Amchitka by another plane.

Well, with the Boeing gone, I was broke again—back where I started. That was no novelty. But the aircraft engines had a ready market value of $4,500.00 if I could deliver them to Anchorage to another operator with a similar Boeing 80-A.

Badly in need of the $4,500.00 to buy groceries and overhaul my remaining old Fairchild, I traced every movement of the transport carrying the salvaged engines in the voyage to Anchorage. The day they arrived I was out of town on a flight. On my return I lost no time in getting to Elmendorf. There I found three boxes with my name on them, but empty.

"Where are my engines," I demanded. A wall of silence from the surrounding GIs was my only answer, if you could call it an answer. All this time they were surreptitiously glancing at a pile of junk. Looking it over I recognized the remnants of my Hornet A-2s broken up in a thousand pieces.

"Who smashed my engines?" I again demanded. Finally a young GI said "They're yours all right. A General from the states was through here on a whirlwind inspection tour. He saw the engines and he said, "Smash up those Jap engines for scrap." We told him they were yours but he said he knew a Jap engine when he saw one and "smash 'em up right now."

To make it worse, the culprit, Major General "Concrete McMullen" was an old friend of mine. I wrote to him and told him he was now "Sledgehammer" McMullen instead of "Concrete" from then on.

And so climaxed a hectic week. To this old-time Alaska pilot, it was all in the game.

— PREVIOUSLY UNPUBLISHED

It Bears Telling

BY CAPTAIN L. RON HUBBARD

Introduction by Seyward S. Cramer, Editor, *Through Hell and High Water*, 1941

I wish Bill Mann was here today. All that expansion at his Zoo in Washington has kept him too closely confined and we don't see enough of him around the Long Table.

There is one question I particularly wanted to ask him. I wanted to know if it was possible for a man to wrestle with a full-grown Kodiak bear and come out on top. I have heard that they are rather unrefined and that most people have been advised to stay away from them. Yet there is a persistent rumor around town that our redheaded Captain Ron Hubbard goes out of his way to pick wrestling matches with Kodiaks. It has even reached the point where ballads are being written about his prowess.

Now, Captain Hubbard left these parts recently on a supposedly scientific expedition. He was even allowed to carry the Club flag, which meant that his purpose was scientific. His schooner Magician *was well equipped to carry on some badly-needed radio studies and research, but we haven't heard anything about that. Bears are all we hear about.*

Have you anything to say for yourself, Ron?

Gentlemen, not even here am I safe from this continual chatter about bears. I am getting so I can't—oops, I almost made the horrible pun which has been following me about. To begin, the whole thing is a damned lie. I did not make love to the bear and the bear did not die of longing. Further, I do not make a practice of going around picking on poor, innocent Kodiak bears. The day I arrived in New York City, this thing began: I picked up my phone to hear a cooing voice say, "Cap'n, do you *like* to wrassle with bears?" And since that day I have had no peace. How the story arrived ahead of me I do not know. Personally I tried hard to keep it a dark secret—I mean the whole thing is a lie!

A man can spend endless months of hardship and heroic privation in checking coast pilots; he can squeeze his head to half its width between earphones calculating radio errors; he can brave storm and sudden death in all its most horrible forms in an attempt to increase man's knowledge, and what happens? Is he a hero? Do people look upon his salt-encrusted and exhausted self with awe? Do universities give him degrees and governments commissions? NO! They all look at him with a giggle and ask him if he likes to wrassle with bears. It's an outrage! It's enough to make a man take up paperdoll cutting! Gratitude, bah! Attention and notoriety have centered upon one singular accident—an exaggerated untruth—and the gigantic benefits to the human race are all forgotten!

Gentlemen, examine the facts. A Kodiak bear, known in Alaska as the "brownie," is the world's largest carnivorous animal. He stands as tall as two of us and weighs sixteen hundred active and ferocious pounds. This past autumn in two different parts of Alaska men were attacked by brownies and so badly mauled that one man died and the other will never walk again. And yet you imply that a sane man likes to wrassle with Kodiak bears! Why, compared with a Kodiak, a grizzly is a Teddy bear! No, the whole thing is preposterous and I must ask to be excused.

You say that the rumors still persist and insist that there must be something behind them?

Well—there was such an incident as the one you vaguely mention. But I tell you that I had nothing whatever to do with it!

The thing began when a trolling-boat skipper came up alongside a survey—came up alongside a big cutter and asked an officer if he wanted to run up through a passageway generally too shallow and too studded with rocks to admit a larger vessel.

The officer, anticipating nothing, gladly went aboard the small trolling vessel and they shoved off. The boat was about 31 feet long and, because there were only a few pounds of fish in the hold, was somewhat subject to an unstable movement even though the day was calm.

The boat chug-chugged between the steep shores of the winding channel and the officer admired the scenery considerably. However, the whole thing was a bit boring, for there is such a thing as too much scenery, even in Alaska.

After some time the attention of the officer was attracted by a bobbing something out in the center of the wide channel. It might be a log or a seal but it was at least something of interest. As the troller approached, the outline of the head began to sharpen. Evidently it was a small black bear, trying stupidly to make headway against a two-knot current and stubbornly refusing to give up the struggle.

The skipper bemoaned the fact that he had no gun aboard and the officer cursed the lack of forethought that had brought him here without a camera.

"Ay vas thinking it vas a shame to lat the bear go," said the skipper.

"Right you are," said the officer. "Isn't there some way we could get him?"

"Maybe if we vent back and got a gun," suggested the skipper.

"It's miles to the ship and he'd be gone by then. I'll tell you, we'll drop a rope over his head and tow him back!"

Nothing seemed simpler and the officer ran off a few fathoms of rope with a running bowline in it and the trolling boat soon overtook the swimming bear. It was easy to slip the noose over the animal's head and make the other fall fast to the ship. This done, the fisherman turned on power and they began to tow the bear along at about four knots.

The bear, however, objected. Water kept getting in his eyes and mouth and the rope around his neck was choking him. Probably he would have gone on having a hard time of it if water in the gas had not made the engine conk.

The fisherman leaped down from wheel to engine and the officer took the helm to guide the boat with what way it had left. No attention was given to the bear for several seconds.

Suddenly the boat reeled under the impact of a terrific blow. The three top gunwale strakes on the starboard side caved in like lathes. The boat gave a terrible lurch and several hundred gallons of eager water spewed into the hull.

The officer whirled, to see that their tow was coming aboard! Somehow it had come close to the boat and had clawed up the low side!

The fisherman leaped into the pilothouse from below and the officer leaped for the deck, with some vague idea of shoving the bear back into the water with an oar.

More and more bear had been coming out of the water and the trolling boat was heeling and taking in an ocean at a gulp.

With a mournful wail the fisherman cried, "It vas a *brownie!*"

The officer need no confirmation. The brute's head, hair plastered down with water—and naturally small anyway, had been wholly deceptive. Streaming and roaring, the brownie got aboard and dived for the officer.

The officer had no wish to match blows with three-quarters of a ton of Kodiak and dodged back around the lump of a pilothouse which stood out of the deck. The bear, making the little boat rock as though a hurricane had hit it, lunged in pursuit. The bear held a grudge because he did not like to be towed at four knots.

"Come in!" screamed the fisherman, meaning the officer, not the bear, and yanked his human passenger into the pilothouse. Together they got the door solidly bolted.

The brownie bent over and glared through the ports of the house; the ports were too small to admit his paws. He buffeted the structure for a while and then, failing to make an impression, gave it up. Besides, he was tired.

He went aft by the fish hatch and sat down, thus bringing the bows out of the water. He panted and clawed at the rope around his neck and cast occasional promises toward the pilothouse.

Below, the fisherman was bailing madly in an attempt to keep the small vessel from swamping but the water was already up to the carburetor and coil of the engine and more came in steadily.

They decided to let the tide carry the boat near some rocks ahead, in the hope that the bear might feel some gratitude for having been ferried there and so go ashore and leave them. Slowly they drifted to the rocks, slid up on one and were held there by the current.

Belatedly it occurred to the men that the bear was still tied to the boat with a nice, strong rope, and if he was to be put ashore something would have to be done about untying him.

The fisherman opened the door a crack. The officer edged slowly toward the cleat and the rope. With a roar and a lunge the bear remembered his revenge. The officer scuttled back, got in, and the bear hit the door.

The movement of the brownie made the boat heel to starboard and water began to pour in with renewed fury. It was certain that if they had the bear another hour they would have to give him the boat.

The tide went slack and then began to run the other way. Evening approached and with it a wind. The officer and the fisherman took turns at the pump and, by strenuously continuing the operation, were able to keep the water from completely drowning the engine. This could not go on forever, they decided.

Finally they had an idea. They took a pike pole which could be reached from the pilothouse port and to the end of it lashed a long, sharp knife. Then, moving slowly so as not to attract the ire of the brownie, began to saw through the line by this remote control.

But when the line was parted the brownie made no effort to avail himself of the fact. He was not grateful. He had calmed considerably and had become interested in the delicious odor of fish which assailed his nostrils. Finally he located the source and with one tap of his paw knocked the top off the fish hold. There he found a number of beautiful fish and proceed to take one bite from the belly of each, casting the thirty-pound remains overboard.

It was dark now and the tide was falling and soon the trolling boat would be left high on a reef, from which it would probably fall, with no good consequence to itself or anyone aboard.

Desperation caused the two exhausted men to peg chunks of coal at the bear, who had now begun to doze.

The first few blows went unnoticed but finally the bear roused himself, gave the pilothouse a final rush and then, stalking angrily, stepped to the rocks and went ashore.

The men were glad to see him go.

They managed to get the water out of the boat and get the boat off the rocks and the engine going once more. And then they went home.

Now that, gentlemen, is the full and true account of my—of the incident of the bear. It is a lie that anybody broke the bear's heart or that the bear wanted to kiss anybody. It is also a lie that anybody showed the slightest inclination to wrassle that bear. And any song written about it, and any puns made about it, are libelous. It is enough to be teased about it in Alaska without being teased about it here. In short, the whole thing is a damned lie!

—*THROUGH HELL AND HIGH WATER* (1941)

PART THREE

Arctic

Arctic Ghost

BY FELIX RIESENBERG

I t seems to be a principle, if there are principles other than those con-jured by imagination, that quick existence, if I may so qualify it, is pos-sible only between the poles of birth and death. But we do know that there is pre-extension of these limits as far as birth is concerned, but just where does this begin? We do definitely know that life starts before parturi-tion, that intention, of some kind, precedes conception, and that a marvelous complication of circumstances leads to the event called life. We may also conceive of a continuation of the result of this elaborate beginning, following the sudden snuffing-out of material motion. The hereafter, yes—but still here if we only knew. Why should things that take so long to start end with sud-den abruptness? Do the things that are absolutely not of the flesh, such as the conscience and the will, do these things evaporate in an instant, or before the dissolution of their earthly shell? Is memory a thing of mud? Is love a mere assemblage of cells? Is one skull exactly like another? Can we assay the value of a brain by weight and size? There must be something other than the bur-ial of the body to attend the cessation of life. This process is not completed in an hour, or in a day, if there is such an entity as time in the realm of ghosts.

Such speculations are disquieting in the growing gloom of an approach-ing polar night. And under such conditions there were naïve arguments between us as to the vitality of such things as bones, or entire skeletons, once most intimate parts of living men. In other words (if those more fit to discuss this will permit) do the preserved remains carry with them an allegiance of the spirit? Do mummies, tortured and distorted, still demand attendance on the part of their life principle? Is not the flesh and bone an equal, or let us say, a necessary partner with the soul? Is one *nothing* and the other *all?* The ancient Egyptians seemed to think so. And what are a few centuries, or a thousand or more years, in the scale of all time? May not the spirit cling to the bone and play havoc with weak mortality, adjacent in the living, shivering flesh? Even the stoutest might hesitate to sleep among the headstones of a cemetery through an interminable night.

Fear is as great as faith. The mind, grown out of mystery, unable to pierce the unknowable, totters on the brink of chaos when we revolve it on an inward orbit, searching secrets. Even with all of our jumbled heap of practical learning, how little do we know!

One might hesitate to tell the whole truth in matters of unusual moment, even if it were possible to achieve complete expression or to reveal emotion too poignant for words. Who can convey the utter terror of a small child screaming in the dark at the apparition of a shadow on the wall? Perhaps that child is voicing something only a young soul is tuned to fear. And here it may be said that I do not believe in ghosts—I have repeated this to myself over and over again.

Well, this is the beginning, or at least it is the explanation, or the excuse, for the story to follow. Still there is something more to be added before the matter is set forth. If the departed come back, we must be certain that they were there, and suffered, and sinned, and served, and died. Even the most willing mind can hardly conceive of a virgin planet peopled with ghosts.

I spent the dark months of a polar winter prisoned in a little house just beneath the eightieth parallel of latitude on Danes Island, off the shores of the northern archipelago of Spitsbergen. Our square, stout little house was built on an ice-encrusted knoll, the timbers of the floor resting on protruding breccia strewn at the base of a steep cliff. The shoreward ends of the timber had been bedded by hewing into the ice, and the ends facing the sea were supported on piles of stone to level off the floor. The wedge-like sides and front foundation wall were built of loose rock, calked with reindeer moss. To make this solid cellar proof against the wind, the rude masonry was later on plastered with ice and banked with snow.

This snug little house stood opposite to the relics of a camp once occupied by Andrée. In this camp were intimate reminders of the gallant Swede, reminders vibrant with the last moments of this determined, earnest man. But it was a camp haunted only by memories, for no material or actual part of the travelers remained. If the camp held an element of death, it was only that of the last contact with men before disaster, hundreds of miles away. But on every point of the horizon were headlands and mountains and glaciers familiar in the annals of polar suffering and discovery. Here came William Barents and John Cornelius Ryp in 1596—Barents, the ice pilot and discoverer, destined to perish in Nova Zembla, far to the south.

And here, too, past the Pyramids and the great Cape of Hakluyt, sailed the indomitable Heemskerck and the able Hendrik Hudson, also to perish in frozen seas. But the names of those who sailed north to die fill a scroll of ample length. In 1620, the track of the Dutch discoverers was followed by a blaze of fortune that, for a time, transformed the waste of the north into a place of turmoil. The waters were thick with the black flukes of leviathan. The wide lanes between the pan ice spouted continual jets of vapor. Fifteen thousand seamen came to those northern shores in the short summer months. Close to the little house on Danes Island, on an adjacent level plain, stand relics of the abandoned city of Smeerenburg, the most remarkable settlement of all time. It once held shops and bakeries, and lodgings, inns and drinking booths, and brothels, for the whale fleet was followed by women and the whalemen held carnival when they drove their barbs into the huge, fat fishes spouting near the shore. The smoke of the trying-kettles rose upward in thick columns, standing in the summer calm, the trembling black plumes on an unearthly hearse.

This ancient killing (and how tremendous is the killing of a mighty whale!) went on amid the rendering of thousand of tons of fat and the carousing of reckless men and women, smeared with blood and blubber and profligate with life and treasure. It was a time of fabulous fortune spouting golden streams of gore and oil taken from the cold blue sea. Two hundred and sixty Dutch ships visited the Spitsbergen whaling-ground in the few months of a summer season, first fighting and besetting the English ships of the Muscovy Company, for, wherever free treasure was to be had, fighting and license held sway. All of these ancient killing and rendering of fat and roistering of flesh went on shamelessly beneath the unwinking sky of continual day. There was no dark intermission of night to cover them. Thousands left their bones to bleach upon the arctic shores. Countless rude coffins of oak, often fashioned from the staves of casks, lay in shallow graves amid the stones, the ground too hard for deeper burial. The whales were killed off and all this terrific life departed, this summer life of a brief score of years, centuries ago. Never did human beings survive the night; the few who wintered perished.

Then came an interval of a hundred years and still more adventurous prows forced past the site of Smeerenburg and the headland of Hakluyt. The *Racehorse* and the *Carcass*, commanded by Phipps, with young Horatio Nelson, a midshipman, in the steerage of the *Racehorse*, sailed by the gruesome souvenir of graves. These were followed by Buchan and John Franklin and Parry, by sailors who dragged heavy boats over hummocks, rupturing themselves in the hopeless battle with the ice, breaking hearts by inhuman labor on the polar field. These, too, left their corpses on those shores to join the great colony of perpetual bones, for in those regions there is no decay. Then followed Nordenskiöld, Malmgren, Fabvre, Leigh Smith, Wellman, Nobile, Amundsen, continuing the struggle northward, leaving their trail of death and hopes behind.

Three sailors left in this bleak surrounding were simple men. One was the veteran of many winters in the polar seas and one was only a sailor, a far voyager who believed the things he saw and knew and who had heard many things he could not understand. The first, Paul Bjoervig, bearded, bent with years, was sturdy and uncomplaining. The second, Morten Olaisen, was more voluble and uncertain, for to him the creeping on of the Arctic night came with grim precision, each darkening hour casting deeper shadows across his mind. I was a youth, but with a fair record of sailing, long miles of sea spun out in the wake of my experience. I was the navigator, the officer, and in charge. Upon me devolved the command, the responsibility, in the changing world slowly sinking from light and life.

For a time we busied ourselves by tasks, setting our house in shape amid the increasing powderings of snow—piling driftwood and lighting huge bonfires on the dim line of the beach, taking cheer from the crackling flames, noting the shooting of blue-green tongues of light, catching the alternating waves of heat and cold that circled about the flames of driftwood in a world of endings. Always the fires left us more cold. Once, as the blaze burned low, a ghastly knob protruded from the ashes, a grinning skull burned black, the eye sockets filled with glowing coals of wood. This was our last fire. Morten muttered something about smoke in his eyes; then, too, the deepening snow buried the driftwood. Our conversation became less buoyant; small things took on sinister importance in our evasive contemplation of the long black months ahead.

And then we began to talk of the dead.

"Did you see it?"

"What?"

"The coffin," Paul whispered, bending over his pipe, slowly puffing, while Morten worked at the kitchen stove. Pungent smoke filled the small kitchen.

"No. I piled the wood. The rocks and wood is gray. It's getting dark. You can't see so well. No, you can't see."

"It rolled over."

"It rolled over—hot—red-hot."

"The dogs ran."

"Yes, they ran."

"I went back. It's gone."

Fragments reached me. I was determined to be cheerful. Further fall of snow prevented fires; the subject was dropped.

The silence came very close as November shaded into a monochrome of gray, blackening toward the night of inky gloom. The birds left the cliff, and the snow, constantly falling, gave an illusion of upward motion; one could feel the friction of impalpable flakes scratching the ether. It was the silence of interstellar space, of complete insulation in the midst of an enormous cemetery draped in white.

So much had happened in that world of close, deceiving snow. So much was bound to happen again. Silence hung over us like a threat. Often I would wake from deep slumber startled by a dream in which I found myself far aloft, high over the black side of Smedburg's Mountain, with its cap of ice, looking down into the valley to the shore where stood the house, a nub of white almost buried. Once I noted its strange resemblance to a small headstone; a shudder came over me, I seemed to see the mound heave up as if from the struggle of three men buried alive. Everything for many hundreds, and for a thousand miles, was absolutely dead. I would have these dreams during periods of moonlight, for by December the curtain of polar night had drawn its fold across the midday skies.

Once the dream came when the moon was gone. I jumped up in the cold and stole to the small double window and saw a strange light without. Cautiously opening the outer door, having thrown on a heavy robe, I saw a vault of sky covered with waving plumes of fire — the aurora. I ran back to my bunk and prayed, shivering for an hour until sleep came.

That night the only black thing in a world of ghostly white was the moving shadow cast by a curious stone on Deadman's Isle, the great Sarcophagus Stone, standing above the snow where the Isle lifts from the plain of the frozen sea, like the mound of a mighty grave. And it was a grave, a gruesome grave holding the bones of a company of ancient sailors under the snow, graves revealed in ghastly bareness in the lazy summer when the ground is clear and lidless coffins show their skulls and skeletons bleaching in the sun.

If you could look to the north over the festering tidal crack, groaning in the calms with unearthly mutterings, noises that sometimes sound like uncouth words, great mumbling words and moans given back again by the distant glacier fronts and cliffs, if you could look across the smooth white sheet of Dane's Gat to the mount of Deadman's Isle and see the Sarcophagus Stone lifting above the place, the fantastic light of polar winter playing its pranks with the things that are, you would sometimes also see wreaths of mist above the ice. You, too, would see things moving where nothing should move. Graves are thick on Deadman's Isle—and also along the shore where stood the house sheltering three sailors.

Once in the night, night by clocks rather than by any change in the complexion of the sky, a shiver ran through the solid little house, the timbers creaked for a moment and all was silent again. For many days before, the growing gloom carried with it an increasing sense of melancholy, a gradual burdening of the spirit as the mounting depth of snow lifted to a level with the eaves of the house, buried completely but for a hollow scooped out by the scouring wind, a providential trench that bared the narrow windows. It was then that old Paul Bjoervig began to talk of his dead comrade, Bentzen, Brent Bentzen who lay dead in the snow hut in Franz Josef Land while Paul slept alongside the corpse of his companion, in fulfillment of a mutual promise that the one to survive, in the event of death, would not cast out his shipmate to the prowling bears.

Bjoervig was constantly talking *with* Bentzen, talking with him in his sleep, and denying the conversation when awake.

Morten Olaisen became a man of monosyllables. His brows lowered with a haunting frown as his eyes sought the face of Paul, always smoking, smoking and grave. The wind whined over the top of Smedburg's Mountain. Crashing down the valley in harsh gusts, screeching across the ice-crusted tar paper on the roof of our house, whirling the metal Jack-in-the-wind that topped the chimney. These winds seemed to suck the heat from the fire, to drain off the vitality of the little house, as if some force without was determined to extinguish all alien life clinging amid the snow.

"Was you awake—last night, sir?" Morten ventured the question after a day of silence.

"You mean the house?"

"Under the house." Morten nodded to the bare floor. Paul, pipe in mouth, looked in from the kitchen door, his face serious, his eyes troubled.

"Only the snow bearing down—timbers adjusting." I had plenty of explanations.

"But the voice. Paul heard it, too. It spoke."

"The voice?"

The house seemed so much colder than before. The weak, asthmatic fire coughed, its consumptive splutter burning up precious coal, with no return in heat. Then, too, the oil lamp seemed so dim, and the wind—it was blowing a gale from the northeast—backed into the valley, recurving down on the little house in violent counter-blasts.

"Perhaps it was the dogs. You know they howl. It might have been the echo coming down the chimney. You hear lots of things in the calm. It was calm last night. The wind began at four, according to the anemometer." I pulled on my finskoes and, slipping into a gabardine, left the house, picking a rifle from the rack and murmuring something about "bears." Anything to get outside of the house—away. I stepped into skis and slid to the lee side of a large hummock a quarter mile away. Two dogs followed. I was glad. Of course it was not a voice, it was merely a sound, a human-sounding sound. I had thought it the voice of a woman. But it was *not* a voice, certainly not a woman's voice.

For days nothing was said about this happening—if it was a happening. The sky had cleared and the aurora smothered us under a covering of flashing beauty, painfully vivid, like leaping blood gushing over a milk-white breast. It was an overpowering brilliance that caught us, looking upward into the magnificence and mystery of the polar night. Was the truth so utterly gorgeous? Why, I wondered, why? With eyes wide open, our puny minds were blind.

For a time we could not sleep. We hung awake, tired, with staring eyes and agitated minds. We crept into bunks and tossed through sullen hours devoid of rest. Every moment seemed laden with significance. We were listening, always listening for the voice. At last we hardly dared address each other, for even our own voices took on a chill of fear. And then we heard the *thump*.

It came suddenly. We had almost forgotten that they were awaiting its summons. The chill of the room suddenly increased. Dogs howled—that unearthly howl, lifted from the canine throat in long-drawn agonizing moans. The men lifted their covers and looked at me accusingly. Something was moving beneath the floor of our house. Below, everything was sealed against the inrush of wind and cold. Many feet of snow banked the walls. There was but one entrance, the square trap in the middle of the floor.

By an almost superhuman effort I left my bunk and braced myself in the cold, the dim lamp throwing my shadow on the wall. I stood over the trap, the cold sweat trickling from my forehead. Behind me Paul and Morten peered with breath suspended.

I lifted the trap. It seemed to lift itself, to yield without weight. My whole balance was disturbed for the effort I had nerved myself to exert.

"Look!"

Both men in the bunks shrieked at once. The open trap gave out a musty draft; it was impenetrable to sight. A fog swam before my eyes, my breath halted, my legs shook. Someone besides us was in the room. Oh, how cold it became—how unnaturally cold! We shook violently. I pushed down the suspended trap and the men huddled in their bunks.

A white form came up out of the trap and dissolved when the door was back in place. It was only a mist—the colder air of the cellar condensing in the warmth of the room, for the room was certainly warmer than the dank hole below. But does cold air rise against warmer air? And the thump?—

We were again in our bunks. That morning we said nothing. Already we had talked too much—too lightly, perhaps—of the relics of men scattered about us under the snow. The continual night made us secretive, morose. We could not sleep; then, of a sudden, we could not stay awake.

Everything was asleep about us; everything dead. A resistless gravity pulled down our eyelids, smothered our thoughts. When we slept, we were warm, were secure and, in the depth of delightful dreams, we heard ravishing music and bell-like laughter. Limpid water cascaded over sunlit falls and we again knew the beauty of flowers.

But these slumbers were also interspersed with the low grumbling of men talking in their sleep, and the fire went out and the lamp burned its wick to a brittle carbon. The outside chill penetrated the room and the increasing snow mounted each day in a shroud of dull white already many fathoms deep above the house-top. Even Deadman's Isle was levelled in the thickening pall and the high Sarcophagus Stone became a mere bulge on the surrounding plain. The black sides of Smedburg's Mountain, too steep to afford a hold for snow, towered in stark grandeur, a giant sounding-board, against which the wailing of hungry dogs set up a constant din.

The chronometer had run its indicator down to "wind," the anemometer clock died down and the scratch of the pen on the cylinder and the metallic click of the ratchet were silent. Everything seemed prepared for our burial. The dark was thick with the hoarfrost of men who still breathe and, in a moment, voices were apparent in the gloom. I lay still, as if dead. My feet were cold, devoid of feeling. Then low words, guttural and slow, told me my companions were still alive.

"I saw it." A voice, thick and indistinct. "Below the house."

"The grave is under my bunk. I have just been down there with *her*."

"Did she touch him?"

"Yes. He's dead now."

"He's dead."

I heard no more. I drifted into oblivion. Was this also a dream?

The dogs, flattened close against the house door, moaned with pitiful insistence. An avalanche descended upon the house, shocking it to its creaking frames, and a sluicing rain, a terrific downpour of warm black water, swept through the valley, washing deep canyons in the piled-up snow. The room was heavy with damp. The warm, sweet odor of fresh rain lifted me from my bunk like a green stalk striking upward. I tottered on clay-like feet, the dead nerves tingling with the shooting pains of a million needles. The impossible had happened—rain in the Arctic night!

I stumbled toward the corner of the room. My numb fingers sought the shelf of the medicine chest; a bottle of whiskey was stowed behind the bandages, an almost forgotten bottle. I lifted this and drank. For a while there was no taste, nothing but a bitter, nauseating trickle down my dry throat and along my spine. Then my heart seemed to awaken, my brain began to throb, I stumbled to the door and the wet dogs burst in from the storm, and great draughts of moist air filled the house. The skinny dogs jumped on me, howling incessantly. This, with the thunder of an internal tornado in my head, steadied me. The northern shores of Spitsbergen were being laved by the freak intrusion of a violent southern storm. Unholy clouds of fog rose upward from the melting ice, mists and humors upset the frozen equilibrium of the night.

I found matches and a can of oil; I lit the smudgy lamp and searched for hard tack and canned beef. My head was light as I reeled about and dragged half a sack of coal to the fire, lighting it with precious scraps of newspaper and kindling wood. I walked about and talked like a fool. The dogs were snapping at the half-frozen beef, panting and snuffing and nuzzling the cans. I kept away from the two silent forms lumped up under the blankets in their bunks. Then the half-empty bottle standing on the table looked at me accusingly. I pulled back the blanket from Paul's head and forced a thick tumbler of whisky between the reluctant teeth, spilling the stuff on the old man's matted beard. The sailor grunted. I went to Morten, forced his jaws apart and poured down a fiery shot. For an hour I fed them, drinking myself whenever the clutch of cold seized me. The room reeked of liquor; the fire roared; the dogs, giving off wet vapor, were clustered at the base of the red-hot stove, sometimes thumping their tails on the floor and barking in short, ecstatic grunts.

That night the wind veered into the north. The cold came back and the country lay beneath a frosting of translucent ice. We sat before a stew of reindeer meat, bending our heads, our eyes dimmed, our minds humble.

In a few weeks the twilight told of the returning sun. A month later three thin, yellow-faced men, with long, light-colored beards, stood on the summit of Smedburg's Mountain, gazing to the south at noon. The upper limb of the sun lifted for a moment above saw-toothed crags of ice. A purple, wind-sped cloud rode across the brilliant arc of day. Without comment we slid back down into the dimming valley of our experience and entered the small house filled with memories.

When our relief ship burst into view past the Cape de Geer in the early weeks of June, summer and daylight had long returned and the world of birds and song replaced the blackness of night.

The surgeon, in charge of commissariat, was seeking stowage for additional stores. He reported finding the remarkable skeleton of a female resting below the trap. The coffin boards, better than usual in those rude graves, lay in a heap below the bunk of Paul.

—*TOLD AT THE EXPLORERS CLUB* (1931)

Felix Riesenberg earned his title of "Captain" by fifteen years' active service at sea. He was a master mariner in sail and steam, his last command aboard the Newport, *then serving as the New York State nautical schoolship. He was also a graduate of Columbia University and an engineer.*

He was a member of the Wellman Polar Expedition of 1906–1907 and spent that winter in charge of the camp established on Danes Island, on the north shore of Spitsbergen, where occurred the nerve-racking experience here described.

In September, 1907, he took part in the first attempt to fly over the polar regions in a dirigible balloon. On account of poor material and adverse weather conditions, the venture met with failure, the balloon being blown back and wrecked on Foul Glacier, in northwest Spitsbergen.

He was the author of twelve books, among them Standard Seamanship *(used throughout the English-speaking merchant service),* East Side, West Side; Endless River; Shipmates; Red Horses; Under Sail.

At Close Quarters with a Polar Bear

BY ANTHONY FIALA

O n our expedition ship we had a number of old Henry rifles of a caliber .45/90. The bullets were copper-capped and paper-patched and the cartridges were made of very thin sheet brass, wound in diagonal strips and quite delicate to the touch. We also had some .45/70 Springfields and an assortment of Marlins and Winchesters in calibers .30/30, .303, and .45. For our sled party I had provided 8 mm. Mannlicher carbines; these, of course, were the most effective weapons of our equipment.

I had an experience with the 8 mm. which I would not care to have again. I had given instructions to the expedition that no bears were to be killed unless we needed them for food. On one occasion when we needed bear meat, I happened to be out walking about a thousand yards from our hut, watching the motion of the ice fields off the west coast of Crown Prince Rudolf Land, where we had lost our ship. Looking down into the bay, I noticed one of our men, Sergeant Long, taking a tide observation in the ice crack where the ice of the sea met the shore ice. A couple of hundred yards from where he was in the rough ice, I noticed an enormous polar bear approaching him. As I was unarmed, I did not waste any time, but ran into the hut, seized the 8 mm. Mannlicher and two clips of ammunition and ran as fast as I could toward Sergeant Long. When I reached him, I told him to go to the hut, as a bear was stalking him. He thanked me and moved off.

I looked for the bear, but could not see him, even when I searched for him from the highest point of ice. I knew then that he was sneaking along somewhere and it occurred to me that it would be unnecessary work to look for him and that, if I would find a big cake of ice and lie on that, he would undoubtedly come and try to get me. Besides, it would be very difficult to haul him in from the rough ice after he was shot, while on one of the large cakes of ice near shore, it would be a simple matter to haul the carcass to our hut.

I put myself down into the center of a cake of ice about two hundred feet square and made out that I was a seal by bobbing my head up and down, lying down as if asleep every once in a while and then kicking my feet to imitate the tail of a seal.

The temperature was at least forty-five degrees below zero and, lying on the ice cake in feigned sleep, I was becoming rather anxious for Mr. Bear to come. I flopped around every once in a while, as it would be rather embarrassing if he came from behind while I was looking out toward the sea.

Once, just as I put my head down again to simulate sleep—with my eyes open, of course—I saw to the left, where an enormous piece of ice went up toward the sky, the tip of a big, hairy paw. I kept very quiet and then the entire paw and a black nose and two black eyes came in sight. I remember they looked like the eyes of a fiend. I kept quiet in spite of the cold and then, with a spring, an enormous bear jumped with all four feet on the cake of ice.

I had loaded my rifle just before lying down on the ice and all I had to do was to jump up, raise it, aim at that big head, and pull the trigger. The bear was only about seventy-five feet away from me and so I expected to have him drop in his tracks with the bullet through his brain. Instead of the crack of the gun, however, there was just a little sucking noise and, to my horror, the firing pin simply struck the cartridge with a gentle tap.

Despite the below-zero temperature, the perspiration started to run down my face as I realized that my gun was useless. Some time before, I had instructed one of the sailors to clean the Mannlichers and remove all the oil from the firing pins and locks, but he must have left some oil on the firing pin of this gun.

I passed the gun to my left hand and drew my knife. I looked at the five-inch blade and then at that big beast coming toward me, and put the knife back in its sheath. I knew that, if I retreated an inch, it would be my end, so I advanced on the beast, called him all sorts of names as loud as I could and told him to move off the cake of ice. To my joy, he stood still in his tracks and observed me, hissing like an enormous snake. He was mad all the way through, but somehow or other lacked the courage to charge.

I took advantage of this and tried to make him feel that I was going to jump on him and bury my teeth in his neck.

It occurred to me that possibly I could get the gun to work by warming the bolt with friction. While talking to the bear and telling him what sort of a fool he was and what I was going to do with him, I rubbed the bolt back and forth, losing some cartridges that way, for I was so intent on watching the bear and talking to him that sometimes I pulled the bolt all the way back, and, of course, flipped the cartridge out. It was a difficult thing to watch the bear and the gun at the same time and so, when my five cartridges were gone, I put in another clip, which was my last, and drove the first cartridge in that clip with all my might, as I was getting a little mad at that old bear.

In spite of my scathing remarks and threatenings, the big beast came slowly toward me and now we were only fifteen or eighteen feet apart. I had put the rifle to my shoulder a number of times with only that sickening misfire when I pulled the trigger. As I put the rifle up this time and pulled the trigger, there was a snapping explosion and, though I missed the bear, not having expected the rifle to go off, the powder undoubtedly filled his face, as he went head over heels backward.

When I saw him again, he was running like a jack-rabbit, fully two hundred and fifty yards away. I aimed at his nose and hit him in the hind-quarters and then worked my way slowly through the rough ice to where he was and ended his troubles with a bullet through his brain.

On coming back to the hut, I found that the sailor who had cleaned the rifles—a very thorough man, by the way—after cleaning all the guns from the barrel to the lock, as I had explained, thought it was absolutely necessary to put a thin rubbing of oil on the firing pin, because it had always been required in the naval service of which he had been a member.

—*TOLD AT THE EXPLORERS CLUB* (1931)

Before becoming the outfitter of explorers par excellence, *Major Fiala saw much active service in widely separated fields: first as photographer of the Badwin-Ziegler Polar Expedition, 1901–1902; then as leader of the Fiala-Ziegler Expedition, 1903–1905, which, although its ship was lost, explored and mapped a large area in the Franz Josef archipelago; later in Brazil with Theodore Roosevelt on his River of Doubt expedition, in charge of the equipment, and on independent exploration of the Papagaio, Jureuna, and Tapajoz rivers.*

His books on exploration are Fighting the Polar Ice *and* Scientific Results of the Ziegler Expedition.

The Compass That Talked

BY EDWARD WEYER

Introduction by Seyward S. Cramer, Editor, *Through Hell and High Water*, 1941

I called on Dr. Weyer at his office the other day. I feared he might be holding an editorial conference on a coming issue of Natural History Magazine, *and was rather surprised to find him poring over some old maps, old books, and photostats. He told me a story that will appeal to two of our members in particular.*

It is fortunate that your duties as Secretary of The Explorers Club *aren't so arduous as to take up all your time, Don Upham. Otherwise you wouldn't have time for those week-end cruises on the* Northern Star. *You may have had trouble with your compass, Don, but you don't know what real trouble is.*

And, Jim Allis, you will like it because it bears out your contention that much has been written that is no longer read. In this case, an article was written in 1508 that had a definite bearing on an event that occurred more than four hundred years later.

It is amazing to read of the findings of the explorers of the sixteenth century. I wish there were more of their books available today.

But, Dr. Weyer, won't you tell us that story of your compass on the Morrissey?

This is the story of a compass, an ancient map, and a blank wall of rock that couldn't be where we found it.

There it was, where no land could be. Picture yourself standing in the bows of Captain Bob Bartlett's schooner *Morrissey*. A low-lying fog hangs close to the gray water. We have sailed northward through Baffin Bay and ice-choked Melville Bay. We know that no land lies ahead of us in the broad sea between northern Greenland and Ellesmere Land. It is near midnight, and the vessel is plunging ahead in utter silence.

Then the sharp cry from the forward lookout, "Land dead ahead! Hard to starboard!"

The sheer, black cliff came at us out of the fog directly ahead. It was so close you could have hit it with a biscuit, and you could see the white foam breaking at the foot.

Our little vessel came alive with all the noises of a ship in sudden danger—bells in the engine room, heavy boots hitting the deck, and voices so surprised that they could express no surprise but only the rock-bottom need for action.

The angry black wall came closer. Because the layer of fog was low, you could look right up through it and see the full height of the cliff. The wall towered a thousand feet overhead. We clearly heard the waves smashing against the sharp rocks to port and starboard.

Captain Bob, on the quarterdeck, spun the wheel, and the stern swung sharply as the motor in reverse slackened the schooner's speed. He then leaned out over an oil drum at the rail, looking a hole through the fog and grinding a piece of chewing gum between his teeth. He was the statue of an animal that waits motionless for his enemy to make the next move. For a long moment he crouched there; and the ship, which only a minute before had bustled with activity, waited in a spell for his order, rising and falling as quietly as a sea bird.

His boot scraped on the deck as he straightened; then he spoke to the sailor beside him.

"Put her back on her course, George."

"East-by-north she is now sir," said George.

"That's impossible," the Captain said bluntly, bending to look at the compass.

East-by-north it was.

We were precisely on the compass course we had set on leaving Cape York. This course was geographically almost due north, the compass variation being caused by our having left the north magnetic pole some 500 miles to the southwest. This known variation could not possibly have been wrong.

The Captain was raking the line of surf with troubled eyes. "Where in the mysterious blazes are we?" he muttered. "Whatever it is, we can't sail through it. George, take her away. Take her out of here." His hand pushed the lever of the engine-room bell. The signal clanged, and the engine began to churn us ahead. "Work her offshore exactly the way you came in."

We eased slowly away from the cliff, which melted into the fog. As we came about you could barely see it sliding off to starboard like a flat piece of scenery.

We continued offshore for ten minutes after the land disappeared. There was no knowing how narrowly we had avoided piling up on those shore rocks. And what lay head of the *Morrissey* in the perplexing sea was anybody's guess.

I ventured to ask Captain Bartlett whether we could have been carried so far astray by currents or tide.

"Certainly not," he snorted. "But whatever that was we brought up against, there's got to be a way around it. There's plenty of water to the north. Nobody's built a wall across Smith Sound." Smith Sound was over a hundred miles wide here.

Presently he ordered the helmsman to proceed at right angles to the course we had been following.

Although talk on deck about the apparition died for lack of an explanation, many a puzzled glance was pointed into the circle of fog that walled us in. Gradually we broke up; some went back to their tasks, others drifted below.

For ten minutes as I sat on the rudder box the skipper did not shift his eyes. Then, before I was aware of anything, his hand was on the engine-room signal again. There was the jangle of the bell and again the shout of the look-out: "Land dead ahead!"

The fog had thinned some and we were not quite so close this time; but from the look of the cliff we seemed to have brought back to exactly the same spot.

"By gar, it's got to be our deck cargo!" exclaimed the Captain. "That's what it is. All those tins we moved aft to make room for the dogs have put a jinx on the compass."

We had put some sixty sledge dogs ashore the day before, but the gasoline tins still stood against the cabin house.

"Take her offshore, George," the Captain said, and then called, "All hands on deck!"

We all threw ourselves into moving the tins; and with a sensible explanation the talk was even cheerful.

At length, with the tins well forward, and confident that we could trust our compass, we again tried to give the cliff a wide berth. Curiosity, however, kept us all on deck.

Fifteen minutes later we were right back under the cliff.

Was it any wonder, I thought, that the ancients, with so many mysterious misadventures awaiting them beyond the unknown horizon, made up all manner of dangers? I recalled the fabulous mountains that were supposed by mariners of old to pull luckless ships irresistibly onto their rocks.

Captain Bob stomped across the quarterdeck, peered forward, and stomped back. "We're chasing around like a mazed capelin!" he thundered. "The compass itself must have gone *pibblooktoo* [Eskimo for 'bughouse']!"

He slammed the companion cover back and lowered himself into the cabin, grumbling. When he emerged he had a new compass, one he kept for use in the whaleboat on side trips.

"Once a compass or a chronometer fails you, you can never trust it again, never. This one I know is good." He laid it at the wheelman's feet for him to follow. His bulk bent lower. "What in the name of the blessed!" he sputtered. "They're both alike. George, could there have been any iron stowed aft in the lazarette or in her counter?"

"Not as I know, sir."

"Well, whatever it is, we must find a place on the vessel where the compass reads right and follow it." He handed me the smaller one. "Take this forward and sing out the reading."

I did as he said. As I set the compass on the forward hatch, I noticed that the dial seemed uncertain of itself. It came to rest at south-by-east, and I called it out.

"I'm all different," came his answer. "You must be out of the influence. All right, George, follow Ed on a course east-by-north."

The vessel had not begun to respond to the wheel when I was startled to see the dial of my compass lazily swing over a 30-degree arc to take a new position. "Hold on," I called. "this compass is no good either."

Two other compasses had now been brought on deck by men who had gone below to rummage in their personal equipment. All four compasses at different points on the deck showed different readings, as did presently a fifth. Thus our efforts at the usual methods of navigating came to a ridiculous end.

Billy Pritchard, our Newfoundland cook, with the mysticism of a true sailorman declared, "We be a fine ship, thinkin' we can find a port, yet never a compass on board in fit mind for sailin'."

Fortunately it was growing clear, and we could feel our way along the cliff, which continued without a break. As we moved away from the strange spot, which had drawn us to the brink of disaster as by an invisible hand, I think we all felt we had tasted of the dark powers that haunted the seas of old, to the confusion of bold but anxious mariners. Three days before in Melville Bay we had forced our way northward through towering cathedrals of icebergs which overshadowed our spars and scarcely left us room to turn and which once almost crushed our vessel. For such is the difficult approach along the coast to Smith Sound. Even these obstacles seemed less hostile than that cliff, hiding in the fog and luring us with its magnetic fingers.

Because such a force it did exert. A meteorite larger than those known to exist in the region might be the cause of it. More likely the mountain itself contains magnetic ore which exerts a strong local pull. At any rate, its existence was later verified by Captain Bob on voyages in clear weather.

A half hour farther north the sun came out bright over a sparkling sea. Now, this corner of the arctic stands in startling contrast to the region immediately to the south. It is rich in game, and in summer it offers gorgeous scenery and a mild climate. Shadows of clouds chased one another across the green mountainsides. We could see hares hopping among the flowers, and the birds wheeled in large flocks over the capes. The sea beneath a clear sky took on that rich blue which one rarely sees outside the deep water of the Greenland fiords.

We lay about the deck soaking in the warm sunshine long after we should have gone below to our bunks, singing and telling stories. Our spirits grew mellow, for we had entered a strange new world.

The sequel to this story is as curious as the story itself. This part of Greenland was discovered in 1818 by Sir John Ross, according to the books. This is the northernmost inhabited land on the face of the globe, and its discovery is not to be passed over as a trivial event. Yet if past explorers get together in the special Valhalla set aside for them, we may imagine that Sir John Ross met with some lively argument over this.

Eight years have passed since our encounter with the magnetic cliff. Not long ago I came upon an old chart, tucked away in the archives of a large library. It was dated 1508 and was drawn by a geographer by the name of John Ruysch. This was more than three centuries before Sir John Ross made his celebrated discovery of northwest Greenland. It was a fascinating map, showing grotesquely that day's lack of knowledge of the Western Hemisphere.

But Greenland was marked on it, though as a peninsula of northern Asia. At about 80 degrees north, between the coast of Greenland and a string of eighteen islands, there was a legend which ran: "Here begins the Amber Sea; here the ship's compass is useless, and vessels carrying iron cannot return." North of this legend were again four islands, and beyond them another small one, with this inscription: "At the Arctic Pole there rises a lofty rock of lodestone, 33 German miles in circumference . . . ."

Where did this map maker get his information three hundred years before Sir John Ross? When he drew his chart neither North nor South America had taken any definite form in the minds of men; and you might suspect that he had let his pen go pretty much where fancy led.

But it would not be the first time that an explorer who is honored with a discovery was not the first to get there. The Vikings, who were almost more at home in their small boats than they were on land, are now known to have discovered America centuries before Columbus. The region I am speaking of is well north of any land that is supposed to have been visited by civilized man in that day or much later.

Those daring northern seamen wrote little of their achievements, but who is to say that the true spirit of exploration did not reach its peak in them? They did not write books about their adventures, but that does not mean that they did not know what they were about, nor that they could not thrill to the discovery of a new corner in an old, old world.

I like to think our compass and that ancient chart were speaking for men whose voices had long been silent, and saying, "We were the first." And I like to picture them in their tiny open boat, pushing northward, ever northward, thousands of miles from their homeland. We can hear the lookout calling out the same warning, and can visualize their struggles to outwit that mysterious cliff of magnetic rock. And we can sense their rejoicing when they evaded the peril and entered that sunny, lively little corner of the arctic, under conditions doubtless much like those we encountered more than four centuries later.

— *THROUGH HELL AND HIGH WATER* (1941)

The Last Resort:
Cannibalism in the Arctic

BY ANNE KEENLEYSIDE

T he idea that anyone could intentionally consume the muscles, skin, blood, and brains of others is undeniably repulsive. Yet there is an instinct that overrides all others—the instinct to survive. In the Arctic, the harshest of environments, that instinct has driven more than one man to that last desperate measure. A glimpse into the history of Arctic exploration reveals how far some men have gone to save themselves from an almost certain death. In some cases human flesh was their salvation; in others it only prolonged their suffering.

Rumors of cannibalism first surfaced during Sir John Franklin's overland expedition of 1819–22. The expedition succeeded in surveying more than 500 miles of the Arctic coastline east of the Coppermine River. On their return journey across the barrens of Canada, Franklin's crew, weakened by starvation and illness, split up—several of the men remained in a camp while Franklin and the rest, including a number of Canadians, pressed onward toward their final destination. A day after their departure, four of the Canadian voyageurs decided to turn back and rejoin those left behind. Only one of the four, an Iroquois named Michel, made it back. According to published accounts of the incident, Michel returned bearing what he claimed was the meat of a deer slain by a wolf. Accepting the voyageur's story, the starving party ravenously devoured the meat, but commented on its strange taste. A short while later, however, John Richardson, the expedition's doctor, became convinced that Michel had murdered at least one of the voyageurs and that the crew had consumed the body.

In June of 1845, Franklin and his crew of 128 set sail from England in search of a passage that would lead them to the Far East. In September of

1846, after spending the first winter at Beechey Island, their two ships, *Erebus* and *Terror*, became trapped in the ice several kilometers off the northwest coast of King William Island. Unusually severe weather in 1847 kept the ships locked in the ice until April 1848. At that time, the ships were abandoned and the crew, now reduced to 105, headed south along the western shore of King William Island. Their goal was to reach the Back River, which would eventually lead them to a Hudson's Bay Company post on Great Slave Lake. They never reached their destination; the last survivors perished at a location now known as Starvation Cove.

Though numerous expeditions had been sent in search of the Franklin party, it wasn't until the spring of 1854 that news of their fate came to light. John Rae, a Hudson's Bay Company employee who had been surveying the coast of Boothia Peninsula, encountered an Inuit at Pelly Bay, who told him that six years earlier, a group of 35 to 40 Europeans had been seen pulling a sledge and a boat down the coast of King William Island and that their bodies were discovered near Starvation Cove. More shocking to Rae were Inuit reports that the bodies had been cannibalized. In his report to the British Admiralty, published in the *Times* of London on October 23, 1854, Rae wrote: ". . . from the mutilated state of many of the corpses and the contents of the kettles, it is evident that our wretched countrymen had been driven to the last resort—cannibalism—as a means of prolonging existence."

In Victorian England, where cannibalism was considered to be perhaps the most dreadful of all crimes, public response to Rae's report was one of outrage and denial. Lady Jane Franklin refused to accept Rae's account of cannibalism, and in the eyes of the public who could not accept the idea that any man could turn to human flesh for sustenance, the Inuit themselves had murdered and eaten the crew. Charles Dickens echoed the public's skepticism. Attempting to discredit the Inuit, Dickens described them as "covetous, treacherous, and cruel . . . with a domesticity of blood and blubber," and considered it ". . . in the highest degree improbable that such men as Franklin would, or could, in any extremity of hunger, alleviate the pains of starvation by this horrible means."

Despite public opposition to Rae's account, Inuit stories of cannibalism among the Franklin crewmen continued to surface. In 1869, during a trek across the southern coast of King William Island in search of the missing expedition, the American explorer Charles Francis Hall encountered Inuit who gave him eyewitness accounts of cannibalism among Franklin's men. In one account, the Inuit spoke of seeing ". . . some long boots—some that came up as high as the knees and that in some was cooked human flesh—that is, human flesh that had been boiled." In another account, "one man's body when found by the Inuits, flesh all on and not mutilated except the hands sawed off at the wrists—the rest, a great many had the flesh cut off as if someone or other had cut it off to eat." Interestingly, Hall's narrative also includes an account of cannibalism that had reportedly occurred among the deserters of a whaling vessel some years prior to his trip to King William Island.

Similar accounts of cannibalism among members of the Franklin expedition were gathered by Lieutenant Frederick Schwatka, who conducted a search for the missing crew on King William Island in 1879. According to one report, an Inuit ". . . saw bones from legs and arms that appeared to have been sawed off . . . the appearance of the bones led the Inuits to the opinion that the white men had been eating each other . . . His reason for thinking that they had been eating each other was because the bones were cut with a knife or saw."

Franklin was not the last Arctic explorer to be associated with cannibalism. Reports surfaced again in 1884 when, on August 12th, *The New York Times* published an account of the Greely expedition, an American expedition whose quest for the pole ultimately claimed the lives of all but six crewmen. The paper's front-page story reported that "many of the 17 men who are said to have perished by starvation had been eaten by their famished comrades." Exhumation of the bodies by one of the search parties revealed that six had in fact been mutilated. A medical examination of one of the bodies revealed that strips of flesh had been neatly removed from the thigh and trunk by a sharp knife or scalpel, and the crew physician, Dr. Pavy, was implicated.

Until recently, such accounts were the only evidence of cannibalism in these early Arctic expeditions. It was not until 1981, when Owen Beattie, a forensic anthropologist at the University of Alberta, recovered the skeletal remains of one of Franklin's crewmen from a site on the southern coast of King William Island, that concrete evidence of cannibalism came to light. A close examination of one of the bones, a right femur, revealed cut marks on the shaft, marks made by a knife used to remove tissue from the bone. The skull of the same individual showed evidence of having been intentionally broken, possibly for the purpose of extracting the brain for consumption. Other signs that cannibalism had occurred included the fact that most of the bones recovered at the site were those of limbs that possibly were retained as a portable food supply. As well, many of the bones were found clustered outside a tent circle, as if purposely deposited there.

In 1993, an expedition in which I participated discovered a previously unrecorded Franklin site on the southern coast of Erebus Bay on King William Island that has yielded the best evidence of cannibalism to date. An analysis of nearly 400 human bones and bone fragments recovered from the site revealed that 92 of the bones had cut marks, and more than half of these had multiple cut marks. Approximately 25% of the bones had cuts in the vicinity of the joints, a pattern indicating intentional dismemberment. In addition to the cut marks, three of the long bones had been fractured, possibly for the purpose of extracting the marrow.

Though cuts were found on bones from many different parts of the body, those found on bones of the hands and feet are particularly telling of the desperate situation in which the men found themselves. In documented cases of cannibalism, the meatier parts of the body, such as the thighs, buttocks, arms, and legs, are consumed first, while the most recognizable aspects, the face, hands, and feet, are consumed last.

That cannibalism occurred in these Arctic expeditions is not surprising given the desperate circumstances in which it occurred. Weakened by starvation, scurvy, and lead poisoning during the final trek across King William Island, Franklin's crew had no other resource. John Rae remarked, "I consider it no reproach, when suffering the agony to which extreme hunger subjects some men, for them to do what the Esquimaux tell us was done." Even in modern times, individuals confronted with death have had to resort to this measure. As recently as 1972, 16 of the 45 passengers who survived a plane crash in the Andes escaped death by consuming the flesh of their dead companions. In the same year, the crash of a small plane in the western Canadian Arctic left two of four passengers dead. The harrowing ordeal of the two survivors is described in vivid detail in the book *The Survivor* by Peter Tadman. The pilot, Martin Hartwell, who was rescued 32 days after the crash, survived by eating pieces of one of the victims. The second survivor, a 14-year-old Inuit named David Kootook, refused to do the same and died 23 days after the crash.

It is likely that Hartwell's will not be the last incident of cannibalism in the Arctic, just as that of Franklin's men was probably not the first. The Arctic is perhaps the most unforgiving of environments, and we challenge it at our peril. While most of us would share Dickens' horror at the prospect of eating one another, we must ultimately side with John Rae, and hope we never find ourselves stranded in an Arctic winter.

Transcription of the *Times* of London, Monday, October 23, 1854:

THE ARCTIC EXPEDITION

Intelligence which may be fairly considered decisive has at last reached this country of the sad fate of Sir John Franklin and his brave companions.

Dr. Rae, whose previous exploits as an Arctic traveller have already so highly distinguished him, landed at Deal yesterday, and immediately proceeded to the Admiralty, and laid before Sir James Graham, the melancholy evidence on which his report is founded.

Dr. Rae was not employed in searching for Sir John Franklin, but in completing his survey of Boothia. He justly thought, however, that the information he had obtained greatly outweighed the importance of his survey, and he has hurried home to satisfy the public anxiety as to the fate of the long-lost expedition, and to prevent the risk of any more lives in a fruitless search. It would seem from the description of the place in which the bodies were found that both Sir James Ross and Captain Bellot must have been within a few miles of the spot to which the unfortunate countrymen had struggled in their desperate march. A few of the unfortunate men must, he thinks, have survived until the arrival of the wild fowl about the end of May, 1850 as shots were heard and fresh bones and feathers of geese were noticed near the sad event.

We subjoin Dr. Rae's report to the Admiralty and a letter with which he has favoured us: —

The following is Dr. Rae's report to the Secretary of the Admiralty: —

REPULSE BAY, JULY 29, 1854
"Sir,—I have the honour to mention, for the information of my Lords Commissioners of the Admiralty, that during my journey over the ice and snows this spring, with the view of completing the survey of the west shore of Boothia, I met with Esquimaux in Pelly Bay, from one of whom I learnt that a party of 'white men' (Kabloonans) had perished from want of food some distance to the westward, and not far beyond a large river containing many falls and rapids. Subsequently, further particulars were received and a number of articles purchased, which places the fate of a portion, if not all, of the then survivors of Sir John Franklin's long-lost party beyond a doubt—a fate as terrible as the imagination can conceive.

"The substance of the information obtained at various times and from various sources was as follows: —

"In the spring, four winters past (spring, 1850), a party of 'white men,' amounting to about 40, were seen travelling southward over the ice and dragging a boat with them by some Esquimaux, who were killing seals near the north shore of King William's Land, which is a large island. None of the party could speak the Esquimaux language intelligibly, but by signs the natives were made to understand that their ship, or ships, had been crushed by ice, and that they were now going to where there were deer to shoot. From the appearance of the men, all of whom except one officer, looked thin, they were then supposed to be getting short of provisions, and they purchased a small seal from the natives. At a later date the same season, but previously to the breaking up of the ice, the bodies of some 30 persons were discovered on the continent, and five on an island near it, about a long day's journey to the N.W. of a large stream, which can be no other than Back's Great Fish River (named by the Esquimaux Oot-ko-hi-ca-lik), as its description and that of the low shore in the neighbourhood of Point Ogle and Montreal Island agree exactly with that of Sir George Back. Some of the bodies had been buried (probably those of the first victims of famine); some were in a tent, or tents; others under the boat, which had been turned over to form a shelter, and several lay scattered about in different directions. Of those found on the island, one was supposed to have been an officer, as he had a telescope strapped over his shoulders and his double-barrelled gun lay beneath him.

"From the mutilated state of many of the corpses and the contents of the kettles, it is evident that our wretched countrymen had been driven to the last resource—cannibalism—as a means of prolonging existence.

"There appear to have been an abundant stock of ammunition, as the powder was emptied in a heap on the ground by the natives out of the kegs or cases containing it; and a quantity of ball and shot was found below high water mark, having probably been left on the ice close to the beach. There must have been a number of watches, compasses, telescopes, guns (several double-barrelled), etc, all of which appear to have been broken up, as I saw pieces of these different articles with the Esquimaux, and, together with some silver spoons and forks, purchased as many as I could get. A list of the more important of those I enclose, with a rough sketch of the crests and initials on the forks and spoons. The articles themselves shall be handed over to the Secretary of the Hon. Hudson's Bay Company on my arrival in London.

"None of the Esquimaux with whom I conversed had seen the 'whites,' nor had they ever been at the place where the bodies were found, but had their information from those who had been there and who had seen the party when travelling.

"I offer no apology for taking the liberty of addressing you, as I do so from a belief that their Lordships would be desirous of being put in possession at as early a date as possible of any tidings, however meagre and unexpectedly obtained, regarding this painfully interesting subject.

"I may add that, by means of our guns and nets, we obtained an ample supply of provisions last autumn, and my small party passed the winter in snow houses in comparative comfort, the skins of the deer shot affording abundant warm clothing and bedding. My spring journey was a failure in consequence of an accumulation of obstacles, several of which my former experience in Arctic travelling had not taught me to expect. I have & c. John Rae, C.F.

Commanding Hudson's Bay Company's Arctic Expedition"

Among the Articles recovered by Dr. Rae: A small silver plate with "Sir John Franklin, K.C.B." engraved on it; several spoons and forks with the initials of the following officers — vix. Captain Crozier, Lieutenant G. Gore, Assistant-Surgeon Alexander M'Donald, Assistant-Surgeon John S. Peddle, Assistant-Surgeon Harry D.S. Goodair, Second-Master Gilles S. Masbean

—THE EXPLORERS JOURNAL, WINTER 1994–1995

Anne Keenleyside, Ph.D. teaches in the department of Anthropology at McMaster University in Toronto.

On Stefansson

BY ROALD AMUNDSEN

---

*In publishing this article, in the belief that it is the first adequate, literal trans-
lation of a portion of Amundsen's* Mit Liv Som Polarforsker, *in the chapter,
"Om Stefansson og Andre," the editors have acted without desire to promote
any controversy, and only in the interests of polar research.*

*For the work thus condemned by Amundsen, for his general career in
northern exploration, Stefansson has received the formal thanks of the
Canadian Government, honorary doctorates from four universities; medals
from the geographical societies of Berlin, Chicago, London, New York, Paris,
and Washington. He is honorary member, medalist, past president, and present director of* The Explorers Club.

*Amundsen also had a long list of similar distinctions, among them a
medal and honorary membership of this Club.*

*The square disagreement and contradiction on facts between men of such
standing is a material issue for science, and especially for geography. It is serious for exploration.*

Amundsen's volume has been widely accepted as authoritative.

*While agreeing with him that no evil should be spoken of the dead, a tenet
that has tied the hands of Dr. Stefansson against his own defense, it is mani-
festly unfair that the living should suffer from statements that may not be
buried with their utterer.*

*It is more than possible that Amundsen was misled, since Stefansson cer-
tainly never made many of the statements attributed to him. It is a fact that
Stefansson, Storkerson, and Andreasen maintained themselves in 1914 for forty-
one days by hunting on the sea ice, and for eighty days on Banks Island. In 1918
a five-man party of the Stefansson expedition, commanded by Storkerson,
maintained themselves and their dogs by hunting for five months at distances*

of from 100 to 200 miles from land. These and many similar things diametrically opposed to Amundsen's statements are matters of record. Burt McConnell and Sir Hubert Wilkins of The Explorers Club, among others, so testify.

Be all this as it may, it has seemed to the Publication Committee a fitting thing to do to clear the record, without rancor or recrimination, solely in the cause of scientific exploration.

The full consent of Dr. Stefansson was secured to the publication of this article.

J. A. D.

I always characterize the first of Vilhjalmur Stefansson's two famous "discoveries" as about the most palpable nonsense that ever has come from the North, and the second not only as nonsense, but even as harmful and dangerous nonsense. I refer to his widely circulated book, *The Blond Eskimos*[1], and also to his equally famous *The Hospitable North*[2].

Let me first deal with *The Blond Eskimos*. It is, of course, not beyond the limits of possibility that one or another little Eskimo tribe may have escaped up to now being found by white men;[3] but to say that this is probable is to stretch the limits of possibility further than one can agree to, and really to

---

1. Amundsen's reference to a "book called *The Blond Eskimos* " (in Norwegian *Blonde Eskimoer*) is puzzling. Stefansson does not appear to have written a book with any name resembling this. The nearest, perhaps, is *My Life with the Eskimos*, 1912. Nor does this book have a name suggesting "Blond Eskimos" in either of the two languages into which it has been translated. It is called *Mit Liv med Eskimoerna* in Swedish (Stockholm, 1925); in German, *Das Geheimnis der Eskimos* (Leipzig, 1925).

2. With *The Hospitable North* (Norwegian: *Det gestfri Nord*) Amundsen probably had in mind Stefansson's *The Friendly Arctic*, 1921.

3. On whether Stefansson claims to have been the first to visit the so-called "Blond" Eskimos, see his *My Life with the Eskimo*, 1913, pp. 199–200.

have any faith in it would be impossible unless the discovery were supported by irrefutable proof. Stefansson has never produced any such proof.

The probable explanation of "blond Eskimos" is quite obvious. The Arctic regions have for four hundred years been the favorite field of the explorer.[4] Expedition after expedition of white men has gone into these regions, and most of them have wintered there. Besides these discoverers, innumerable fur traders have journeyed to the North, generation after generation. In all these enterprises the British and the Scandinavians have been in the majority. The man who is married to a native woman is a phenomenon constantly met with here, in the same way that the unavoidable mixed connections have sown the American West Coast with half-breeds, the South with mulattos, and Latin America with mestizos. The morality of the Eskimos is not higher than that of other human beings—note the offer which an Eskimo made to one of the crew of the *Gjoa:* in return for a needle he offered to lend his wife to the white man.

Blond Eskimos are almost certainly halfbreed grandchildren of halfbreed Eskimo mothers and light-haired, blue-eyed white fathers from the northern lands.[5] Anyone who has even a fair knowledge of the Mendelian law of the inheritability of physical characteristics knows very well that in the second

---

4. It is generally considered that the first expedition to go into the region here debated was Franklin, 1821; Dease and Simpson's was the second expedition, in 1938. Neither of these expeditions wintered; both reported seeing "Blond" Eskimos. But see Note 5.

5. With reference to Amundsen's view that the "Blond" Eskimos are descended from whalers, trappers, traders and explorers, it is pertinent to consider a statement by the first white man who (so far as the editors are aware) ever visited the region in dispute, the Coronation Gulf section of Arctic America. This was Sir John Franklin. He says:

"The countenance of Terregannoeuck was oval, with a sufficiently prominent nose, and had nothing very different from an European face, except in the smallness of his eyes, and, perhaps, in the narrowness of his forehead. His complexion was very fresh and red, and he had a longer beard than I have hitherto seen on any

generation of such connections (whether of plants, animals or human beings) the issue will as a rule bear the character of one of the parents in its pure form. Stefansson's tale of a special race of blond Eskimos[6] merits no more serious consideration than a sensational news item in the boulevard press.

Stefansson's *Blond Eskimos* is merely an amusing figment of the imagination. His *The Hospitable North*, on the other hand, is a dangerous distortion of the real conditions. It would not harm credulous people if they believed that some Eskimos are blonds. But it is quite certain that one or another who is in search of adventure and new experiences up in the North will be led astray by this prattle about the "hospitality" there, and that he will actually attempt to do what Stefansson declares that he has done, namely, to venture into these regions equipped only with a rifle and a little ammunition. If they do this it is certain death. A more unreasonable distortion of conditions in the North has never been set forth than that a skilful marksman "can

---

of the aboriginal inhabitants of America. . . ." (John Franklin: *Narrative of a Journey to the Shores of The Polar Sea, in the Years 1819, 20, 21, and 22*, London, 1823, p. 353.)

This quotation from Franklin, who knew intimately and at first hand the Eskimos of Hudson Bay, and the Indians south of the Coronation Gulf Eskimos, is in brief compass practically the description which Stefansson gave from the same district nearly 100 years later. So Amundsen is here taking issue quite as much with Franklin as with Stefansson. Indeed, Stefansson's own books claim in this respect only that he confirmed (and amplified) the observations and reports of Franklin in 1821 and Simpson in 1839 (Thomas Simpson: *Narrative of the Discoveries on the North Coast of America, effected by the Officers of the Hudson's Bay Company during the years 1836–39*, London, 1843, pp. 346, 347).

Stefansson cites the above and other authorities in Chapter XII of *My Life with the Eskimo*, where he discusses various theories that have been advanced, including the one here maintained by Amundsen.

6. As to whether Stefansson really favors the view of "a special race of Blond Eskimos," consult his cited work, Chapter XII and elsewhere. For a discussion of the "Blond" Eskimo controversy, see the Appendix to the revised and abridged edition, *My Life with the Eskimo*, New York, 1927.

live off the land." Stefansson has never done it, although he says he has. Furthermore, I am willing to stake my reputation as a Polar explorer, and will wager everything I own, that if Stefansson were to attempt it, he would be dead within eight days, counted from the start, provided that this test takes place on the Polar ice, which is constantly adrift over the open sea.[7]

There is just enough truth in what he says so that this statement sounds plausible. A trifle of game is to be found on the mainland and a little on the large islands within the Arctic Circle. If a man were expert in finding it and very skilful in capturing it, and if luck and the season were good, he could just barely live along the coastal strip, though it should be pointed out that it is not uncommon for Eskimos to starve to death—they who here have every advantage and experience and thus, better than anyone, have the qualifications for being able to exist.

But when one sets out on the endless Arctic ice fields, out of sight of land, then the chances for whoever it may be to "be able to live off the land"

---

7. As to what Stefansson and those who were with him have said on the matter here in dispute, see:

> Vilhjamur Stefansson: *The Friendly Arctic*, New York, 1921, really the whole book, but especially Chapters I, II, XIII–XXII.
> Storker Storkerson: "Drifting in the Beaufort Sea," *MacLean's Magazine* (Toronto), March 15 and April 1, 1920.
> Storker Storkerson: "Living off the Country on an Ice Cake and Never Missing a Meal," *Literary Digest*, August 7, 1920.
> Harold Noice: *With Stefansson in the Arctic*, New York (Dodd, Mead & Co.), n.d.
> George H. Wilkins (Sir Hubert Wilkins): "A Defence of Stefansson's Discoveries," *Discovery* (Magazine), London, January, 1928.
> George H. Wilkins: *Flying the Arctic*, New York, 1928, pp. 3–6.

All these, and others of the same (Stefansson 1913–18) expedition have claimed that they lived by hunting on the drifting sea ice tens to hundreds of miles from land for an aggregate of several months. The issue is therefore squarely drawn between the Amundsen and Stefansson camps.

are just as good as they would be to find a gold mine on the top of an iceberg.[8] There are, to be sure, some few—very few—seals which now and then come up on the ice, but to see a seal and to kill it are two widely different things. Fishing is not to be spoken of, since the ice is from three to twelve feet thick.

Stefansson's foolish tale has also injured the prospects of more serious explorers. I have met here and there in the world men of the very best education who have accepted this yarn as the actual truth about life up there. I have heard them express their astonishment over my elaborate preparations to enable me to take along sufficient provisions in concentrated form for use on my expeditions. By this tale, furthermore, the belief has been spread abroad that a trip to the North Pole is not much more than a hunting trip for pleasure, during which one promenades comfortably over the ice and stops now and then to kill something for food, without having any worry about provisions for the following day. These men believed what they said. "Had not, perhaps, the well-known Arctic explorer Stefansson written a book just to correct the error that it was difficult to obtain enough to live on up there in the Arctic regions?"

I am, naturally, personally acquainted with most of the men who have gathered experience in the Northern regions. I have spoken with many of them about Stefansson's *The Hospitable North.* To mention the book to them is the surest means of getting a chance to hear a string of coarse words of abuse. They know by experience what ridiculous nonsense it is. Just the same, I venture to predict that it will not in fifty years be possible to convince

---

8. Amundsen has apparently nowhere claimed that he has himself tried to live by hunting on the sea ice at considerable distances from land. Stefansson and his associates claim that they did it again and again for long periods during the 1913–18 expedition (see under footnote 7).

Stefansson's method of hunting seals, under the conditions here being discussed by Amundsen, is described in various parts of *The Friendly Arctic,* particularly in Chapters XVII–XXX.

the greater part of the sanely thinking public that money which is used for the sensible provisioning of Arctic expeditions is not money thrown away. Stefansson has done the cause of really serious exploration an infinitely great injury by this fantastic tale.

Stefansson's expeditions have become widely known, but they have always been marked by the same lack of valuable results, and in many instances also by terrifyingly poor power of judgment. Many of Stefansson's companions have returned to civilization as his bitter enemies.

I should not speak of Stefansson in such a disagreeable manner were it not because his prattle about the Polar regions has demonstrably injured all that is called Polar exploration. Poor power of judgment is sometimes understandable, even though it is not always so easily forgiven, but many men have also been forgiven for that. More than one Arctic leader has had dissension on his expeditions. Other expeditions have been unsuccessful. But when one man combines all these common faults with an ungovernable imagination, then it is, in my opinion, the duty of one who can speak with the authority of experience and can do it with profit for the work of all explorers, to point out in clear terms that Stefansson's talk about *The Hospitable North* is merely nonsense.

— EXPLORERS CLUB TALES (1936)

The Norwegian polar explorer Roald Amundsen was the first person to reach the South Pole. He served from 1897–99 as first mate on the Belgica *(under the Belgian Adrien de Gerlache) in an expedition to the Antarctic, and he commanded the* Gjöa *in the Arctic in the first negotiation of the Northwest Passage during 1903–1906.* Gjöa *was the first single ship to complete the route through the Northwest Passage. His account appeared in English as Amundsen's* North West Passage *(1908). He then purchased Fridtjof Nansen's* Fram *and prepared to drift toward the North Pole and then finish the journey by sledge. The news that Robert E. Peary had anticipated him in reaching the North Pole caused Amundsen to consider going south. He was successful in reaching the*

South Pole on December 14, 1911, after a dash by dog team and skis from the Bay of Whales (an inlet of Ross Sea). He arrived there just thirty-five days before Robert F. Scott. This story he told in The South Pole. *In the course of these expeditions, he added much valuable scientific and geological information to the knowledge of Antarctica.*

Rescued from the "Death Trap" of the Arctic

BY BURT M. MCCONNELL

The man sitting opposite me had just finished his first square meal in seven months. For five months, each seemingly longer than a year, he had been marooned on Wrangel Island, a hundred miles off the coast of north-eastern Siberia, with never a sight of sail or a smudge of smoke. His shaggy, matted hair streamed down over his eyes in wild disorder. His grimy face was streaked and furrowed with lines and wrinkles. His caribou-skin clothes were begrimed with seal oil, blood, and dirt and were in tatters. The color of his skin could not be judged from a look at his hands, so stained were they. His full, unkempt beard effectually hid the emaciation of his cheeks, but his sunken eyes told of suffering and want.

This was John Munro, chief engineer of the *Karluk*, flagship of the Canadian Arctic Expedition of 1913.

The story of the dramatic rescue of Munro and his eleven companions is a narrative to stir one's blood. It is the story of a comparatively unknown arctic tragedy—a sturdy whaling vessel, with twenty-two men, one Eskimo woman and her two children on board, caught in the drifting ice fields north of Alaska and carried westward for fifteen hundred miles, only to be sunk by the shifting floes; the dogged retreat of the shipwrecked lot over a hundred miles of chaotic pressure ridges; the needless loss of eight lives before the party reached Wrangel Island; the seven-months' wait by the survivors, camped in flimsy tents, while two of their number pressed southward over another hundred miles of ice to Siberia in search of aid; the death of one castaway by accident and two from scurvy; hardship and starvation; finally, the heroic rescue of the nine men, the woman, and the two Eskimo children after they had abandoned all hope. A small amount of seal meat and a few arctic fox carcasses were the sum total of their food supply. Munro had but twelve cartridges left with which to sustain himself and his companions throughout the winter. Long ago they had given up hope of ever being rescued. They knew only too well Wrangel Island's inaccessibility. They had matches, but their clothing was insufficient for another winter. These survivors of the shipwreck must have perished, had they not been rescued.

In February of that year they had been fairly well clad in caribou-skin shirts and trousers and sealskin boots, but after working, hunting, and sleeping for more than six months in their garments, their bedraggled appearance can better be imagined than described. The nerve-racking suspense suffered by the castaways while waiting for relief must have been terrible. They had no way whatever of knowing whether or not Captain Bartlett had been able to reach the mainland, and very few ships ever pass near enough to distinguish even a smoke signal on the island.

Their rations, even with the strictest economy, had lasted only until the first week in June, for the three months previous to our arrival they had subsisted on whatever they could obtain.

Wood was plentiful and fresh water could be had by melting snow or pieces of year-old salt-water ice that had been exposed to the rays of the sun and thus made into fresh ice. Tobacco, tea, coffee, salt, sugar, flour, and other luxuries they had not known for several months, but still they were alive and well.

". . . You came just in time," Munro was saying. "I had only a dozen cartridges left with which to kill game enough to last us through the winter. We'd have starved to death long ago if it hadn't been for Mr. Stefansson's Mannlicher rifle. One day, after our food supply had become exhausted and we were wondering where the next meal was coming from, I saw a seal out on the ice. I managed to creep to within a hundred yards of him before being compelled to stop to steady my nerves. It seemed to me that the seal must hear the beating of my heart.

"While resting, this thought came to me: if you miss him, you will starve! For seals were very scarce, and we had seen no other game in several days.

"The seal was basking in the sunlight, unaware of his peril. I crept to an advantageous position, set the hair trigger of my rifle and took deliberate aim—or tried to. I think I drew a bead on the head of that seal for at least two minutes, then almost collapsed when I realized that my hand was too unsteady to make my aim certain. Here was meat enough for all of us for a week, our very lives were at stake, and yet here was I with an acute attack of something akin to buck fever! It was a terrible predicament. I lay back on the ice, trying to regain my composure. But then came the thought that, if I waited too long, the seal might disappear into the water.

"I aimed again, but my nervousness still frustrated me; in that state I could not have hit a barn, so I waited. During this wait I kept saying to myself, through my clenched teeth, 'I'll get you!' and calling the poor seal all sorts of names. I was a caveman for a few moments. Then, when I had talked myself into a state of comparative calm and had convinced myself that I simply could not miss, I fired. The seal gave one convulsive shudder and lay still. For the time being, our troubles were over. But you came just in time."

Stefansson, with a scientific staff of nine, of which the writer was a member, and a ship's crew of fourteen, four Eskimo men, one Eskimo seamstress, and her two girls—thirty-one persons in all—had set out in the whaler *Karluk* in the summer of 1913, under the auspices of the Canadian Government, to explore as much as possible of the area lying between Alaska and the North Pole. While Stefansson, Wilkins (now Sir Hubert), Jenness, and I, with two Eskimo dog drivers, were ashore hunting caribou on the north coast of Alaska, the ice in which the ship was imprisoned, eighteen miles from land, broke away under the influence of an unprecedented northeast gale and carried the helpless *Karluk* westward toward Siberia. There, sixty miles north of Herald Island, she was crushed like an eggshell some four months later. Meanwhile we hunters were left marooned on the north coast of Alaksa, but we managed to make our way to Point Barrow. It was not until a year later that the rescue party, of which I was a member, reached the survivors on Wrangel Island. It was a stirring story that the castaways had to tell . . .

A phonograph concert was being given in the after cabin on the *Karluk* when the first warning of disaster came—a tremendous groan from the vessel's staunch timbers as the ice field closed in. Everyone worked desperately to save the necessary articles that had been left on board until the last moment should come. Every care was taken to secure the twenty-seven dogs, for only by their aid would retreat over the treacherous ice fields be possible. It was a weird and dreadful night for the twenty-two men, the Eskimo woman, and her two little girls of eight and four years.

Presently to the creaking of the *Karluk*'s timbers as they were smashed like pencils by the irresistible pressure was added the touching sight of her actual writhings as she twisted and turned like an animal in a trap. Then came the rush of in-going water. A few hours later the ice field which had sealed her doom receded at the whim of an unknown current and the place where lately a gallant ship had floated became a mere blot of black water, strongly contrasted against the spotless white of the surrounding ice and snow.

Nothing like this had ever happened before in the Arctic. True, more than a hundred ships have been caught in its icy grasp and hundreds of adventurous young men have gone down with their vessels or lost their lives in the retreat over the ice to shore, but never in history had a crew been compelled to abandon a crushed and sinking vessel in the midst of the long arctic night, with the temperature thirty-five degrees below zero and a raging blizzard blowing from the northeast.

Captain Bartlett, Peary's ice navigator, was in command; Stefansson and the five of us who made up the hunting party were marooned between Point Barrow and the Mackenzie delta, a thousand miles from the scene of the disaster. Fortunately Bartlett, in anticipation of the crushing of the ship, had removed several months' provisions to a comparatively safe place on the ice. Here, at Shipwreck Camp the twenty-five castaways settled themselves to wait for the end of the arctic night and the return of the sun, so that they might retreat to Wrangel Island, a hundred miles away.

As the hours of daylight lengthened, Captain Bartlett began preparations for the grim race against starvation and the elements. First, an advance party of seven men and two sleds was sent to cut a trail with picks, over which the retreat might be made. Theirs was a heart-breaking task; often it was necessary to haul the sleds up steep acclivities with ropes and let them down on the opposite side in similar manner. Finally, when they arrived at what they believed was Wrangel Island (but which was in reality Herald Island, a forbidding mass of rock rearing itself abruptly out of the sea) they found their way blocked by three miles of open water. Electing to wait until the ice on which they stood drifted ashore, First Officer Anderson and Second Officer Barker, with two seamen—all inexperienced in arctic travel—piled their provisions on the ice, pitched their tent alongside and sent the other three men and the two dog teams back to Shipwreck Camp.

The officers and seamen who stayed with the provisions were never seen again; the shifting ice fields probably carried them off into that region marked "Unknown" on maps of the Arctic. These four were the first pawns to be sacrificed on that white chessboard that has claimed perhaps seven hundred lives since explorers first attempted to find a Northwest Passage to China.

Against Captain Bartlett's wishes and contrary to the advice of their companions, another party of four—three scientists and one sailor, departed from the base camp, poorly equipped and pulling their own sleds. This was composed of Dr. A. Forbes Mackay, Oceanographer James Murray, Anthropologist Henri Beuchat, and Seaman Morris. Both Murray and Mackay had been with Shackleton's Antarctic expedition, but their experience was no match for the furious blizzards that frosted their feet and hands and broke up the ice over which they laboriously made their way. Impatience to reach Wrangel Island ahead of the others cost them their lives. Their bleached bones were found some twelve years later on the wind-swept shore of Herald Island. Four more were thus added to the death list, making eight in all.

The main party, under Bartlett, set out and in three weeks reached Wrangel Island. Their slow advance was marked by innumerable hardships. For five days in succession a blizzard compelled taking refuge in the tents. Trails had to be chopped with picks and spears through rough ice piled into chaotic ridges. Vast floes had been tumbled about and thrust upward into barricades by pressure, as if by the hands of a giant.

On reaching Wrangel Island, a comfortable camp was first established. Then Captain Bartlett and Katarktovik, the youngest Eskimo hunter, set out over the ice toward the mainland of Siberia, a hundred miles away, with seven dogs and a sled. It was a terribly difficult journey, during which Bartlett and the Eskimo lost several dogs and broke through the ice many times. Later in the spring the trip could have been made safely in Eskimo *umiaks*, but none of these sturdy walrus-hide boats had been brought from the wreck.

Reaching the mainland, the two travelers continued to East Cape and thence to Emma Harbor, a distance of several hundred miles. They were then taken on the whaler *Herman* (Capt. Pedersen) to St. Michael, Alaska, at the mouth of the Yukon, where Bartlett was able to communicate with the Canadian government by telegraph. At its request the United States government sent the Revenue Cutter *Bear* to the rescue.

On her first journey the *Bear* was only able to get within twenty miles of the ice-encrusted island. The Russian government, which also responded to Canada's appeal for aid, sent two ice-breakers, but Fate played another trick on the castaways—war was declared and Russia recalled her vessels by wireless. An effort was also made by an American whaler to reach the survivors, but, blocked by heavy and densely packed ice, they were unable to make a landing. At least three other whaling ships would have made the attempt from Point Barrow, but everyone seemed to feel sure that the *Bear* would be able to reach Wrangel Island on her first voyage.

Meanwhile, I had reached Point Barrow. When the *Bear* did not succeed, I became alarmed for the safety of the shipwrecked party, came down to Nome on a schooner, and telegraphed to the Canadian government, suggesting that it charter a vessel to proceed independently of the *Bear* and approach the island from a different angle where, presumably, there would be no ice. When this suggestion was rejected, I went to talk the matter over with Olaf Swenson, an old friend, owner of the *King and Winge*, a tiny trading schooner, and urged him to attempt the rescue. He agreed to join in the race and invited me to go with him.

We left Nome for Wrangel Island, six hundred miles away, on September third. September fourth we reached East Cape, Siberia, where Swenson engaged fifteen Eskimos and secured an *umiak*. This was for use in case the schooner should find herself, like the revenue cutter, unable to get near the island. Light in weight and covered with walrus hide, this Eskimo boat could be dragged over the ice which might surround the island, and launched in the open water beyond. On September fifth we sighted loose ice fields and the next day entered the pack within a hundred miles of our goal.

We were not in serious peril, save as anyone entering an ice pack is in peril. An ice field is a danger zone; it is always in motion and at the mercy of winds, tides and unknown currents. The possibility of having your ship crushed by the ice or frozen in for the winter, when you have only two months provisions on board, is not pleasant to contemplate. Therefore, in undertaking this rescue, Swenson did a fine and admirable thing. In the Arctic he is known as a "white man."

First came several hours of ice bucking. The staunch little vessel, only one hundred feet long, but with excellent engines of 140 horse-power, forged her way through seemingly impassable fields. When Captain Jochimsen, the ice pilot, encountered an ice field through which the schooner could not force her way, he skirted its edge until he found an opening. His fearless and skillful seamanship and uncanny knowledge of ice conditions contributed largely to our ultimate success.

The ice was moving all this time under the influence of a southwest wind, which made the situation all the more dangerous for the *King and Winge*. The field became heavier and more densely packed as we neared the island. We passed pressure ridges almost as high as the masts of the schooner. Sometimes, when sent full speed into the ice, she would slide clamberingly up on the floe, like a polar bear struggling out of the water, and break it down with her sheer weight.

At midnight, when it became too dark to see clearly, the fight was postponed until daylight and Captain Jochimsen, who had been on deck for more than twenty-four hours, retired for a three-hour nap. Progress was resumed with the coming of dawn, and slow and discouraging it was.

After three hours of bumping, crashing, and grinding against the densely packed ice, we emerged from the hundred-mile field within sight of the precipitous granite cliffs and the sandy beach near Rodgers Harbor, where Captain Bartlett had told us the survivors would be found. Within five miles of the beach open water appeared, after which the approach became a comparatively simple matter.

When we were within two miles of shore, a tent was sighted by the lookout in the crow's nest and, as we came nearer under full speed, a flag-pole and a cross could be seen near the tent. When within half a mile of the camp, Captain Jochimsen began blowing the ship's siren at intervals. When no one appeared in answer to its blasts, our spirits fell. We had expected to find twenty-three people at this place, yet we could discern only a dilapidated four-man tent, a flag-pole and a cross. No sleds or dogs were to be seen.

Suddenly a man emerged from the tent on hands and knees. I shall never forget his actions. He did not show signs of joy. He did not wave his arms and shout for sheer happiness when he sighted the ship, as some of us had expected the survivors would do. He did not run up and down the beach to attract our attention, but rose and stood rigidly beside the tent, gazing at us as if dazed.

It was plain enough that he at first refused to believe the evidence of his eyes, as he had first refused to believe the evidence of his ears when he heard the sound of the siren. Indeed, he brushed his hands across his eyes more than once, as if to clear away something which might be there, deceiving him, before he finally decided that the *King and Winge* was a real ship come to rescue him.

As soon as he reached this conclusion, apparently, he turned abruptly and entered the tent without another look toward us or even a friendly wave of the hand. Almost immediately, however, he reappeared, bringing with him a British flag, which he raised to half-mast. This confirmed the news con-veyed by the cross—someone had perished. At first we were apprehensive that the entire party, with the exception of the one man we saw, had died, but this gloomy possibility was dispelled presently by the appearance of two other men. But still we were wondering. Could it be possible that but three remained of the twenty-three?

None of this strange trio made any demonstration. Each seemed dazed by his sudden good fortune and stood near the tent and stared at us.

The first mate hastened the launching of the Eskimo *umiak*. When it came within a hundred yards of the beach, the man whom we had seen first started toward us, taking a rifle from its case as he came. He seemed to be loading the magazine with cartridges, at which our Siberian natives became greatly frightened. They pointed to their foreheads and muttered, "That man long time not much eat; him crazy." Swenson quieted their fears, however, and they kept on paddling.

The greatest moment in Swenson's life and mine came when we landed upon the beach and advanced to meet this strange individual, who proved to be Munro.

"How many are left, Chief?" I asked, almost timidly.

"There are nine at Cape Waring, all well the last I heard, but Mamen and Malloch died last spring and are buried near the tent over there." He pointed. These men had been my best friends in the whole party. With no means of procuring fresh meat, they had fallen a prey to a form of scurvy.

But there was no time for reflection, for Fred W. Maurer, one of the *Karluk's* firemen, then came up. He was pale, weak and emaciated. I did not recognize him until Munro spoke his name. Templeman, the steward, next appeared. He was gaunt and very pale. The caribou-skin clothing of these two men was in the same condition as Munro's; they had worn it and slept in it for seven months.

The belongings of the rescued men were collected in a very few minutes, while I sat in the tent and wrote a message for any rescue that might arrive later. The tent was left standing to serve as a beacon. We then hastened aboard the ship, which was immediately headed for Cape Waring, thirty miles to the eastward. After breakfast I played the phonograph for the three guests and gave them a glad surprise when I played "Pierrot's Serenade," a violin solo by Kubelik, which had been our favorite record on the *Karluk*. I had bought this record in Nome, just before starting, for this very occasion. That shows how much confidence I had in Swenson and Captain Jochimsen.

Although Munro had lost about thirty pounds in weight in the preceding months, he was found to be in remarkably good condition and insisted on piloting the schooner to the other camp. He was soon coaxed below, however. Our obliging Japanese steward prepared a delicious breakfast for the castaways, who consumed quarts of coffee in a few hours, huge spoonfuls of both sugar and condensed milk going into each cupful. An hour after a meal they were hungry again. It seemed impossible to fill their long-neglected stomachs. Each man devoured a whole can of condensed milk with a spoon, as though it were ice cream.

On the way to Cape Waring each survivor indulged in a bath—a luxury they had not known in six months or more. They were given clothing from the ship's stores and by almost everyone on the ship. Their tattered skin garments were thrown overboard.

We reached Cape Waring almost before we were aware of it. With the aid of glasses we could see two tents on shore and near them little black figures running up and down the beach to attract our attention. These survivors were regarding our arrival with far more manifestation of excitement than had been made by the Rodgers Harbor group.

We were again able to take the schooner to within two miles of shore before being blocked by the ice. Kurraluk, the expedition's best Eskimo hunter, fearing that we would not see the tiny tents, had gone out over the ice to intercept us. His look of wonder and astonishment at seeing me was laughable; he thought Stefansson and his hunting party had been lost in the same gale which carried the *Karluk* to the westward. As he shook hands with me, he muttered to himself and insisted on feeling my arms and shoulders to see if I really were flesh and blood.

The early morning had been cold and clear, but now snow began to fall so thickly that the schooner could not be seen at a distance of a quarter of a mile. Several of the marooned men rushed out upon the ice to meet us. They had hunted every day, we were told, but had not been able always to kill enough game, so that at times the little band had gone hungry. They were in a desperate plight when we arrived and had abandoned hope of rescue for that year. They had but forty cartridges left—forty cartridges with which to provide meat for nine hungry mouths for a whole year! Their flimsy tents were torn and full of holes, and their food supply was almost exhausted. George Breddy, fireman, we learned, had accidentally shot himself and was buried on the hill near the camp. They had intended to move their camp that day to the north side of the island, where driftwood was known to be comparatively plentiful. They would have done this but for the snowstorm, in which event we would have been compelled to search the island for them.

Thus twelve of the original ship's company were rescued; three were known to be dead and eight were missing, while Captain Bartlett and one Eskimo reached Siberia safely. Such was the fate of this section of the most elaborately equipped expedition that ever went into the Arctic.

Only three dogs out of twenty were left and but one sled of their original three. The rest had been lost, with their loads, in the water between Wrangel Island and Herald Island. The survivors had a plentiful supply of matches, but their clothing was woefully inadequate. One man had frozen the great toe of his foot in March and it had been amputated with a butcher knife and tin-shears. Another man had fallen into the water, and had frosted the heel of one foot; he was still limping. They made a weird-looking procession as they walked out to the *King and Winge*, by twos, with the Eskimo baby on her father's sled. They climbed aboard the little rescue ship and we sailed away in the direction of Herald Island, where we hoped we might sight some of the eight missing men. But a solid field of heavy ice barred our progress and, although we skirted its edge for forty miles, no sign of the missing adventurers was to be found.

The next afternoon we met the revenue cutter *Bear*, on which Captain Bartlett was a passenger. Bartlett boarded the *King and Winge* and, after thanking Swenson for the trouble he had taken, ordered the survivors to transfer to the *Bear*. So the revenue cutter, instead of the *King and Winge*, still gets credit for the rescue. Captain Cochran, of the *Bear*, took me also to Nome, where we arrived September thirteenth, gratified with our success, but feeling only too keenly the loss of three members of the expedition and our inability to find any trace of the eight missing men. Their names, with the names of the three who perished on Wrangel Island, are to be added to the staggering toll which the Arctic has taken from the ranks of adventurers since the fourteenth century.

— *TOLD AT THE EXPLORERS CLUB* (1931)

Arctic exploration, gold mining, aviation, and writing have been Burt McConnell's principal occupations to date.

In 1913–1914 he was meteorologist and secretary to the commander of Stefansson's third arctic expedition and, as he here relates, organized the rescue of the Karluk *survivors, marooned on Wrangel Island.*

Then followed a year as assistant editor of Recreation Magazine, *two of war service, and ten on the editorial staff of* The Literary Digest, *with a special interest in aviation and the air mail.*

In 1929 he went into the woods of northern Quebec, sixty miles from the nearest known inhabitant, without food, clothing, matches, weapons, or shelter, and maintained himself by bow and arrow for two months (September 21–November 26) just to show that it could be done.

The Royal Road to Humdrum

BY VILHJALMUR STEFANSSON

My favorite quotation is Stefansson's dictum: "Adventures are a mark of incompetence."
— Roy Chapman Andrews, *Saturday Evening Post*, August 22, 1931.

I n a book of adventures I like the chance to defend by anecdote and narrative a saying that has been quoted frequently with disapproval, although I managed to discover a favorable vote on it to place at the head of this article.

There is a bit of exposition and argument in the quotation itself, if it is taken somewhat *in extenso* from page 43 of "My Life with the Eskimo" (New York, 1913):

"An adventure is a sign of incompetence . . . If everything is well managed, if there are no miscalculations or mistakes, then the things that happen are only the things you expected to happen, for which you are ready and with which you can therefore deal."

In that book a narrative which supports this thesis is found on pages 165–167. Condensed and adapted, it runs:

"Through incompetence, I came near having a serious adventure; that I did not actually have it was due to the incompetence of a polar bear.

I was hunting caribou eastward along the sea front of the Melville Mountains that lie parallel to the coast (Dolphin and Union Straits) a few miles inland. . . . I had seen no caribou all day nor the day before and our meat was low; therefore I stopped whenever I came to the top of a commanding hill to study the country with my binoculars . . . Ptarmigan there were but they are uneconomical for a party of four that is to go a year on nine hundred and sixty rounds of ammunition; even the foxes were too small for our notice, but a wolf that came within two hundred yards seldom got by, for a fat one weighs a hundred pounds.

This day the wolves did not come near, and the first hopeful sign was a yellow spot on the sea ice about three miles off. It was difficult to determine whether or not it was merely yellow ice. I put in a half hour watching this thing that was a bit yellower than ice should be. Now and then I looked elsewhere, for a caribou or grizzly may at any time come out from behind a cake of ice, or a seal out of his hole. On perhaps the sixth or seventh sweep of the entire horizon with the field-glasses, I missed the yellow spot. It had moved away and must therefore have been a polar bear that had been lying down; after sleeping too long in one position, he had stood up and lain down again behind an ice hummock.

In a moment I was running as hard as I could in the direction of the bear, for there was no telling when he would start traveling or how fast he would go. I had taken careful note of the topography of the land with relation to the rough sea ice, for it is as difficult to keep a straight line toward an invisible object among pressure ridges as it is in a forest. I kept glancing back at the mountains as I ran and tried to guide myself towards the bear by their configuration.

When at last I got to the neighborhood of where I thought the animal would be, I climbed an especially high pressure ridge, and spent a longer time than usual sweeping the surroundings with the glasses and studying individual ice cakes and ridges, with the hope of recognizing some of those I had seen from the mountains. But everything looked different on near approach, and I failed to locate myself definitely. I decided to go a quarter of a mile or so farther before beginning to circle for the bear's tracks. My rifle was buckled in its case slung across my back, and I was slowly and cautiously clambering down the far side of a pressure ridge, when I heard behind me a noise like the spitting of a cat or the hiss of an angry goose. I looked back and saw, about twenty feet away and almost above me, a polar bear.

Had he come the remaining twenty feet as quietly and quickly as a bear can, the literary value of the incident would have been lost forever. From his eye and attitude there was no doubting his intentions; the hiss was merely his way of saying "Watch me do it!" Or possibly the motive was chivalry and the hiss was a way of saying "*Garde!*" Whichever it was, it was the fatal mistake in a game well played to that point. No animal on earth can afford to give warning to a man with a rifle. And why should he? Has a hunter ever played fair with one of them?

Afterwards the snow told plainly the short—and, for one of the participants, tragic—story. I had overestimated the bear's distance from shore and had passed the spot where he lay. On scenting me, he had come up the wind to my trail and had then followed it. The reason I had not seen his approach was that it had not occurred to me to look back. I was so used to hunting bears that the possibility of one of them assuming my role and hunting me had been left out of consideration. A good hunter, like a good detective, should leave nothing out of consideration."

A thing I have too frequently left out of consideration in my travels has been my high-school education, whereupon I have had distressing and thrilling physical adventures. By considering my education, I have sometimes had intellectual adventures that were equally thrilling but less disagreeable.

One of the fundamentals in the training and belief of explorers has been the theory that, when lost or unable to find shelter in a blizzard or in very cold weather, you must on no account go to sleep; if you did, you would never wake again. There is still vividly in mind the thrill I had when I first applied to this belief what I have learned in the eighth grade about physiology and in high school about physics.

I show the problem and background of this adventure by quoting the most famous of American polar explorers before Peary, the physician and popular hero, Elisha Kent Kane. In describing a winter march in extremely cold weather, he says ("Arctic Explorations: The Second Grinnell Expedition." Phila. 1857. Vol. I, pp. 194–197):

"Bonsall and Morton, two of our stoutest men, came to me, begging permission to sleep. 'They were not cold, the wind did not enter them now; a little sleep was all they wanted.' Presently Hans was found nearly stiff under

a drift; and Thomas, bolt upright, had his eyes closed and could hardly artic-
ulate. At last, John Blake threw himself on the snow and refused to rise. They
did not complain of feeling cold; but it was in vain that I wrestled, boxed, ran,
argued, jeered, or reprimanded. . . . Our halts multiplied and we fell half-
sleeping on the snow. I could not prevent it. Strange to say, it refreshed us."

Refreshed as he was and impressed as he was by the startling discrepancy
between belief and experience, Dr. Kane was not jolted out of his folk-belief
that going to sleep in cold weather is dangerous. To him evidently this experience was a strange and unaccountable break in the orderly process of what
he thought was natural law.

The belief in the danger of going to sleep out of doors in cold weather
flourishes even today and even in the schools, side by side with opposite
teachings.

In the physiology class you learn that the body is kept warm by the com-
bustion of food that has become fuel in the blood stream. You can get more
warmth by burning more fuel. It takes fuel also to move the body around
from place to place. The motion itself does make you warmer but only at the
expense of disproportionate fuel consumption. While you are still, most of
the fuel is being used for warmth, but when you are moving, although you
use still more for warmth, you use in addition something extra to produce
motion. This means that, with a certain amount of food in your belly or a certain amount of fat distributed through your tissues, you can keep warm
longer if you move less. Accordingly, when in danger of freezing, you should
move only when, in your judgement, it is absolutely necessary either to avoid
some outside risk or to increase temporarily the body warmth.

In the human body there is not only less use of fuel during idleness than
action but also less during sleep than wakefulness. Apparently, then, wanting
to live long without meals in cold surroundings, you should be as idle as possible and you should sleep as much as possible.

In the physics class you learn that the body is a heat engine and can do
only a certain amount of work on a certain amount of fuel. Your teacher adds
that fuel used for one purpose cannot be available for another.

In physics you learn, too, that air is a comparatively good non-conductor of heat, which means in everyday speech that it keeps away the cold. Air useful for this purpose in human clothing is found inside hollow hairs or imprisoned between hairs or in cavities. Water, on the other hand, is a good conductor. If you move around too much you perspire. The perspiration gets into your clothing, fills the air chambers and displaces the air, making the garment a good conductor and preventing it from keeping out the cold. One of the most important things, then, if you are lost out in the cold is to guard against perspiring. One way of doing that is to move around as little as possible.

A matter of such common knowledge that it is seldom if ever mentioned in the schools is that you do not sleep soundly unless you are comfortably warm. There are few in the United States, even in Florida, who have not been awakened in the night by too great a chill coming in through a window. They have either closed the window or found an extra blanket.

But the same man who knows from experience that a chill wakes you up in a bedroom believes also that a chill would put you to sleep under other conditions, this reversal of the familiar natural law taking place only when you are lost somewhere, preferably in a snowstorm and best of all in the Arctic.

I had not as yet read Dr. Kane as quoted above when my first turn came to stage an encounter between schooling and inherited folk-belief. This occasion was a starlit night with a temperature probably around fifty below zero. I was coming home from a long hunt. As I walked along with fifty or a hundred pounds of caribou meat on my back, I became gradually sleepier—and quite reasonably, for I had been on my feet for something like twenty-four hours. So I stopped, lay down on the snow with one of my arms for a pillow and went to sleep.

I don't suppose it can have been more than five or ten minutes till I began to have the old familiar feeling of being in bed on a chilly night with too few blankets. That feeling woke me up. I was as refreshed as I discovered twenty years later that Kane had been fifty years before.

This being a volume of adventures, I have tried above to produce a thrill and to make myself a bit more of an adventurer by holding out on the reader. I fear I may have known at the time of our story the Mackenzie Eskimo rule for what to do when lost in a blizzard. According to them, you sit down on something with your back to the wind and go to sleep if you can. During the storm you move about as seldom as possible, only to get your blood into circulation when you feel cramped or to warm up if you are getting unendurably cold.

The first Eskimo I knew to be lost in a storm was an old woman who was poorly dressed in comparison either with the rest of the Eskimos or with us explorers. That blizzard lasted three days and she had been sitting it out only about a half-mile from the house. She came home smiling and cheerful when the weather cleared and explained that she wasn't even so very hungry because she had slept most of the time.

Another winter two sailors ran away from a whaling ship at Herschel Island. They were better dressed than the old woman, but they believed, if they went to sleep, they would freeze to death. Their bodies were found by a search party a few days later. Following their belief, they had kept moving and, when going to sleep became imminent, they had tried to keep awake by moving about so violently that they had perspired and their clothing had become wet. Under that condition of extreme exhaustion and with garments which no longer protected them from the cold, they had been able to substantiate at the cost of their lives the theory in which they had so firmly believed. They had gone to sleep and never waked again.

It was the soda counter rather than the high school which furnished the background for another of my early polar thrills. My mother had cautioned me when I was growing up in North Dakota that on a cold winter's day I must not eat snow but was always to come into the house for a drink if I got thirsty. Then I got to know people who had traveled in Switzerland and who had learned from their mountaineer guides that under no condition must you eat snow when you are scaling one of the tourist peaks. Eventually, on my first journey to the Arctic I met a Hudson's Bay Company trader on the average every two hundred miles for the 2,000-mile stretch of the Mackenzie system and I think nearly every one of them cautioned me—the accent usually Scotch and the words usually to the effect that some time I would find myself in bitterly cold winter weather where there was no possibility of liquid water;

under those conditions I must not eat snow. And they fortified the warning by tales of men they had known who had eaten snow and taken violent cramps, dying or nearly dying if they were alone, or becoming burdens on their companions otherwise.

One arctic day a few months later, when I got thirsty, I began wondering what would be the difference between eating snow and eating ice cream. I experimented gingerly, for, after all, these folk-beliefs are not always wholly without rational foundation. A little snow did not hurt and so I ate more. I continued the practice through ten winters and all the members of our various expedition have done the same. We begin eating snow in the morning to forestall, rather than quench, thirst and we eat it all day. It never has hurt one of us.

However, most things can be done in a way that is injurious. The reason why there has been some injury in polar exploration from eating snow is found in a combination of a strong belief with a weak will power. If you believe that eating snow will hurt you, you refrain until the thirst becomes so intense that your will breaks down. Then, if you try to eat the snow fast enough to quench thirst, you will also be eating it fast enough to freeze your lips, tongue, and even your gullet. The whole secret is to have the amount of snow you put in your mouth at any one time so small that the chill of it shall be easily neutralized by the warmth of your mouth.

You can safely swallow snow as snow if the temperature of it when swallowed is only a little below freezing. If you try to swallow it in great quantities while its temperature is still sixty or seventy degrees below freezing you will produce almost the effect of applying liquid air.

That brings us to another of our small adventures with folk-belief. According to revered precept, the thing to do when you freeze your nose is to rub snow on it. But you learn in your physics course that, if you bring together two bodies of different temperatures, the warm one becomes colder and the cold one warmer. Assume now that the skin on a nose which is beginning to freeze is at a temperature of a degree below freezing. The snow on the ground is always at the same temperature as the air, and you are not likely to freeze your nose unless the air is at least fifty below freezing (twenty below zero). If now you apply to a body (a nose) already slightly frozen another body (a mittenful of snow) which is fifty degrees colder, there is going to be that transfer of heat about which we learned in school. The snow will become a little warmer and the nose will become a whole lot colder.

According to the physics course, you ought to bring a warmer body near the cold one if you want the cold one to grow warmer. But the only warm thing you are always sure to have with you at the time of a frostbite is the rest of your body. So you naturally apply your hand to your face. The hand is not necessarily the warmest part of your body, but it is peculiarly well situated for applying to the face and usually it is quite warm enough.

On a cold day, with a moderate head-wind, we freeze our faces dozens and scores of times, but we thaw them out just as often, and we never allow the frost to become more than skin deep, in which case it is no more serious than a sunburn. Neither is it more painful.

A case where a folk-belief really had me going was about the well known depressing effect of the long arctic night. Why should a long night be depressing when a short one isn't? The first winter, I was so firmly convinced it would be that I don't remember ever posing to myself the contradiction beween that belief and the well known hilarity of city nights, with their midnight revelry against which the clergy inveigh. I actually felt the midwinter polar depression, even with the Eskimos about me behaving as if Billy Sunday ought to come and scold them for it.

That winter I rejoiced at length in my diary when the sun returned, but now believe this to have been due to auto-suggestion. Anyhow, I have never been depressed by any of the nine following arctic winters. More convincing, I have noticed that the conservative and uncritical members of our expeditions have been depressed the first season by the sun's absence, while the younger and more intellectual have been able to convince themselves in advance that the gloom, if it came, would be only the result of auto-suggestion.

The thrill of conquering arctic blizzards did not come to me in any particular blizzard. I had at first been a good deal worried by several of them, and then it occurred to me one day to ask myself what was it that made an arctic blizzard so much more terrible than the ones I grew up among in North Dakota. The answer came in a flash and, with elation of a newish kind, for here it was not high-school training but a university course in logic that had slain the dragon. If there was no difference in strength of wind or degree of cold between polar and temperate-zone blizzards, then the different effect on me had to be due to something in me. All I had to do was to recapture my commonplace attitude toward blizzards. I did, and they never worried me thereafter.

A whole series of intellectual adventures came when I discovered that you could overcome many of the arctic terrors by simply changing their names. The dreaded Barren Ground becomes reasonably innocuous if you think of the grass and flowers and then name the treeless country "prairie." The Long Arctic Night is deprived of half its gloom if you call it the Time of Short Days. That is more descriptive, too, for out of doors you have daylight enough to read a newspaper around noon at very midwinter—for instance on the Ross Sea, where most of the famous antarctic expeditions have had their base, and at Smith Sound, where Peary used to winter.

An adventure in part physical, though it concerned also a tussle between the biological sciences and folk-belief, is foreshadowed by the reading of the typical polar book. The case is put in a nutshell by Raold Amundsen on p. 211 of his "My Life as a Polar Explorer" (*Mitt Liv Som Polar Forsker*), Oslo, 1927:

"A more indefensible misrepresentation of conditions in the North has never been advanced than the claim that a good hunter can live there by hunting. Stefansson has never done it, although he says he has. Moreover I am willing to stake my reputation as a polar explorer, and to wager everything I own, that, if Stefansson were to try it, he would be dead within eight days, counted from the start, if only he makes the experiment on the polar ice which is steadily drifting about on the open sea."

The view here so clearly stated by Amundsen had not yet been specifically contravened, so far as I know, by any book in print before 1914, when three of us (Storker Storkerson, Ole Andreason, and myself) made the experiment of living under just the conditions laid down by Amundsen—on polar ice that was steadily drifting about on the open sea at distances varying between scores and hundreds of miles from land.

The thrilling side of our adventure was the intellectual—that we were staking our lives on the rightness of what we had learned in school. According to physics and physical geography, no sea water could be colder than twenty-seven Fahr., and waters of that temperature were known to be crowded with animal life in other parts of the world. Why not equally crowded in the polar seas, too, especially as the great fisheries of both the northern and the southern hemispheres are found exactly in the coldest water? The ice on top of a sea could not deprive the life in the water of the necessary oxygen for at any temperature it is broken into drifting cakes by the stresses of tides, winds, and currents, so that it does not come so near hermetically sealing the water as does the heavy unmoving and shore-fast ice of lakes like Winnipeg or Great Slave, which are known to be excellent fishing grounds toward spring.

Just as the same man will tell you that a chill wakes you up in a bedroom and puts you to sleep out of doors, so the same book will tell you in general that all the conditions of the Arctic Sea are favorable to animal life, and then in particular that little or no animal life exists there. We decided to be logical, to conclude that two opposed statements could not both be right and to bet our lives that animals would be found in places known to be suitable for them.

The reasoning which led to the decision was simple. We had examined all the arguments and had come to the conclusion that they were the kind that would appeal to a philosopher but would probably not appeal to a fish. To begin with, we did not believe that the fish knew the philosophers had drawn a line in the ocean beyond which they must not swim, and secondarily we believed that, if the fish knew enough to turn back at the right place, there were nevertheless ocean currents which would carry with them all over the polar sea millions of tons of those sea animals and plants which do not swim but float wherever the water takes them. We would live on these directly or indirectly—most probably indirectly, on the swimming seals that follow and eat the drifting shrimps.

There was, however, a certain nervous tension about traveling north from the known arctic lands with provisions for less than two months and a plan to be gone a year. For, as said, not every folk-belief is wrong and there are cases where high-school knowledge fails through the omission of something true or the inclusion of something untrue. It was not merely the scientists who clung to folk-belief despite their contradicting knowledge; nor merely the explorers like Amundsen, who believed that animals sufficient for a hunter's life would not be found beyond a certain limit. The whalers, who had been seeking the bow head in the western Arctic since 1889, and the Eskimos, whose forefathers had been there for generations, held the same view.

The thrill, both physical and scientific, came after several weeks of travel on the "polar ice which is steadily drifting about on the open sea," when we were two hundred miles from land and our food gone. For it appeared, then, that we three and our six dogs were about to lose our lives through a condition as little expected by us as it had been by Amundsen. He was wrong in believing the seals would not be there, but we were really equally wrong, for it seemed we were not gong to be able to live on them because we would not be able to get them. We killed them all right, but they sank.

The explanation proved simple—there had been something missing from our high-school training. The ocean is salty by Scripture and by the schools. The salt makes things float readily by the physics textbooks, but by an omission in the geographies it had not been pointed out to us that the reason why most oceans are fairly uniform in saltiness is that winds keep churning them up. If you have half a glass of brine and pour fresh water into it gently enough the fresh water will float unsalted on top of the brine.

In summer on the polar sea it rains and the sun is warm between the showers. The rain and the thaw-waters flow gently off the ice. They are as fresh as if distilled and float on top of the brine sometimes for a depth of ten or fifteen feet. If the seal we killed was at all far from us, he sank from our sight; because of the gap in our high-school training, we were unaware that he would stop sinking ten or fifteen feet down, where the salt and fresh waters met. Against that situation we could use a harpoon with a long handle, we could convert our sledge into a boat by wrapping a tarpaulin around it, we could paddle out where the seal had sunk and harpoon the carcass as it lay floating and clearly visible to anybody who was straight above him.

Not understanding these things, we had out there on the ice a day or two of semi-panic, if not exactly despair. Then one of the killed seals, instead of sinking, floated and we thought it must have been because he was fatter or for some other reason more buoyant. They may have been so, but we realize now that more probably the motion of the ice cakes or a direct breeze had churned up the sea in that particularly locality, mixing the salt with the fresh.

There is much to be said, then, for polar adventures. The hardest are usually the easiest; the most dangerous, safest. Doing in the Arctic what the public believes impossible frequently becomes the safest possible routine after you have gone through a bit of mental gymnastics, such as changing your mind where you are obviously wrong, or filling up, by reasoning or experience, a gap or two in your education.

— *TOLD AT THE EXPLORERS CLUB* (1931)

"Stefansson will stand for all time as the Great Interpreter of the North," is the apt characterization of Dr. Isaiah Bowman, director of the American Geographical Society.

Born in Manitoba, he began his work as an explorer with two journeys to Iceland in 1904 and 1905. Between 1906 and 1918, he made three extensive expeditions along the northern coast of Alaska and Canada, among the Canadian arctic islands and over the unknown polar sea, adding islands, rivers, lakes, and mountains to the map of those regions and bringing back much scientific information.

Eleven years among the Eskimos, some of whom had never seen a white man before, gave him an intimate knowledge of their language and ways of living.

He was president and a medallist of The Explorers Club and gold medallist of the leading geographical societies of the United States, Great Britain,

France, and Germany. For his field work and writings he received in 1921 an official vote of thanks from the Canadian government—the only time in Canadian history that this honor has been given to an explorer. An alumnus of the University of Iowa, he held a graduate degree from Harvard and doctor's degrees from the universities of Michigan, Iowa, North Dakota, and Iceland.

In addition to scientific reports, he wrote My Life with the Eskimo; The Friendly Arctic; Hunters of the Great North; The Adventure of Wrangel Island; The Northward Course of Empire, *and a gem of Voltairian Satire,* The Standardization of Error.

PART FOUR

Asia

1990 American Everest-Lhotse Expedition

BY GLENN PORZAK

A fter flying from Kathmandu to the mountain airstrip of Lukla, a week of trekking brought us to the village of Periche. Situated in a wide river valley at an elevation of over 14,000', this village has always put into perspective for me the awesome nature of trying to climb Everest. When in Periche you are nearly equal to the highest point in the continental United States, yet you are still some two to three days' walk from base camp where the climbing first begins. The magnitude of it all is overwhelming.

Once above Periche, the terrain has a special feeling which is totally unique. You know that you are entering the throne room of the world's highest peak. While the mountain is still hidden from view, the cold thin air, approaching glaciers, and rock memorials to those climbers who never returned, tell the story.

After passing two more acclimatization days in the hamlet of Lobuche, the last village en route to base camp, the team headed to the final trekking campsite known as Gorak Shep. Located on the edge of the Khumbu Glacier, which flows from Everest's southern flank, this campsite lies at the foot of the 18,600' trekking peak of Kala Pattar. On the afternoon of March 28 the team members all ascended Kala Pattar from where we enjoyed the first unobstructed view of the King and his court. Rising over 10,000 vertical feet, the icy black pyramid of Everest is absolutely stunning in its immensity.

From our vantage, I could see where we had placed our high camps in 1981 and 1989. Rising steeply above are the summit slopes of Everest's southeast ridge. Mentally I climbed those final 3,000 feet, all the time wondering if I would finally get the chance to experience the mountain's last mile.

People ask why climb Everest? Why take all the risks? Why spend years engaged in such a useless endeavor? Well, if they could stand atop Kala Pattar and witness firsthand this monarch among mountains, they would know why.

The next day was cold and overcast. After crossing an old lateral moraine, we finally set foot on the Khumbu Glacier. To the left is the beautifully formed Pumori and on the right is 25,750' Nuptse. At the end of this glacial corridor is the Nepalese-Tibetan border, with Changtse (the north peak of Everest) looming behind. Two hours of weaving through the ice pinnacles and climbing a never ending series of plateaus at long last brought us to our home for the next two months—Everest base camp. At an elevation over 17,600', it is a desolate world encased by towering walls of rock and ice.

Since there is not a flat place around the base camp area, we immediately set to work with pickax and shovel leveling out platforms for our tents— hard work at such altitudes. As planned, expedition members Pete Athans and Andy Lapkass had arrived at base camp with a number of our Sherpas four days ahead of the main group. Due to the tremendous efforts of this advance party, the major construction work had already been completed.

Khumbu Ice Fall

A couple more days of organizing personal gear and sorting out group equipment, and it was finally time to begin our first forays into the dreaded Khumbu ice fall. Between base camp and the tractional site of Camp I is a distance of only 4 miles and just over 2,000 vertical feet. Yet what lies between these two camps is perhaps the most dangerous section of the entire climb. An ice fall is to a glacier what rapids and waterfalls are to a stream. And the Khumbu ice fall is the grand daddy of them all. A twisting maze of towering seracs and gaping crevasses which is constantly moving and exposing even the most cautious climber to hideous risk.

In 1981 it took less than a week to establish a route through the ice fall. In 1989 the route was radically different and 19 days were required to find a way through the labyrinth. That year the route was exposed to the constant threat of collapsing seracs and significant avalanche danger from Everest's west shoulder. A more dangerous day of climbing cannot be imagined. The fourteen times I traveled through the ice fall in 1989 were all terrifying experiences and when descending it for the last time at the end of that expedition, an enormous serac collapsed in on itself less than 10 yards from me. I didn't stop moving until I reached Periche later that evening. Surely, I rationalized, the ice fall would be kinder and gentler next year.

However, Everest rarely lets up its guard. While the 1990 ice fall route was a bit more direct and less exposed to avalanches, there was considerably more movement than in past years. During the course of the expedition, the route underwent a series of radical transformations and had to be continually reestablished. Unfortunately, with each change the ice fall became more and more dangerous such that by the latter part of April, the route was as bad as I had ever seen it.

Moreover, the last 400 or so vertical feet of the route were like nothing encountered on my two prior expeditions to the mountain. It consisted of a series of 100 foot vertical ice towers, which had to be climbed and descended with the aid of fixed ladders. Then a heavily crevassed area and final 75 foot head wall had to be negotiated before reaching the site of Camp I. This section had a deadly beauty and was simply awesome. To summarize my feelings about the Khumbu ice fall: after 32 separate trips through the ice fall over three expeditions, the best thing about having Everest behind me is knowing that I will never again have to set foot in this dreaded death trap.

The Lower Camps

By April 6 the route was completed through the ice fall and we began to make our first carries up to Camp I. Located at an altitude of just under 20,000', Camp I is at the foot of a long, narrow corridor known as the Western Cwm. Bordered by the west ridge of Everest on the left, Nuptse on the right, and Lhotse at the head of this corridor, the Western Cwm is the highest valley on earth. More importantly, it provides access to the upper slopes of Everest.

Taking full advantage of good weather on the lower portions of the mountain, we immediately moved two members and two Sherpas up to Camp I while the remainder of the team continued to carry our supplies through the ice fall. In short order those at Camp I established a route through the crevasse ridden lower section of the Western Cwm and located the future site of Camp II. Situated below Everest's huge southwest face at an altitude of 21,300', Camp II is approximately 3 miles up the Cwm and by mid April served as our advance base camp. Once fully acclimatized, we eventually eliminated Camp I and Sherpas and members alike would make the climb to Camp I directly from base camp.

The Lhotse Face

After a week-long effort of load carrying, half the team had moved into Camp I and we were ready to begin pushing the route up the Lhotse face and ultimately towards the south col. It took two hours of steady, but easy, climbing above Camp II to reach an enormous bergshund at the base of the Lhotse face. From this point, 1,500 vertical feet of ice, at an average angle of $35°$ to $40°$, had to be ascended to reach the site of Camp III.

This portion was always one of the most physical sections of the climb for me. As the mountain was extremely dry, the bergshund had opened up and we were forced to bypass it by climbing a steep, diagonal pitch, and then traversing back to the main part of the Lhotse face. Above this traverse stands a $70°$ head wall of pure water ice. At over 22,000' this head wall involved two of the toughest leads of climbing on the route. Even when fixed with rope, the jumaring of this section was extremely exhausting.

Above this head wall, a seemingly endless series of fixed ropes inched us ever closer to the site of Camp III. A final series of short, but steep, water ice sections led to a platform in the center of the Lhotse face where we pitched two tents. The altimeter registered 23,500' and the view looking down the Western Cwm was stunning. Equal to the height of Pumori, we could look out at Cho Oyu, the sixth highest mountain in the world. But the most powerful sight was of the ever present wind plume streaming off Everest's south summit for thousands of feet into the sky. While cold and windy at our perch on the Lhotse face, it was painfully evident that the conditions 5,000 feet above were far worse.

From Camp III another 600 to 700 vertical feet of ice climbing led to a diagonally sloping traverse towards a large rock outcrop known as the Yellow Band. After an exhilarating climb up a notch where the snow meets the distinctive yellow granite, one encounters the first of three sections of fixed rope which led across the rock band. Climbing the Yellow Band is like being on a small island in a huge sea of snow and ice.

Geneva Spur

At roughly 25,000' the rock ends and an easy stretch of snow was reached which gradually led to an enormous buttress known as the Geneva Spur. Far bigger than it looks from a distance, the Geneva Spur was a welcome mixture of snow and rock scrambling. But while the terrain was straightforward, the severe altitude and accompanying cold make their presence felt. The pace slows markedly, and every step requires considerable effort.

Yet as we climbed higher on the Geneva Spur, the excitement began to mount. After nearly seven hours of climbing from Camp III, the 8,000 meter mark was at last in reach and the south col of Everest was just around the corner. Then, after a beautiful 75 foot pitch of steep snow, the corner was finally turned—there ahead was the south col. The views of the summit pyramid of Everest to the left, Lhotse to the right, and the Western Cwm now far below cannot be adequately described. Simply put, if we hadn't realized before that we were on the highest mountain in the world, we knew it now.

By the third week in April the route had been established and fixed to the top of the Geneva Spur and we began our first carries of supplies to the south col. At an altitude of more than 26,000', the col would be the site of our fourth and last camp on Everest. While most of our team began the work of stocking this camp, a small group was given the task of establishing a Lhotse-Camp IV.

The Lhotse Route

The routes on Everest and Lhotse are identical up to roughly 25,250'. Then, at a point approximately halfway between the top of the Yellow Band and the place where you begin to ascend the Geneva Spur, the routes diverge. For Lhotse you head southeast from the Geneva Spur towards a small platform which is just to the right of the start of the pencil-thin couloir which dissects Lhotse's west face. This couloir is without a doubt one of the most aesthetic mountaineering lines in all of the Himalayas, and up till then was the only way Lhotse had been climbed. Two thousand vertical feet in height, this couloir is all the more impressive as it leads directly to Lhotse's final 100-foot summit cone. With such a beautiful route as this, it's a wonder that Lhotse is the least climbed of all the world's 8,000 meter peaks. The combination of the ice fall approach and the lure of Everest must be the reasons.

While we had originally hoped to have our team climb Lhotse first, it was clear that circumstances were drawing us towards Everest. Nonetheless, I felt that if we had not at least put in the high camp on Lhotse prior to any summit success on Everest, the likelihood of maintaining our resolve to climb Lhotse would be slim. Thus, I was relieved when we were finally able to get a tent pitched and stocked with supplies at 25,800 feet on Lhotse's west face.

First Summit Attempt

Less than a month after we had arrived at base camp we were ready for our first summit attempt. Unfortunately, the mountain was not yet ready for us. When eight of us made the final traversing descent into the south col from the top of the Geneva Spur, the mountain was engulfed in storm. It was April 27, 1990, and my fifth trip to the 26,000' mark on Everest over three expeditions. The horrible weather conditions were like an all too frequent nightmare, only these nightmares had all been real.

Physically and logistically, one simply cannot recuperate or hang out at 26,000' and realistically hope to climb a mountain as high as Everest. But, turning back now meant a very strenuous and difficult descent on significant sections of water ice, and then two days of tortuous climbing back up the

Lhotse face, Yellow Band, Geneva Spur, and to a camp which is higher than the summit of all but the 14 highest mountains in the world. Faced with such a choice one does not turn back lightly, especially when you realize that weather conditions on a mountain like Everest are extremely fickle and can change in a moment.

Unfortunately, though, the weather can always change for the worse, and that is exactly what happened. When we finally reached the south col, we were barely able to stand in the 80 mph winds. In temperatures of -20°F with the wind chill off the chart, we endured an hour of absolute torture as we struggled to set up the tents.

No one slept that night and by the morning of April 28 all agreed that we would have to descend as it was obvious that these weather conditions were not going to change anytime soon. However, before retreating I set off alone across the south col and up the lower slopes leading towards Everest's southeast ridge. It was a desperate gesture of a desperate man hoping against hope that perhaps if I climbed a few hundred feet above the windswept col, just maybe the winds would not be so severe.

But at an altitude of 8,100 m I realized that the entire mountain was engulfed in storm and the winds were only getting worse. We simply did not have the weather needed to make an attempt on the summit. Everest was not ready to be climbed and until the King grants permission to his subjects, there is no chance of success. It was time to retreat while we still had a chance.

Retreat

By late that afternoon after a difficult descent, we were all back in Camp II. As the storm continued to rage the following day (April 29), those of us on the first summit attempt decided to pull back to base camp to wait for better conditions. While none of us relished the thought of having to make another round trip through the ice fall, we knew that we had a far better chance of mounting another serious summit attempt after recuperating at the lower altitude of base camp. This proved to be a wise decision for the storm continued for six of the next seven days.

Meanwhile, the Lhotse summit team of Wally Berg, Scott Fischer and Lapkass waited at Camp II for the weather to break. Finally, on May 3 the storm abated and the three set off for Camp III for the first serious attempt on Lhotse. That same day Charlie Jones, our excellent team physician, and I hiked from base camp down to Gorak Shep just to stretch our legs a bit. Even in the relative comfort of base camp, four continuous days of storm can really be confining. As we did not want to begin re-ascending the mountain until we were sure that the weather change was more than a one day aberration, a day trip to Gorak Shep seemed just the ticket.

Before departing, however, we had to say goodbye to one of our most popular team members, Ron Crotzer. The day before the mail runner brought family and business news that required his immediate departure. Had Crotzer been able to stay, I'm sure that he would have climbed Everest or Lhotse as he was very strong and a real team player.

Psychologically, the hike to Gorak Shep was an important day for me. I could accelerate at will and realized that I had reached maximum acclimatization. But I also was keenly aware that we were starting our sixth week on the mountain. It is usually the sixth or seventh week when personal fitness peaks and then rapidly deteriorates. The good weather would have to come soon.

Unfortunately the next day (May 4) a fierce snowstorm engulfed the entire mountain forcing the Lhotse summit team to immediately descend. The blizzard conditions continued the following day and I was so frustrated that I hiked with Jones all the way from base camp to the village of Lobuche, a 3¼ hour descent. After having a cup of tea and some fried noodles at one of the Sherpa guest houses, the two of us walked all the way back to base camp that afternoon in a blinding snowstorm. Altogether, we walked nearly 7 hours for a lousy lunch of fried noodles! It shows you what effect high altitude cabin fever can have.

The morning of May 6 dawned beautiful. Aside from Brent Manning and a few Sherpas who were in Camp II, the entire team was at base camp. As a day of good weather was needed after a snowstorm before it was safe to travel through the ice fall (not that it is ever really safe), preparations were begun to move the Everest team back up the mountain the following day.

The Lhotse team, which had only just returned to base camp, would follow a couple of days behind.

Rather than spread out and stage summit attempts over a week or more in small groups of 2 or 3 climbers, we were determined to summit the entire Everest team on the same day, to be followed close by the Lhotse assault group. While logistically far more complex, it was important that everyone have the same summit chance. We were going to succeed or fail as a group.

The evening of May 6 was almost warm. As we were certain that the weather would be good the next morning, there was an air of excitement and I doubt that anyone on the Everest team slept that night. But so much for predicting weather in the Himalayas, for when the 4 A.M. wake-up bell was sounded, snow was lightly falling. Nevertheless, Sherpas and members alike decided it was time to move up to Camp II.

Setting Out Again

An hour later we were on our way with the mountain still in darkness. The only light was from the flame of the juniper being burned by the Sherpas, a ritual they religiously adhered to anytime someone on the team started up the ice fall. The flame was bigger than ever. Maybe they sensed something. I wondered what.

That morning the climb through the ice fall was physically demanding and very eerie. The snow intensified and we soon found ourselves having to take turns breaking trail in deep powder. Also, with the snow was a heavy mist and all but the immediate surroundings were blurred from view. Given these conditions, it was a great relief when we finally reached the site of Camp I. There to meet us were the Sherpas who had remained at Camp II. They had descended that morning to help break trail, and to pick up a few loads of kerosene.

As we continued together towards Camp II, I marveled at what incredible work-horses the Sherpas are, a truly remarkable group of people. Always so friendly and willing to do more than their share, I knew that if we succeeded it would be due in large measure to these "tigers of the snow." Some people exalt over climbing a big Himalayan peak without having Sherpas along. But after climbing 8,000 m peaks with and without Sherpas, I've found their companionship is one of the primary reasons I like to climb in the Himalayas.

Early the morning of May 8, Peter Athans, Mike Browning, Dana Coffield, Brent Manning, and I left for Camp III, to be followed later by Sherpas Ang Jambu, Nima Tashi, Dawa Nuru, and Ang Dorje. Throughout the climb up to Camp III and into that evening the weather was variable. Snowing one moment and clearing the next, the weather put us on edge.

But there was no mistake about the weather the following morning. It was very cold and windy. Setting out for the south col around 7:30 A.M., we almost turned back before the Yellow Band because of the adverse conditions. I felt miserable. My toes and fingers were stone cold and hurt. Yet we continued on and once above the Yellow Band we could hardly believe it when the wind began to die down. Usually it was the other way around. While the upper 2,500' of Everest were still engulfed in clouds, there was hope.

South Col

Just after 2 P.M. we reached the south col and I was relieved to see that most of our tents were still standing. It had been 11 days since we left the col after our first summit attempt and I was concerned that we might find our high camp in shambles. Throughout the afternoon we kept brewing liquids and testing our oxygen apparatus. During the summit assault, we would each carry a 13 lb. bottle which would provide 8 to 9 hours of oxygen at a flow rate of 2 liters per minute. In addition, we each had a bottle for sleeping at Camp IV which was set at 1 liter per minute.

Around 6 P.M. the near balmy weather we had been enjoying for the last few hours dramatically changed. It started to cloud up, began snowing, and the winds returned. However, after two hours the storm blew itself out, the mountain cleared and the stars came out. In a few hours we would have a full moon. More importantly, there was no wind. After so many unsuccessful attempts and all the years of waiting for just such an opportunity, it was time to act. We could sleep the rest of our lives. At 9 P.M. I called over to those in the adjoining tents and announced that we would leave in two hours.

Night Ascent

The mark of an experienced team, everyone was ready precisely at 11 P.M. Totally clear above with a brilliant full moon, the temperature hovered around -25°F. Cold to the bone, it was all we could do to start moving.

After crossing the south col, the slope immediately steepened, and we quickly began to encounter deep snow. For the first 3½ hours we climbed up a series of steep snow gullies which led towards the southeast ridge, with Athans breaking trail most of the way. An incredible display of heat lightning on the southwestern horizon and the elegant view of Makalu and Lhotse to the south were the only relief from the physically demanding climb.

At roughly 2:30 A.M. we reached the southeast ridge. We were now at an altitude of over 27,500', just above the site of the highest camp historically used to climb Everest. After a very brief water stop and an unexpected crevasse which had to be bypassed, we began to inch along the treacherous southeast ridge. Here the slightest misstep would send one plunging 9,000 vertical feet down the Kangshung (east) face. With the deceptive shadows cast by the moon, the climbing was tricky and we had to completely concentrate on each step.

Continuing upwards ever so slowly, above 28,000' the slope leading towards the south summit began to steepen radically. I had heard from more than one Everest summiter that this section, not the Hillary step, was the crux. It was 4:30 A.M., still pitch dark, and the slope was not only steep but avalanche-prone. This was scary and I wished that it would soon get light and we could feel the warmth of the sun. It was so cold.

South Summit

Then, when we were less than 300' below the south summit, all of a sudden the sun exploded out of the sky. The transition from darkness to sunlight was almost instantaneous. With nothing to block the view to the east, at a vantage just 500 feet below the highest point on earth, the awesome sight of the rising sun was indelibly etched into our minds. Thirty minutes later, we were standing on top of the 28,700' south summit of Everest, the second highest summit on earth.

But we had come to climb the highest and a formidable ridge separated us from our goal. Whoever coined the phrase "knife-edged" ridge must have had the final 300 vertical feet of Everest in mind. Leave it to the King to save one of the hardest sections for last. Composed primarily of steep snow flanks with massive cornices, the constant winds had exposed far more rock than is typically seen on the photographs of this ridge. However, the most impressive aspect is the mind numbing exposure on both sides: 8,000 vertical feet on the left (west) and over 10,000 feet straight down the east face. With such an obstacle barring the way, it was hard to rest. So we didn't stop for very long and set out from the south summit at approximately 6:20 A.M.

Hillary Step

After a short descent into the notch below the south summit, an awkward rock step was first encountered. Above this section I remember totally focusing on each foot placement and making sure that I was on firm snow, yet not too close to the cornice. Fifteen minutes later I was at the base of the famed Hillary step, a 40 foot pitch which surprisingly was composed of two sections. The first was a left-angling snow gully which led to a large boulder. Wedging myself between the boulder and the snow wall on the right, I reached the base of a short but near vertical chimney. More strenuous than technically difficult, this chimney was virtually the only portion of the final summit ridge offering temporary escape from the exposure.

At the top of the step I spent a few minutes trying to catch my breath and taking in the surroundings. What appeared to be the summit looked tantalizingly close now. But as it turned out, it was not the summit but a final cornice which unbelievably extended some 30 feet off into space. I thought to myself that it was a good thing the weather was clear, because I'd hate to traverse a ridge like this in marginal conditions.

Just then Athans came into view. Running dangerously low on oxygen he had not delayed on the south summit and climbed immediately ahead. Upon reaching the top his oxygen bottle was on empty so he spent less than 5 minutes on the summit before heading down. As we passed we embraced and he indicated that I was almost there. Not only was I happy about that, but I was glad he had made it first. More than anyone on the team, he deserved that honor.

The Summit

Minutes later I had passed the final cornice and for the first time that day the terrain eased up. Ahead of me was a rounded crest of snow with a small outcropping of rock just below. There was no mistake about it. This was indeed the summit. A wave of emotion briefly swept over me. Then all at once it was gone and my dominant thought was of all the years of effort to get to this one moment in time. A few more steps and I stood alone on the highest point on earth. It was 7:15 A.M., May 10, 1990.

Shortly after summiting I was joined by Ang Jambu. Usually so controlled, I had to laugh at how excited and emotional he was. I remembered our disappointment after being forced to evacuate the high camp during the 1981 expedition. Who would have thought that 8½ years later we would be standing together on the summit. It was a special moment.

During the next 30 minutes we were joined by Nima Tashi, Coffield, Manning, Browning and finally Dawa Nuru. Only Ang Dorje was forced to turn back just below the south summit when his oxygen regulator malfunctioned. Only 22 and exceptionally strong, he will have many more opportunities and some day will stand on the top. But for the eight of us that made it, our time together on top was a wonderful experience.

While windy, it was absolutely clear and you could see a hundred miles or more in each direction. To the west the Nuptse wall, base camp and the Khumbu Valley were far below. Turning counterclockwise, the plains of Nepal and India were far in the distance. Due south was Lhotse with the summit couloir looking ever so impressive, while to its left was

Makalu, absolutely stunning in appearance. And behind these two giants, on the distant horizon was Kanchenjunga, the third highest mountain in the world.

Perhaps the most stark sight, however, was the view looking east into Tibet. Unlike the ice and snow views in the other directions, the Tibetan plains are arid and dry. But the view looking north was my most favorite. Framed by the deep blue sky above with the northeast and west ridges of Everest plunging down toward the ground below, Shisha Pangma and a sea of countless peaks over 20,000' spread before us. The curvature of the earth could be seen, and for a time I just stood there trying to memorize it all.

Yet, it was all just too much for the mind to comprehend and it made me feel so insignificant. After taking some photographs and unfurling the same Club flag which had accompanied me to the summits of Makalu and Shisha Pangma, I had been on top for nearly an hour and it was time to go. Together we began a slow but steady descent back to the south summit. Below there, for the first time we roped for the next 500 vertical feet during which all of us at one point or another ran out of oxygen. Somehow it no longer really mattered as we were on our way down.

By 10 A.M. the weather had deteriorated and we were descending in near white-out conditions. But by that time we were below the southeast ridge and it made no real difference. The late night start had paid off. I hate to think what the outcome might have been if we had started much later.

Tired, but very happy, in small groups everyone reached the south col by 2:30 P.M. We were met by Lapkass who had changed his mind about attempting Lhotse first and was determined to try Everest. As luck was with us, that evening the weather cleared and on May 11 he summited Everest with our good friend Tim McCartney Snipe. Five years earlier he had become the first American to climb Mt. Everest and was back to repeat the ascent with only the assistance of two Sherpas. With their success, nine of our members (6 Americans and 3 Sherpas) had reached the summit of Everest and we could now turn our full attention to Lhotse.

Lhotse

So it was that on the 12th of May, Berg, and Fischer moved up to Lhotse-Camp IV. It was evident that the good weather of the past two days was starting to change for the worse and a try at Lhotse would have to be made now or never.

That evening, now safely back at base camp, few of us slept as we lay in our bags wondering how the Lhotse team was faring. The mountain was totally shrouded in mist so it was evident that any summit attempt would be made in less than ideal conditions. Nonetheless, we were confident an attempt would be made as two stronger climbers cannot be imagined. To them would hopefully go the prize of becoming the first two Americans to summit this elusive peak.

At 10:45 A.M. the next morning (May 13) Berg's voice burst over the radio. He and Fischer were on the summit of Lhotse! The entire camp erupted in cheer. As the shouting subsided we learned that they had departed their high camp at 4 A.M. and climbed the west face couloir in near white-out conditions. The 45° couloir was continuous except for a 40-foot rock constriction encountered at approximately 27,000'. Once surmounted, the couloir continued to the base of the final summit pinnacle, a 90-foot rock pitch. The summit itself was a cone of snow just big enough for the two climbers to straddle between their legs. Their dramatic summit photos bear this out and are graphic evidence that the peak of Lhotse is one of the most spectacular of any big mountain.

By the late morning of the 14th of May the entire team was all together safely back in base camp and the celebrating could begin in earnest. Over the next few days our equipment was cleared from the mountain, and as the last ladders were brought out of the ice fall on May 18, I could finally savor the fact that all of the members of the climbing team had summited either Everest or Lhotse. It had been a fine team effort by a super group of individuals.

The next day Browning and I were the last two members to depart from base camp. The mountains were shrouded in clouds and as we neared Periche it started to rain. I had hoped for one last view of Everest, but the rains continued the entire walk out. However, the weather no longer mattered. If anything, it provided an opportunity to reflect on our Everest-Lhotse expedition and my Himalayan adventures over the past decade.

Was it worth the effort or the risk? Probably not for most. After all, climbing a big mountain is somewhat a useless endeavor. Nevertheless, for those who long to reach the heights where clouds lie beneath their feet, experiencing every facet of a mountain like Everest is indeed worth the effort, and perhaps even the risk.

—THE EXPLORERS JOURNAL, SUMMER 1991

Glenn E. Porzak is a partner with Holmes, Roberts & Owen, one of the oldest and largest law firms in the Rocky Mountain West. A former chairman of the Club's Rocky Mountain Chapter, Porzak is the current president of the American Alpine Club. He resides with his wife and two children in Boulder, Colorado.

Cheetah Hunting

BY COL. C. SUYDAM CUTTING

A whole literature has grown up around the fox and the hound, but of cheetah hunting, a more ancient sport and a much faster one, very little has ever been written.

The cheetah is one of the most curious and interesting animals in existence, and the sport in which he becomes the leading actor deserves special attention in a book on travel and exploration.

Although cheetah hunting has dwindled today in India to such an extent that there are but few places where it may be witnessed, it was once quite common, and we learn from miniatures that it was popular with the Mogul conquerors of North India many centuries ago.

One of the places where it survives with its old-time vigor is the native state of Kolhapur, situated in the Deccan of South India. The Maharajah, an ardent sportsman and famous pigsticker, is enthusiastic about the cheetah.

While my wife and I were staying with the Maharajah he arranged a hunt for us, although it was not the proper season. I regarded it as a completely new experience—outside the usual hunting tradition. I write about it now as a novelty unknown to most sportsmen and hunters.

It was an impressive sight to walk into the long, high buildings in which the Maharajah housed his cheetahs and see the animals stirring on their individual charpoys or native beds along the wall. Each cheetah wore a hood, a black hood fitting snugly around the head. Two personal attendants were watching over the animals as if they were royal infants.

There were thirty-five of them lining the walls, the youngest being around three years old, the oldest eight or ten. Since the animal is becoming scarcer and the African breed not only grows bigger and stronger but acquires greater speed, the Maharajah imported his from Kenya. Brought to India, they had to be domesticated and trained. Each animal was worth something between 200 and 250 pounds.

It was obvious that the cheetahs took kindly to their keepers and mode of training. They responded much better than leopards, on which the ruler had conducted some abortive experiments.

Having trained his imported cheetahs in admirable fashion and revived an ancient sport, the Maharajah sold some of his surplus animals to other princes of India, including the late Gaekwa of Barioda, his uncle by marriage.

The cheetah, a member of the cat family, has many qualities of the dog. The height of the shoulders is about the same as those of an adult greyhound. The torso and legs also resemble a greyhound's. The cheetah lacks the back leg knee-bend common to the lion, leopard, and tiger. Again the feet are those of a hound with heavy, nonretractable claws. In size, however, the feet are much larger.

Yet, for all these resemblances to a dog, one glance classifies the cheetah as a cat: his markings are spots, his skull, eyes, and teeth are feline, his habits are purely carnivorous. Lastly the cheetah has a definite purr.

Like falcons, cheetahs wear hoods at all times except when they are being fed and exercised and at the moment when they take part in the chase. The hood on the cheetahs serves the same purpose as it does on falcons. It keeps them quiet and tractable. Contrary to what one might expect, it does not cause their eyesight to become any less keen.

One of the first things I learned about the Maharajah's cheetahs was that fondling them even when they were in their charpoys, properly hooded, was a risky pastime.

In Kolhapur the quarry was always black buck. The cheetah was strictly trained to kill none but adult males. Because these are readily distinguishable in any herd by their dark color, a slow and curious process of familiarizing the cheetahs with this shade was carried out. The men who fed them dressed exclusively in black, while the regular keepers wore white. Having killed, the cheetah was invariably allowed to feed providing he had dispatched a buck. But if he killed a female he was haltered and pulled away: the punishment soon taught its lesson.

The cheetah's daily exercise varies. Usually he is led up a road on a halter by one keeper in white and then encouraged to run back to another keeper in black, who holds a piece of meat in his hand. Unlike whippets, on the leash the cheetah does not strain, and released he carries out his act without enthusiasm. Another exercise is a real black-buck hunt to keep him in good trim for big occasions.

The speed of the cheetah is amazing. He is well aware that no other animal can rival him in this regard. The tiger, lion, and leopard rarely rush their quarries more than a hundred yards. After that they desist, knowing they cannot catch up with game that has attained its maximum speed.

Trained cheetahs proceed slowly and methodically, choosing their quarry out of the herd. Only when the quarry has attained its greatest speed does the cheetah run him down with that tremendous burst that has no parallel in the entire animal kingdom. The cheetah's lasting powers lie somewhere between a cat's and a dog's, but nearer to a cat's.

This ancient sport of India does not affect the abundance of game, for no great numbers of bucks are destroyed and the herds are plentiful. Furthermore, the slain bucks are eaten.

The day of the hunt a car called for my wife and me at six in the morning. An hour later we arrived at the plains where the hunt was to be held. Here the Maharajah, the Maharani, the Maharajah's sister, his niece, and two male guests, both Indian, greeted us.

The genial Maharajah, who tips the scales at 300 pounds, is one of India's greatest sportsmen. His cheetah hunts are famous. He is an expert pigsticker, a daring cross-country rider. His stables hold 300 horses of Indian, English, and Australian breeding, his kennels bird and hunting dogs of every kind, 275 in all, and his fields fine herds of Brahminy cattle. Even his pets are unusual. Near his house were to be seen at that time a young lion and lioness and a pair of two-year-old tigers gambolling around on thirty-five-foot leads. Formidable sloth bears, the most dangerous of animals that attacks without provocation and has been known to tear a man to pieces for no reason at all, were sometimes seen walking down the village streets with their keeper.

The Maharajah's sister also has a unique place in the Indian sports world. She is the only woman pigsticker in all India. White women are not allowed to join the clubs, and native women do not participate. But at the age of forty, the Maharajah's sister has made a great reputation in a difficult sport. An active rider and hunter, she is a handsome woman, but belongs to a type that may be found among sportswomen of England and America, never in India. She is keen, trained down, alert.

The Maharajah usually followed the cheetah hunt from a brake or light wagon, specially built according to his own designs. It carried one eight feet above the ground and was drawn by four Australian walers. But although it was not early October, the beginning of the dry season, the grass, still high from the recent monsoon rains, covered many blind ditches that would have made riding in a brake impossible. So for this special, off-season hunt, the Maharajah elected specially built motor-cars with high shelves for the cheetahs. In addition there were two lorries, one for additional cheetahs and their attendants, the other to supply us with tea and sandwiches.

After a cup of tea we were off on a wild ride by seven o'clock, bumping and crashing along at thirty-five miles an hour. In one car went the Indian ladies and one of the guests. In another my wife rode in front with the driver, while I was sandwiched in between the Maharajah and his other guest.

A cheetah, still hooded, was lying on a platform built into the car at about the level of my knees. His keeper, crouched on the running-board, a precarious perch, had to keep his eyes on the animal and also get out at times and have a look at the trappy ground. On we careened, sometimes on lanes, but more often across open country where our thirty-five miles an hour was a dizzy speed. Every one held on like mad.

Having found a herd, we maneuvered for a proper position. Then began the real strategy. In confronting a large herd, an attempt was always made to detach the males, as they were quarries for the cheetahs. They were kept in a continuous stampede. Since they did not run in a straight line, the car bucketing along was able to keep up with them.

I was trying to operate a camera, and because it required two hands I had to relinquish my grip. The car swerved violently. The cheetah and I were thrown forward, landing on my wife's neck. No more did we get settled than it happened again.

Then, with everything perfectly timed by the Maharajah, the car stopped. The cheetah was unloaded, unhooded, and hustled out on the grass. For a half minute he stood there sizing up the situation. At a gentle, slow lope he started off toward the herd. The black buck, about two hundred yards away, began to move off. The field was alive with galloping forms, their bounds increasing progressively in length. By now the cheetah had chosen his particular quarry. He rushed towards it with incredible speed.

The quarry, realizing too late that he could not match the cheetah's speed, attempted a downhill slope. The cheetahs prefer to run uphill: going down they are liable to a false aim and then a bad tumble.

Undaunted by this maneuver, the cheetah soon overtook his buck. He sprang with front paws directed at the hindquarters of the quarry. The violence of this blow threw the animal. Then the cheetah caught him by the throat.

At this point we arrived on the scene. The cheetah lay full-length with the buck's throat held tightly in its slightly curved canines. Gradually the victim ceased his violent attempts to tear himself loose. He was choked to death. The cheetah lay perfectly still in apparent ecstasy. Slowly he opened and closed his great greenish eyes, gently emitting a soft, rumbling purr.

The cheetah was allowed to feast on one hindquarter of the buck. Then he was gently and firmly led aside while one of the attendants disemboweled the victim. Some of the blood and the steaming viscera, placed in a long spoon like bowl, was offered to the cheetah. This was his reward, and he seemed quite satisfied.

Another cheetah was brought from the lorry. The motor was started and off we went again. This time the car, overtaxed by the speed over such rough terrain, broke down. The Maharajah coolly beckoned for another car, of which there were several for such emergencies. It zoomed over and we continued the hunt.

There were dramatic variations in all the seven hunts staged that day. Once a cheetah, forced to carry the pursuit downhill while going full speed, landed in a blind ditch and turned head-over-heels. He was given a rest and drink and the mud was cleared off his head, but he refused to run again.

Another cheetah killed a female, a regrettable incident. He was dragged off his feed so that he would never repeat the performance.

Once again a motor broke down. Sometimes the staff had difficulties in maneuvering the herd. Sometimes we drew close to them but they succeeded in escaping. Then, perhaps, we would pick them up again. To add still more variety, the cheetahs were unloosed at various distances; so we had a good chance to watch all phases of the approach and attack.

By eleven o'clock we were through. Six cheetahs had overtaken animals. The cars and lorries went back to the bungalow rest-house. Then, with the Maharajah and his party, we made merry at breakfast, later viewing the kills or what remained of them, as they lay in line on the grass. Natives in a carnival spirit brought wreaths of flowers to hang around our necks. Made of plumaria and jasmine, they were larger versions of the leis of Honolulu.

One last word about the speed of the cheetahs. To begin with, one should remember that when they are apparently running fast, they are by no means running their fastest. Any one who has had experience with cats will realize that it is extremely difficult, owing to their peculiar temperament, to train them to perform any action out of keeping with their normal behavior. Cheetahs would probably never run at their maximum speed on a track. Furthermore, it is doubtful if they would sustain their greatest effort for any distance beyond two hundred yards. But in their natural habitat, when pursuing buck, their final charge is terrific. It must surely attain a speed of sixty-five or seventy-five miles an hour—for a hundred or more yards.

—PREVIOUSLY UNPUBLISHED

The Elephant-Headed Deity Ganesh

BY STANLEY J. OLSEN

F or a considerable number of years I have been conducting research into the origins and early domestication of animals in Asia. My investigations have led me to monasteries and temples in China, Tibet, and Nepal where animal materials play an important part in the religious rituals of the various sects concerned. Not the least of these associations are the human/animal figures of deities such as the yak-headed Yamantaka or the monkey god Hanuman.

One of the more striking animal representations is the elephant-headed deity Ganesh (at times, incorrectly referred to as Ganesa or Ganesha). He is associated with the Hindu religion, particularly in the Kathmandu Valley of Nepal where a number of shrines are located for the worship of Ganesh. Perhaps the combination of a portly human body with an elephant head and possessing four arms is enough reason to cause more than a passing interest in Ganesh from non-Hindu visitors to Nepal.

The story of Ganesh's origin has been offered in several variations but essentially it is as follows: Ganesh's father is the god Shiva (i.e., Siva) and his mother is the goddess Parvati. Shiva is said to have returned to Parvati after a journey lasting 14 years. Arriving home at night he found Parvati asleep with a young boy beside her. Suspecting her of infidelity he immediately lopped off the boy's head and then discovered too late that it was his own son. Shiva was very sad and said that he would bring his son back to life if the first thing seen in the morning was brought to him. The first living thing turned out to be an elephant so Shiva took its head and joined it to the body of his son who then became Ganesh.

Ganesh is revered by Hindu believers who consider him as a god of good luck who can cast obstacles aside and one who is consulted by one and all before any journey or task is undertaken. His help is usually invoked in the early morning of Tuesdays or Saturdays. He is believed to decide between the success or failure of his worshipers. His elephant head has only one tusk, the other has been broken. His four arms hold a conch, a discus, a mace or goad, and a lotus or water lily. He is usually presented as a light-skinned deity having a fat, round belly.

Ganesh travels on a shrew and is greedy for food, particularly fruit. The shrines, honoring Ganesh in the Kathmandu Valley, all have representations of the shrew. Some are several feet in length. Many of the small bronze statues also depict the shrew at the foot of Ganesh. Fewer examples have Ganesh astride the shrew as his method of travel. Some references state that this vehicle of transportation is a rat, but on examination the depicted bronzes are most surely a shrew and not a rat. The head alone of a shrew is long and pointed while that of a rat is more blunt and rounded.

Two mammalogists, H. R. Mishra and D. Mierow, who are specialists in the fauna of Nepal even go so far as to state that the animal carrying Ganesh is the large musk or house shrew (*Suncus murinus*) which reaches a length of 10 inches or more. It emits a peculiar chattering noise as it runs about which is described as "a jingle of coins." For this reason the natives of some regions call it a "money mouse." It is not an uncommon resident of houses in Nepal but also frequents marshes and the margins of ponds. It feeds mainly on insects. There are several species of shrews in Nepal including a water shrew but these are considerably smaller than the house or musk shrew. I too agree that the bronze and brass depictions of Ganesh's shrews are of *Suncus murinus* and not another species of shrew or a rat.

The finest example of one of these large brass portrayals of the shrew of Ganesh is in front of Ganesh's temple in Jal Binayak in the Kathmandu Valley. Here the shrew is portrayed as offering fruit to Ganesh with one paw extended, holding a native durian (*Durio zibethinus*). This fruit has an intolerable odor but is available in the durbar market in Kathmandu. There is another superb brass rendition of Ganesh's shrew in the market of durbar amidst the stalls of produce. Both of these figures are several feet long.

Most of the depictions of Ganesh are as chiseled cameo reliefs in stone. The smaller representations are of cast bronze or brass as well as amulets for wearing as suspended personal talismans. Most of the public figures are heavily coated in the traditional red or yellow paste that adorns all Hindu shrines.

It is difficult to learn with any certainty when the deity Ganesh was first established but there is some evidence, arrived at by comparing datable contemporary art, that Ganesh was not known before ca. 50–200 A.D. but was well established by 700 A.D. Without a doubt he is a well-revered deity today and one who is sought out by Hindus for the many favors that he is able to bestow on his followers.

— *THE EXPLORERS JOURNAL*, JUNE 1990

Stanley J. Olsen, Professor in the Department of Anthropology, University of Arizona and zooarcheologist at the Arizona State Museum is a member of our Science Advisory Board and a frequent contributor to the Journal.

The Elephant that Walked to Vienna

BY J. MONROE THORINGTON

n the golden age of Indian courts, it took up to twelve servants to keep
the royal elephants well and happy.

In 218 B.C. when Hannibal brought African elephants through
Spain and France, invading Gaul after crossing the Alps, his army
caused both astonishment and fear, the impact of which vanished long before
the Middle Ages.

In the year 802 an elephant named Abu'l Abbaz, still known in
Westphalian dialect as "Bulebaz," arrived in Aix-la-Chapelle as a gift from
Caliph Harun al-Raschid to Charlemagne, and was the earliest of its kind to
reach the soil of present-day Germany. One is recorded in Frankfurt in 1443
and another in Cologne in 1482. The latter animal, exhibited in many cities,
was to be taken to England, but unfortunately drowned with its keeper when
overtaken by storm while being transported on a canal.

In India an elephant, after capture, received a name in the language of
the principality for which it was broken in and trained. Selected animals were
regarded as holy in India and Ceylon, where Hindus and Buddhists lived.
The Khmers of Cambodia, where the Portuguese were influential in the 16th
century, supplied countless numbers for the court and army. Court elephants, of which the maharajas had many, received special training as parade
animals, throne elephants or for use in hunting. The lowest caste were the
work elephants.

Every court elephant received rich food and much care, waited on by a
crowd of attendants. At times of parades or journeys, the beasts wore gala outfits embroidered with pearls and jewels, trappings of silk and satin, ribbons
with silver bells, and gold tuskrings. Head and trunk were painted with red
and green arabesques, between which were golden spangles. The caparisons
extended on both sides between the front and hind leg, and under the belly

were united by a band of gold cloth. Sometimes there were great coverings of purple, with gold and silver embroidery over the entire animal except for the head. On the middle of the back was a gilded wooden seat.

In the Golden Age of Indian courts, each elephant had its own caretakers, usually twelve. Two were mahouts, two saw that the beast did not get out of control, and two looked after food and drink. Two rode with lances in advance of the Moguls and kept crowds at a distance, and two set off firecrackers before and behind to accustom their animal to smoke and noise. Another attendant kept the stall clean, and finally a servant drove the flies away and doused the animal with water.

Every tame elephant, whether for parade, hunting, or work, had its own keeper or mahout. The keeper of a work elephant was answerable not only for its well-being, but also that it did not run away when returning from the forest. The keeper sprang on the back of a recumbent animal, or stepped on the joint of the bent forefoot to gain its neck, taking his place in the riding position. The elephant was usually controlled vocally ("Hu" or "Hott"), rarely by the iron hook or ankus. A close relationship formed between the elephant and the driver on its neck, with obedience to the faintest whisper.

All of this made for costly upkeep. Animals were shipped from Goa and Malacca, 16th-century colonies of Portugal, the sea voyage around the Cape of Good Hope to Lisbon taking five or six months, with limited food and water. On arrival they were brought through the whole city and shown to the king, before whom they made the obeisance that court elephants are taught. In the royal zoo the newcomer could live with others of its kind, cared for by trained keepers and often petted by distinguished visitors.

Elephants in war were the predecessors of modern tanks, and this led to the depletion of the North African species which was somewhat smaller than others of that continent, and of which there were few left in Europe by the end of the 17th century. Indian elephants reached Rome in the early Middle Ages, the cost of maintaining them, however, being so great that European princes must be satisfied with simpler accoutrement even if they had only a single specimen.

King Emanuel I of Portugal, in 1514, included in a gift of exotic animals to Pope Leo X a gigantic "white" elephant, with a richly dressed Moor as keeper. Raphael immortalised it in one of his Gobelin tapestries and placed its portrait on a tower of the Vatican. When it died two years later it received an epitaph worthy of a cardinal.

In 1548 Archduke Maximilian of Austria (1527–76) went by command of his uncle, Emperor Charles V, to take over the regency of Spain for his cousin, later Philip II. On arriving at Valladolid, when he was barely 21 years of age, his marriage to the Infanta Maria, daughter of Charles V, was celebrated with great pomp. In the following spring Maximilian was given a title of royalty, which brought upon him the duty of a state visit to Lisbon, the young couple being received with ceremony and colorful festivities, including visits to the zoological garden which had an exceptional collection of African and Indian mammals and birds.

Maximilian was from boyhood an animal lover, as was his brother Ferdinand. He spent many hours in the Lisbon zoo, feeding the elephants with his own hands and expressing to everyone his desire to possess one. King John III of Portugal, good-natured and open-handed, promised his nephew that a later shipment would bring an enormous court elephant from India, together with its ornaments and escort. It arrived in Valladolid early in the summer of 1551, accompanied by a letter from King John in which he suggested giving the animal a new name: Sultan Suleiman, the deadly enemy of all Christians, but thereafter Maximilian's slave.

The elephant endured two sea trips, first to Barcelona and thence to Genoa, en route to which it narrowly escaped capture by a French privateer. It then led a triumphal procession through Liguria, Lombardy, and Venezia, an especially enthusiastic reception being received at Trent where the council-fathers were assembled.

Maximilian and his wife reached Bozen on December 17. There, because affairs of state held him, he sent her and their two young children ahead to spend Christmas in Innsbruck with Emperor Charles, a part of their train as well as Suleiman accompanying them as far as Brixen, where the tired animal spent two weeks in a stable adjoining the inn "am Hohen Feld," as Hotel Elefant was then known.

The appearance of a live elephant, known only by hearsay, was sensational and many curious people came to see the animal quartered near the inn. It was natural that the hostel should take the name of this rare guest and as Hotel Elefant it remains, more than four centuries since the beast, after short stay, departed and crossed the mountains. As some visitors arrived too late for the show the innkeeper, Andreas Posch, was urged to put an accurate picture of the elephant and its entourage on the house wall. The fresco-painter, Leonard Mair, had probably been an eye-witness of the elephant's entry into Brixen and had seen a crude version of an elephant painted a century earlier in the third arcade of the cathedral cloisters, where the animal "looks like an overgrown goat with a French-horn trunk, bearing on its exiguous back a monumental tower carrying armed men." But artist Mair, although producing a better likeness, was far from portraying the anatomy correctly.

The 16th-century fresco on the outer wall by the hotel entrance records the departure for the Brenner Pass. A giant in Spanish costume, with curls, plumed hat and belted sword, bears a long lance and leads the procession, followed by a figure half his size with turban and blue smock, holding a short halberd. Then comes Suleiman, with an expression almost cat-like and raising the right forefoot. A window of the hotel left the artist no room for placing a mahout on the beast's neck, but a red and gold cloth serves as a saddle on which a rider in Spanish costume, with beard and broad hat, swings a whip with his right hand and holds a spear-like ancus in his left. In the rear a small figure, with white turban and crimson robe, raises a whip. On the interior staircase of the hotel there is a later painting showing Suleiman's arrival in Brixen with a crowd of on-lookers.

On January 2, 1552, the court elephant, with feet well-upholstered against the cold, spent a night in Sterzing and then crossed the Brenner Pass to Innsbruck. Suleiman continued down the Inn River by way of Hall, Wasserburg, and Braunau to Passau, and thence along the Danube to

Vienna, arriving on March 6. On May 7 the animal was the main attraction in a festive parade through the city's streets.

Maximilian was often away from Vienna and so was not able to see Suleiman frequently. The elephant, bereft of proper keepers, all of the Indians having apparently departed, died of neglect on December 18, 1553, to the grief of its owner. This was the untimely fate of the first elephant in the Vienna zoo. However, it was not the last offering of Portuguese to European monarchs, Indian and African elephants being shown in the 17th century in the Versailles park of Louis XIV.

For centuries many inns and public houses of Europe had borne the names of wild and domestic animals and birds, signs over their entrances depicting bear, wolf, stag, eagle, and other creatures, not a few being mythological. Following Suleiman's arrival the elephant began to appear in many places, first at Brixen where the old tavern of "am Hohen Feld" became Hotel Elefant, the name spreading to Salzburg, Linz, and Graz as well.

When a visitor to Vienna in 1555 inquired about the renowned elephant, he was told that Suleiman was now only a stuffed body. When it was shown to him he noted that the figure of a Moor with full-drawn bow was seated on its back. In this way it is represented as a hunting elephant on the inn signs of Brixen and other towns.

Even this was not the end of Suleiman. Maximilian became Emperor Maximilian II in 1562. His brother-in-law, Duke Albert IV of Bavaria, who had seen the elephant when the royal cortege came through Wasserburg on the Inn in 1552, visited him in Vienna in 1564. Albert was a patron of the arts and a collector of curiosities; on discovering the elephant "mummy" he requested it for his museum, to which the emperor acceded in 1572. It was taken by ship up the Danube to Passau, thence overland to Munich and placed in the royal art-gallery. In the past century it became a showpiece in the State Zoological collection and in 1928 was transferred to the Bavarian National Museum where, until about 1941, it was called the "Brixen Elephant." Later the remains (the tusks had been replaced by toned plaster) were stored in a bomb shelter and there disintegrated from dampness.

One relic exists, still shown in the Kremsmünster Abbey, near Linz on the Danube: an elegantly engraved chair of elephant bones with an inscription saying that when the royal family returned from Spain to Vienna in 1552 "they brought with them an Indian elephant which through carelessness of an attendant died on December 18, 1553." The dead body weighed 42 hundredweight, 73 pounds, which indicates starvation as half-grown Indian elephants in the Berlin zoo weigh from 79 to 90 hundredweight.

The right forefoot was sent as a gift to the burgomaster of Vienna, who had the chair made in 1554. Other bones were given away and used for various purposes. None, sad to say, reached Brixen.

—THE EXPLORERS JOURNAL, JUNE 1973

Dr. Monroe Thorington was a retired physician much addicted to mountain climbing. He was Past President of the American Alpine Club, former editor of the American Alpine Journal, and author of many articles on mountaineering and Alpine history. His climbs took him to the Alps, the Canadian Rockies, and the interior ranges of British Columbia, where a peak bears his name. He was honorary member of the Alpine Club (London), the Alpine Club of Canada, and the Appalachian Mountain Club. He was Honorary Trustee of the International Folk Art Foundation, Santa Fe, New Mexico.

A Gobi Adventure

BY ROY CHAPMAN ANDREWS

Introduction by Seyward S. Cramer, Editor, *Through Hell and High Water*, 1941

I don't suppose the time is far off when motorcars and airplanes will be common in all parts of the world. It wasn't so long ago that many Mongols hadn't even heard of a motorcar. I can't imagine their reaction when they saw and heard the motor fleet of the First Central Asiatic Expedition going across the Gobi. That was a great accomplishment—to get those cars and trucks onto the desert and keep them running.

Bayard Colgate was transportation officer on that expedition and he had a full-sized job cut out for him. He not only had to keep things going but he had to anticipate whatever spare parts might be required and see that they were on hand.

I've often wondered if he had any spare steering wheels around, because a little time later Dr. Andrews was going to need one. Won't you tell us that story, Dr. Andrews?

An adventure that happened to me in Mongolia is a mystery today and always will be. I was driving across Mongolia, from Kalgan to Urga, with a friend who later was murdered in China. We were in an open Dodge touring car, traveling hard, trying to make the crossing in less than four days. Three hours at the wheel and three hours' rest was our schedule.

I was driving when we reached Ude, a collection of five or six Mongol *yurts*, in the center of the Gobi. The trail ran about four hundred yards from a rocky promontory which juts out into the desert. Charlie was asleep in the rear seat and I was half dozing over the wheel, for the road was good.

Suddenly five men appeared on the end of the promontory and, without the slightest warning, opened fire on our car. They couldn't have been

Chinese because they were doing awfully good shooting, and a Chinaman is the world's worst shot. The bullets were zinging above our heads and plumping into the motor every minute. Boy, did I wake up! I humped over the wheel, trying to make myself as small as possible, and stepped on the gas. The speedometer showed fifty miles an hour but the bullets were still hitting us. Charlie got our guns out from under a robe and I yelled:

"We'd better do something about this or we'll be killed. Pass me my rifle."

I leaned backward to take the gun. At that very second a bullet smacked against the steering wheel, shattering the whole lower side, where my body had been pressed only a second before. Call it Fate, Divine Protection, what you will—the fact remains that if I had waited a fraction of a second before leaning back I would have been a dead man. That bullet simply wasn't marked with my name.

The trail led round a high wall of rocks into the soft sandy bed of a dry stream. It was a bad place, and we knew that we never could get through without some strenuous pushing on the car. Sure enough, we were stuck in a few moments, but at least we were completely out of sight of the men who had been shooting at us.

Leaving the motor running, Charlie and I climbed the rocks and peeped over the top. Five men were standing in plain sight, about three hundred and fifty yards away, evidently consulting about their next move. They knew, of course, that we would be stuck in the sand. Moreover, since we had not fired in return, I suppose they thought we had no rifles. Anyway, they started to climb slowly down the rocks to come across the open plain to our car. Something had to be done about it, as apparently they were bent on murder.

Charlie selected one fellow, who was standing silhouetted against the sky, and I lined my sights on another, just in front of him. I was shooting a Savage .250–3,000 and Charlie had a Ross .280. As our rifles crashed, both men crumpled. The other three disappeared like shadows behind the promontory. We waited for a time, but none of them showed himself. Then we scrambled down to the car, trying desperately to push it out of the sand. It took more than an hour of hard work to get through the canyon, for every few minutes we had to climb the rocks to be sure that we were not being stalked by the remaining bandits. I don't mind saying that we had the jitters.

Who those fellows were and why they attacked us I could never find out. They were dressed in Mongol clothes but that proved nothing. That they were not Chinese we felt certain, because they shot too well. They might have been Russians, but I hardly think so. Probably Mongols with Russian rifles.

THROUGH HELL AND HIGH WATER (1941)

The title Roy Chapman Andrews gave to his autobiography, Ends of the Earth, *was peculiarly appropriate. At middle life he had already traveled over nearly every important body of land and water on the surface of the globe. "I wanted to go everywhere," he once explained, in commenting on his ready acceptance of an assignment to make an expedition to Borneo.*

Graduating from Beloit College in his native town in Wisconsin, he went to New York and insisted that the Museum of Natural History employ him in any capacity. He remained connected with that institution and became its vice-director.

From 1908 to 1914 he made extensive studies of whales, seals, and fishes, covering a wide territory from Alaska to Celebes and building up a remarkable cetacean collection for the Museum.

Then turning to very dry land, he elaborated a plan for the thorough scientific exploration of the Gobi Desert, as the possible place of origin of northern mammalian life. The field work begun in 1916 continued, with interruptions, to the present year and has yielded, in addition to the far-famed dinosaur eggs, a rich harvest of fossil remains, geological data, and geographical, botanical, and zoological information concerning that hitherto unexplored territory.

For his scientific achievements Dr. Andrews was awarded the Hubbard Gold Medal of the National Geographic Society and, by Brown University, an honorary degree of Doctor of Science. He was a President of The Explorers Club.

In addition to many scientific treatises, he published Whale Hunting with Gun and Camera; Camps and Trails in China; Across Mongolian Plains; On the Trail of Ancient Man; Ends of the Earth.

Hang-Gliding on K-2: An Emergency Descent of 7,600 Meters

BY JEAN-MARC BOIVIN

I n preparing for K-2, I thought of taking along a hang glider, thinking that this expedition might provide an opportunity to make a magnificent flight. Also, it might have practical applications. For example, in crossing a torrential river where the bridge had been swept away in a flood, I would land on the opposite bank with my glider to secure a line that my comrades would throw to me from the other side. This might obviate a five-day march to circumvent the river. During the expedition such a situation arose, but there was no need for our hypothetical solution because the porters of another expedition appeared by chance on the other bank.

Bernard, the expedition leader, authorized me to take a glider along. This 14-kilogram model had the special feature of being collapsible. When folded, it was only two meters long, greatly facilitating its portage. I already knew that the spur of K-2 we had chosen for our ascent involved great technical problems. There were difficult vertical rock climbs over large sections, thus the glider's lightness and relative ease of portage were essential. A large six-meter classic glider could not be used except in areas and conditions where no technical difficulties are involved, where there are only ascents of snow-covered slopes or easy rock climbs as, for example, in the normal route for Everest.

Under such conditions, a large glider could be dragged or carried without great difficulty. However, such a model could not be used on the southwest ridge of K-2, because the difficulties of the route and steepness of the slope would not permit either portage or launching. But I had been chosen for the K-2 expedition as a mountaineer, not as a glider specialist. My primary objective was, above all, to ascend the spur with the entire team; the hope of accomplishing a magnificent flight was only secondary.

I had received my new glider only a few days before the expedition's departure, and was unable to test it in France because of bad weather. Thus, I had to count on doing so during the approach march.

It was between Chapco and Chongo that I was able to make my first flight. Until that moment our approach followed the river in the middle of the valley. Before leaving Chongo, we had to cross a rocky ridge. I wanted to fly from its summit and rejoin my comrades, who already would have descended the other side on foot.

I had gone ahead with the porter who was carrying my glider, in order to arrive first on the summit. Assembling it on a very rocky terrace was difficult, even though Chouca and Bernard helped me. It was the first time I had done it. The fabric had shrunk because of the high temperature, and we had to pull very hard before the cross bar could be threaded through the tension eyelets of the wing. The sail was excessively tight and complete assembly took nearly an hour.

The launching took place in strong up-drafts caused by the heat. I had to pull hard on the control bar to stabilize the wing, which was bucking. The flight was fast and difficult. I landed on a flat area at the edge of the river, in the midst of several amazed porters, a 40-minute walk from my point of departure.

I made my second flight above Askolay, a small village of about 2,000 inhabitants. The approach march to the village was very pleasant, among wheat fields and trees. During the evening a porter of Askolay, who was not yet a member of our group of porters but wanted very much to join, offered to carry my glider to a point 300 meters above the village. I also was accompanied by Karim, a Pakistani climber. After ascending a gorge, I positioned the glider on a big rock. The fabric of the wing remained much too tight. The wind was coming up the gorge. Flight conditions were excellent. I didn't take a leap; two steps and I was off into space. I flew in circles above the village; people were running from every direction. I landed in a cemetery and immediately was surrounded. Everyone wanted to touch the wing, a cable, a bolt, the tubing.

Five days later, I made my third flight at Peju, the last wooded place. After having taken off 400 meters above our camp at 4,000 meters, I landed without difficulty. The warm air, channeled into the corridor, caused strong thermal updrafts. The wing was shaken in every direction. The tubes, of small diameter and each made in three pieces, bent. The fabric flapped. The landing posed a problem. The grass was strewn with huge boulders and I had planned to land on one of them.

Unfortunately, at ground level a breeze from the slope was blowing in the opposite direction to that at altitude. This sudden wind from behind forced me to the ground just beside a large block of stone. I have never found such strange conditions elsewhere.

A tubular support of my trapeze was broken in this very abrupt landing. Faced with the possibility that I might not be able to fly my glider anymore, I immediately set to work trying to repair it. I searched for a piece of straight wood the same diameter as the tubing. The porters found a likely one which Daniel helped me thread into the two parts of the broken tube. I added a small nail from each side so there would be no play. I placed a tent stake parallel to the tube and bound everything together with adhesive tape.

During this same repair period, I sawed pieces from the keel and the two attack edges. Now the shrunken sail no longer was excessively tight. Two days later, during a day off, I tested it. I had to wait before takeoff because of a strong wind from the rear. When it had resumed its normal direction, I dived downward.

All went well and I was satisfied with my improvised repairs. However, the glider's weight was increased a good kilo, and I was apprehensive about the possible fragility of the repaired area. Before our departure from France, I had ordered some spare sections of tubing, knowing that repairs during the expedition would be almost impossible and that a tube is easily damaged. I hadn't received them in time and depended on Robert Paragot, who was leaving later, to bring them with him.

Our Base Camp was established, then Camp I. From that moment all our efforts were devoted to assuring success in scaling the spur, so the glider was left there, where it remained for a month and a half. In the meantime, I received the spare tubes and made proper repairs. Starting the ninth of July, I suffered from dysentery, which weakened me. None of our medicines were effective.

On August 31, after we had spent many days at Base Camp immobilized by bad weather, Bernard authorized me to take my glider to a higher altitude. In the afternoon we left in the direction of Camp I, which was buried under a meter of snow. We spent the rest of the afternoon there shoveling snow, reforming the platforms for the fixed tents, digging out the supply cache, searching for the equipment, ropes, and food needed for our ascent to high altitude.

My glider also was buried in the snow. I partially dug it out before the evening meal and continued after dark by the light of a forehead lamp. I was the last to retire. The next day Daniel volunteered to carry the spare tubes and I readily accepted his offer. I hoisted the wing onto my pack and lashed it in a vertical position. I had no frame and it swung about. I had about 20 kilograms on my back; a load for altitude normally doesn't exceed 10 or 12. I finally arranged my wing horizontally for the rest of the climb. I passed Patrick, who was taking photos and didn't seem to be in a hurry. I arrived after the others but wasn't too tired.

At Camp II some of us spent the next day cleaning it up, while the others continued on toward Camp III. Xavier offered to take the sail, which weighed about one kilogram, to Camp IV. The rocky climb between Camp II and Camp III increased our altitude by 600 meters. I located a portage key and attached my wing vertically, the only way it could pass through the vertical chimneys. I again climbed up the fixed ropes. My wing knocked against the rocks but didn't get wedged.

At Camp III I added the rest of the spare tubes to my pack because Daniel couldn't take them any higher. His pack already was heavy and the expedition's ropes obviously took priority over my glider. The weight of my load increased proportionately. I also added the down vest and trousers I had previously left at Camp III. With more than 20kg on my back, I left the next day for the vertical wall where Laskaran had died. It was 50 meters high with overhangs for the first 10 meters.

I was most grateful to Xavier, Yannick, and Pierre for their assistance in this difficult climb. They pulled the wing from above while I pushed from below, and freed it whenever it became wedged in the overhangs. This was the most difficult passage for my wing. I continued the traverse, then up the interminable snow corridors. My load became heavier and heavier, the wind rose, snowflakes began to fall. I advanced more and more slowly, too slowly, a little mechanically, my muscles chilled quickly and my feet became very cold.

Finally I decided to put down my wing and anchored it with a piton on a snow bank at the lower end of a chimney, 80 meters below Camp IV. I set off again for Camp IV, where I arrived about two hours after the others. In the tent I found warm fellowship. Xavier prepared hot chocolate for me while Chouca massaged my feet. I didn't get around to eating. All night I was shaken by fits of coughing.

The next day I tried to make a portage to Camp V but had to give up. I was completely exhausted from having carried such unusually heavy loads during the past three days. The following day when I awoke I found that I could see only hazily. Red spots floated before my eyes. Curiously, one of them had the profile of a skull. Luckily there were no cross bones below it, but then I am not superstitious. I couldn't even make out a climber crossing the plateau 30 meters from the tent. Only his heavy breathing enabled me to locate him. Dominique thought it was a retinal hemorrhage and advised me to descend as soon as possible.

We had two days of good weather and attempts were made to reach the summit. I knew that I had to go down and preferred to do so by glider since the return to low altitude would be so much faster. Although I couldn't see a man at 30 meters, I could distinguish the general topographical relief. I went down to search for my wing, located it, and spent five minutes hoisting it onto my back. I found my way up to the glacier by following the fixed rope, stopping to breathe with each step. I became too tired to carry my wing further, left it, and returned to camp.

When I awoke, the sun was still shining. I knew more than ever how imperative it was for me to descend, and this time Bernard, who would have liked to delay my flight until victory was achieved, authorized me to fly down. He and Dominique went down for my wing and brought it up to the camp while I readied my other equipment and the harness.

We took the assembled glider 50 meters above Camp IV to a spur only 15 meters high, a little to the right of the fixed rope, a spur I had climbed many times. Moving it up the 30° slope was difficult without crampons, and we slipped on the flat, snow-covered stones. It took an hour. I checked the entire operation twice and Bernard, who had normal vision, also verified everything. I tested the harness to see if the straps were properly adjusted. The wind was blowing across the spur, but I was apprehensive that it might not be strong enough to lift me clear of the hanging glacier below. The takeoff would be the most critical moment. The density of the air at this altitude, 7,600 meters, is about one-third of normal and the lift very weak.

My mittens slipped on the control bar; I took them off just before throwing myself into space. I went very fast, about 70 miles per hour, and cleared the glacier by several meters. The glider was shaken; the sail clacked in the wind. For a moment I thought of landing on Angelus, a peak of about 7,000 meters opposite the rib of K-2. I decided that it wouldn't be prudent since I didn't have the climbing equipment necessary for a descent in the event that something went wrong.

I continued my trajectory over the face of Angelus, then made a turn at 20 meters above Camp II. I heard my comrades shouting, but couldn't see anything other than the tents. My hands were very cold. I flew very high over Camp I, then over Base Camp. I couldn't see anything except a mass of blue tents. I tried in vain to see the fire about which they had told me on the walkie-talkie, the smoke of which would indicate wind direction and the landing place. However, I landed only 50 meters away, 13 minutes after takeoff. The porters greeted me with wild cheering.

I had just made the most beautiful flight of my life.

— THE EXPLORERS JOURNAL, SEPTEMBER 1982

Jean-Marc Boivin, a 29-year old French Alpine guide and mountaineer from Chamonix, received the 1980 International Award for Valor in Sport, in recognition of his daring descent from the 7,600-meter level of K-2, the second-highest mountain in the world. At the time of his descent, he was partially blinded by retinal hemorrhages suffered during the ascent. This personal account was provided in French by M. Boivin for The Explorers Journal *in response to the request of Stanford F. Brent, who made the translation.*

Mongolian Interlude

BY WILLIAM J. MORDEN

ontrary to popular impression, most of those who go into distant and little known areas or who collect specimens in far places, are not impelled by a desire for "adventure." I do not mean that they do not enjoy pitting themselves against and overcoming difficulties encountered. What I mean is that their purpose is to procure their information and collect their specimens with as little labor, as little danger and as little "adventure" as possible. I have heard several explorers say that, if they find themselves facing a situation against which they have not prepared and which seems likely to bring their work and possibly their lives to an end, then they have been guilty of an error. Carefulness in making plans and in working out the major details of a project should cover every contingency, so that, should danger arise, an expedition will have within itself means of eliminating or overcoming the difficulty.

But, no matter how carefully plans and preparation have been made, now and then a situation may arise where a desired result can be obtained only through a course which involves risk. As an instance of this I will relate a story of an "adventure" which occurred in Central Asia in 1926.

I was the leader of the Morden-Clark Asiatic Expedition of the American Museum of Natural History. My companion was James L. Clark, assistant director in charge of the Department of Preparation at the Museum. Clark and I left Kashmir on the first of April, crossed the Himalaya and Karakoram ranges, collected *Ovis poli* in the Russian Pamirs during May and then traveled northward to Kashgar in Chinese Turkestan.

My original program, worked out in conjunction with Roy Chapman Andrews, had been to make contact with his Central Asiatic Expedition at the town of Hami, in Eastern Chinese Turkestan. Clark and I were to collect ibex, roe-deer, and other specimens in the Tian Shan Mountains during the summer. The Central Asiatic Expedition expected to be working in the western Gobi that year and the plan was for one or more of the expedition's cars to push through to Hami, where Clark and I would join them on the first of September. Unfortunately, a civil war raging around Peking prevented Andrews from taking the field that season. A message from him, received by us at Kashgar in June, made it necessary to re-arrange our plans.

For several reasons, I wished to cross Mongolia. First and foremost was the possibility of collecting specimens of saiga antelope, a rapidly disappearing species. A few of these little animals are still to be found in part of Mongolia and I hoped we might be fortunate enough to locate their limited range. Another reason was that the American Museum wished Clark to study the Mongolian Plains, as his department was charged with the preparation of the zoological collections of the Central Asiatic Expeditions from that region. Should we turn back and retrace our steps to Kashmir, after completing our work in the Tian Shan, neither of these objectives would be attained. We considered the matter for several days and decided to attempt to cross the Gobi to Urga with a camel caravan.

We could get little information in Turkestan. The Chinese could tell us almost nothing, nor could the Soviet consuls at Kashgar and Urumchi give us much help. Chinese domination over Outer Mongolia had ended some years before and, although Russian influence, we understood, was in the ascendency in that country, the Russian consuls themselves could tell us little about conditions at the moment. They did, however, offer to advise Moscow that we were starting and ask that Soviet representatives in Mongolia be instructed to assist us where possible.

There was no Mongolian representative in Chinese Turkestan, so it was impossible to procure Mongolian credentials before entering the country. Our proposed route across the Dzungarian plains had never been traversed by white men, though it was occasionally used by native caravans. We knew that we were taking a chance, but the results to be obtained seemed worth the risk.

On arrival at Kuchengtze, the starting-point for caravan travel across the Gobi, we had with us one assistant, Mohamed Rahim, who had been with us several months. Although he spoke no English, his Hindustani was excellent. In addition, he spoke Turki, the language of Turkestan, and a useful amount of Chinese.

I had expected no difficulty in hiring camels at Kuchengtze, but, when the Chinese caravan agencies learned that we intended to enter Outer Mongolia, there were suddenly no camels available. At last, however, we obtained a native caravan of thirty camels, together with a caravan *bashi*, or leader, and five men. We hired a guide who was said to know the route to Urga and to speak fluent Mongolian. There was no way of checking up on this individual, so we had to take him more or less on faith. As it turned out, he had been over part of the route several years before and, when not excited, could speak some dozen or so words of Mongolian. Under stress, he could not only speak no Mongolian but little of anything else.

We left Kuchengtze on October twenty-third. Immediately the weather broke and, from then on, snowstorms were of almost daily occurrence, with the temperature much of the time considerably below zero. Plainly, winter was under way.

About three days out, one of the caravan men stole a horse and deserted. We were pretty angry about it at the time, but, looking back, we decided that he was the only one of the party with good sense.

Most caravan travel in Central Asia is done by night, for the Bactrian camel is a cold-weather animal and travels best during the cooler hours. On halting, it is customary to picket the camels until daybreak and then turn them loose to graze. Our marches usually began some time in the afternoon and continued into the early morning.

At dusk one evening, our caravan *bashi* rode ahead to try to locate a Mongol post known to be somewhere near by. Shortly after dark we came upon him, sitting on his horse and looking intently down a slope to the right. While questioning him, we heard voices below and three dark figures rode rapidly up the hill. The first was a bare-headed individual, who began to shout in a gruff voice at our party. We could not understand what he said, but his tone gave us the feeling that all was not well.

Clark and I thought it time to show ourselves and explain that we were white men on our way to Uliassutai and that we wished to find the post; so we called the interpreter and instructed him to tell who we were. One of us took out a spotlight and we flashed it on our faces to show that we were not natives. The fellow was evidently startled, for he blinked in the light, then lighted a match and by its flickering rays scrutinized us closely. He was a repulsive-looking individual with a badly scarred face. As he wore no uniform, we wondered if we had not met some Mongol bandits, instead of Mongol soldiers. Then several more horsemen came tearing up from different directions and we realized that unawares we had been well surrounded.

In the starlight, I could see that the newcomers wore the winter headgear of the Red Army, peak-topped felt helmets with Soviet stars in front. All carried rifles slung over their shoulders and rode active little Mongol ponies. They seemed a wild lot, but the fact that they had uniforms of a sort reassured us and we felt certain that, as soon as we located the commanding officer and told him who and what we were, everything would be all right. We instructed our guide to tell them that we wished to go to the post with our whole caravan. A guttural reply and a gesture indicated that we were to turn down a steep slope to the right. On the way, they surrounded us closely and evidently commented on the fact that we were armed, which seemed to displease them, though there was little opportunity to do more than notice their expressions.

So far as we could see in the darkness, the post consisted of two yurts. Into one of these we were hurried by our escort. Inside the yurt, about a dozen savage-looking individuals were seated around a small dung fire, while a single bowl of grease with a floating wick gave a dim light, which but added to the gloom. All wore sheepskin coats and pointed felt helmets with red stars in front. Some wore heavy felt boots with leather soles, others Mongol leather boots with toes turned upward. Around the wall hung belts, rifles, and various articles of equipment.

We had brought three of our men along and we five, added to the dozen or so already there, crowded the small yurt nearly to capacity. Lowering looks met us as we entered, but a place was made in the circle around the fire and we were motioned to sit. Through the interpreter I asked for the commanding officer, but it appeared that there was no officer present. We tried to explain who and what we were, where we were coming from and where we wished to go, but they took no interest in our explanations. I produced our papers, which included passports, letters in Russian from Soviet authorities and a number of documents with large red and gold seals on them. The latter had never failed to impress local officials in Turkestan. We endeavored to explain the papers, emphasizing the Russian permits and a personal letter of introduction to the Russian consul in Kobdo.

We said we were Americans, but it was quite evident that they had never heard the word. One unfriendly individual, who seemed to have a good deal to say, asked us if we were Russians. Fearing someone might speak Russian, I answered that we were not, but said that we had many friends among them. That, however, made no impression on their stolidity. One of them suddenly asked if we had Mongolian passports and, when I replied that we had not but expected to get them through a Soviet consul, there were ugly looks and whisperings. Then we began to sense trouble ahead.

One by one, Mongols left the yurt, until but a single man remained by the door. In spite of our distinctly hostile reception, it seemed best to pretend that we felt sure of ourselves, though we were far from it. We supposed, however, that we would at least be free to make camp over night, so, when we heard the caravan outside, we arose and moved toward the door. Mohamed, who was nearest the entrance, went first, As he neared the door, the Mongol standing by it struck him in the face and knocked him down. Then he growled what seemed to be an order and pointed to the floor, which probably meant that we were to sit down. That we did not do so at once may have been one reason for what followed. We had not yet realized what sort of savages we had met and probably a bit of the "dominant white man" feeling still remained. But not for long.

The guard shouted and the whole crowd came pouring into the yurt. Several carried ropes and, before we knew what was happening, they set upon us in overwhelming numbers and we went to the ground under a mass of Mongols. Probably in normal moments we would have realized that resistance was useless, but at the time coherent thought was suspended and we fought our assailants as best we could in the crowded yurt. But we never had a chance and our struggles only served to infuriate them. As I lay on my back, I saw a Mongol take a vessel of boiling water from the fire and start to pour it on my face. I rolled my head to the side and closed my eyes. Fortunately the water went wide of its mark.

We finally ceased the unequal battle and lay back, while they forced our arms in front of us and passed ropes around our crossed wrists. Then we were jerked to a sitting position and the ropes tightened. Men seated themselves on each side of us and, with feet braced against our wrists, jerked the ropes as tight as possible. The pain was pretty severe. I felt my wrist crack and thought it was broken. During the struggle, the back of my right hand was torn by a rope and this was very painful. When they had us bound, the ropes were soaked with water, so that they would draw even tighter. The whole mob shouted continually in a sort of excited frenzy and each seemed anxious to take a hand.

Completely trussed up, we were roughly thrown on our backs, our pockets were turned inside out and our clothes torn open in a very thorough search. It was not a gentle process, either, for we were rolled over and over on the ground and each roll caused a hard jerk on the rope stretched between us. During the search, one chap kept his foot on my head.

When the fracas started, Clark was smoking a pipe and this a Mongol knocked clear across the yurt. I was chewing a bit of gum but fortunately no one noticed it; before I finished with it, that was probably the hardest chewed piece of gum in history. They took everything from our pockets and clothing and tossed the articles across the yurt, where they were tied up in one of our handkerchiefs. We were searched twice before we were permitted to sit up. Even then, we were not allowed to warm our fast-numbing hands over the tiny fire. I tried to do so a couple of times, but on each occasion was struck in the face and knocked back. One big savage seemed to take a particular dislike to me and lost no opportunity to get in an extra bit of unpleasantness.

Our three men were tied up at the same time as ourselves and were badly beaten in the operation. Mohamed received a worse pounding than the others and his cries of pain were not pleasant to hear. The beating of our men was pure savagery on the part of the Mongols, for they did not struggle when being tied.

For some reason our captors did not prevent our speaking together, so we were able to discuss things. There could be no doubt that we were in a very serious fix. I asked Mohamed if he had learned anything from the interpreter. Mohamed, a bit dazed, moaned and replied that the interpreter had overheard the Mongols saying that we were to be shot. I asked him whether it was to be at once or in the morning, but he had learned nothing beyond the fact that we were to be shot.

It was quite evident that, as matters stood, we could expect no mercy. The only thing we could do, lacking some break in our luck, was to take whatever might come as stoically as possible and not give our captors the satisfaction of seeing us weaken. Clark and I talked now and then, but not very hopefully. There seemed little chance that we would come out alive. We wondered how long we could stand the probable torture.

A series of rather disconnected thoughts passed through our minds, but except for the natural dread of torture, we both agreed that we felt no actual fear of death. Neither Clark nor I was particularly frightened at the thought of being shot. To both, however, it seemed such a futile thing to be shot by a group of savages on mere suspicion.

The things which caused me the most concern were: first, the terrible period of waiting and the anxiety which my wife must go through when we did not arrive in Peking and the equally distressing interval that must be spent in trying to find out what had happened to us; secondly, a very sincere hope that the Mongols would make it quick and short. I had no panorama of my past life, such as I have read comes to one facing practically certain death. As for the future, there was a complete blank; it had ceased to interest me.

By and by a newcomer entered the yurt. Apparently, this individual was not a soldier, for he was dressed in a blue coat instead of the usual sheepskin. He and Mohamed talked in low tones and I could catch enough to gather that Mohamed was carefully explaining who we were, where we had come from and what we had been doing and, as I had told him to do, strongly emphasizing the fact that we had many friends among the Russians. The fellow seemed interested and understanding; his attitude was noticeably different from that of the soldiers. At first I thought he might be their officer, but Mohamed told me that he was just a Mongol civilian who could speak Chinese and was thereby able to converse directly with Mohamed. Our interpreter was practically useless, for, while he had not been badly injured during the *mêlée*, he was thoroughly frightened and spent his entire time kneeling on the ground, mumbling prayers interspersed by deep groans. The Chinese-speaking Mongol went out after a while and we were left to our thoughts, with several armed soldiers standing guard over us.

How long they kept us in the yurt we had no means of knowing. After what seemed an age, during which time our hands grew more and more swollen and painful, several of the group entered and motioned us out through the yurt door. Our three men went first, then Clark and I followed, with the rope dragging between our bound hands. In the starlight we saw several dark figures with rifles. We felt sure they were leading us out to a firing squad. Clark and I said goodbye to each other.

We were led off into the gloom, fully expecting to be halted and shot at any moment. A dim shape, appearing vaguely in the light of the stars, resolved itself into a small caravan tent. We were roughly thrust inside the entrance and again thrown to the ground. Our big dogskin helmets were put on our heads and these came so far down over our eyes that we were practically blindfolded. Moving feet were all we could see. Presently we were dragged to the rear of the tent and forced into a sitting position back to back against the tent-pole. Our arms were trussed to the pole by a rope passed around the two of us.

After we were tied so tightly that movement of arms or bodies was impossible, they again pushed our caps low on our heads and threw a few sheepskins over our legs. It was away below freezing in the tent—how cold we did not know, but certainly close to zero.

It looked as though we were there for the night. That was worse than being shot, for it was certain that, even should we live, there was little chance that we would ever again have the use of our hands. Even though they did not freeze—which they probably would—with circulation entirely stopped for many hours, they would undoubtedly be paralyzed by morning. We were hundreds of miles from any possible medical attention and, though we might be finally released, there seemed nothing ahead but a most unpleasant lingering death by blood poisoning. It was a thought I tried to keep out of my mind.

Now and then the soldiers felt our hands, though at the time we could not understand why. It occurred to us that they might know how long the hands could remain bound before numbness would intervene and the pain no longer be felt. The fact that they covered our feet and legs with sheepskins simply meant to us that we were to be tied up in that position until morning, in which case our hands would be lost and little else would matter.

That period seemed endless. At first we hoped that they might loosen our bonds for the night but, as time passed, we were in too much pain even to hope. We could not move our fingers and there was no sensation in the hand when the Mongols touched them, although, curiously enough, they burned as though scalded; sudden pains shot through them now and then and flashed up wrists and arms. By the dim light I tried to see my hands each time they were examined, but could only tell that they were badly swollen and out of shape.

The last time the man felt my hands, he must have decided that they had reached the limit, for he said something to the others and they at once began to untie us. He tried to loosen my rope himself, but it was so tight that he had to call for assistance. When at last it was off, I felt a surge of blood down my wrists and into my hands. I had expected it to be painful when the rope was loosened, but it was not; on the contrary, it was decidedly pleasant.

The removal of our bonds was like an unexpected present. One moment we had been without hope; the next, though it still seemed likely that we would be shot, at least we were not to be tortured to death. We were probably closer to fainting just then than at any other time. Before, we had rather hoped we might.

After freeing our wrists, the Mongols gave us our goatskin coats. Then, seated back to back, we were again bound to the tent post by ropes which passed about our arms and bodies. The wrists of our three men were unlashed and their arms were tied by ropes above the elbows, but they were not otherwise bound. Sheepskins tucked about our legs and feet made us fairly comfortable, though we were so limp by then that we could only lie back and rest. Nothing to eat since early morning, added to the strain of the last few hours, had weakened us badly.

A little later, the Mongols brought us bowls of their tea, a rather dirty and most unpleasant concoction made of brick tea and salt. But it was hot, so we gulped it down. Shortly afterward we were agreeably surprised to have them put a couple of our own cigarettes in our mouths and light them for us. Certainly that cigarette tasted better than any other I ever smoked.

The sudden change from pure savagery to more humane treatment was bewildering. We talked it over but could not understand the motives for either the original outburst of ferocity or the change. At all events, for the present out hands had been saved and the night ahead promised to be less unpleasant than we had expected.

Our hands still hurt severely; in fact, bruised nerves gave us trouble for many days. The rope burn on the back of my right hand became infected and it was a month before I finally got it under control.

All night Mongols wandered in and out of the tent, squatted by us, scrutinized us closely, felt our clothing, and generally satisfied their curiosity. A guard was always seated at the tent door with a rifle across his knees. One of these chaps amused himself now and then by aiming his rifle at one of us and curling his finger suggestively around the trigger. He would hold the position for several seconds, then put the rifle down and laugh uproariously. He evidently enjoyed his little joke.

The night dragged on and on, for we were still in suspense regarding the outcome. With no means of keeping track of time, we could only watch a tiny bit of sky visible through the tent door and hope for the dawn. We managed to slip our ropes down the post until we could lie partly stretched out and ease the strain on our back. We even slept in snatches.

Shortly after daylight we were taken outside, with our arms still bound above the elbows. Several soldiers stood guard with rifles at the ready. Where they expected us to run in that open country, with our arms tied, was a mystery, but each time any of us were taken out of the tent for a moment, one or more soldiers always had their rifles pointed in our direction. It was really funny, though the future was too uncertain for us fully to appreciate the humor.

Later our caravan men, who had not been molested and had made camp near by, were allowed to bring us some of their tea and hard bread. The tea, while not good, was far ahead of the salty Mongol variety and, by soaking the bread, we could soften it enough to obtain a little much-needed nourishment.

Sometime during the morning Mohamed was led out of the tent. Almost immediately we heard two shots. I said to Clark, "There goes poor Mohamed. I wonder who's next." For two hours we waited in suspense; then, to our amazement, Mohamed was led back to the tent. He had merely been taken out to open our boxes, so that the Mongols could examine the contents. The shots had been fired by someone experimenting with my automatic pistol.

Late in the afternoon a snappy-looking stranger rode up. His long coat was of blue silk, lined with sheepskin and tied with a yellow sash. Mongol boots with turned-up toes and decorative stitching of red and green, a closely fitting leather cap and sheepskin trousers completed his clothing, while a large Mauser automatic pistol hung prominently in its wooden holder at his side. With him came a younger man who spoke Turki and acted as interpreter.

The newcomer, very evidently a Buriat, was of a much higher type than the soldiers we had hitherto seen. He proved to be in command of the post and, about an hour after his arrival, we were conducted to the yurt. Our papers, which had been taken from us with everything else, were opened and examined, though it was quickly apparent that the officer could not read them. He seemed to have control of the situation, however, and the soldiers did not have so much to say as formerly. We found our firearms, field-glasses and other articles of kit piled in the yurt.

After the commander had asked a number of questions, we were taken back to the tent, still bound and with no information as to what was to happen. Nothing was told us, nor were any of our questions answered. The one-sided conversation between the officer and me was carried on through Mohamed and the young Mongol interpreter.

Our own interpreter was still worthless, for what little Mongolian he could speak originally he had lost completely in his fright. He did, however, tell us that we were thought to be spies and that a patrol had been sent back along our trail to learn if we were the advance party of some invading force. Again, he said that the real commanding officer of the post was at a place some two days north, that a messenger had been sent for him and that we would be kept prisoners until he arrived. All sorts of stories were passed on to us. Probably none of them were true, though anything seemed possible. The Mongols themselves treated our inquiries with insolent indifference.

Shortly after we re-entered the prison tent, a big bowl of rice and meat was brought in by one of our caravan men. We had had practically no food since breakfast the day before, so the whole five of us pitched into the rice. Clark and I ate native fashion. Squatted by the bowl with the men, we dipped our hands into the sticky mess and made the rice into balls. With arms still tied at the elbows, it was impossible to reach our mouths, but we threw balls of rice at our mouths and inhaled deeply to catch as much as possible of the precious food. It was a wonderful picture—two white men, three Turkis, and a couple of Mongols feeding noisily in the dimly lighted, filthy tent. It was getting pretty close to nature—a bit too close—but the rice and meat were good and strengthened us considerably.

That night was even colder than the previous one and, as the Mongols had taken away many of the sheepskins for their own use, we were so chilled that we got little sleep. Much of the time we just lay and shivered. It had been a bit of good fortune that, when captured, we both happened to be wearing felt boots. Had we been wearing leather footgear, our feet would have frozen, for certainly our captors would not have permitted us to get our heavy boots from the caravan. My injured hand throbbed and ached, but my request to be allowed to get something for it from the medicine kit with the caravan stores was curtly refused.

Our boxes already had been opened and our arms and ammunition, of course, had been confiscated. During the day our two pistols had been proudly worn by various soldiers who took a huge delight in strutting past us. The officer later took these to himself and appeared, wearing his own Mauser and both our revolvers.

The next morning the commander came in and looked us over. Shortly after that the ropes were removed and we were ordered to go to our camels and make camp. After being bound in the freezing tent for thirty-six hours, it was a great relief to be out in the air and free to move about again. We put up a tent and attempted reorganization of our much-scattered belongings. The officer had made one inspection of our kit the day before; that morning he inspected it again, to the great edification of a group of curious soldiers, who fingered everything and constantly pushed us out of the way so that they might better see what was going on. All that day we were bothered by soldiers who sat about our tent and followed us everywhere.

Later in the day we were again called into the main yurt, where another inspection of our papers and the contents of our saddle-bags was made. A few small articles were given back to us, but most of our possessions, such as field-glasses, compasses, thermometers and extra camera lenses were not returned. It was interesting that the Mongols seemed anxious to have us take their photographs. We doubted if they knew what the cameras were, but they liked to stand in front of the buzzing Eyemo and hear the hand cameras click.

Our experiences in the yurt and prison tent began to seem unreal and dream-like—the sort of thing one reads about, but which makes little impression because it could never actually happen. My infected hand, however, which I had at last been able to bandage, was a constant reminder of stern reality. After our release the Mongols were not aggressively unfriendly, although they treated us as their inferiors and felt free to come into our tent at any time and demand cigarettes.

In the days following we were sent from one post to another. Evidently no one knew what to do with us. Each post passed us along to another one, always under armed guard. At each post a further examination of our baggage and papers was made. We asked to be sent to Uliassutai, as that was on our route to Urga and China. This was curtly refused. We asked to be allowed to return to Turkestan. That was also refused. We were finally informed that we were to go under guard to Kobdo, which is the headquarters of Western Mongolia.

It was a most unpleasant march of some two hundred and seventy miles across the Mongolian Altai, by a trail which I do not think has ever been traveled by white men and which in winter is not even used by Mongols for camel caravans. After struggling for twelve days to force our tired camels and horses through deep snow, up and down steep slopes and across several passes, near the end of November we arrived at Kobdo.

I had hoped that we might persuade the authorities there to allow us to continue our journey to Uliassutai and Urga, but this they flatly refused to do. Eventually, with the assistance of some friendly Russians and the Soviet consul, we made our way by wagon and sleigh to a branch of the Trans-Siberian Railroad at Biisk, a distance of about six hundred miles. From there it was a week's journey by train to Peking.

As nearly as I have been able to determine, the Mongols thought we were spies, and it seems that their code calls for spies to be executed first and investigated afterwards. Apparently, the civilian Mongol who spent some time conversing in Chinese with Mohamed, believed that we had influential Russians friends. This information, passed along to the soldiers, probably convinced them that it might be safer to await the arrival of an officer before shooting us, as Soviet influence was paramount in Outer Mongolia. The officer, with more intelligence and a greater feeling of responsibility than the soldiers, decided that for the moment, at least, we were not dangerous, and thought it best to shift the responsibility to the shoulders of his superiors.

At the time we were at a loss to understand the ferocity of the Mongolians and the seemingly needless agony of the first few hours. Months later I learned from Roy Chapman Andrews that the binding of a prisoner's hands until circulation is stopped is a recognized form of torture among Mongols. Andrews told me that he had seen it practised in the jails at Urga. Clark and I can testify that it is a most effective method.

It would seem that the application of torture was intended to frighten us. Very probably it use was dictated by a feeling of uncertainty and fear on the part of the Mongols themselves. We had arrived unannounced at their post at night from the direction of Chinese Turkestan; we were armed; they could not read our credentials and were suspicious of us. It is quite possible that our interpreter's story about our being considered an advance party of a larger invading force was true. The outburst of savagery was the natural consequence of suspicion and fear, engendered by our unheralded arrival.

Frankly, I am not particularly proud of the foregoing recital, for I agree with others that "adventure" has no place in the world of a scientific expedition. I have been asked, however, to describe the incident and, inasmuch as the specimens and film, which were the objectives of the expedition, came through undamaged, I relate the story as an example of what can happen, regardless of the most careful plans and preparation.

— *TOLD AT THE EXPLORERS CLUB* (1931)

William J. Morden was a field associate in the Department of Mammalogy of the American Museum of Natural History. His record of work in Africa and Asia makes an impressive exhibit of scientific activity crowded into a short space of time.

In 1922 he led an expedition to East Africa, Uganda, and the Sudan; the following year he headed another to Baltistan, Ladakh, Kishtwar, and Kashmir, and in 1924 one to Nepal and Upper Burma. He organized and led the Morden-Clark Asiatic Expedition of the American Museum of Natural History in 1926, of which this story tells the most dramatic episode. He left

Kashmir that April first; collected in the Russian Pamirs; crossed Kashgaria; collected zoological specimens in the Thian Shan Mountains; crossed the Great Turfan Depression, the Dzungarian plains and western Outer Mongolia, and made a new crossing of the Dzungarian plains and the Mongolian Altai, traveling eight thousand miles and obtaining a comprehensive series of Ovis poli, *Thian Shan ibex, and roe-deer, besides specimens of other fauna of the various regions. The full story is told in his* Across Asia's Snows and Deserts.

In 1929–1930 he led the Morden-Graves North Asiatic Expedition for the same institution, spending eight months in Russia, Tashkent, Samarkand, Bokhara, and eastern Siberia, and covering about seven hundred miles by camel caravan on the steppes of Kazakstan, obtaining a series of the saiga antelope and making a general collection of the fauna of the region. He spent the winter in the forests of the Amur River country, getting three fine specimens of the "long-haired" Siberian tiger, as well as a comprehensive general collection.

Over the Khyber to Kabul

BY LOWELL THOMAS

Introduction by Seyward S. Cramer, Editor, *Through Hell and High Water*, 1941

Philip Cummings is one of the happiest men I have seen in ages and his pleasure comes from his ownership of a single envelope. Many of us are philatelists and would shake dice with the devil for first-day covers. Philip's envelope, though, has no stamp and that fact, believe it or not, makes it all the more valuable. It carried a letter halfway around the world. It was handled by the postal services of several foreign countries—and honored by them. Up in the corner, in place of a stamp, is this notation: "Quetta Earthquake—Postage Free." It was mailed by the General Commander of Baluchistan from Quetta.

Yes, that letter was mailed from Quetta after it had been nearly leveled by a severe earthquake in 1935. For centuries Quetta had been an important city of Baluchistan. Its importance had reached out to the entire Orient and its market was one of the most colorful of the section. But that seismic catastrophe destroyed the bazaars.

Lowell Thomas was in that country at one time carrying out a series of explorations. Harry Chase was with him, acting as his cameraman. You weren't our Vice-President at that time, Lowell Thomas. In fact, you were just doing the field work that qualified you for membership in our Club. But we do take pride in claiming you as our First Vice-President now.

You had the unusual distinction of being invited to visit Afghanistan. Until a few years ago, foreigners were extremely unpopular in that country. They were never invited in and many of those who managed to get in were immediately shipped out—often in a box.

I wish you would tell us about that experience, Lowell.

IT IS ABSOLUTELY FORBIDDEN TO CROSS
THIS BORDER INTO AFGHAN TERRITORY.

Thih warning stands in large letters at the western end of the Khyber Pass, where Alexander the Great, Mahmud of Ghazni, Timur-i-Lenkh, Baber, Akbar, and other conquerors had ridden. In case you don't know enough to take that warning seriously there is a thick tangle of barbed wire to pull you up short. In addition, a camp of British Tommies guards one side; on the other is a company of armed troopers of the Amir of Afghanistan. Over all looms the invisible but strict taboo of the British Raj.

For two years before I ever saw it, that signboard haunted me. While traveling through India, Burma, Borneo, the Malay States, I had been moving heaven and earth to break down that taboo and walk through that barrier with my camera colleague, the late and unforgettable Harry Chase. We had wangled, intrigued, pulled wires. We had tried to work the governments of the United States, of Great Britain, of India.

Finally we had given up hope and were waiting at Bombay for a steamer. We had trunkfuls of notes and good film from remote parts of Asia but the more we were forbidden to approach Afghanistan the more fascinating it had become. Luck arrived when we least expected it, real luck in the shape of an invitation from the Amir, King Amanullah. For it, I had to thank, of all people, the United States chargé d'affaires at the court of the Shah of Persia, Mr. Cornelius Van H. Engert. Where the British Raj had been obdurate, one of Uncle Sam's diplomats had got me through.

Let's skip everything that happened to us from the time we left Bombay until we saw for ourselves that signboard at the foot of the Khyber Pass. There were days filled with excitement, experience, color—the spectacle of the bazaars in Quetta, since destroyed by the big earthquake of 1935, the Pink Mountains of Baluchistan, trying to swim across the flooded Indus on an inflated goatskin bag, the desert of Sind, the wolflike folk who inhabit the barren horrors of Waziristan. You calculate the length of your journey from the

Indus to the Khyber not by days but by the number of motorcars that break down under you: our record was thirteen.

Probably they would have been more but for the extraordinary versatility of Harry Chase. An amazing fellow, truly of the breed that challenges, dares, and tries anything to get a good shot on his film. Aside from his imperturbability, Harry had a mechanical aptitude that was almost incredible. He ground his own lenses like the best German experts at Jena. After a desert simoon—which could blow dust into a watertight steel vault—Harry would take his cameras to pieces, clean them thoroughly and, while putting them together again, improve their mechanism. He could do the same for your watch or patch a broken-down motor with baling wire and a couple of leather straps.

Among the experiences we skip is a sojourn in Peshawar, the Paris of the Pathans. A city of "a thousand and one sins"—that describes it accurately if inadequately. What tales old Abdul Ghani told us, pulling on his hubble-bubble on the balcony overlooking the Street of the Storytellers!

Four of us left Peshawar for the Khyber Pass. The third American was David King, then representing American jute interests in Calcutta. A Harvard man, he had fought the war in the Foreign Legion, was buried alive thirty-six hours at Verdun, and since the war had traveled and acquired an invaluable knowledge of Asia and Asiatic peoples.

The fourth of our quartet was Niam Shah, whose shadow I trust has not decreased. What a man! A Goliath of the Afridi tribe—there was a real soldier of fortune for you! He had served in German East Africa and Mespot, fearing nothing and nobody but Allah. With the strength of three ordinary men, he watched over us, twirling his fierce mustachios, as though he were an ayah protecting the young or an asylum orderly guarding three harmless lunatics. He had one warning phrase: "Sahib, naughty man shoot," with which he plied us, from the moment we crossed the Afghan border until we returned. It was no empty phrase either.

We left Peshawar on a July morning, a typical day during which the average of heat strokes and sunstrokes from dawn to sunset was around a hundred. Hot as it was there, we did not realize what heat really was until we crossed the Afghan desert and four ranges of barren mountains between Peshawar and Kabul. All three of us Americans were literally swathed in thick woolen clothing—to keep out the heat. It wilted even Niam Shah.

Before we entered the Khyber Pass we had to show our firman from King Amanullah to a British Tommy with a red flag. Remarking that it was "'otter than 'ell" he obviously wondered why any three white men should want to go where it was even 'otter.

In the Khyber the road winds up and up. Running parallel was another highway for caravans of camels, asses, mules, bullocks, and shaggy ponies. Still a third carried heavy motor lorries, mechanized army units. Over the cliffs above and the canyons below we saw aerial cable tramways, such as carry ore from the mines in our own western mountains. Just below the narrow walls of Ali Masjid Gorge, where the Khyber opens into a wider valley, we overtook a caravan of merchants on the way to Samarkand, each man astride a tiny donkey, the camels loaded with bales of cotton. Along that golden road to Samarkand two hundred thousand tribesmen pass back and forth every year, Turkomans, Tartars, Afghans, Povindahs, Persians, Hazaras.

As we approached Dakka, a walled town on the banks of the Kabul River, our car was surrounded by a swarm of bearded tribesmen, headed by an aged hadji in a green turban and a henna beard. He was followed by a smart young Afghan officer in a black astrakhan cap, Sam Browne belt, and Turkish cavalry boots. He welcomed us in the name of His Majesty King Amanullah. Colonel Abdul Ibrahim Khan gave us tea while he waited for orders over the military telephone wire from Kabul. He turned out to be a man of education, owning a Rand-McNally atlas, vintage 1900, brought from Australia by an Afghan camel driver. Colonel Ibrahim Khan accompanied us across the Afghan desert as far as Jalalabad.

That fifty-mile ride was more than any of us had ever experienced, even our faithful Niam Shah, who was born and reared less than a hundred miles away. It took us over four hours, with a puncture every hour. In the midst of it all a desert simoon overtook us. How the car survived that boulder-strewn, crater-pitted hell's causeway is a mystery to this day. Dave King had the wheel and it nearly tore his arms loose. And it cheered us vastly to learn that on that identical stretch of road a German engineer employed by the Amir had been murdered by the Afghan officer in command of his escort only a few weeks before. Moreover, some encouraging soul showed me a copy of the letter, written in Pushtu, which is sewed into the coat of every British aviator who flies over Afghanistan. It reads "to whom it may concern," that anybody returning the bearer unharmed to British lines will receive ten thousand rupees. It is hardly necessary to add that none of us carried any such letter on the road to Kabul and we knew nobody who would have paid ten thousand rupees for the three of us put together!

However, we reached Jalalabad without casualty or need for ransom and, frankly, it was worth all the agony and trouble of getting there. Laid out by Baber nearly four hundred years ago, the place was still the winter capital of the amirs, in the seasons when Kabul is snowbound. In the midst of a fertile plain, and surrounded by lush orchards, Jalalabad, as we saw it, seemed virtually unchanged from the days of Akbar, Baber's grandson. Nearly every man within the high, thick mud walls carried a rifle slung over his shoulder. All the gates are double or treble so that a besieger would have three fights to break through.

The royal palace, where we were put up for the night, offered a curious mixture of *Arabian Nights* with Marseilles boulevard and Jersey City decorations. But the trees in the park around the palace had been planted by the Empress Nur Jehan, consort of Jehangir. And the dinner that was served to us at midnight would have been fit for Haroun-al-Raschid himself.

Right here let me pay a tribute to Afghan food. Never before or since have I tasted more delicious fruit and vegetables. No wonder virtually all the men we saw on the streets were huskies, since even the poorest Afghan is fed on all the vitamins and minerals that the fussiest dietitian could desire. On the protein side the fare leans rather preponderantly to mutton and goat. But anywhere you go in Asia you have to expect that.

Both Chase and I craved to take a look at the Jalalabad bazaars, but Niam Shah wouldn't listen to the idea: "Naughty man shoot, sahib!" And apparently the description "naughty man" fitted nine-tenths of the inhabitants of the amirs' winter capital.

We entered Kabul through the Gate of the Trumpet and Drums but there was no fanfare for us. Frankly, we were a bit jumpy. The Afghans to this day are as xenophobe as they were in the days of Baber. The Amir Habibullah, King Amanullah's father, had paid for his friendship toward the British with not only his throne but his life. The only man who ever really subdued the country was Alexander, whose name is still a byword.

As we passed through the gate a policeman in scarlet tunic and black astrakhan helmet jumped on the running board and made us turn to the right. Then a one-horse tonga pulled up beside us, driven by a character in spectacles, clad in a Prince Albert coat, gray trousers, vivid red necktie, suède gloves to match his trousers, and on his head an astrakhan tarboosh. He addressed us in perfect English, with a scowl on his face, not a word of civility but the peremptory order: "You are to go with this man, he will show you to the quarters that His Majesty has placed at your disposal." He turned out to be no less a dignitary than the counselor to the Foreign Ministry, by name Feizi Mohammed Khan, and we gathered unmistakably from him that King Amanullah's invitation to us had not pleased his advisers.

Our quarters, on the western edge of the city, were comfortable enough. We were lodged in a house called the Londoni Khoti, because it was supposed to look like something in London. Nasrullah Khan, who seized the throne upon the murder of Habibullah, had built the palace and really made a handsome job of it. But we were unable to congratulate him—he was in prison when we visited Kabul.

A retinue of twenty-seven servants waited on us and a detail of soldiers protected us, though we never were quite sure whether they were escort or wardens. Over all was one whom we nicknamed Boots-and-Spurs. In the house he functioned as a major-domo but we never were able to go anywhere without him and were convinced that his most important job was to spy on every move we made, every word we spoke. He was surly, as are most Afghans to foreigners, especially British and Americans, and pretended to speak no

English. But he had his uses: if any of the Afghan citizenry showed reluctance to pose before Harry Chase's cameras, they soon changed their minds after a round of kicks—literally, kicks—from old Boots-and-Spurs.

Maybe we owed our lives to him: maybe he prevented us from being shot or cut down by some bhang-crazed religious fanatic filled with the idea that our assassination would provide an instant passport to the throne of Allah. If so, he got little collaboration from us. Countless times we tried to lose him, sliding down the banisters, sneaking out the windows. But always old Boots-and-Spurs caught up with us. Even Niam Shah did not approve of our ducking him. "Naughty man shoot, sahib."

One night at dinner we thought even the Amir's precautions for our safety had failed. The massive candelabrum over the table swayed madly, dishes shot across the room, and outside was a roar as of heavy cannon. But that was the least of our perils: only an earthquake which we learned to expect almost regularly for hors d'oeuvres.

The big bazaar of Kabul, a maze of narrow tunnels in the heart of the capital, presents perhaps the most kaleidoscopic spectacle in all Asia. Not even Shanghai, Singapore, or Constantinople is more shaggily cosmopolitan. Through miles upon miles of alleyways we elbowed and shoved: we never would have got through without the "Khubardar, Khubardar! (Out of the way, dogs!)" shouted by Boots-and-Spurs. Here was no end to the variety of people we saw—Uzbegs, Kizilbashes, Ghilzai; merchants from Isfahan and Khorasan; mighty phalangists; Turkomans from Bokhara, Mongols from the Gobi, Orakzai, Ysafzai, Hazara, Tajik; shaggy men from Tashkent, Kazan, and Yarkand. And that's not all the list.

Though we were Amanullah's guests we had plenty of waiting before we were admitted into the Presence. But finally even that hour arrived. We approached the palace through a leafy tunnel formed by the interlocking branches of an avenue of beautiful *chinar* trees. Through the trees we could see a gathering of men on their knees. Kneeling in front of them was not an imam but a stout man in black tunic, riding breeches and top boots. It was King Amanullah, leading his court in prayer.

Passing through an archway we pulled up and were greeted by the friendly smile of a man dressed like a race-track tout who said, with an American pronunciation: "Pleased to meet you, Mr. Thomas. I am Tewfik Bey. I'm mighty glad you have turned up at last: I thought I would have to look you up." He saw us gazing at his costume and explained: "His Majesty wants us to encourage home industries." Tewfik had been a secretary at the Turkish embassy in Washington, a salesman in Philadelphia, a Hollywood extra, and finally a student of scientific agriculture. It was as agronomical adviser that Amanullah employed him.

"I am very glad you have come to Afghanistan," said the King most courteously when we finally were presented. "I want you to have everything to see and photograph everything. Tell me if there is anything particular you want."

"What I really would like," I replied, "is to stay a year in your fascinating country and explore it thoroughly."

"Just where do you want to go?" asked the Amir.

"To the headwaters of all the rivers."

King Amanullah laughed uproariously.

"It's lucky for you and your family that I can't let you do that," he chuckled. "You never would come back. We are still in a—well, disturbed state.

Amanullah was as good as his word and allowed Chase to take plenty of shots with both still and motion cameras. That nearly got me into trouble. I had the job of posing the Amir and once I made a too sudden gesture to alter his position. I was promptly warned: "You are in danger of being instantly shot if you make such violent movements in the direction of His Majesty. Armed men, whom you cannot see, guard him day and night. Only recently his life was attempted."

Not long after we were there a revolt broke out against his rule: the mullahs resented his attempts at modernizing his kingdom. That one was suppressed but Amanullah had caught the reform fever from the Ataturk Kemal and tried to defy the Moslem priesthood. So in 1929 the rebellion of

Bacha-i-Saqqao, the Water Boy, toppled him off his throne. Amanullah and his family escaped to India and thence to Europe. In 1930 his uncle, Nadir Shah, turned the tables on the Water Boy and hanged him. Nadir Shah in turn was assassinated but his son, Muhammad Zahir Khan, then a boy of nineteen, was seated on the throne where he sits today—for who knows how long.

—*THROUGH HELL AND HIGH WATER* (1941)

Through the Wilderness of Northern Korea to the Long White Mountain

BY ROY CHAPMAN ANDREWS

I am averse to writing about adventures, for I dislike them. They are a nuisance. They interfere with work and disrupt carefully laid plans. Still, even the best prepared explorer cannot always avoid what may be called adventures. It is impossible to foresee everything. I suppose that I have had many adventures during twenty-three years of wandering into the strange corners of the world, but in retrospect I cannot say which single experience was the most exciting. At the time it was happening, each one seemed more interesting than any other.

It might be of some interest to tell of an exploration I made of the wilderness of northern Korea in 1912—not that it was particularly exciting, but things happened which might easily have had unpleasant results. It was my first prolonged land expedition, although I had worked along little-known seacoasts for four years, with short trips into the interior. My object was to explore the forests of the Korean-Manchurian border lying south of the Paik-tu-san, or Long White Mountain. No one knew what that wilderness contained, for until the Russo-Japanese War Korea had remained a hermit kingdom.

I went up the east coast on a tiny freight vessel, accompanied only by a Japanese interpreter who spoke Korean. As my knowledge of Japanese was passable, our conversation was conducted in that language. From the little village of Seshin, we went inland to the ancient walled town of Musan. There I engaged eight diminutive Korean ponies and four men for the trip into the border wilderness. The Koreans did not want to go. They never had been there and were frightened. It would have been impossible to obtain a caravan without the assistance of the Japanese gendarmes. They ordered the men to go. The ponies carried our camp equipment and food; all of us walked.

It was only fifty or sixty miles to the edge of the forests. There I camped for a few days, trying to get information, but it was useless. None of the natives had been more than a few miles into the wilderness. My Koreans were sad-looking men when we started northward. Every few miles, they stopped to built tiny shrines of birch bark, leave little offerings of food and pray to their own particular gods for protection from the unknown terrors which awaited them. I took compass directions, laying a course straight for the Long White Mountain.

The first day's march was fairly easy, up a broad valley through a thin larch forest. The second was not so good. By the middle of the third afternoon, we were fairly in the wilderness and making slow progress. The forest was dense, the ground littered with moss-grown logs and spongy from underground water. At the end of the fourth march, I camped two days, for the men were very tired and much depressed. I thought a rest and fresh meat, if I could find game, would revive their spirits. Luck was with me and I killed a bear. That bear haunts me yet, for I did not give the poor brute a chance. It was almost murder. He came ambling along while I was resting on a fallen tree. Totally unconscious of my presence, he walked to within thirty feet of me. The bullet caught him squarely in the heart. My one consolation is that he never knew what had happened.

The bear meat did much to improve the morale of my men. Bear's paws are a great delicacy and the Koreans feasted like children, forgetting for a time that they were far away from home and mother.

For days we did not see another sign of life. The forest became denser at every mile, with more swamps and surface water. Time after time, our ponies were mired and had to be lifted out of the mud. Lush ferns and rank grass made walking dangerous. The trees were interlaced with great festoons of gray "Spanish moss", which formed a thick canopy overhead. Down where we were, there was only a gloomy half-light, occasionally shot through with patches of thin sun. No sounds broke the stillness except the calls of the men. No birds or animals, not even a squirrel. To make matters worse, it began to rain—not a hard, refreshing rain, but a dull drizzle which continued for a week.

The men were completely disheartened, frightened at the gloomy stillness of the forest, and exhausted by strenuous work. They began to talk furtively among themselves and, when we camped, were ominously silent if I passed their fire. The interpreter told me they were planning to desert that night with the ponies and food, leaving us to die or get back as best we could. It would have been fairly serious to be left without the caravan. I could find my way out easily enough but no game meant possible starvation.

We were only two days' march from the base of the Paik-tu-san and I had determined to complete my traverse against all odds. To leave it in mid-air meant that all our efforts were wasted. I told the men that we must reach the mountain; that I would give them double wages; further, that I should watch at night and, if anyone touched a pony, he would be shot without mercy. They did not like it much. My ultimatum was received in silence. The interpreter and I watched by turns through the night. Now and then, one of the men got up to replenish the fire, but they made no move to leave the camp. The next night was a repetition of the first. Both the Japanese and myself were utterly exhausted from lack of sleep and hard work. We wondered if we could stick it out another twenty-four hours.

In the late afternoon, we emerged into a great burned tract and the mountain rose majestically right in front of us. Banked to the top with snow, it looked like a great white cloud that had settled to earth for a moment's rest.

The open sky and the mountain acted like magic on my men. They began to talk and sing and call to each other in laughing voices. I knew then that the strain was over; they would not desert me. That night we camped in the shadow of the mountain, well out in the burned area, beside a pond of snow water. I slept for fifteen hours, utterly exhausted.

In the later afternoon, I shot a roe deer, and that completed the contentment of our party. One cannot wonder at the fears of the men. They knew that our objective was the Long White Mountain, but it seemed hopeless that we could get there. They had never seen a compass. To them, we were merely wandering aimlessly through the forest. When we actually arrived, and all by means of that little disk with the turning needle, their admiration knew no bounds. Of course, they did not understand how it worked, but it had brought us to the Paik-tu-san and that was good enough for them. Now they would follow anywhere I wished to go; they had complete confidence that I would not leave them to starve in a gloomy wilderness.

Four days at the Long White Mountain were sufficient. It was futile to attempt its ascent, for the snow was piled in great drifts from base to crown. But in any case, there would have been little to be gained, for James and Young-husband had reached the crater from the Manchurian side. My object had been to find what lay within that Korean wilderness over which they had looked thirty-three years before. I had a compass line straight through the forest to the base and a rough map of the surrounding country.

I determined not to return by the way we had come but to strike through the forest to the headwaters of the Yalu River, which could not be far to the west. It was a difficult trip, just about like what we had experienced on the way to the mountain. Dense forests, swamps and drizzling ran. But the men pushed on with light hearts, laughing at difficulties and hard work, supremely confident that my little compass knew the way.

We discovered a beautiful lake, set like a jewel amid the green larch forest, its shores a gray line of volcanic ash. Near by were two large ponds, swarming with mallard ducks. I shot three roe deer and a wild boar and trapped many small mammals. Birds were everywhere; flowers made a brilliant carpet in the park-like openings of the forest.

A day before we reached the Yalu, while hunting roe deer, I stumbled into the camp of eight Manchurian bandits—tall, brown, hard-bitten fellows, armed with long flintlock rifles. I suspected immediately what they were, but they saw me as quickly as I saw them. My rifle did not help any. They had me covered from several directions. There was nothing to do but bluff it out. Fortunately I knew a little Chinese. I said I was a friend, laid down my rifle, and advanced.

After a little, they resumed eating and offered me tea and millet. Then they went to my camp. They looked over all our stuff, but there was absolutely nothing they could use except my rife. I told the cook to get busy as he never had before and prepare a dinner of roe-deer meat. The bandits were pleased and accepted the invitation to eat with alacrity. My interpreter spoke bad Chinese but enough to tell them all about us.

After dinner the brigands became most friendly. They admitted that they were part of a band which held this region near the Yalu. All merchants sending goods between villages must pay them taxes. As we were not merchants and had been so hospitable, they would charge us nothing. Moreover, they told us how to avoid others of the band who might not be as friendly.

The next day, we camped on the bank of the great river, which at that spot was less than thirty yards across. Following down the stream for two days, we came to a Korean settlement. There was great rejoicing among my men, for they were heroes. Had they not been to the Long White Mountain and faced the terrors of the unknown wilderness, and all with the aid of a tiny compass? If I had given it to them, they would certainly have placed it in a shrine to worship as a god. Every villager came to see it. Reverently they passed it about, the old men wagging their heads and saying little, the younger explaining volubly how it worked.

Further down the river, we came to the first logging operations conducted by the Japanese. Here I dismissed my caravan and arranged to float down the Yalu on a log raft. The men made me a little house of bark and I had a huge deck for a playground. Sometimes at night we tied up to a bank, but usually the raft floated on, guided by two men with huge sweeps. I shot ducks and geese for specimens, retrieving them in a small boat towed behind the raft.

I watched the Yalu grow with every mile, for we passed dozens of small streams, each of which contributed its share to swell the giant river. The trip was very restful after the strenuous days of continued travel. With plenty of birds and fish, I lived like a king.

But I was a sorry sight in the way of garments when we reached Antung at the mouth of the river. My shoes and trousers were completely gone. I was dressed in Korean clothes, except for coat and hat. In this garb I reached Seoul and registered at the Sontag Hotel.

A cable to the Museum elicited a delighted reply. For nearly five months, I had dropped out of the world and the usual reports of death in the Korean wilderness had been cabled far and wide. I have "died" so frequently since that I am quite accustomed to it; it seems to be the best little thing I do.

The Museum was pleased with the results. I had explored and mapped a considerable area of unknown country and brought out a large collection of mammals and birds, many of them new to science.

— *TOLD AT THE EXPLORERS CLUB* (1931)

Traversing Arabia's Rub' al Khali

BY JENS MUNTHE

Deserts cover one-fifth of the Earth's land surface. Only one-fifth of these, however, are actually sand seas. They are seas indeed, with dunes constantly moving and breaking like waves under the power of the winds—the largest remain virtually untouched by humankind. The Rub' al Khali—Arabia's fabled Empty Quarter—is by far the largest sand sea. At 600,000 square kilometers it is the size of Texas, or of France along with the Low Countries. Its closest rival is the Kara Kum sand sea of central Asia, which covers 380,000 square kilometers. The great ergs of the northern Sahara are all less than half the size of the Empty Quarter. The longest dunes in the world are in the southwest Rub' al Khali, and the world's highest dunes, excepting only a few in two Algerian ergs, rise from the sabkha flats of the southeast Empty Quarter. Overall, the Rub' al Khali has more dune variety and greater scope for study of eolian geomorphology than any other place on Earth.

Yet, with all its research potential and appeal to explorers, the Empty Quarter remains virtually unknown. This is partly due to obvious physical problems of access, but more significant is the historic cultural milieu of the world's last theocratic monarchy: the Kingdom of Saudi Arabia. During the great Age of Exploration from the sixteenth through nineteenth centuries, when so many blanks on the map were filled, rulers of disease-ridden coastal states and fiercely territorial bedu tribes kept Western explorers out of central Arabia. Early in the twentieth century the Empty Quarter was one of the Earth's last unmapped places and a primary objective of explorers, but only the most determined individuals had any chance of being the first to cross the Rub' al Khali.

It finally came down to two well-connected Arabists: Harry St. J. B. "Jack" Philby (father of Russian spy Kim Philby), confidant of King Abdul Aziz Ibn Saud of Saudi Arabia, and Bertram Thomas, Wazir to the Sultan of

Muscat and Oman. Both saw the crossing of the Empty Quarter as the last great goal of exploration. Although Philby had the advantage of being in Saudi Arabia during the planning stages, it was Thomas who managed the first crossing in January of 1931. Thomas sprinted through the shortest possible crossing, traversing 730 kilometers of Rub' al Khali sand from Mughshin north to Qatar. He spent only 17 days in the sand, which was wise since he had neglected to ask Ibn Saud for permission to enter Saudi Arabia.

"Damn and blast Thomas!" wrote Philby, who had gone so far as to convert to Islam in hopes Ibn Saud would allow him to attempt the Empty Quarter crossing. "I have sworn a great oath not to go home until I have crossed the Rub' al Khali twice!" He got his chance in January of 1932. Leaving Al-Hasa, the world's largest oasis in the northeast Saudi desert, Philby traveled south into the heart of the sand sea. He stayed in the Empty Quarter for 40 days, following a complex route across 1,400 kilometers of dunes before emerging at Sulayil far to the west. His primary goal was to find Wabar, a legendary city lost in the sand. What he actually discovered was the meteorite impact site of Hadidah, which had inspired the tales of a city destroyed by fire from the heavens. Philby's was a great journey. He saw more of the Rub' al Khali than anyone before or since.

And that was all. There were no other crossings of the Rub' al Khali in the days of camel expeditions with bedu guides. Wilfred Thesiger crossed 300 kilometers of the Empty Quarter's east rim in January of 1947 and journeyed through 200 kilometers of its southwestern fringe early the following year, but by then automobiles were common in Arabia and Aramco was about to begin its oil exploration of the northeast Rub' al Khali. Aramco established a supply base and airstrip in the northern Rub' al Khali in 1950. This base at Ubaylah was permanently occupied until 1960, while Aramco shot thousands of kilometers of seismic surveys, drilled many water wells, and finally drilled a dozen deep wildcat exploration wells. But oil was found only at the far northeast edge of the dunes along the Abu Dhabi frontier, so Aramco too withdrew from the Empty Quarter. The drill sites are slowly being overridden by the dunes, although bedu still manage to keep hot, sulfurous water flowing from a few of the abandoned wells.

When my wife Kathleen and I arrived in Dhahran in 1988—I was a geologist on loan to Aramco from Mobil Oil—we met Hal McClure, a 30-year veteran of Saudi Arabia, who had crossed the Rub' al Khali with three other Aramcons in 1982. We immediately began planning a similar crossing, but as we learned more about deep desert driving it became obvious that we could not cross the Empty Quarter alone.

While we tried to interest others in attempting to cross the huge sand sea, we read everything we could find about the Empty Quarter. We learned that the Rub' al Khali has been a sand sea for only the past 700,000 years. By the late Pleistocene all the quartz sand had been dumped into the shallow Rub' al Khali Basin by rivers flowing northeast from the highlands of Yemen, Oman, and western Saudi Arabia. Increasing aridity dried up the rivers, and winds swirling clockwise around the persistent Arabian High began to mold the sand into dunes as the vegetation cover disappeared.

Sometime around a million years ago early man arrived in western Arabia. Paleolithic stone tools are found today north and west of the Empty Quarter, however, there is no evidence that humans penetrated the sand sea during this time. And, Acheulean tools found today on the gravelly interdunes of the far southwestern Rub' al Khali may well predate the sand sea itself.

The Arabian climate became moist once again from 36,000 to 17,000 years ago, during which time many small lakes formed in the southwest Rub' al Khali. Though no implements have been found associated with the limestone deposited in these ponds, thousands of Neolithic stone tools have been found around another series of lake deposits in the western Empty Quarter. Many of these have been radiometrically dated at 9,000 to 6,000 years old, demonstrating that humans hunted deep in the Rub' al Khali during this wet interval.

But man has never been able to tolerate the Rub' al Khali for long during arid times. Even at the height of the frankincense trade in the second century A.D., camel caravans carrying the precious resin avoided the Empty Quarter. Starting from Dhofar in what is now western Oman, the caravans skirted the sands to the south and west, making their way to the Mediterranean through Marib, the legendary capital of the Queen of Sheba, and the

Nabatean cities of Mada'in Saleh in northwest Saudi Arabia and Petra in Jordan. Even as the human population slowly grew throughout coastal and northern Arabia, and tribal areas grew into Arab nations, and wars raged all around the peninsula, the Rub' al Khali remained untouched and mysterious.

In late 1989, following the publication of Hal McClure's *Aramco World* article describing the first four-wheel-drive crossing of the Rub' al Khali, a few of us in Dhahran finally got serious about attempting to duplicate the feat. Kathleen and I were now joined by Norbert Kremla, a well-traveled and meticulously organized Canadian, and his girlfriend Christine Bullock. Their desert camping partners Mike Yelle and Steve Glover—both with families who supported the venture despite not being able to participate themselves—signed on next, and then we got two absolutely critical expedition members in, Peter Simmonds and Steve Gent. Simmonds is a vehicle mechanic extraordinaire, and few know their way around Blazers and Jimmies like Gent. Our token German, Manfred Reccord, rounded out the group.

We began planning the expedition in September of 1989, holding weekly meetings to discuss objectives, parts lists, tool requirements, weather, routing, fuel and water requirements, safety and medical plans, and contingencies in the event of a vehicle breakdown. The toughest problem was finding room in each of our five vehicles for 500 liters of gas and 120 liters of water. Yelle and Glover took on the navigational responsibilities and began working with a sextant.

Like Thomas, Philby, and McClure before us, we knew the risk of the dreaded *shamals* (sand storms) and killing heat was lowest in January. On January 20, 1990, we drove from Dhahran to Selwa with all our excess fuel tanks empty as a hedge against the possibility of a traffic accident on the highway. It took over an hour to top off all our tanks in Selwa, after which we set up our first camp in the sand.

When we lined up the vehicles for a ceremonial photo session the next morning, Simmonds' 1974 short-wheelbase Toyota Land Cruiser looked rather forlorn amidst the late-model V-8 Nissans, Jimmies, and Land Rovers. His primary objective was to nurse this "classic" vehicle through the greatest four-wheel-drive challenge of all. He got his chance to start tinkering that same day when the Toyota-From-Hell's clutch master cylinder failed. Reasoning that he needed the clutch more than brakes in the Rub' al Khali, Simmonds converted the brake master cylinder to serve the clutch.

We eased into the expedition by following bedu truck tracks 300 kilometers from Selwa to the abandoned water well at Jirwan. Here, we filled our tanks again from a fuel cache we had buried the month before. At Jirwan, the Jafura sands merge into the northern edge of the Empty Quarter, so when or heavily laden vehicles rolled out of Jirwan our Rub' al Khali crossing really began. Ahead of us lay 1,100 kilometers of dunes.

We perfected our sand driving over the first few days. All of us had studied bedu techniques, and knew that tires and tire pressure are the keys to driving in soft sand. We "aired down" our oversized sand tires—featuring soft-rubber tread, six-ply sidewalls, and very strong tubes—to about eight psi. Then it was simply a matter of maintaining speed to avoid sinking into the sand.

In trackless sands, the lead driver does all the work. The leader must make route decisions without slowing down, keep the vehicle moving up or down rather than across slopes, and avoid closed topographic lows with their notoriously soft sand. Most importantly, the leader must avoid taking dune slipfaces too fast or at too great an angle. This is not easy; driving downwind in flat light with no plants for scale is very stressful. Even the best dune drivers make mistakes in these conditions. Despite all his experience in the Rub' al Khali and innumerable other sand-sea penetrations, Gent carried too much speed onto a Jafura barchan slipface in early 1992. He planted the winch and flipped the Jimmy on its roof. It took a while to dig him out of the cab, but his careful welding on the auxiliary gas tanks paid off. The 500-liter fuel load did not explode.

Following is easy. We merely stayed well back and judged sand conditions by the leader's tracks. With five vehicles, we changed the lead every half or three-quarters of an hour, giving everybody a share of the excitement.

Our first objective was the meteor craters at Hadidah (Philby's Wabar). We knew Hadidah was about 100 kilometers southwest of our camp near

Aramco's old Ubaylah airstrip, but the craters were devilishly hard to find as their position never had been precisely determined. We reached the general area at midday, but well-spaced sextant LOPs (lines of position) and several five-kilometer box searches failed to reveal the craters by nightfall. We found Hadidah the next morning when we saw a dark plain from the crest of a dune. It was one of the famous "glass gravels."

When the meteorites hit the Hadidah dunes 6,000 years ago, the intense heat and pressure vaporized the quartz sand. The silica condensed into liquid drops, which fell back on the dunes as a rain of black beads. One-hundred-fifty meteorite impact structures are now known around the world, but only Hadidah is littered with these shiny "Saudi pearls."

We found only one of two craters sketched by Philby in 1932. The rim of this crater, just 100 meters in diameter, was still exposed when Aramco sent an expedition to collect the 2,045-kilogram Camel's Hump meteorite from Hadidah in 1966. But in 1990 we found that the dunes moving from the north had covered all but a quarter of the rim.

We spent a half-day at Hadidah, finding bizarre melted blocks of silica and limestone among the silica beads and rusted meteoritic fragments, before heading south into the center of the Rub' al Khali. We now crossed the last barchan-dominated rolling sands toward the beginning of the great linear ridges. The plan was to follow the linear trends some 700 kilometers southwest to the new Shororah highway.

The December and January rains had not hardened the sand this far south, and we began to get stuck. This, of course, is what people fear most about desert travel. There are tricks to getting unstuck, though, and a party with three to five vehicles should not be seriously slowed due to vehicles stuck in the sand. Progress through sand seas is mostly a matter of hard work. Our vehicles were stuck many times during the expedition, but they were quickly pushed, dug, towed, or winched out.

The linear ridges became higher and more continuous as we moved farther to the southwest. The interdunes were surprisingly soft, so we stayed low on the northwest slopes of the ridges. Three or four times every day we had to correct our course by crossing ridges to the south, so we had many exhilarating rides down the 35° south-facing slipfaces.

We began to see Pleistocene lake and pond deposits between the dunes. On one of these we found a single Neolithic projectile point. This find, at 19°51'N and 49°22'E, proved that Neolithic hunters penetrated 400 kilometers farther east into the Rub' al Khali than previously thought. A small brown rock at another lake bed attracted my attention, simply because it was 500 kilometers from any other rocks. It was very dense, and later petrographic analysis showed it to be a stony meteorite which extended the limits of the Rub' al Khali tektite field 200 kilometers to the southwest.

Old bedu truck tracks began to appear on the interdune plains, which were now frequently littered with both Paleolithic and Neolithic tools. We finally drove onto the new asphalt of the Sulayil-Shororah highway only 10 kilometers from the exit point we had projected months earlier. It had been expected that we would cross about 1,100 kilometers of Rub' al Khali sand from Jirwan to the Shororah highway; our Land Rover actually covered 1,106 kilometers.

Although elated at such a smooth crossing, we did not think of attempting another as we drove back to Dhahran in early 1990. Yet, less than two years later, we were planning a much more ambitious venture into the eastern Rub' al Khali. Mainly intent on reaching the giant sand mountains and pinnacle dunes, we planned a 1,700-kilometer loop south and east of Jirwan.

This new expedition would have been impossible for us in 1990, but in 1992 we had two dramatic navigational upgrades. I had gained access to the new 1:100,000 topographic maps of the Rub' al Khali, and four of us brought Garmin-100 GPS (global positioning system) receivers into the kingdom. The maps were of course photogrammetric and had not been field-checked, but the sand topography was shown precisely enough to allow identification of dune types and allow navigation through them if vehicles could be accurately positioned. The GPS technology had been available in Saudi Arabia for some years, and I had field-tested GPS against Loran receivers for Aramco, but it was the Gulf War of 1990–91 which brought full activation of this satellite system to the Middle East. With the maps, GPS units, and low-power radio receivers, we were now able to function as a single unit navigating "on instruments."

Many of the 1990 expedition members returned, but this was definitely a far more serious undertaking than the previous venture. Gone was the Toyota-From-Hell, replaced by a 1982 Blazer whose 350-cubic-inch engine Simmonds modified to deliver 350 ft. lbs. of torque at 1700 rpm. He also added four individually valved 100-liter fuel tanks. I replaced the clutch and put new 8.25" x 16" sand tires on our 1984 Land Rover 110. Gent and Kremla teamed up in Gent's 1985 Jimmy; Walter Schrick and Glover rounded out the four-vehicle team with another Blazer.

The GPS navigation worked superbly right from the start. We needed two fuel caches this time and were able to place them in featureless sand, where the bedu couldn't find them, because we could now reoccupy these locations months later with +/- 10–15 meters accuracy.

The first few days out, we crossed relatively easy rolling sand of the northern Rub' al Khali, and then moved into a unique belt of vegetated *dikaka* (hummocky, soft sand) which stretches down from Abu Dhabi. Tortuous progress in this maze gave way to rather more straightforward route-finding when we moved eastward into a broad zone of feather dunes. The crests of these dunes are so sharp that each vehicle bottomed on at least one and had to be pulled off. Since the feather dunes are elongated north-south with irregular slipfaces on the east, it was necessary to cross many of them and we needed a consistent way of approaching them from the west. Gent and Kremla gradually developed a complex technique which brought us to the tops of ramps splitting the eastern slipfaces. This type of navigation and route finding proved absolutely fascinating. It was rather like three-dimensional small-boat navigation through fixed waves hundreds of feet high.

After the feather dunes we entered the Zone of Death, as we had named this area of star dunes when we studied it on the maps. Only 80 kilometers wide, this band of complex dune topography was the last barrier between us and the great sand mountains of the far southeast Rub' al Khali. After a day of extremely complex route-finding, we emerged on a high balcony with a superb view down a sabkha valley receding eastward between two staggering ranges of sand mountains.

Here at last were our objectives. These sand mountains stand 180 meters above the perfectly flat plain over which they migrate. In the southwest Empty Quarter the linear ridges stretch for 100 kilometers parallel to the wind direction, but here in the east the sand supply is limited and the mountain ridges are normal to the north winds. Still farther east, as the sand supply is reduced even more, stand the unique pinnacle dunes. These completely isolated and star-shaped peaks rise as much as 190 meters above the plain. It was our intent to locate, climb, and photograph the highest sand mountain and the highest pinnacle dune.

The entire route to this point had been planned to bring us out of the Zone of Death at the head of a sabkha valley bordered on the north by Arabia's highest dune. We felt like midgets in toy trucks as we dropped down to the sabkha and started east, hemmed in by the monumental heaps of sand. The sand ridges have couloirs, aretes, and cols like those of the Alps, but here they endlessly shift with the wind. It wasn't long before one stupendous dune began to fill up the sky.

The highest dune rises 218 meters above the flats. We climbed it in a howling wind; I was glad I'd brought my climbing snowshoes. We took two GPS units to the summit and enjoyed a spectacular view while they acquired five satellites. The position was 20°40'43"N and 53°42'38"E.

The next morning, we drove on southeastward to our final outbound objective and turnaround point: the world's tallest pinnacle dune, 190 meters (623') high, at 20°N and 54°E. For hours we made good progress, crunching across the sabkha.

Then Gent's voice crackled over the radio: "Walter's wheel fell off." He didn't need to explain. When we'd gotten turned around and pulled up to the knot of Blazers, Gent was sitting on his roof rack staring down at Schrick's vehicle. He stayed there a long time, thinking, transfixed. Finally he said, "It's the C-clip."

Knowing which part had failed determined the problem's solution. We had no spare C-clips, but Simmonds was able to fabricate one from a nut of the right size and grade of steel. It took three hours and 20 minutes to repair the Blazer and turn it into a front-wheel-drive hybrid.

The outbound journey was at an end. Now, our GPS navigation capability was critically important as we planned the easiest possible exit route. We had to get back out of the east-west oriented dune mountain ranges and through the Zone of Death. West of Qalamat Tawil we knew there was a relatively easy "seam" through the heart of the eastern Rub' al Khali—an area where the high feather dunes marching down from the north gradually die out and the huge linear rides still lie to the southwest.

Climbing up out of the sabkhas proved difficult for the wounded Blazer, but we made good progress through the southern feather dunes and reached Qalamat Tawil in two days. Soon we began to see remnants of the 1950s Aramco exploration camps. Unusually steady rains hardened the sand and old Aramco junk became so common that we began calling our route the A-2030, as we were staying near 20°30'N. When we at last turned north along 51°E, we referred to the route as Interstate-51. We put air back in our tires and occasionally used our vehicle's highest gear as we flew along at 60 kph.

All five vehicles bounced through the puddles and back onto a paved road at Nibak in a driving rainstorm one day ahead of schedule. We had not achieved all our objectives, but had traversed 1,700 kilometers of the eastern Empty Quarter. We had navigated precisely through some of the world's most spectacular trackless desert, climbed Arabia's highest dune, and escaped with all our vehicles despite major mechanical problems. Our second crossing of the Rub' al Khali was over.

The most important single result of the 1990 and 1992 expeditions is that our small team is now able to operate in any part of the Rub' al Khali and locate any feature within it entirely independently. The type of research recently completed in Oman's Wahiba Sands is now possible in a sand sea 33 times larger.

Philby wrote that he would cross the Rub' al Khali twice and "leave nothing in it for future travelers." He did cross it once, and I have crossed it twice, but it remains a treasure chest waiting to be opened by all future travelers.

—*THE EXPLORERS JOURNAL*, FALL 1994

Jens Munthe, Ph.D. has conducted stratigraphic and paleontologic field programs in Wyoming, Nepal, Pakistan, and Libya. He has been a geologist with Mobil Oil since 1981, and explored many seldom-visited corners of Arabia while seconded to Saudi Aramco in 1988–1992.

Woman, You Are a Beast

BY JØRGEN BITSCH

"**W**oman, you are a beast" was the best compliment a Mongol could pay a woman at the time when Djengis Khan and his wild escorts flooded the greater part of the world.

The compliment was no doubt very flattering for the woman because it implied that he estimated her almost as dearly as his beloved cattle.

Today the population in Mongolia is stabilizing, but there are still many nomads in the steppe, and there you can still hear the old compliment: "Woman, you are a beast". It must be said, that the Mongolian woman is very flattered at hearing this, and until a few years ago she piled up her hair on top of her head so that it resembled a cow's horn and she made her dresses with high shoulders for the sole purpose of inspiring the men to make the flattering comparison.

When you have seen a Mongolian woman in her heelless riding boots with the turned-up noses, dressed in a silk cloak reaching her feet, which may not be too clean as she is probably busy collecting dried cow dung with a fork made from the ribs of a sheep (cow-droppings are the only kind of fuel on the treeless steppe)—then you understand why the Mongolian men have not felt inspired to use more romantic words of love. But still, the Mongolian woman works very hard for him and their children. Who then has got the time to be vain and to expect romantic declarations of love?

In the old times it was customary that the Mongol must carry off his wife, but this abduction was only a pretense—the Mongolian woman has always had a prominent position in the family—just like the women we hear about in the Icelandic sagas. She had authority, and when her husband was away it was she who bossed the cattle drivers. The Mongol often had to be away for a long time either going to war or on caravan trips, or maybe he went to stay in one of the Mongolian lama monasteries for a while. At one time more than one-third of the male population was enrolled in the many monasteries. During the revolution in 1922 there were more than 1,700, but today all the monasteries have been closed. The mile-long camel caravans have been replaced by railways or trucks speeding across the flat steppe, where there is seldom road or path.

Milk Foods

In the country the cattle people have established a thriving agriculture, but still many of the men work as herdsmen. The women tend the daily chores at the yurt.

Cooking does not take up much of her time. The only available vegetable is the wild onion and the main part of their food consists of milk foods, but not milk foods known to us. In the summer when you can milk the mares, Mongols eat nothing but fermented mare's milk, called *Kumys*, morning, noon, and night. There are weeks between meals of mutton. On the other hand, in the winter they get nothing but mutton.

The fermented mare's milk is alcoholic and therefore the Mongols' favorite dish. They get a little tipsy from it, which makes the Kumys all the more beloved.

If they can afford it, they make a salted tea. In order to make it taste good, it is necessary to add a big lump of butter.

150 Miles to the Nearest Neighbor

In the steppe, where there are often several hundred miles between neighbors, a visit is so unusual that it is a welcome excuse for celebrating.

Because of the great distances guests almost always come uninvited. They do not catch the housewife unprepared, however as she usually sees them from several miles away because of the crystal clear air of the steppe.

When a stranger approaches a settlement, it is good form for him to walk slowly until he is close. Then, he must stop and pretend to be adjusting the saddle — or find some other excuse for stopping — in order to await a message from the leader of the settlement that he is welcome. A stranger must always visit the yurt of the leader first.

In the meantime the housewife has had time to clean the yurt and to change into her prettiest silk-del. It is customary that the housewife sits to the right of the door with her pots and pans, a barrel of the fermented mare's milk, and—not to forget—a pile of dried cow dung for the open fireplace or for the oven, if there is one.

In the second part of the yurt the master of the house sits together with the leading men of the settlement. In the third part of the yurt, the most exclusive, the guest is placed on a small settee.

In the last part of the house, next to the door, the rest of the guests sit, one of their boots serving as stools. There are often many guests, if for no other reason than because they are curious to see the stranger.

Mongols slaughter their best sheep when guests arrive. I have often been invited to such a dinner and I always managed fine with the tea and Kumys. However, I must admit to having a hard time with the main course, as the guest of honor has to eat the sheep's eyes.

Watch Your Nose

After the guest of honor has swallowed the eyes, the others cut a slice of meat or intestines from the dish on the table. There are often tendons that cannot be bitten into. Then you have to use your knife so close to your teeth that you have to be watchful not to cut your nose.

Well-to-do Mongols serve *arkhi*, which is spirits distilled from milk. It hits you hard. When the meal is finished, the knife and fingers are dried on wearing apparel. Mongolian women do not wash dishes.

In a time when there is plenty of milk, the cream is dried into something resembling cheese. It is excellent for provisions if you are going far away. They dry it on the sloping roof of the yurt and it creates an odor which can be smelled a mile away.

Tending of the children is an easy task for the Mongolian women. They never have to wash diapers because there are no bottoms in the children's pants — not even in winter, when the temperature drops to 40 degrees below zero.

The older children can do almost as they please. Six and seven-year-old boys race over the steppe on the half-wild horses and spend a good part of the day helping the herdsmen or in play imitating their skills.

The Yurt

The rest of the housework is also easily done, because the Mongol's home consists of only one room only. The yurt, in fact, is worth some more discussion here.

When you approach a settlement, you can see the yurts from far away, each resembling a big white mushroom growing above the flowers of the steppe: It is the home of the Mongol. A yurt is a sort of one-family tent. The walls are made from wooden frames, resembling snow fences. Every unit can be folded, because the whole yurt must not be larger than can be carried by two camels or in a camel cart.

The wooden frame is about a meter high, and from the top there are poles gathered in a wooden ring in the middle. The outside of the yurt is covered by a sheet of linen which keeps out the rain, and on the inside are at least two layers of felt. In the wintertime, when the temperature drops, up to eight layers of felt are used for insulation. An open fireplace or a small oven serves to warm the interior as well.

In the old days rain could come through the opening in the roof, but modern ovens have metal pipes that cut through the wooden ring in the roof just like chimneys.

When television first appeared, it was often a matter of prestige for inhabitants of developed nations to have an aerial on the roof and it is the same with the Mongol's chimney pipe. They often buy one before they can afford the oven itself.

I Got Him Cheap

The furnishings of the yurt are simple in approach, as everything must be transportable. Most of the domestic utensils are kept in chests painted in bright colors. At the same time they serve as a kind of chest on which knick-knacks can be placed.

One of the first families whom I visited had for example a plastic bird, of which they were all very proud. They had bought the bird at the big market in Ulan-Bator on one of the national holidays, when a large number of nomads gathered in the capital.

On such occasions, the Mongolian is always tempted to have his picture taken by one of the many street photographers who do good business. A photo is considered a valuable possession, and it is placed together with other pictures and cuttings from newspapers in one big frame.

In many yurts Mongol families keep pictures of non-family members, and although the Mongols are very peace loving, they seem to prefer pictures of soldiers. When I saw such a picture in a yurt, I asked if the soldier had on a Russian or a Mongolian uniform.

"I do not know, I do not know the man!" answered the owner of the yurt—"but it does not matter, I got him cheap!"

The first thing one notices in the yurt is all the saddle gear hanging to the left of the entrance and the big wooden barrel to the right. In this barrel is *airak*, which is similar to the kumys—fermented mare's milk. Every day the women of the yurt pour fresh mare's milk into the barrel and mix it with the old and fermented milk. It is good form to help them in their work by stirring it every time you go in or out of the yurt.

A guest is received with a refreshment consisting of tea and very lean, pungent cheese. If the hosts want to honor a special guest, they offer him a lump of sugar or a caramel.

The people of a yurt rarely use more than a couple of kilos of sugar a year. Sugar is the family's only luxury. The tea which is served is made from leaves that they have gathered, or it may be a cheap Chinese tea, which is often used as means of payment instead of money. The tea is drunk out of politeness only.

Then the airak is served. It tastes a little like buttermilk and is served in bowls, containing 3/4 of a liter. If you want to continue being polite, you must drink at least two such bowls. When you are luckily through, you can risk being offered *arkhi*, a sort of spirit usually made from wheat, but in some places in the country they distill a similar fluid from airak. *Arkhi* is about 50% proof.

If you cannot pronounce "arkhi," you just have to swallow some; then you can pronounce anything. The airak and other products made from mare's milk play an important part in the nourishment of the population. Bread is virtually unknown in the country, as they do not grow enough wheat. Besides milk foods, they eat various kinds of meat. Intestines are considered a delicacy.

Progress is on its Way

The housewife is not overworked. You can see the women sitting for hours outside their yurts talking in the spring sun. They have much free time. And even though the Mongols have had about ten different written languages through the ages and still use three or four of them, there are no newspapers on the steppe.

In a few years the nomad life will come to an end. Formerly they traveled the steppe—not looking for grass, but for water for the cattle. During the last five years, hundreds of wells have been dug and dams been built, thus making it possible for them to settle down in one place. At the same time thousands of wooden houses have been built for the nomads.

The capital, Ulan-Bator, which in the old days was called Urga, consisted at the time of the revolution in 1922 of a few clay houses besides thousands of yurts. But today Ulan-Bator is a modern city with broad avenues and modern centrally heated flats. Horses are not allowed in the city, for Ulan-Bator must be kept clean.

Pretty Flower

About half the Mongols are dressed according to Western fashion, and the old "guttal," the boots with turned-up toes, are seldom seen in town today, thanks to a new factory that is now making millions of modern riding boots per year.

Most women wear riding boots, which is the most practical footwear in the cold and windy climate. Besides, shoes are considered a luxury and they cost more than boots.

Names such as Deligertzetzek, "Pretty Flower," describe the Mongolian woman of today better than the dubious comparison with a beast, because one thinks of colorful flowers when he sees a Mongolian girl in silk-del, shopping in the department stores in Ulan-Bator or enjoying the sun by the monuments on the broad avenues, or on the campus of the new university in Ulan-Bator.

The time is past when the most esteemed compliment was: Woman, you are a beast.

— PREVIOUSLY UNPUBLISHED

Born in Denmark during 1922, Bitsch is a member of The Explorers Club and had previously been President of The Adventurers Club of Denmark for five terms. Specializing in primitive cultures, he is a published author, with books circulating 18 countries, as well as a producer of documentary films on travel and exploration. A seasoned traveler, he has visited nearly all the countries in the world; his most frequent stops include the jungles of Borneo, Africa, and South America, and fifteen crossings over the Sahara Desert. Bitsch has since stopped writing books and instead gives tours with adventurous clients because he feels it is more important to share the places he has been with others than to write about them. Here, he shares his observations on Mongolian Women after traveling to Outer Mongolia four times.

Yeti Expedition

BY THOMAS BAKER SLICK

H aving read and heard numerous reports regarding the occurrence of an ape-like creature in the Himalayas, my interest in further investigation of this animal began to develop. I fully realize the scientific value of discovering even a new ape variety in a new area. If the creature should prove to be a man-like ape or possibly even a primitive human, as some of the reports seemed to indicate, the discovery would be of unique scientific importance.

After checking the various areas where the Yeti, as the reported animal is called, had been seen, we selected an area in the Upper *Arun* River Valley as being the most likely area. In this area leading off from the River, are three large parallel valleys known as the Iswa Kola, the Choyang Kola, and Sankua Kola. Slightly north of these lies the Barun Kola. The first three valleys which we covered to a considerable extent were, from all previous reports, completely unexplored by Europeans.

Most of our operations in this area were carried out at an altitude of between 12,500 feet and 17,000 feet. At the time of year that we were in this region the snow level was roughly around 12,500 feet. In the course of the trip, we came upon three sets of tracks with very considerable evidence that they were of the Yeti. One other set of the very small tracks might have been of some other type of primate, but this seemed less certain.

From discussions with the natives, as well as from previous reports, we believe that there are at least two types of ape-like animals in this area and perhaps three or more types. The large type is known as the Yeti. From eyewitness accounts, of which we had some fifteen, this animal would seem to average about eight feet in height, to be generally similar in appearance to a gorilla, to have long black hair which, curiously enough, is reported to point upward on the upper part of the body and downward on the lower portion.

Two reports describe a white band of hair around the middle. The face is similar to that of a gorilla but the head is very pointed in shape. The animal apparently normally walks erect on two legs and there were no reports of it being seen on four legs. It is fairly definitely tailless, according to eyewitnesses.

The other type of animal of a generally similar nature is referred to as the Meti. This animal seems to be generally similar but has reddish hair and is about five feet six inches in height.

There is a third type of animal, which the natives generally block together with the Yeti and the Meti in their discussions, called the Chutay, or as it apparently sometimes is spelled, the Dzu The. The reports on this Chutay are confusing but I believe that the chances are very good that it is the Red Himalayan Bear.

However, it might be a new animal of some other type and perhaps even could be a more primitive primate of some type. The Chutay walks on four legs, is tannish-colored, has a long snout, and is carnivorous.

In the course of our travels, we came upon three sets of what we believe are Yeti tracks. There is some confusion due to a difference in the shape of these tracks. One set of tracks was very human-like in general shape but larger than average (about 13 inches), broader, and with two sides of the tracks going back almost parallel, with no indentation for an arch being present.

The toes, which had a generally human arrangement, differed by cutting off almost even, with no drop back from the large toes toward the small toes, as in the case of a human foot. Besides the one set of tracks of this description that we saw, the natives generally describe the tracks from the Yeti as of this type. A set of tracks that Peter Byrne saw last year in Sikkim, which he was confident were the tracks of a Yeti, had this exact same description.

On the other hand, the other two sets of tracks were somewhat shorter (about 10 inches), considerably broader, and with the large toe and the toe next to it, fairly widely separated from the other toes. These tracks bear a very great resemblance to the tracks photographed by Sir Eric Shipton on the slopes of Mount Everest a few years ago. Both of these types of tracks seemed to be of a large animal walking in an erect, two-legged posture. We have no way to account for the difference in the shape of these tracks.

Alongside of these two sets of tracks, a fair number of long, coarse, black hairs and a few white hairs in one case, were found caught in the bushes and almost certainly originated from the animal making the tracks. A quite good plaster cast was made of one of the tracks of the Shipton type.

Some excrement was found near the set of the other type of tracks, although we were doubtful as to whether this originated with the same animal, since it appeared, judged by its appearance, to be more likely from a member of the cat tribe, perhaps from a snow leopard, although it was found near the Yeti tracks and no cat tracks were apparent. This excrement seemed to consist almost entirely of gray hair from some type of animal with some medium-sized claws contained, which might have been from some small gray cat-like creature.

Two sets of tracks were very fresh of the same day, and there were some considerable hopes that the animal would be caught up with. However, after following the tracks for about a mile and a half in each case, they were lost in rocky ground. All three sets of tracks were found near the snow line at around 12,500 feet. During the course of the trip, many natives were talked to, who had seen tracks of these animals, particularly in the wintertime when the heavy snows seem to drive the animals lower in the valleys and nearer the villages.

Winter certainly seems the most favorable time of the year to try to come upon these creatures, when they are lower and more concentrated and more available. Also, the call of the animal seems to be fairly well known and quite frequently heard in the wintertime, being described as a sort of yelping howl which the natives immediately recognize.

In the course of the trip, we talked to some fifteen eyewitnesses who have seen the Yeti. Besides the description that they gave us, as recounted above, we gave them a group of about twenty photographs which had been selected as being of animals that might be expected to resemble the Yeti, or conversely of animals that some of the scientists think might be confused with the Yeti. We asked these people to select the photographs that most resembled the Yeti.

It was quite impressive that there was a unanimous selection (of these photographs), in the same order, with the first choice being a gorilla standing up, the second choice an artist's drawing of a prehistoric ape-man, Australpithecus, and the third choice an orangutan standing up, which they liked particularly for the long hair.

When they came to the picture of the bear, which many authorities have thought may be the explanation of the Yeti, every one of the observers immediately said that this was a bear and not a Yeti.

Similarly, when they came to the picture of the langur monkey, which some other authorities have thought may have been confused with the Yeti, they immediately recognized this as a monkey rather than a Yeti. All in all, the eyewitness descriptions and the selection of photographs were most impressive evidence of the existence and nature of the Yeti.

In the course of the trip, we heard frequent accounts of the Yeti killing yaks, which it apparently accomplishes either by breaking its neck with its hands or by throwing the yak off a rock or a cliff. This does not happen frequently but a few cases occur almost every year.

The Yeti, which does not seem to be primarily carnivorous, in no cases eats the yak and seems to kill them from other motives than food. The diet of the animal is thought to consist of bamboo shoots, which are plentiful in this region, possibly roots of various types, insects, small rodents, and very possibly a variety of edible fern which is fairly prevalent in this region.

We also heard of a few cases, three identified by name and village within the last three years, where the Yeti has killed men. When it kills men it apparently has a normal pattern of eating the eyeballs, the fingers, the toes and the testicles, which might seem to resemble the practices of ritualistic cannibalism of certain primitive tribes, and which might indicate a fairly high position on the evolutionary scale.

From the various items of information that were collected, it seems almost certain that there are at least two types of ape-man-like creatures present in certain Himalayan regions which, from their erect two-legged posture, the advanced shape of their feet, and some of their habits, seem to be considerably above the development of the gorilla in the scale of evolution.

From the description, and the apparent size of the animal, an interesting conjecture, which has been suggested before by several anthropologists, is that the animal might be related to the extinct ape man *Gigantopithecus*, relics of which were found by the anthropologist, Von Koenigswald, in the caves along the Yellow River in China.

This ape man could easily have migrated through the Himalayan region. From its description, the Yeti could well be an isolated group of this creature which had been cut off and managed to survive under the unusual environment of this area. This of course is a conjecture, but one apparently with some likelihood of being true.

On our return, the hair and the footprint were turned over to the Department of Anthropology of Delhi University for analysis, and the preliminary report was of the opinion that they came from some sort of ape-like creature and not from a bear or any other routine Himalayan animal. The evidence seems very promising that the possibility of a most interesting natural history discovery exists, with the likelihood of a higher ape or primitive human type creature existing in the Himalayan region.

— *THE EXPLORERS JOURNAL,* DECEMBER 1958

Ruler of the Bush

BY G. VIC HURLEY

As every member of The Explorers Club knows, the deliberate seeking out of danger or adventure, is only an evidence of bad planning. Those of our membership accept the fact that there are certain elements of danger resident in the jungle or desert that we traverse, as we accept our reason for being there. Certainly not the least of the occupational hazards of travelling in south-eastern Asia and the islands that lie offshore, is the presence in all of that area of the King Cobra.

Professional herpetologists are not always in agreement as to the behavior of this great snake, and certainly the jungle-man, encountering the King in its habitat, may differ greatly with the scientists.

The terrain of the King Cobra is usually a tangled patch of high *cogon* or *tigbao grass*, and its den will be found in a cleft of rock, or in the tangled buttressed roots of a fallen tree. The meeting with a King Cobra might happen in this manner.

The man might be a timber cruiser crossing a clearing in the bush. As he approaches a huge fallen tree, there is a slight movement in the maze of interlaced roots, and there are eyes that are calculating and unwinking. An olive-bronze length, faintly striped with black, rises four feet from the forest floor. On the throat, flanked by the spreading hood, is a patch of orange. The head is small, the mouth open. The round brilliant eyes have an intense and penetrating stare. There is no sway in that erect and muscular length. The snake will stand rigid, watching the approaching man, in a position of calculating readiness. Behind the raised head, and half concealed in the twisting roots, is an awesome length of venomous creature; sixteen feet or more of undulating flesh, curling and sliding in the grass.

A hiss, loud and almost human in quality, proclaims the King's presence. The man notices a spot of orange on the neck of the raised length. The man stops. He is in the presence of *Naja hannah*—Ruler of the Bush.

No man, however brave, can face the King Cobra, particularly the female with young, without a flutter of the heart. It is an experience that may result in uncompromising peril. The man faces death, and the arena of action favors the snake.

This King Cobra is the greatest of the Elapidae, possessing a venom that disintegrates the nerve centers. A struck man or beast is left a quivering spastic mass in a few moments. There is no reprieve. The King is one of the most dangerous of all living creatures, for nothing that breathes can survive the unattended bite.

Even the elephant makes way. In the teak forests of south-eastern Asia, the timber companies occasionally lose tuskers. The great animals, bitten on the end of the trunk where the skin is thin, are stricken dead by a few drops of venom as casually as if the victim were a rabbit. Truly ruler of the bush, it is a creature with a weapon that can fell an elephant.

That weapon is a neuro-toxic venom lying behind the short, always-erect teeth. It is introduced by an aggressive chewing motion. The attack is prolonged, to allow time for the venom to run down the grooves on the outside of the teeth. The cobra does not possess the hypodermic-needle fangs of the viper; it bites and hangs on until the poison has been introduced. It is a dreadful appendage for a man to find attached to himself, with the tenacity of a bulldog.

Although the King has been documented to a length in excess of eighteen feet, it is not an impressive sight when viewed through the glass walls of a zoo. Save for those malevolent eyes and that awesome length, it can appear almost harmless. The King Cobra weighs barely a pound to the foot, bulking small in comparison with the massive *Reticulated Python* with which it shares the jungle. It is no more than half the weight, per foot, of the Texas Diamond Back Rattlesnake.

But the King can strike fear that can crescendo into panic. Confused and slow in tangled grass, a man is in grave danger. Let it be said—and let it not be the postulate of a thrill-seeking adventure writer—that the King will attack a man. The ground the reptile selects for the offensive maneuver is admirably suited to the proposition that the attack will be pressed home with success. Terror is always a possibility in the patches of high grass on the jungle edge, in Mindanao or in any other area where the King reigns.

A man is eye to eye with immediate death when that long bronze length slithers at him through the grass roots. One of the most breath-clogging sights in the world, might be that flutter and ripple of high grass, when the King rises to scan the victim with those bright shoe-button eyes.

There is no retreat. A man has to stand his ground as he faces a creature of dreadful venom, that is also standing its ground. That slither and rattle of scales in the grass-roots, can become the most terrible sound in the world.

A shotgun insures survival. Shot cartridges in a pistol are a handier expediency. A rifle or a hand-gun with ball ammunition, demands almost impossible accuracy at a twisting, looping target only half in view.

In Indo-China, the tiger hunters sometimes balance the odds with the use of double-barrelled rifles; one barrel with ball for the tiger, the other charged with bird-shot for the King. The jungle career men usually depend upon a belt weapon with shot cartridges. A shot-gun is an unhandy weapon in jungle.

The cobras belong to a large and lethal family. Their cousins are the *mambas*, black and green, of Africa, incredibly swift arboreal members of the family; the *krait* of Asia, small, aggressive, emaciated, and diabolical in temper; the marine *Hydrophidae* in all tropic seas, *banded sea cobras* as venomous as their cousins on land.

Australia is doubtfully blessed with the *black snake*, the *brown snake*, the *tiger snake*, and the *death adder*—nephews of the cobra, and as venomous. The island continent also supports a giant variety of the brown snake in the Cape York Peninsula. Until recently this large snake was believed to reach a maximum length of about eleven feet; it is now thought that it may be considerably larger, as a possible rival to the title of longest venomous snake now held by the King Cobra.

The Americas support one member of the cobra family, the bright ringed *coral snakes* of southern United States and Central America. These are sluggish and degenerate little reptiles but the fangs are dead-loaded.

The head of the family, the King Cobra, commands the jungle of all Indo-Malaya. It slithers in Burma, all of the Malay Peninsula, all of the larger islands of Malaya, the Asiatic mainland as far north as central China, and the islands of the East Indian Archipelago as far north as the Philippines.

On Mindanao, the King is in residence all along the coast of Cotobato Province, and in much of the interior. The King Cobra is not a rare snake, as scientists once assumed. All too frequently it is encountered in the half-felled jungle that has been hewed out for the coconut and rubber plantations. In sections of Cotobato, the inspection of young seedlings is a detail of some hazard.

This most intelligent of all snakes is insolent, curious and not to be bluffed. Everywhere in its habitat, the King is a citizen of bad repute. It will dispute passage of a jungle clearing and it will invade the bush house of an isolated planter.

The most dangerous characteristic of the King is its fondness for the haunts of men. A planter's house in the bush breeds odors, and results in an accumulation of waste products. Garbage draws rats from the jungle and the snake is attracted by the rats. It is inevitable that the house of the planter will sooner or later be investigated by the curious snake.

All of the King Cobra country supports stories of planters awakened by an awesome presence; of constabulary soldiers on outpost probing with flashlights to disclose alert death reared beside their cots. The sound of those scales, sliding across the grass matting on the floor, have brought men trembling from sleep to face death in the dark. Men have suffered horrible room-fear, confined within four walls, with a length of bronze death rearing an alert head in a corner.

The white man's house, or his plantation, is not wholly his own in King country. There in the shadow of the bush, or in the darkness of a room, the attention may be rivetted at any time, by a blotch of orange and a pair of bright and calculating eyes.

— THE EXPLORERS JOURNAL, MAY 1959

G. Vic Hurley, Lcdr Ret. Former war planning officer on staffs of Admirals Halsey and Nimitz; former cocoanut and rubber planter in the Philippines. Author of: Swish of the Kris *about the Moros, and* Jungle Patrol, *of the Philippine Constabulary.*

PART FIVE

Atlantic
Ocean

Rowing Across the Atlantic: Husband-Wife Team Proves it Can be Done

BY CURTIS L. SAVILLE

My wife, Kathleen, and I decided to row across the Atlantic Ocean to be part of a great new era of exploration. We also wanted to demonstrate the potential of solar energy and efficient design, to establish new standards for speed and safety in ocean rowing and to take advantage of a small, slow-moving craft close to the water to make contributions in oceanographic research.

Our Transatlantic Rowing Expedition was endorsed by The Explorers Club and awarded a grant. Flag #175 was carried on the voyage.

Edward Montesi designed a craft specifically for the expedition and supervised its construction. For seven months, beginning in June 1980, we worked at building the ocean rowing boat in a barn in Touisett, Rhode Island. Several friends from the Narragansett Boat Club in Providence, specifically Peter Wilhelm, a rowing coach and builder of racing shells, assisted in the building.

Using the "one-off" construction technique, a disposable wooden framework was built in the shape of the hull. Sheets of ¼" thick Airex foam core material were tacked to the framework and layers of fiberglass mat and cloth were laminated to the outside of the hull. The wooden framework was released and the hull turned over to apply the inner fiberglass skin to complete the basic hull fiberglass sandwich construction. Watertight compartments and cabins were added.

Twenty-five feet five inches long with a beam of five feet three inches, she has enclosed cabins fore and aft and an open, central deck area with two rowing stations. Sliding seats and oars of the type used in racing shells permit rowing with the efficient sculling technique used in competition. The boat has no auxiliary motors or sails.

Two banks of Solarchargers, solar electric panels, mounted on the roof of the larger forward cabin, supplied electricity to two heavy-duty 12-volt marine batteries stored below deck in the smaller aft cabin. Electricity was used to power radios for communication, navigation lights, cabin lights, and an electronic self-steering device attached to the rudder, which enabled us to maintain a precise course without the need to row harder on one side or the other.

Ocean trials were conducted in Narragansett Bay, Rhode Island Sound, and Chesapeake Bay. At the U.S. Naval Academy in Annapolis, where we were guests of the Navy crew, the craft was christened *Excalibur*, complete with a bottle of champagne.

A number of companies donated supplies and equipment. Included were hatches, ports, bilge pumps, paints, oars, navigation and weather instruments, clothing, radios, and safety equipment. Because ocean rowing, as in space exploration, has critical weight and space requirements, we contacted the U.S. Army Natick Research and Development Command, which plans the diets for the astronauts. With their assistance, menus were planned to provide 3,600 calories per person per day. Canned goods, dehydrated and freeze-dried foods, and fresh foods were taken.

Dr. Elijah Swift of the University of Rhode Island and Dr. James Butler of Harvard University assisted us in preparing to conduct observation and sampling programs in bioluminescence and pollution.

On February 18, 1981, we boarded at Baltimore the Yugoslavian freighter *Zvir* with our gear and *Excalibur* as deck cargo and headed across the Atlantic to Casablanca, where our rowing expedition would begin. We made friends among the crew and passengers who helped us work on our boat, stowing supplies, and making preparations for our return voyage.

In the congested, cosmopolitan port of Casablanca, *Excalibur* was lowered directly into the harbor waters. We said good-bye to our friends on the *Zvir*, climbed down a rope ladder and started rowing. The president of the local rowing club, Jean Francois Polizzi, and fellow oarsman Patrick Everarts de Velp, a diplomat from the Belgian Consulate, rowed up in a coxed pair, or skiff as it is known there. They escorted us the half mile to their club, the Société Nautique de Casablanca. Jean Francois, Patrick, and their families were our hosts for a week-long stay, helping us to procure last-minute supplies, treating us to banquets and showing us around Casablanca.

On March 18th, we climbed into our boat, heavily loaded with food, water, and the gifts our kind Moroccan friends had given us. The waving crowd receded as we pulled on the oars. One by one the escorting sailboats and rowboats turned. We rowed beyond the breakwater, out into the choppy seas of coastal Morocco.

The first leg of the voyage from Casablanca to the Canary Islands was a real horror. Adverse winds threatened to blow us onto the rocky shore. Ships came frighteningly close without seeing us, despite our radar reflector and navigation lights, slim protection against this danger in the storm-rattled highway of freighters, tankers, and fishing trawlers along the African coast.

The second storm pushed us 200 miles off course, into a region of the sea which is part of a war zone in the conflict over control of Spanish Sahara. Late into the night we pulled at the oars, rowing westward toward the Canary Islands.

Like shells exploding in the water around our boat bioluminescence excited by the stroking oars gave off the most spectacular display of living light we had ever seen. It was dark and clear and we felt suspended in a void. Bright stars reflected in the night-blackened sea, alive with thousands of sparkling points of organic light. From this now seldom visited region of the ocean we collected samples of the bioluminescence and sea water to take back to Dr. Swift at the University of Rhode Island.

The passage from Casablanca to Fuerteventura in the Canary Islands was completed in 24 days. The corrosive effect of sea water damaged wires leading from our banks of solar panels. Some of the watertight hatches leaked because of the constant pounding of waves during the storms. Some of the canned goods rusted, in spite of precautions to remove the labels, paint the cans with coats of varnish, and wrap them in plastic. Through a fortunate radio contact we rendezvoused with the yacht *Jangada* and were towed to the island of Tenerife, where the wiring was repaired and our stores replenished. *Jangada* once again towed us to Hierro, the westernmost island of the Canary chain. From there we began our row across the Atlantic to the West Indies on April 21st.

We were impressed by the power of the trade winds and waves in the Canary and North Equatorial Current systems, the great conveyor that has carried crafts large and small across the Atlantic for centuries. Our last sight of land disappeared from view in a cloud bank along the horizon early in the morning of April 22nd as we rowed westward. We knew only too well that there was no turning back. We were not strong enough to row against the wind and waves which helped push us along.

We wondered about possible voyages over this same route in ancient times. Major voyages in crafts such as Heyerdahl's Râ were certainly possible, but what of voyages in smaller boats? Would a fisherman blown off the African coast in a small boat strive to return against the unbeatable sea and die? Or would he conserve strength and continue patiently westward to arrive at some distant unknown shore and survive by gaining acceptance and adapting to a new culture?

Communication is an important element of safety on ocean voyages. Kathleen obtained her amateur radio operator's license and as a novice was allowed to transmit in Morse Code and receive code or voice. Biweekly contacts were made with Peter and Kurt Wilhelm in Rhode Island. At times of difficult transmission, other amateur operators relayed messages so that our families and friends could keep track of our progress. A TR-7 unit donated by the R. L. Drake Company was used for these contacts, as well as for time signals and weather reports. Dr. Van Cochran, who advised us on medical needs for the expedition, supplied us with a copy of DH MEDICO code for use in medical emergencies. In addition, a Sommerkamp handheld VHF radio was used for line-of-sight voice communication with ships, planes and stations on the island of Antigua.

During the voyage, we usually rowed between seven and eight hours each per day, mainly in the early morning and late afternoon and evening, to avoid excessive exposure to the hot, midday sun.

Birds were sighted almost every day, especially jaegers and petrels. We were surprised to see the birds so far from land. They would dive down and grab flying fish which seemed to be startled as we rowed through their oceanic backyards. Sometimes birds tried to land on our oar-shaft mast, used to support the radio antenna, navigation lights, radar reflector, and flags. But we were rocking around so much in the waves that they couldn't land.

We were also surprised to see bioluminescence virtually every night in the form of points of light that glowed briefly in the waves that broke against the side of the boat. Dr. Swift as well as the U.S. Navy, which has become involved in bioluminescence through research in submarine detection and communication, were most interested in these observations, which seem to suggest that living light at sea is more widespread than previously thought.

We were also able to collect samples of tar balls and plastic with living organisms growing on them. Pollution was seldom sighted except above the African coast and near the Canary Islands. Near Fuerteventura, samples of rain were collected containing appreciable amounts of Sahara sand. An ocean rowing boat is a unique platform for oceanographic research, from which significant discoveries could be made.

The early advent of the hurricane season made it imperative to complete the crossing as quickly as possible. We put on a big push to increase our daily mileage. Precise navigation was important for steering a straight and efficient course across the Atlantic. H.O. 249 Volumes I & II were used as well as noon sights. Easterly storm systems and the associated clouds and heavy seas sometimes gave us problems.

On June 3rd, we met the Spanish freighter *Atlantico*. They gave us a position check and supplies of fresh food. We found we had become very run down, perhaps due to a lack of vitamins found in fresh foods. (Our supply of vegetable stew, an important dinner menu item, had turned out to be rotten and inedible.) Bolstered by fresh green salad, cold milk, fruits, and vegetables, we continued on to Antigua, where a successful landfall was made on June 10th.

We and *Excalibur* were later transported to the Virgin Islands on a 96-foot schooner. From there, we obtained a complimentary passage from the S/S *Norway*, the largest cruise ship in the world, up to Miami, where we were met and hosted by Col. Gerry Bass of The Explorers Club and his wife, Carol. From Miami, we drove *Excalibur* back home to New England.

The voyage of *Excalibur* was more than an exploration of the sea. It was an exploration of ourselves. "Be a Columbus to whole new continents and worlds within you," wrote Thoreau, "explore the private sea, the Atlantic and Pacific of one's being. . . ."

Significant contributions can be made by amateur scientists. Man really knows very little about the complex relationships of the living creatures at sea, the probable birthplace of life on earth. How important are those relationships to the survival of life on the planet? How does man, the creature who alters his environment, affect the sea? Discoveries will be made which will gradually illuminate the answers to these and many other questions as we move forward into a great new era of exploration.

— *THE EXPLORERS JOURNAL,* MARCH 1982

Kathleen and Curtis Saville continued their small boat travels through the years; sailing/rowing expeditions to Northern Labrador and Baja California; a rowing trip down the length of the Mississippi river; and various other small boat adventures, including a number of solar motor trips on the Atlantic coasts of the United States and Morocco.

PART SIX

Canada

Pagans of the Pasquas

BY DONALD A. CADZOW

I t was during the summer of 1929. I was working among the Prairie Cree Indians on the Little Black Bear reserve north of Regina in Saskatchewan. I was endeavoring to piece together the almost forgotten fragments of their social organization and trying to collect ethnological specimens.

One day, old Buffalo Bill told me about a band of Salteaux Indians who lived about 150 miles northeast of Prince Albert, on the slope of the Pasqua Hills. He said they were real wild Indians; that they would not take treaty from the Government, refused to talk to missionaries, and that all the white people were afraid of them.

Two days later I was on my way to the country of these "bad" Indians. To an anthropologist, doing his stuff in the field, the story of an untamed, pagan band, hating white men with a fierce, vindictive passion, was just too good to be true and had to be investigated.

It is too long a story to tell how, after days of travel with a saddle horse and two pack horses, I finally found the camp of this band. It was pitched in a nice little grove of pines beside a good fishing stream.

My arrival was not an auspicious occasion. Two children playing on the bank scampered to the shelter of a dirty tipi, and to all appearances the place was deserted. But I could feel eyes watching me from every direction and hatred seemed to fill the air.

When I dismounted, half-starved dogs snapped at my heels. So I very carefully tied my horses to some handy willows and, going up to the nearest tipi, threw the door aside and in my best Cree asked politely for the Chief. I half expected a bullet or a knife for an answer, but a spoken reply came from the darkness: "He is in big tipi."

The big tipi was at the end of the row, at the farthest point from where I had tied my horses. My progress down the shore was made in absolute silence, except for the snarling, mangy curs that followed me.

I banged on the canvas door and, speaking again in Cree, asked to see the Chief.

After a few nervous minutes an answer came from inside, in surprisingly good English.

"Come in and tell me what business you have with me."

I threw the door aside, stepped inside, and stood waiting for some indication of friendliness. As my eyes became accustomed to the darkness, I saw a very dignified, white-haired old Indian sitting propped up on some skins and blankets on the opposite side of the tipi.

Walking around the fire in the center, I offered my hand to the Chief, but he ignored the gesture and told me to sit down.

At this time silence on my part was the best policy. So I sat down, filled my pipe and waited.

The old man stared at the fire for several minutes, and to my great surprise I saw that his eyeballs were white and that he was unquestionably blind.

Finally he said: "What can I do for you? Are you a missionary? Do you represent the Indian Department? I know from the way you act that you are not a trapper." This was all said in excellent English with a decidedly Oxford accent.

I carefully explained that I was an anthropologist.

"Oh," he said, "you are from the Museum in Ottawa."

When I told him I was from a Museum in New York, and was an American, the old chap seemed to be a bit more friendly, and the next two hours were the most interesting I have ever spent in an Indian camp.

He told me that he was called "Blind" Nippy, that he was the half-breed son of a great English Lord and had been educated in England. He elucidated emphatically and clearly several reasons why his long-haired people hated white men, "but," he sad, "an anthropologist is different; you are trying to understand us."

We talked economics, social organization, religion, and about the Great War in which he had lost two sons.

He was still friendly when I left to cook supper and pitch my camp about a half mile away, and I looked forward to seeing him again the next day.

I am still waiting to see Blind Nippy again. In the morning he and his band had vanished. Something seemed to tell me not to follow them.

I sincerely hope the old Chief still roams the Pasqua Hills with his unseen, wild band of long-haired pagans.

— EXPLORERS CLUB TALES (1936)

Donald Adams Cadzow was an authority upon North American Indians, particularly as concerned the Indians of the Northwest. His extensive and intensive expeditions into Northern Alaska, along those rivers of enlivening nomenclature—The Crow, Porcupine, Peace, Sucker, Slave, and Great Slave, his exploits in the upper Rockies and Mackenzie Delta, brought him in touch with such unique peoples and experiences as he describes to us.

PART SEVEN

Central America

Carmelita

BY TOM GILL

You go to woman? Remember your whip! —NIETZSCHE.

J ust at dusk we saw her.

She was standing knee deep in the lagoon, washing a cotton shirt, wearing only a skirt twisted about her waist. She may have been half-Indian or more, and her hair hung black and thick over her shoulders— the kind you want to run your fingers through. Firm, full breasts and satin-smooth skin with a ruddy warmth of healthy blood beneath, she made a lovely picture standing there in the Orinoco twilight. A superbly voluptuous animal—the kind you find only in the *tierras calientes,* and not often even there. She was probably no more than seventeen, just at the very height of her physical flowering.

Up the bank between her stood a palm-thatched hut, and beyond that the dark shadows of the jungle.

Jack couldn't take his eyes off her—which was natural, for Jack was just nineteen. I'd brought him up from Trinidad, a likable, clean-cut boy of British parents, extremely sensitive and filled with the ideals that youth picks up, God knows where, and that middle-age spends years in discarding. Jack's father held a tight little job in the British Government, and planned to send Jack to Oxford next fall. Until then the boy was to help me look up timber.

I paddled the *cayuka* nearer shore, and, seeing us, the girl gave a shrill cry back toward the house.

The man I was after came out.

He called himself Felipe Rojo, which was probably a Spanish form of Philippe Rouge; and, when I heard his French accent, I believed what they said about him lower down the Orinoco—that long ago he had drifted in from over Devil's Island way with no more luggage than a pair of striped trousers and a bullet festering in his thigh.

I had heard of Rojo for years. He was the one man who knew that pestilential part of the Orinoco, and made his living trading with the Indians, but very seldom going to any of the white settlements. A hard-eyed, big, hulking brute, with a deep, resonant voice. A man without fear or any of those cultural luxuries we call "finer feelings." There were no gradations about Rojo, no damned subtlety—black was black and white was white. He had a vocabulary of filth and invective that would have awed a Port Said prostitute, but in the two days I spent with him I found myself liking him. You knew where you stood with him—and so did Carmelita.

A word from Rojo, and she would scurry about the place, getting his meals, fetching demijohns of villainous raw brandy, oiling his boots, taking care of her man. A strange pair. At first I thought she was his daughter. He must have been a good twenty-five years her elder.

God knows whether she loved him or not, but she certainly had a healthy fear of him. Rojo was a pure specimen of the dominant male—not pretty, but thoroughly consistent.

Then and there Rojo and I made a deal. We would stay with him two days and he would show me where the best timber grew. So we talked, while the moon rose and the bats came out, and later I opened my flask of Fundador cognac. Rojo drank it like goat's milk, and when Carmelita helped him to the inner room, about midnight, he was singing in French. Later I heard a scuffle and the sound of Carmelita crying—crying in a low monotone, as an animal cries. Jack got up and went outside so that he wouldn't hear it, and next morning I saw two bruises on the girl's arm.

Jack stayed in camp that day, while Rojo and I fought mosquitoes through the bush, and, when we got back to the lagoon that night, Jack was in a ferment with the story of Carmelita's wrongs. Rojo beat her, abused her, led her a dog's life, until she prayed the saints for death—she had wept the tale to Jack, and the boy was ready to do violence. I quieted him down. Later a great yellow moon came up and Jack sat with Carmelita on the river bank, very close, talking lisping Spanish to one another while Rojo squatted on his threadbare haunches, with my brandy, paying no attention to them, launching his bellowing laughter out over the river. Meanwhile, Jack proceeded to fall in love.

It was a tough combination for nineteen sheltered years to buck—tropics, full moon, springtime, and beauty in distress. Jack didn't even try to buck it. That night he put his head under my mosquito net and whispered that he couldn't endure a lovely girl like that wasting her life on this big, brandy-sodden brute. Then he begged me to take her with us as far as Ciudad Bolivar. Rojo would be going down the river soon—there would be no trouble. Carmelita was willing, and at Bolivar she and Jack would catch the steamer to Trinidad. "We love each other," he ended.

I tried to picture those two very British parents when Jack brought home a half-caste Indian girl who hadn't the least idea whether the world was round or flat, what the pages of a printed book looked like, or, for that matter, how a water-closet flushed. I felt a responsibility toward those parents, and I counseled delay. We would go to Bolivar first and then make plans. But Jack wouldn't budge—if I wasn't willing to help him, he would find some way to go it alone.

So for the second day Rojo and I headed for the jungle, and when we got back Jack was more in love than ever, and Carmelita was having a marvelous time herself. She had braided brightly colored ribbons in her hair, the way the Maya women do, and I could see she was excited and very happy and a little tremulous. Her black, slanting eyes sparkled, and every time she looked at Jack I could see her breasts rise and her little hands clasp and unclasp.

It was a touching picture, but it might be even more touching if Rojo caught its significance. With a thoroughgoing realist like Rojo, the wise thing would have been to buy Carmelita. I suggested that to Jack, but he was properly shocked, as every good British schoolboy should be. There is simply no romance in buying a wife, and Jack really meant to marry her.

It was a job keeping Jack civil to Rojo, for the girl had shown him marks on her legs and shoulder, and a cut across her back that Rojo had given her.

"He even bites her," Jack fumed, and seemed indignant when I had no comment. "See here, you've got to help me," he pleaded at last, almost in tears. I gave in.

Next morning Rojo left for a trip down-river, and we waited around the bend in our *cayuka* until Carmelita joined us.

We made good speed all that day, for I didn't care to think of what might happen if Rojo got back unexpectedly and came after his woman. By the time we quit paddling the moon was up, and I turned my mosquito tent over to Jack and Carmelita, while I curled up on a poncho a little way down-stream. For an hour I sat smoking, thinking of those two children inside the tent, and of Rojo, and of laying in a supply of quinine when I got to Bolivar, and of this and that, and then I went to sleep.

Next morning Jack was unusually quiet, but I was busy getting ready for a three-day trip into the jungle. Jack's affairs weren't my business—my business was to find timber. So I left them together, and when I got back to camp I could tell something had gone sour. Carmelita was querulous. For one thing, her stomach may have been upset. She had got into the syrup and what little the termites had left of my sugar, while Jack sat at her feet, adoring and worshipful.

He was devotion itself. He had bound up her cuts and bruises and given her his wrist watch. He wouldn't let her cook. I think he even washed her hair. Jack was a great artist, only he didn't know it—he was creating a work of purely imaginative art out of a red-lipped little barbarian.

But they certainly weren't a picture of conjugal bliss. That night they went into the mosquito tent early, and soon I heard the angry tones of Carmelita's voice, telling Jack in Spanish to go away from her, and later Jack came out of the tent and walked over to where I sat.

"Quarrel?" I asked.

"I can't please her. Nothing I do pleases her. She says she is sick of me— sick and tired of the way I treat her. God! A person couldn't treat her any better, could they?"

I wasn't so sure. From Carmelita's standpoint I could think of many better ways to treat her. For whether she knew it or not, life for Carmelita demanded a touch of the strong-arm. She had to be dominated, even at the risk of a few bruises. It gave a zest to things, like red chile in your soup. Jack couldn't give her what she had been getting from Rojo in the matter of slaps, blows, and curses, and all this was bound up in Carmelita's simple psychology of love. I tried to get that across to Jack, but who can speak from one generation to another? I think I quoted Schopenhauer and Nietzsche, but it was futile to demand of Jack something he didn't have. He just wasn't the big, dominating male. He could have brought anything in the world to a woman except the thrill of physical violence. And Carmelita needed that.

I did suggest that he put off marrying her until he had seen his parents. He looked at me for a while, then he said, "But I've got to marry her now."

I went to sleep. When a boy looks at you in just that way and says just those words, the Gods themselves are powerless.

Jack shared my poncho that night, and when we woke the sun stood high above the jungle. The *cayuka* was gone, and Carmelita had gone with it— gone back to her brandy-soaked lover, where once in a while she could count on the supreme ecstasy of a wallop across the buttocks.

I wasn't surprised, but youth has an infinite capacity for suffering, and Jack took it pretty hard. So did I when I thought of the stolen *cayuka* and of the long tramp to Bolivar.

"What will become of her?" he asked me once.

I answered with unnecessary heat: "She'll go back and get hell beaten out of her. Then she will lie in his sweaty arms and she will be content."

"You mean she'll be happy?"

"Neither happy nor unhappy. Her life will be too simple ever to ask questions about happiness or unhappiness. And it will be utterly unimportant, just as your life and mine."

So we hacked our way up the river to Bolivar, where Jack left me and went back to his snug little Trinidadian home to prepare for Oxford, and I wandered around the upper Orinoco, sending back samples of timber to the States, fighting army-ants and scorpions and drinking water not fit for a hog to wallow in. And ten months later I came down to Bolivar again.

I asked about Rojo. They told me he was still living on the lagoon. Yes, Carmelita was with him. Did he still beat her? Not so much now. You see, she has a baby—only a month old.

I wondered about that baby.

—*EXPLORERS CLUB TALES* (1936)

Tom Gill surveyed forests from the air contiguous to the Caribbean. He explored the delta of the Orinoco. That he surveyed other matters than those purely arboreal, with a keen sense of humanity, is evinced in this yarn of "Carmelita".

Eyes in the Night

BY SEYMOUR GATES POND

My comrade and I had been pushing up river through the steaming Darien jungles for three days and parts of three nights. We had two *cayucos* or native dugouts with four Darien Indians poling and paddling. It was mid-November, the height of the Rainy Season, and on this particular night the heavens had been sluicing down over us with unbelievable torrent. Even though in oilskins, we were soaked to our skins and haggard from lack of sleep and heavy dosages of quinine.

Our *cayucos* were sloshing with rain water and much of our equipment, though protected in pure rubber bags and coverings, was wet. Our destination was the reptile country at the headwaters of the Rio Yape on the Panamá-Colombia frontier, which we expected to reach in about three more days; and this, it might be explained, was for us the most opportune season for our work.

We needed a respite, though, badly, as did our Indians. We were seeking a plantation along the river for such rest when, about three in those morning hours of deluge and wind, a livid flash of lightning revealed momentarily the wet-shiny tin roof of a planter's *finca* some two hundred yards back from the river bank. Pulling against a swift current our Indians caught the small dock where we made fast. Six water-soaked humans, we wended our way between two wind-lashed lines of coco palms to the jungle home.

"*Oye, de la casa!*" I yelled through the boom of the storm, and:

"*Despiertese!* Awake!" shouted our Indians.

The house was a two story frame building. Presently from the circular veranda above, a door banged. The arc-white glare of a portable carbide gas lamp revealed a huge German with six-gun strapped over his pajamas. Rubbing the sleep from his heat-riven eyes, he growled, in Spanish:

"What's the trouble?"

In brief we explained that we wanted shelter from the storm and a few days' rest, if possible, on his *finca*.

"Well," he grumbled, in what amounted to: "This ain't no country boarding house, you know! Go in, downstairs, to the kitchen. Here, take this light." He lowered it over the balcony through the rain. "I'll get some clothes on and be down. Hell of a night to be out."

A few moments later in his kitchen the German surveyed us with his steel gray eyes. We stood, on his handmade cement floor, in six abundant pools of water, a mighty bedraggled six. It was very apparent that as guests we were not at all welcome. The corpulent German said:

"Well, get your wet things off. I'll build a fire. You'll need something to eat and—drink."

Our equipment was brought up from our *cayucos*. From somewhere out of the shadows of the German's establishment there appeared a tall Darien Indian. He was a splendid specimen, well over six feet, broad shouldered, muscular, coal black hair and eyes, and intelligent. To him the German said:

"Mocoa, make coffee. Make it strong."

"*Si, Señor.*"

Soon the German had bacon and eggs on the fire. Conversation went on apace, all in Spanish, as the planter spoke no English. Mocoa, the big Darien Indian, glided about, efficiently getting things done, and it was a joy to watch his each lithe, unwasted movement. Through it all, though, we could feel those cold gray eyes of the German watching us surreptitiously, critically, almost—we felt—with suspicion.

When we finally pulled up to his big round eating table with the rain booming down outside and the thunder rocking the jungle, he faced us questioningly from the opposite side of his table. He had produced a square-faced quart bottle of Gorgona Rum. Glasses were waiting. For a brief, awkward moment the German stood there looking at us oddly, one hand on the cork of his rum bottle undecidedly. Then he put a question to us, our answer to which, it appeared, was to determine whether or not we would obtain the hoped-for drink. He said:

"You fellows say you're here on an expedition. That's all right. Maybe you are. That's none of my business. But tell me, what do you do when you're—when you're *not* exploring? Naturally you don't do this exploring and adventuring *all* the time. What do you do, I mean, when you're up home there in the States?"

I looked at my comrade who shifted a bit uneasily in his chair, and then back to the German.

"Why," I replied, "we—we both write. You know—articles for the newspapers, stories for the magazines, and so on."

And somehow that explanation sounded very inadequate there in the storm-thundering forest night. Apparently the German felt so, too, for his jaw clicked to, unpleasantly. With a scurrilous tone he commented:

"Hmph! Oh-h, *writ-ers*, ehh!" There was a sarcastic whip to the enunciation of the word *writ-ers*. He still held the cork of his waiting rum bottle, just as if, after all, he might decide that we were not worthy of the drink he was considering. But finally after an uncomfortable silence, he said condescendingly:

"Oh, well, hell! I guess none of us is perfect. Have a drink, anyway!"

We drank, but that drink was a long-remembered one. We knew he must have something on his chest against writers, and it wasn't long in coming off. He was that kind. With a deep, unpleasant grunt he stated:

"You know there was another *writ-er* through here a few months ago, too. His name was — —. You know him, eh? Yeah, prominent, I guess. Well, he stopped here on much such a night as this. Said he had come here to go jaguar hunting. Hmph!" he snorted. "Some hunter!" He cinched up his belt savagely. "Maybe you fellas'd like to go jaguar hunting, too, eh-h?" His heavy bull neck shot forward, and he eyed us questioningly. It was a challenge. We felt the viciousness is of his glare.

I looked at my comrade. He returned the look with a wry smile. Neither of us had ever been on such a hunt. It sounded exciting.

"We, yes," we replied, we thought we would.

"Oh-h, so you do, eh-h? You think *you'd* like to go jaguar hunting, too? Ha-hah!" he chortled, and it wasn't a pleasant laugh. "Well," he explained in a more natural tone, "I sure would like to get a few more of those big cats. They've been bringing down my cattle almost every night, and killing my hogs wholesale."

After our meal, and once more in dry clothes, our host showed us to a clean bedroom with two spacious and comfortable beds.

"Sleep well," he suggested pointedly. "Tomorrow night we hunt *El Señor Tigre.*"

Left to the privacy of our quarters, my comrade turned to me thoughtfully and said:

"Well, *compañero*, it looks as though we sorta got ourselves in for something, doesn't it?"

"It does," I admitted. "Just how much, tomorrow will tell."

The night arrived. Mocoa, the big Darien Indian, sitting on the ledge of his nipa hut, faced us. His black eyes were shining with the eager anticipation of the hunt.

"So! Thy first jaguar hunt, *Señores*? *Dios*, you will love her! No, the *Señor* German *dueño* will not be able to accompany us. You see, we just got word the fruit company's boat will be here tonight for bananas. But, *Señor*, you are a good shot? That is well, for sometime if the jaguar she have left enough strength, she charge, and that is not always pleasant.

"The jaguar, you know, she is always hunt by the night in Darien. After the midnight is best, when the animal think man asleep. The darkest night is better, then our lamps shine brightest. This night she be very dark. It is well. Thy first jaguar hunt must be profitable and—exciting."

It was about two A.M. when Hartwell Ayers, my boon traveling companion, fated to be killed a few months later in the Panamá revolution, and I gathered at the big *piragua* or large dugout at the German's dock. The night was stifling hot with intermittent showers. The five of us dropped into the long, narrow *piragua* and pushed out into the strange river now swollen from the torrential November rains.

It was a never-to-be-forgotten night. On the black, roaring waters we dipped and swayed precariously between the shadowy, clifflike walls of the jungle on either side. Great tree stumps torn from the river banks by the angry waters bobbed their grotesque heads like shaggy water monsters at us, or grated menacingly under our hull as we raced in speechless speed down the current, our Indians struggling with poles and paddles.

After about an hour Mocoa guided our *cayuco* into a dark, swirling lagoon. As I bent out onto the bank, one foot on the shore, the other holding our dugout, an ear-splitting explosion flamed over my shoulder. There followed a terrific lashing of the waters under me between the dugout and the bank. A dark object some nine feet in length hurled past me and plunged into the churning waters. Mocoa had shot an alligator between myself and the bank! The cruel and powerful tail, able to mash a human body to pulp, had barely missed me.

"In the jungle one needs to have eyes in the back of the head!" complained Mocoa in a low voice.

We now pushed up into the jungle and with our *machetes* cut our way to a clearing. Here Mocoa, Ayers, and I put on our hunting lights, small carbide lamps like miners' lights, with straps to fit around the head. Carefully we adjusted our lamps so the light beams would shine down our rifle barrels and over our sights for accurate shooting. Mocoa assigned a single Indian to Ayers and the other to me to carry our rifles, while we took *machetes* in hand.

The desolate jungle brush through which Mocoa now took us reached for the most part over our heads. At times banana plants made a sixteen to eighteen foot ceiling above us. Heavy perfumes of *dama de noche* flowers mingled with the dank odors of decaying ferns and acrid miasmic exhalations. As we moved through abysmal tunnelings of foliage and darkness the shadows thrown from our light beams made Indian and white man appear huge and fantastic gargantuans stalking through some unbelievable land of giants.

There came a low cry on the trail. Suddenly Mocoa's *machete* flashed down a light beam. We stared into the oozy-wet ground. Two severed parts of a gorgeous vermilion and ivory reptile twitched and wriggled over the morass. "*Corál!*" spat Mocoa. "Bad!"

No larger round than a lead pencil and not more than a foot long, this little reptile, known as the *corál*, is deadly venomous. "The twenty minute snake" the Indians ironically termed it, for within this time the venom from its tiny fangs spells end to its victim. We continued on, cutting and slashing with our *machetes* until we came to a distant clearing. Here our guide astonished us by saying abruptly:

"Now we make three parties into one triangle. Mocoa go 'up' end of triangle. One white man go shore end, other white man go deep forest end triangle. Jaguar she in middle, then we close, so . . ." Under his light beam Mocoa sketched a crude diagram on the morass enclosing the imaginary jaguar.

"And remember, *Señores,*" he cautioned emphatically. "Go so very still. In jungle Indian have saying: 'He who go gently go safe, he who go safe, go far!' That is well remembered."

We rose to our feet. The breath caught in my throat. We were to go into this lonely, mysterious forest to look for wild jaguars—alone! Ayers looked at me, and I looked at Ayers. Our first jaguar hunt! Both of us had cold chills, but neither of us secretly would admit it before our Indians. Mocoa unheedingly added:

"Mocoa go alone. White man each take Indian to carry gun. Make careful no shoot at mans. Also take much care for snakes. We go!"

Go, we did. We parted three ways, my companions' two lights vanishing in the blackness of the wild forest. My Indian padded along silently behind me. We did no cutting of brush now, but poked into the darkest pockets, squeezing quietly between the thickets. Now and then the Indian would tug at my shirt and we would study the trail. We found jaguar prints, four little toe pads in front, and one in the rear. Their ridges were moist, indicating the animal was near. It was becoming exciting.

Every now and then we would halt and I would throw my long beam into those dark holes or grottoes before us and we would poise, listening, watching. Once two eyes gleamed from the end of a dark tunnel, low down. My Indian was tugging at my arm fiercely, silently; there was desperation in his movement. Softly I raised my .30-.30. The two coals of fire lifted and went waveringly, ghost-like upward. It was a tinamou bird.

I realized now that my Indian had been trying to urge me to caution against an unnecessary shot which would frighten away our jaguars. He had patience and stealth, this Indian, and the soul of a hunter. I was losing my awe for the forest night in the thrill of the hunt, catching something of the magic of the hour, when very suddenly two jets of flame blazed up my light beam alertly. This time my Indian did not tug at my elbow. He was all silence. I stared with trembling thrill. Was it . . .?

Softly, again I raised my rifle. My light beam found the sights. Careful aim. It was deathly quiet. Just the drip-drip of moisture from the banana plants to the morass below; somewhere a perdiz bird called dismally. Finger drawing back steadily on trigger.

Crash!

The explosion echoed and reverberated through the deep jungle to the hills, and back again. Two eyes, blazing larger as they came, charged up the light beam and fell with a dull thud almost at our feet. There was a low, savage snarl, a twitching, and quiet. A soft, tawny body some three and a half feet in length stretched before us.

"*Tigre!*" breathed the Indian, bending over joyfully.

Another jaguar with his insatiable curiosity had come too close to the white man's powder stick. And the Indian—until now, never a sound, never a tremor, all patience. Truly, he had the soul of a hunter.

Too, he seemed the embodiment of Mocoa's fine jungle adage, which was so often to recur to us on the expedition: "He who goes gently goes safely, he who goes safely, goes far." What a meritous expression, we often remarked, for any explorer, any adventurer, any expedition!

* * *

The next day when we were on the German's small dock loading our equipment back into our *cayucos* to be along on our journey, now rested and
refreshed, we saw the old German talking intensely with Mocoa, obviously
getting all the details of our hunt. And while, from the beginning, he had
obviously not been at all anxious to have us appear at his *finca*, nor to have
us around, he now came over to us eagerly, and with his characteristically
gruff, and almost angered tone, admonished us with:

"So, you're going up river, eh? Leaving me already? Going to stop at that
Swede's place, too, eh? My rival! Well, what's the matter with *my* place, huh?
Why don't you stay *here* a while? We can do some hunting together, and
there's plenty of snakes right here. We can find them together. The Swede's
place is rotten anyway. He's overrun with red bugs, *niguas*, scorpions, taran-
tulas, mosquitoes, and snakes. His camp's reeking with fever. *He's* drunk all
the time and fights like hell. What's the matter with *me*? Ain't I good enough
for you? This is just as good a jungle as you'll find at that Squarehead's *finca*.
Maybe I'm too sour, eh?"

"You're tops with us," we replied smilingly, and we meant it. We thanked
him for his liberal hospitality and the interesting hunt. "But we have to be
pushing on. Maybe we'll see you again, though. Perhaps coming down river,
if it's in the daytime. So long!"

"Well," he grumbled, half under his breath, "anyway, *buena suerte*, good
luck, and good hunting to you."

— *EXPLORERS CLUB TALES* (1936)

Seymour Gates Pond trailed in Mexico, Lower California and South America,
as explorer, correspondent, and navigator. He was last seen heading out of
Panamá. This yarn of his, with its setting in Columbia, is, of course, a personal
experience.

Men Who Can't Come Back

BY W. E. AUGHINBAUGH

T he out-of-the-way places of the world are filled with the men who can't come back. I have seen them all over the earth and, due to the fact that I have attended many of them professionally in their last illness, have learned from their own lips the reasons for their exile—the secrets that they were hiding from their fellow men.

They have crossed my path in the most remote localities. In the Khyber Pass, that hostile thoroughfare between Northern India and Afghanistan, I met one serving under the British flag. At Oran, in Algiers, the headquarters of the famous French Foreign Legion, I ran into a lawyer from home who had killed two men—and disappeared. Others I have met in Persia, in Arabia, in Somaliland, and in Jerusalem. Two years ago I encountered at the Assuan Dam in Egypt an old schoolmate in charge of a group of laborers. The reward for his return to the States had reached five figures. Hongkong, Shanghai, Port Said, Korea, and the Mediterranean littoral harbor these social outcasts, scattered about in profusion; the islands that dot the dreamy Pacific conceal many from inquisitive eyes. But, of all countries, those of Latin America, owing to their nearness to the States, seem to offer the quickest haven to the frightened offender. Each of these republics has far more than its quota of men who are endeavoring to hide themselves and forget!

Many are trying to drown their remorse in drink and, in their efforts to accomplish this purpose, have sunk lower in the scale of civilization than beasts. I knew an ex-bank president from this country, a defaulter, who by some means had attached himself to a tribe of Carib Indians. Ignored by the men of the clan, he carried water for the women and did their chores. His feet had not seen shoes for years and his matted beard and disheveled hair reached the waist-line of his ragged undershirt, which with his trousers formed his only raiment.

At the sea wall of a Central American port, gazing eastward with inquiring mien from dawn to dusk, stands "Napoleon." When he came there or how, no one knows. Even his name has been lost in the years that have passed since his arrival, for he is now over seventy. But a faded soldier's uniform, his precise mannerisms, a hat such as the famous military genius affected, the wisp of hair on his forehead, the fingers of one hand concealed beneath the front of his coat make him a startling reproduction of the Little Corporal and give him the name by which he is locally known. He speaks to none, but stiffly salutes all passers-by. Mild and inoffensive, the police let him sleep in the balmy tropic air of the little park; the local tailors patch his tattered uniform; the charitable hand him food or money, and each morning for more than twenty years he has been the first customer of the local barber, whose tonsorial attention he repays with a gracious elevation of his hand to the brim of his *chapeau*. Rumor has it that he was a West Point graduate who in a fit of passion killed his fiancée and escaped. Fate has been kind to him, for time has blotted from his mind all recollection of the tragedy. Yet each sunrise sees him at his post and each sunset finds him on guard, wistfully, sadly looking out to sea.

In nearly every instance that I recall, a woman has played a leading rôle in the drama which has left its principal actor stranded on these foreign shores. I know that I could fill a book with the pathetic stories told me by these world-weary ones in their faltering journey to meet mine host of the inn at the end of the road.

Of all that I knew in my twenty years' practice of medicine, the one that surges to the front when I think of these men is White—at least, that is what we called him, but we knew it was not his right name. In the outposts of civilization it does not behoove one to be unduly inquisitive. I knew him as "White" for nine years and learned his real name only two hours before his tired spirit entered the next country.

I was the surgeon of a railway in a Latin American country, which out of respect to the memory of White shall be nameless. The road ran from a typical coast town on the Caribbean Sea, with its pastel-shaded adobe houses, up through coffee *haciendas*, perched high on the side of verdant mountains, and on into the rich hinterland. Its termini were the capital, in a valley of the interior, and the port I have just spoken of, which is today, as it was then, a hotbed for beri-beri, bubonic plague, and yellow fever epidemics. The hospital of which I was in charge was situated half-way up the mountain, so as to be readily accessible to both ends of the line and in order that the patients might benefit by the salubrious air.

The station-master at the port end had just died of yellow fever when White walked into the office of the general manager and applied for the vacancy. He spoke Spanish perfectly, was well built, deeply tanned, and heavily bearded. His clothes were torn and travel worn. He told the road official that he had walked over the mountain into the city. A few questions elicited that he was an experienced railroad man, and, despite the fact that he was without testimonials or references, he was employed, for men were hard to get who would stay in the heated inferno of the port.

The new station-master made no friends. The English-speaking engineers, conductors, and others could not fathom him. He was polite, but distant, and had no confidant among them. He knew his business—kept the docks free of cargo and ran the trains on time—and that was all that was expected of him.

His palm-thatched adobe hut was in a coconut grove, so close to the beach that during the equinoctial storms it was often splashed by the spray from the restless, troubled sea. Its furniture was meagre. An old hag of an Indian woman cooked his scanty meals and spread the news around that each night, after the cares of the day were over, the *señor* drank rum until he became maudlin drunk and then, alternately talking and crying, went to sleep. He was always the first to be up and around the railway yard in the morning, however, and none the worse for his debauch.

He never received any mail. He never borrowed books or asked for papers from the States, the one thing that outcast men crave. Once each month he would give the chief engineer of a ship that came from New York a letter to post. What he did with his money, no one knew. What he thought, no one cared. Thus he lived for the nine years he was with the company.

In the sixth year of his service, he sprained his ankle by jumping from a shifting-engine in the yards. I attended him, but he refused to go to the hospital, preferring to remain in his hut by the sea. During the first few days of his illness, I came down the mountain to treat him and was conscious that my ministrations were being appreciated. Although he was decidedly taciturn, it was apparent that he had had a thorough education. I recall him quoting Omar Khayyam, another time Thanatopsis, once Virgil, and also Confucius.

Twice a week after his recovery, he would send me a live fish in the water tank of the engine, for we had no ice, and once in a while, a large lobster. These were the nearest approaches to friendship which he made toward anyone. My repeated efforts to get him to spend Sunday or the week-end with me were politely declined. To the consul, the only other American in the town, he was distant and cold.

One day a case of plague, that dreaded tropical disease, was reported at the port. Before the week ended, there were three hundred new victims and the "Angel of the Darker Drink" was gathering a rich harvest. The town was suffering from its usual epidemic, which this year was attacking Europeans and Americans and was of a particularly violent type.

The engineer of one of the "up-trains" sent me a note saying that White's old Indian servant had hobbled to the cab door to tell him that her *señor* was complaining, and she asked that I be notified. I had the operator telegraph White, asking how he felt, and received an assuring reply. The evening train brought up a large lobster, as proof of his ability to be around. The next day he did not report for duty. I telegraphed again and was informed that he felt all right. About midnight the watchman came to the hospital with orders from the general manager for me to meet the light engine which would arrive shortly and accompany it to the port, where I was to attend White, who was reported in a precarious condition from the disease then so prevalent.

I can never forget that night ride down the moonlit mountainside, with the sea at its base. Two o'clock in the morning found me at White's bedside. His was a typical case of plague and it was apparent that medicine could do nothing to aid him. I told him of the seriousness of his condition and stated that dissolution was usually preceded by a period of coma, from which one passed into the great beyond. "Have you any message to send? Do you wish to make a will? You can trust me," I urged.

Telling me where to get paper, ink, and pen, he dictated his last testament, leaving his money to a daughter, whom he named and whose address he supplied. After signing the document, he turned to me and said:

"Doc, my name is not White. It is, as you see, _____. I was the manager of the (here he named a famous Latin American road). I graduated from Cornell, married a beautiful girl from my home town, and took her with me to live in a bungalow facing the sea. Our happiness was ideal. A girl was born, to whom I have left everything.

"My assistant was a Jamaican—a half-caste with sufficient Negro blood to make him positively handsome. He was as lithe as a deer and strummed a guitar as he sang romantic songs of Spain. It was the old story. The spell of the tropics came over my wife. If a woman is to go wrong and a hundred men are to know it, her husband's number is one hundred and one. I came home one day and the mother of my baby was gone. So was the Jamaican. When I expressed surprise, everyone intimated that they had expected such a thing for a year or more.

"I took our baby home and left it with my sister, who has devoted her life to raising and educating her. Then I came back to locate the woman who had seared my soul and the man who had wooed her from me. I knew I'd find them with some railway in these lands, and so I wandered for four years from road to road seeking them.

"At last, in the mountains of Peru, I found them. In the dead of night, with the winds howling a requiem and the snowflakes to soften my approach, I entered their home. Sleep was heavy on their eyes as they lay together, and, by God, I cut their throats!"

I can never erase from my mind the dramatic fervor of the man—his tense emotion, as tremblingly he raised himself from the bed and, with glaring eyes and shaking hand and rasping breath, drew an imaginary dagger across their throats. The moan of the wind through the palm trees, the lisping, sobbing waters as they lapped the shore, and the shimmering light of the tropical moon, all added a nocturnal accompaniment that intensified the scene.

Then, after a pause, he resumed.

"I closed their books forever and gloated over my work that night. With the coming of day, I made my escape from the scene and walked and walked, a haunted man, through the backwoods of Peru, Bolivia, Ecuador, Colombia for nearly six years, until I found myself here and secured the position I now hold. Every month I send a draft to the little daughter that I carried home in my arms. She has now grown to early womanhood. I have never seen her and don't want to, for she is a replica, I am told, of the mother in beauty and mannerisms. She does not know that I live. That is why I have kept from my fellow men and from you. That is why each night I sought forgetfulness and solace in drink. I have but one favor to ask—promise never to tell my family name to anyone."

When the sun rose, its rays filtered through the window blinds and rested on the quiet form of White—peaceful in the majesty of death. And I, his only friend, the only one to whom he had confided his life's secret, fulfilled his every wish and buried him and kept my promise.

—*TOLD AT THE EXPLORERS CLUB* (1931)

Physician, lawyer, university professor, editor, author, and worldwide traveler, Dr. Aughinbaugh had a life of rich and varied human contacts. Important academic and journalist positions in New York City alternated in his active career with more than a score of years spent in medical research and practice among primitive surroundings on the far-flung frontiers of civilization.

He saw service on the Bubonic Plague Commission in India, Burma, Arabia, Afghanistan, and the Shan States, also in the investigation of the pneumonic plague in China. He was in charge of leprosy hospitals in Latin America and has battled verrugas in Peru, trachoma in Egypt, Arabia, and The Levant and the hay-fever problem in Labrador!

He published Selling Latin America *and* Advertising in Latin America *and planned three volumes based on his experiences, of which the previous story was a foretaste.*

The Capture of an Ant Army

BY HERBERT F. SCHWARZ

Mr. Schwarz, I have been after you for some time to get you to tell us something about those ant armies you like so much. Before you do, I have another martial story to tell, really a record story.

Seyward Cramer claims that one phase of his military career established a record for speed in promotion.

Cramer was living in Tsingtao, China, at the time. The European colony had planned a fancy dress party but, being upcountry at the time, he knew nothing about it until he returned the day of the party. Those affairs were rather rare and not to be missed. It was too late to have a costume made, so Cramer had to rely on something ready-made.

He finally hit upon an outfit, a bit macabre but quite appropriate as there was a bit of bandit trouble in the area and the military execution squads were working on regular schedule. He would wear the uniform of a member of the squad, beheading sword and all. The tailor made the uniform in a couple of hours, and it was a good fit.

Late in the afternoon, during the social hour among the Chinese, Cramer hopped into a carriage to call on the Military Commander, General Pi Shin Fong. General Pi was used to the odd ways of these foreigners and treated them all as his friends.

After several cups of tea and much small talk, Cramer finally broached the subject. Could he borrow a beheading sword to complete a costume to be worn at one of those foolish parties that the foreigner seemed to like? Pi was horrified at this—it was impossible! It was absolutely against regulations—regulations that specified a colonel was to head each such party.

Cramer was all for letting the matter drop. He certainly didn't want to bring a large part of the Chinese army to the party. But General Pi wouldn't let the matter drop. His friend had made a request and if he, General Pi, couldn't grant that favor he would lose face.

Finally, he turned to Cramer and said, "My friend, I have made you a colonel on my staff. You may order your squad to remain in quarters and carry the sword yourself, if you so desire. It has never been done, but there is no law against it."

Cramer went to the party. He had a good time even if, before the party was half over, the wife of the British Consul did demand that he "put that disgusting thing away before somebody gets hurt."

He could never drill his men as well as your ants are drilled, Mr. Schwarz. Tell us something of them, will you?

Collecting insects may seem like small adventure to those of you who have had encounters with game animals or have been the discoverers of dinosaur bones. And yet the mere size of an animal is not an altogether reliable gauge of its interest. To see a leaf-cutting bee deftly and unhesitatingly snipping, with its mandibles, a perfect disk out of a leaf, is a reminder of what a small creature can do without the aid of compasses, and those who have had the good fortune to watch a *Sphex* wasp smoothing the earth about its nest, with the aid of a pebble, will be forced to the conclusion that man is not the only tool-using animal. But for sheer drama I know of no activity in which insects engage that is comparable to a raid by a colony of army ants.

It was during the second day of our stay at Barro Colorado Island, in the Canal Zone, that I saw one of these armies on the march. It had selected as the scene of its ravages the very clearing in which we lived. Some species of army ants surge forward in rather dense masses, attacking whatever looms up in the way of a living thing along the broad field of battle. Frantically scurrying and leaping, insects seek escape—but for the most part ineffectually—from the oncoming host and sometimes such armies attract the so-called ant birds which, to the detriment of the ants, take their toll of the little fugitives the ants have flushed. One such mass raid I witnessed on a later occasion but the species of which I am about to tell you has a different but no less interesting method of attack.

Instead of advancing as a surging mob, this army moves in extended columns that divide and subdivide into tributary raiding parties, eventually covering a large area. Such a ramification of activity had already taken place at the time I arrived on the scene. The ant columns were marching not only on the surface of the ground but up the sides of the buildings of the Institute for Research in Tropical America. Here was a jet of fast-moving brown units spurting up the wall of one of the cabins straight into a wasp's nest suspended under the roof. The adult wasps were flying about the nest in futile rage while their nurseries were being robbed. A return stream of ants laden with wasp larvae flowed back along the same line of march followed by the ascending column.

The column moved close to the nest of a community of small stingless bees built in the wall of the cabin. A tiny tube gave access to the interior of this nest, and filling the orifice of that tube was the watchful little head of a guarding bee. The rapacious column of ants went upward without deviation from its main objective.

The raiding column of which I have just spoken was a spur from a longer column moving along a concrete pathway that led to the house belonging to our fellow member, Dr. Frank M. Chapman, who has written two delightful volumes on Barro Colorado, which he regards as his tropical air castle. The speed with which these ants moved along the pathway again suggested a narrow flowing stream but the flow was not all in one direction. Some ants were ascending the concrete steps while a stream of laden ants was cascading past them down the steps in counterflow. As the two opposing streams moved side by side with great rapidity there were frequent collisions between individual ants.

In marching, the antennae are held low, almost like a fourth pair of legs. This may be partly for the purpose of obtaining tactile impressions but it is to be remembered that the sense of smell is located in the antennae and that these insects are probably largely dependent on smell in following the ant trail, their organs of vision being poorly developed.

The ants were of many sizes and sometimes the captured prey was too large for the carrying capacity of a single ant. In such cases two, or even three, individuals bestrode the burden and moved along in tandem formation, with their mandibles clutching the object of their solicitude.

In a sense, all the foraging individuals of an ant army are to be thought of as military units, but the term "soldier" is usually reserved for a particular caste, distinguished by its larger size and notably large head. Though these soldiers are conspicuous in the marching column, it is only when they are viewed under the microscope that one can fully appreciate how devastatingly nature has equipped them with weapons of aggression. Their mandibles are considerably longer than their heads, incurved and sharply pointed. In their shape, as in their disproportionate length, they suggest the tusks of a mammoth that have been transferred, through some Alice-in-Wonderland legerdemain, to the head of an insect. It was easy to arouse the pugnacity of these soldiers and to induce them to stray from the column by teasing them with a blade of grass or a wisp of vegetation.

I followed the column along the concrete path to Dr. Chapman's house. Here again raiding was taking place among the wasps' nests. The booty was abundant but what particularly caught my attention was a cluster of ants that formed a little brown patch at the base of the building. This patch was stationary in contrast to the moving column and it somewhat suggested a small sample of some textile material. I picked up a long nail, inserted it above and behind the patch, and pulled gently forward. The impression I received was that of a thinly woven, rather elastic cloth. The comparison is not altogether inept, for these ants have a habit of uniting, usually by interlocking their tarsal claws, and thus forming a sort of living fabric.

The march of the ants did not end at Dr. Chapman's house. Another fork of the column extended into the jungle beyond the cluster of buildings on the clearing and raiding columns were thrust out into other directions as well.

But where was the nest, the fountainhead of this great river system in reverse, in which the tributaries represented the ultimate reaches of a great stream of life? To discover the center of energy the obvious course is to follow the booty-bearing ants, for ultimately their destination is the homesite. But the solution is not always simple. The trail is likely to be lost in the dense undergrowth of the forest and the treasure hunt often presents false clues in the form of branching trails that lead away from, rather than toward, the nest. Happily, owing to the nature of the terrain, my task was a relatively easy one. Journeying along with the returning ants I moved past the buildings of the Institute for Research in Tropical America, on toward the forest, and there just beyond our temporary homestead the ants had built theirs.

I had read of nests of these ants but seeing the living reality is, I assure you, far more impressive. I use the word "living" advisedly, for the building blocks of the army ants' nest are the ants themselves. A while back I told you of the little patch of interlocked ants that I noted far up the ant trail. It was an evidence, in miniature, of the technique employed in the building of the nest. For the site of the nest the ants had in this case chosen the space between the ridgelike roots of a tropical tree, where a pendent liana offered a surface of attachment for the ant tapestry. A small irregular curtain of ants hung dropping from this liana. There were several layers of ants, giving the curtain thickness. One was reminded of its living character by individual ants that moved about over the animate drapery.

After taking a good eye-filling look at the nest, I hurried back to report the find to Dr. Frank E. Lutz, who headed our field trip to Barro Colorado island. He was at once impressed with the opportunity of collecting this nest and re-creating it in the form of a permanent habitat group with identical natural background in the American Museum of Natural History. So a plan of campaign was formulated for the capture of the ant army.

The attack upon the insects would almost certainly invite reprisal, for these ants are powerful biters. Their capacity for imbedding their jaws in their victim and holding fast is comparable to that of the soldiers of the leaf-cutting ants and the latter, as some of you may know, are used in primitive surgery for the stitching of wounds. In such a case, the flesh at each side of a cut is drawn together, an ant is held over the narrowed gap; the ant responds by biting, and after its mandibles are firmly locked in the flesh, thus closing the gap, the ant's head is severed from its body. This is repeated until a row of tiny heads makes a beaded line along the cut in place of stitches.

We did not want to be subjected to the bites of these little savages if we could prevent it. First the earth in front of the nest was sprayed with kerosene; if the nest dissolved into an attacking army of ants, the insects might be chemically repelled when attempting to cross the saturated terrain, and a Flit atomizer was kept handy. Another item in the equipment was a large pail filled with formaldehyde in solution, and finally an ordinary shovel. This shovel Dr. Lutz wielded with aggressive dexterity, plunging it into the heart of the nest and then quickly transferring his load of ants to the pail with its deadly fluid. Several shovelfuls gave the needed number of ants for the Museum group.

Then suddenly out of the confusion emerged the queen, a rarity in collections and prized accordingly. A quick lunge with a forceps assured the capture of her majesty and now we felt that not only the army, but its most distinguished member, had capitulated.

When the dead ants were taken from the pail, many of them were still locked in festoons, just as they were in the living formation of the nest.

This nest, by its spontaneous character and its impermanence, is admirably adapted to these nomadic insects, which during their period of more active raiding, make only temporary bivouacs, camping here tonight and at some more distant site on the night to follow.

I have talked to you, perhaps too long, about this species of army ant without introducing it by name. It is known as *Eciton hamatum* and, if you would like to know what its queer bivouac looks like, you can see it restored with substantial fidelity in the army ant group a the American Museum of Natural History.

— THROUGH HELL AND HIGH WATER (1941)

PART EIGHT

*Pacific
Ocean*

The Fire-Dog of Asu

BY LEWIS R. FREEMAN

A s we came out on the open veranda from the dinner table, the gold and orange banners of gorgeous sunset had flickered out in the west and the gray gauze of the tropical twilight was thickening into the soft velvet of night. The bay was piling full of purple shadows, through which the foam spurts and patches along the rocky windward wall glowed with increasing luminosity as the darkness deepened and the heavy swells of the Pacific, plunging against the cliffs, signalled their despair with ghostly rockets and bonfires of phosphorescence.

Overhead, save for a few squadrons of hurriedly marching trade clouds, the heavens were clear and, where the sky above the eastern valley wall was lightening before the rising moon, the transient silhouettes of flocks of flying-foxes, dark and spectral in their noiseless flights, flashed and disappeared. Inland, the throaty croak of the wood-pigeon boomed at intervals in the fathomless blackness; above, the lisp of the leaves of the coconut and banana blended to the rustling of crisp silk; seaward, awakening a mile of mellow music, the fingers of Neptune ran up and down the reef's ever responsive keys of coral.

We had come since morning—the Judge[1], the Lieutenant and I—all the way from the naval station at Pago-Pago, toiling up through the sweat-box of bush at the end of the great bay to the lofty wind-fanned summit, dropping again to sea level at Fauga-sa, and from there running down with a fair wind to Mala-toa in the Judge's *malaga*. On the way we had put in at the village of Asu, on Massacre Bay, for a glimpse of the monument erected by the French in commemoration of their countrymen who figured in the event which gave

---

1. Judge E. W. Gurr, for many years Robert Louis Stevenson's friend and lawyer in Apia, later Judge of the American naval station at Tutuila.

the cove its sinister name. Singularly impressive it was, that plain little tablet of bronze set in a base of hewn coral, and eloquent in their simple appeal were the words graven thereon.

MORTS POUR LA SCIENCE

ET LA PATRIE

LE 11 DECEMBRE, 1787

Below were the names and the ranks of those who had fallen—nothing else.

The Judge told us in brief outline the story, whilst we sipped our coffee and watched the moon come up.

The *Boussole* and *Astrolabe*, fitted out by the French government to search for the Northwest Passage, after failing in their original object and cruising for some months on the eastern coast of Asia, extended their voyage of exploration to the South Pacific. In December of 1787 they anchored off the leeward coast of Tutuila, one of the Samoas, to be most kindly received by natives as friendly and hospitable then as they are today. Dances and feasts were arranged for the visitors whenever they landed, no unpleasantness of any description occurring until just before the ships were ready to sail.

At that time a large party, headed by Vte. de Langle of the *Astrolabe* and De Lamanon of the *Boussole*, head naturalist of the expedition, landed at Asu with the intention of inducing some of the natives to accompany them back to France. Failing to accomplish their object by persuasion, an attempt was made to carry off a half-dozen or more of the villagers by force, the ill-advised Frenchmen foolishly imagining that the easy-going, light-hearted Samoans would lack the courage to oppose their high-handed and inhuman plan.

The little bronze tablet tells most of the rest of the story. "For Science and for Country," de Langle and De Lamanon were killed, while the rest of the party saved their lives only by putting off in the boats and abandoning the bodies of their comrades. With the spread of the news to the surrounding villages, the natives gathered in such numbers that the warships were forced to sail without venturing another landing. After some further months of voyaging, both *Astrolabe* and *Boussole* were lost with all hands by being driven ashore in a hurricane on a small island to the north of the New Hebrides.

That was about all the story, said the Judge, except that the natives told of a big dog that was with the landing party, which, after fighting desperately for the lives of its masters, made off into the hills, bleeding from many spear thrusts. Closely pressed, the great animal, after turning many times and scattering by savage charges the horde of warriors that pursued him, finally rushed to the brink of a lofty cliff and threw himself off into space. The natives heard the thud of his body striking the rocks below and fled back to Asu, holding their ears to shut out his dying roars.

Some time later a native, journeying by land from Asu to the next village, failed to return. His friends trailed his footprints to the heart of the deep valley at the foot of the cliff and, while endeavoring to account for their sudden disappearance, were confronted with an apparition so terrible that, though they escaped it and reached Asu alive, the blood in their veins turned to water from fright and they were ever after as little children. Their babble till they died was of a great blood-red dog, as big as a wild bullock, which held the body of their friend crosswise in its mouth, as a pelican holds a fish too big to gulp. The valley immediately became *tabu*, none venturing there even in times of famine, when its great groves of coconuts, bananas, and breadfruit and its beds of yam and taro, might have prevented actual starvation.

The dog, or his ghost, grew larger and fiercer with the years and his color changed—probably through some dispensation of the devil, the natives thought—from red to that of smouldering fire. He was never actually seen carrying off another man, but all disappearances from the village, and in time even sickness and failure of crops and ill-luck in fishing came to be laid at his door. Throughout the Samoas the expression "as bad as the Fire-Dog of Asu" became the superlative of all that was terrifying and dreadful.

The Judge set his coffee cup on the arm of his chair and stepped to the end of the veranda, motioning us to join him.

"You gentlemen see that black wall over there, with the shadow from the moon creeping down it?" he asked, pointing to a towering basaltic barrier that shut off half the western heavens. "That's the cliff the Dog is supposed to have jumped over and the farther side of the big grove of *maupes* is where he landed. And that same dog—or at last the impression the memory of him has left on the minds of the natives—is what made it possible for me to buy this whole valley of Mala-toa for five hundred dollars. He is also responsible for the fact that I have expended five times that sum on it without getting back a single cent, even for copra. He is responsible for my coming over here now, when I should be convening court at Pago-Pago, and before morning he (or the fear of him) will be responsible for us all being waked up to let that bunch of big boobies (indicating the Samoans, where they were grouped around their *kava* bowl in the twilight) inside for protection.

"Every time I get a gang well started at clearing and planting," he continued, as we resumed our seats, "the Dog shows himself and work is off for another year. I tried it first with gangs of natives alone, but after these had been frightened away a half-dozen times I was unable to get any to go without a white man. My first white foreman, a hard-bitten Australian whom I picked up in Apia, was getting things opened up in good shape when he was taken with the fever, upon which the natives, declaring that the Dog had set its mark on him, stopped work and left at once.

"The result of my last attempt to keep men here you will probably have heard about at the naval station. A young Virginian named Brent, whose time in the Navy was up and who was anxious to remain in Samoa, was in charge and, according to the weekly reports he was despatching me, doing very well indeed. Then, one morning last July, a half-crazy native was picked up on the beach and brought to Pago-Pago. From his delirious chatter we gathered that the Dog had appeared at Mala-toa and killed Brent and that the natives, fleeing in an overloaded *malaga*, had been upset in the heavy southwester that was blowing and, except himself, all drowned.

"Accompanied by the naval station doctor, I went around at once in the government launch. Brent was indeed dead. With a revolver full of unfired cartridges tightly clenched in his hand, he was lying across the veranda yonder, his face still rigid in the lines of terror that had distorted it when he died. Death was due to heart failure, the doctor said, and recalled that, some months previously, his stethoscope had shown that Brent had an enlarged valve. The immediate cause of the heart failure was violent nervous excitement.

"Of course, the sight of a huge fiery dog such as the natives described might have caused such excitement, but more likely a fight with his unruly gang of natives was at the bottom of it. This would account for the flight of the latter, thought the doctor; probably they were not drowned at all but only in hiding. This had become the generally accepted theory at Pago-Pago, especially since a pack of bloodhounds I brought over from Apia failed to run down anything more terrible that a lot of wild pigs. Still," the Judge concluded, rising to go inside, "no ordinary encounter with a gang of natives can entirely account in my mind for the look that was frozen on poor Brent's face when we found him."

The Samoans left their fire and brought their *kava* and sleeping-mats up on the veranda as soon as we had left it. After they had kept us awake for a couple of hours by setting up a nervous shuffling and chattering at every unwonted sound from the bush, the Judge, fearing they might take fright and make off with the *malaga*, got up and let them in to sleep on the floor.

The next morning the Judge put his men to work re-clearing for a new setting of cacao trees, while the Lieutenant and I made pigeon shooting an excuse for exploring the valley. It was not until some time after dark that we straggled back to the house, changed from khaki to duck, and re-assembled at the dinner table. We had done full justice in turn to turtle soup, red snapper baked in *ti* leaves, and roast sucking pig dressed with the inimitable *miti hari* sauce and were just turning gloating eyes on dishes of that greatest of all delicacies, coconut-sprout salad, when an ear-splitting yell of terror rang out from the bush. An instant later there came the sound of running feet and, before we had risen from the table, the low west window shivered to fragments under the impact of a great brown body which was launched through it and fell, bruised and bleeding, inside the room. In the wake of the first, followed another brown body, while through the doors the rest of the Samoans came trooping, bellowing with fright.

For five minutes none of them was able to say much but "*Oka, Oka; him dogga come!*" When we finally got them quieted down, it was to learn with disgust that two of the boys, Toa and Luka, the ones who had come in through the window, had gone to the stream a hundred yards away for a can of water. While they were filling their can, the Fire-Dog rushed out of the bush and charged them so savagely that they had barely managed to save their lives by jumping through the window. When we found that Toa's and Luka's wounds were all from broken glass and that none of the other boys had seen the Dog in pursuit of them, our first impulse was to drive the whole lot outdoors and finish our dinner. On second consideration we decided the opportunity for investigation was too good to miss.

Accordingly, the Lieutenant and I with revolvers and the Judge with his shotgun, we set off down the water path after vainly endeavoring to force Toa and Luka to show us the way. The moon had not yet risen and the narrow trail, closely walled in with bananas and guava scrub and overarched with intertangling breadfruit-tree branches, lay in inky blackness, save where the darting fireflies laced the air with evanescent wires of gold. Presently, as we emerged from the bush into the clearing along the bank of the stream, we became aware of a spattered line of dull luminosity running at right angles to our line of advance, such a trail as one might leave by scattering broadcast handfuls of glow worms as he walked. I heard the heavy breathing of my companions and was conscious of something like a gasp from myself at the dawning recollection of how the Fire-Dog was always described as leaving behind him a wake of light.

Glancing nervously to right and left, we advanced to examine the spectral spoor. The glowing matter was cold and wet to the touch and emitted enough light for us to discern the indistinct marks of the feet of some animal on the tender grass. The tracks seemed heading inland and in that direction we followed them for a hundred yards or more, only to find that they ultimately looped around and headed back into the original trail just seaward of where we had first encountered it.

Before long a faint glow, such as might have been thrown from a smouldering campfire, was perceptible through the trees ahead and, as we neared the beach, between the sharp, slashing blows of the surf on the shingle, came the confused but unmistakable sound of coughing, snorting, and wallowing, such as a large animal makes when bathing.

Every symptom of complete and unmixed fear that I have ever heard described—dry lips, trembling hands, quaking knees, going hot and cold, and turning to goose-flesh—I can distinctly recall experiencing in that last fifty yards to the beach and my companions have since admitted as much respecting their own sensations. The coughing and snorting increased in volume as we advanced and the ghostly light flashed on the cliff in quivering lines of green and blue. These, reflecting, struck faintly through the bush, revealing to each of us the tense lines of puzzled apprehension in the faces of the others.

As we struck out upon a bar of pebbles near the mouth of the stream and the hard round stones began rattling underfoot, the noises from under the cliff suddenly ceased and the fluttering waves of light grew dimmer and died low. The deepening darkness descended and wrapped us like a pall. In the ominous silence we waited, tense and ready but undeniably shaken with the grim, unearthly mystery of it all.

As the uncanny sounds broke forth anew, we pressed forward again in the shivering light and reached a point where only a dense clump of pandanus palm shut us off from the foot of the cliff. Around this we were stealthily picking our way when a sea shell cracked sharply under someone's foot and the wallowing ceased again. This time the heavy, sputtering respirations of a large animal were distinctly audible.

It may have been only a few seconds that we waited thus, or it may have been a minute, or two, or three, when the Lieutenant's patience or his nerves—or both—gave way. Without a word of warning, he dashed forward, rounded the clump of pandanus and fired blindly in the direction of the cliff. The next moment there burst forth a hoarse snort of rage and the ghostly light flared up again, to show the young officer, wide-eyed with terror and surprise, staring blankly ahead and discharging his revolver into the coral clinkers at his feet. An instant later the Judge and I had sprung out beside him, to recoil in turn before a fearsome and unearthly sight.

In an angle of the cliff, a dozen yards or so back from the crest of the wave-piled shingle of the beach, was a glowing pool of liquid fire, dimly luminous for the most part but bursting forth in spurts and flashes of green and blue flame where it was churned by the legs of a large animal that was ploughing through it to the bank.

For the beast itself, words fail me. Reeking with fire, snorting fire, scattering fire, it would have seemed terrible enough to an unimpassioned observer watching from a safe vantage at the top of the cliff; the effect of actually standing in the path of its advance, with nerves already racked to the point of giving way, must be left to the imagination.

With a rush and a roar the Thing of Terror gained the bank and charged straight down upon us. The Lieutenant's revolver exhausted itself into the broken coral. My own, unfired, hung loosely on nerveless fingers. But the Judge, who seemed suddenly to have pulled himself together, squared away and discharged both barrels in quick succession almost under the nose of that hurtling Bolt of Wrath. I heard the heavy buckshot grind home through flesh and bone, heard the snorts of anger change to shrill squeals of pain and saw the great gleaming form reel and stagger and tumble forward into a quivering heap at our feet.

For a few moments we peered down at the inert mass, still veined with trickling lines of fire, and stared incredulously at each other as comprehension burst upon us. The Judge was the first to speak.

"Gentlemen," he said, "we have killed a pig! And that pool of 'fire' over there is a 'skim-hole' of phosphorescence, quite the livest and brightest one I have ever seen. We'll see how it formed in the morning. For the present, let us return to our dinner."

The next day we found the "Fire-Dog" still lying where it had fallen. It was of enormous proportions, quite the largest wild boar of which there was any record in Samoa, but must have been almost harmless from the fact that its great tusks had grown back almost into a circle. In the morning light the glowing pool of the night before presented a surface of dirty brown, but so charged was it with phosphorescence that it showed faintly luminous streaks on being stirred with a stick, even when the noon-day sun was shining directly upon it.

Its existence was due to a hollow behind the pile of shingle thrown up by the waves on the beach. The animalculae which are responsible for the phosphorescence in sea water, dying at regular intervals and floating on the surface of the bay in a brown scum, had been washed over into the hollow at high tide. The lowest level of the hollow chanced to lie at the foot of the cliff and to here the phosphorescence had drained, to be left behind as the water drained away through the porous coral.

Such fish as were occasionally washed over the beach were also carried to this pool and it was these, no doubt, which attracted the old boar there to wallow and feed. The half-dozen sticks of dynamite which the Judge set off in the cliff to fill up the obnoxious "skim-hole," brought down a shower of basaltic blocks which piled themselves in a rude mausoleum above the body of "The Fire-Dog of Asu."

Robbed of its terror, there was no longer trouble in keeping native labor at Mala-toa, which soon became a lucrative copra and cacao plantation. When I last visited Pago-Pago, in the course of the 1925 Australasian naval cruise, the Judge had retired and was making his home there.

— *TOLD AT THE EXPLORERS CLUB* (1931)

Athlete, writer, explorer, and correspondent in the Russo-Japanese War and the First World War, Lewis R. Freeman had already at middle life had enough adventure to satisfy two ordinary mortals.

Running a scow down the White Horse Rapids, at the time of the Klondyke gold rush, aroused a special fondness for boating that led him to navigate the principal rivers of north America and many in foreign lands, visit the six continents, and sail the seven seas.

Of the sixteen books that have come from his facile pen, ten deal with these extended wanderings: In the Tracks of the Trades; Down the Columbia; Down the Yellowstone; The Colorado River—Yesterday, Today and Tomorrow; Down the Grand Canyon; On the Roof of the Rockies; By Water Ways to Gotham; Waterways of Westward Wandering; The Nearing North.

"Juah Tada"

BY HASSOLDT DAVIS

Introduction by Seyward S. Cramer, Editor, *Through Hell and High Water*, 1941

There are a lot of expressions in English that are loose and free. Whenever we want to appear melodramatic or slightly hammish, we strike a pose and say, "A plague on your house" or "A plague take you." I, for one, will never use any expression like that again because I was once unfortunate enough to see the results of a cholera plague.

It must be a bit ghastly to live through a pestilential plague—waiting rather helplessly for it to pass or strike. It must also be trying to sit through a locust plague.

Hassoldt Davis spent some time in the South Seas. There are few experiences that he missed while he was carrying on his studies there as an ethnologist. I wish you would tell us about one of those vivid experiences, Dave—the locust plague.

"You must never go there," said little Rinpiog, "'juah tada,' far away, whence your dreams have come."

It was long before the tourists discovered Bali that Jeff and I came to it to gather ethnological data concerning one of the most beautiful and most intricately cultured people in the world. The brown sisters Marini and Rinpiog kept us materially comfortable and aided our research as the profoundest textbooks could never do. We lived in beauty and peace until the goddess Durga shook down our world about us.

Some days before their arrival we heard that the locusts were coming, the hideous swarm of them, the plague. Word was relayed from Singapore to Sumatra to Java to Bali, and all white residents able to do so sailed frantically for Macassar and Banjermasin, which were believed to be aside from the devastating flight. Those of us who remained in Bali reinforced our windows with blankets, chinked the ventilating interstices between the eaves and walls of the house, bought all the food possible, and awaited the horror nervously. The natives were in a panic. The temple yards were filled with suppliants dunning the goddess Durga for mercy. Those rice fields which ordinarily were left to take care of themselves were now surrounded with variously spaced twenty-foot poles from the tops of which little banners dangled, the symbolic napkins of the moon goddess in the periods of her decline; no one, man nor locust, could decently pass beneath them, however attractive the crops.

We waited, our small family, as those who wait desperately for a destruction whose identity is unknown and in consequence most terrible. We were ashamed but could not help the occasional whispers of our conversation. As the danger drew nearer, the natives sat clustered and afraid, as of some unimaginable evil, in their temple, and our own *baboes*—housegirls—forsook us at midnight to attend congresses whereat white men were forbidden.

Marini was quiet in our presence, and sullen, as she watched the western sky whence the plague was to come, whence it would come as a thick dark terror swooping out of Asia and lowly across the loveliness of Java and Bali and all the archipelago eastward. Marini no longer smashed the crockery nor overpeppered the soup; she was deft, precise, despite her glowering. My ridiculous coin trick, hitherto infallible for her laughter, was useless now. It was little Rinpiog who laughed, she whose carven beauty of expression had never altered either for melancholy or for mirth. Rinpiog laughed hysterically and grimaced at the threatening west.

Then one night it was upon us, heralded by yapping hounds and yelling natives and the small house lizards which "chichaked" and instantly disappeared along our ceiling. I heard Rinpiog's choked giggle in the next room and the moan of Marini.

"Oh, Davie," called Jeff, "you got your pajamas battened on?"

We lit cigarettes and stood silently by the lamp while the whir of invasion surrounded us. An unattached blanket end snapped loose from a window and a thousand huge insects burst upon us. We rushed to the next room.

After interminable hours through which we could not sleep for the vibrant drumming of the plague upon our walls, the ripping of foliage,

Rinpiog's laughter, and Marini's whine, morning broke with scarcely a perceptible lightening, so dense was the locust swarm. The single glass window was a mottled pattern of smashed and smashing small bodies through which we could dimly see the devastation of our garden, the orchids whipped to shreds, the huge banana leaves broken and lacerated to the semblance of green fringes. Hibiscus blossoms were shot from their stems and punctured by the locust bullets before they reached the ground.

When we went to the well for water, swaddled in towels and raincoats, it was all we could do to fight our way against the million bodies which battered and burst upon us. Those were nightmare journeys, in which we staggered as through an unreal world, livid and terrible, where all that world's infamies, locust-like, were swirling to our assault.

The gin saved us, I believe, the gin and the drollery of having nothing to mix with it but the juice of coconuts and *langsap*. We contrived to find it hugely entertaining the while we wished profanely we could get a fresh breath of uninfested air, or a moment of surcease from that murderous drone. We tried morbidly to count the bodies as they burst against the window; we were fascinated as we scooped black corpses from the water buckets.

Evening came suddenly, and then night like some monstrous cogged wheel grinding daylight and Bali and our remnant minds to dust. We sprawled in our corners, drunk and prideless, staring with an idiot devotion at the one small lamp, fitfully reading or drowsing or chattering all at once. Our nerves were raw and our tempers ungenial. We had by now come to know each other through such intimate perspective that our separate identities were blurred. We four had become one body of hysteria, jabbering at itself, consoling itself, tweaking its own nose. We poured ourself another drink and flailed limp arms against the stifling tobacco smoke. We were reverently aware that the gongs were pulsing in some temple far away, very far away it seemed as the notes came muffled through the locust swarm. And we jeered at our reverence, for the gods surely could not hear this petty clangor of their suppliants.

We poured ourself another drink and viciously tweaked our nose again, and that more sensible part of us which was Marini deflected and blunted our fears against her charitable flesh.

Little Rinpiog sat huddled in her corner, laughing crazily and the more terribly because she was a drunken child; then Rinpiog screamed, shattering what was left of the world about us, for that which should have been a langsap berry in her drink was in reality a scrunched locust. Thereafter we took our gin neat.

Next morning, when the sun rose awesomely over Bali, the terror ended as abruptly as it had begun, with a lessening drone and a slower plop-plop at the windows. Shouts of ecstatic relief and a few shouts of hysteria arose from the neighboring kampongs. For many minutes we did not move but to uncross our cramped legs. The shouts died into a silence more terrible than sound, and we knew then that our Bali, our blessed exquisite island was a waste.

We sat for minutes longer on the floor, collecting our ravaged wits and saying again and again that it was over at last, that another drink would go nicely, that Bali in a few months would be as green and glorious as ever. Then we went out and broke our last pint of Holland gin across the smirking mouth of an idol.

All over the island that night there were gatherings for supplication and thanksgiving. I walked some distance away from Kedaton, past clamorous kampongs and fields of rice which were ruined yet still piteously stirring in the wind. I walked through a dimly lighted gateway and there we all were, we worshipers, the gamelan orchestra, the white- and black-swathed dancers, the old men chanting together beneath a contorted great banyan tree, the gods. Incense lay heavily upon us like a pall.

The girls danced three at a time, weaving in geometrical patterns through and around each other, their faces expressionless as masks. Each bore a pot of flowers or smoking incense, held high before her. Suddenly they would turn and stride off to a little temple, and after making their offerings slip back again into shadows, while other groups took their place. Constantly the old men moaned and the gamelan played softly.

Four women on a high, roofed platform beckoned to me. I climbed up and sat among them, drinking arrack with them as we watched the ritual. One made a fire of coconut husks and roasted paper-thin wafers of beaten rice.

Gradually the crowd increased, squatting before the little temple. All their eyes were upon an old priest and a boy of about twenty who sat in the front row, their hands lifting now and again to flutter over a large pot of scarlet-burning incense. The dancing girls were changing; they were becoming older, and soon the crones of the kampong were dancing rather pathetically, with their offerings, trying to remember the lost steps and forgotten graces with which they had formerly charmed the gods.

"It is the invocation of the goddess Durga," a native whispered to me, "Durga, the goddess of sudden death and madness. — Look! . . ."

The old priest and the boy in the front row were trembling. Their eyes were closed and their heads tipped back. Their entire bodies were shaking as the goddess filled them and possessed them. Suddenly the priest screamed and flung himself into the crowd, and simultaneously a man swathed in black scarves danced from the darkness and circled him. The priest snarled like an animal, his mouth slobbering, and slid on his belly toward the dancer, recoiled and leaped again, catching a foot which he tried to tear with his teeth. He darted insanely about the abandoned dancing group, intent — and you could believe it — upon carnage. The interpreter of the gods called out loudly to Durga, and the native beside me translated. "Why do you afflict us so? Why do you thus torture our priest?" And Durga answered aptly through the slobbering lips of the madman, "Why do you bother me with your prayers? Have I not been good to you? It has been very long since your island suffered misfortune. Why do you bother me with your prayers? Am I not the judge of the justice of my own wrath? You have been proud and sinful in the pride of your small island, and I have punished you justly." The priest leaped into the air and fell back to the earth, groveling. And after a moment the goddess spoke again, demanding food.

The interpreter rushed forward and broke an egg into the priest's mouth, then gave him arrack from a banana-leaf cup. The priest reeled to his feet and fell fainting into the arms of the dancer, who carried him away.

Now the boy before the pot of incense was trembling more violently, his hands clasped before him and his uptilted head jerking as with palsy. This had been continuing for at least an hour, and it seemed that the only possible explanation of it was that of hypnosis. No man conscious could maintain that terrific tremor for such a time. Certain of the Balinese, to whom the gods have given signs, are trained from childhood for this role of "sangkiangs," the ambassadors between the kingdoms of gods and men, and like the priests they must live under the most rigid discipline. They can eat but one meal a day; they can under no consideration have more than four wives.

Now a girl and an old woman were shaking, slowly at first, then gradually faster, and now another girl, a child, had caught the divine palsy. She was beautiful in a ghastly way, with her bare young shoulders throbbing and her hair flung across her face like dark rain. She flounced about in a fury, beating those who were near her; she moaned and sobbed convulsive words which the interpreter called nasally to the crowd.

The gamelan had steadied to one iterant gong note; the old men whispered their dirge.

And suddenly the boy fell forward with both hands in the burning incense pot. Women rushed to him with a gigantic dragon mask of green and gold and red, and fitted it upon his shoulders. His hands were still among the coals, and the horrible mask bobbed above them.

There was a tremendous report and a blinding flash, then a frightful series of explosions as a long string of cannon crackers, strung to the banyan tree, were set off. Sprayed with fire, the sangkiang leaped into the midst of it, howling and stamping madly upon the spurting flames. And suddenly he stopped limp, blubbering words, the awful dragon head swinging from side to side. Arrack was poured by a dozen hands between the tusks of it, and the boy lifted his own hands to the sky as he reeled over, and I could see that they were unburnt. . . .

People were disappearing; the two girl sangkiangs swung before them bowls with blue-burning arrack; the gamelan wailed into silence.

And I also hurried off homeward, shaking a little, and feeling wholly mad.

— *THROUGH HELL AND HIGH WATER* (1941)

Pitcairn Island After 200 Years: Will the Settlement Survive?

BY PRINCE JOLI KANSIL

itcairn is a rugged island of formidable cliffs of reddish brown and black volcanic rock. Located at 25° south latitude and 130° west longitude, it is a mere dot in the South Pacific Ocean. The island rises to a height of 1100 feet (350 meters), has an area of two square miles, with a forbidding coast and poor access to the sea.

One of the remotest of the world's inhabited islands, unlike Polynesian islands, it has no fringes of white sand, no aquamarine waters; it is just a haunting rock that looms from the sea, where land and ocean meet and form furious spray and foam. There is a quality of eeriness and brooding in the landscape, and to travel there is a journey back to the 19th century.

The only village of Pitcairn is Adamstown, on a northerly slope 350 feet above sea level. The road is a steep and narrow mud path that rises sharply from Bounty Bay below. This little town is the capital of the last British colony in the Pacific, and it is home to all fifty-four inhabitants—a unique community of Anglo-Tahitian descent which turned a naval mutiny into a celebrated romance.

The story of how the ancestors of these settlers came to live and thrive on Pitcairn is familiar, but a few highlights of the account may be in order, if only to put the modern-day plight of Pitcairn into historical perspective. In 1789, the British ship *Bounty* was bound for Jamaica in the West Indies with a cargo of breadfruits from Tahiti. The master's mate Fletcher Christian led a mutiny that set the ship's captain, William Bligh, adrift with eighteen of the crew. (That Bligh and his men navigated all the way to Timor in the East Indies remains as one of the greatest open-sea voyages.) Fletcher Christian and nine of his followers, spurred by the fear of discovery and arrest, set sail for an uninhabited island with six Tahitian men and twelve Tahitian women.

After two months at sea, they landed at Pitcairn. The *Bounty* was stripped and burned, and a permanent settlement at Pitcairn evolved. The Tahitians were treated as slaves and later revolted; by 1794 only four mutineers remained, along with ten women and their children. They built simple houses, they cultivated the land, they cared for the stock of animals, and Pitcairn has survived in good times and bad to the present.

Now, some two centuries later, Pitcairn is inhabited mostly by fifth-, sixth- and seventh-generation descendants, and the number of residents, which reached 233 earlier this century, is now fewer than sixty. If this number goes much lower, how will it be possible for the island to sustain itself as a cohesive social group? With a reduced population there would not be enough labor for growing crops, fishing, building, and the many other chores necessary to run what is, in essence, the least populated country or colony on the globe.

Besides the direct descendants of the original settlers, there are also descendants of an American whaler, Samuel Warren, who came to Pitcairn in the 1850s. Today, two Norwegian women (who are sisters) and a New Zealand school teacher and his wife and child are also living there. A telephone roster for Pitcairn would have only six surnames in it. (Besides, there are only two phones on the island!) There has been much intermarriage with close relatives, but the Pitcairn society is a vigorous one, as I saw during my visit to the island in February 1987.

The S.S. *Rotterdam* was en route from Callao (the port city of Lima) to Papeete, Tahiti, via Easter Island (Rapa Nui), and Pitcairn. I was primarily interested in the last two islands. British Brigadier General Matthew Wilson and his wife followed the same itinerary, and we teamed up to visit the islands.

"Tony" Wilson and I spent a rigorous day jeeping all over Easter Island. Together we outlined our visit to Pitcairn. Even if the weather were ideal, passengers would have to descend a swaying rope ladder from a portal of the ship to one of the three Pitcairn longboats, then onto a rubber "zodiac" craft for the rough sea journey to the island. The treacherous landing itself must be made by swooping through a final wave (barely missing nearby jutting rocks) to the small pier at Bounty Bay.

Having learned some Dutch through my marriage to an Indonesian, I befriended the captain early on and implored him to let me go to Pitcairn. That I was the youngest passenger aboard and a member of The Explorers Club (an organization with which the captain was quite familiar) were helpful. I was the only full-paying passenger allowed to go. Wilson was permitted to go on the first launch with a couple of the crew, and I was on a second launch an hour or so later with one more crew member. The ride to Pitcairn was as turbulent as described, but it was exhilarating nonetheless.

The road from the pier to Adamstown is a steep and narrow mud path that rises sharply, and while the islanders now have a few motorized tricycles, until the last decade the trip was made solely on foot. Off the main path are numerous little lanes with sprawling ramshackle tin-roofed houses partially hidden in dense foliage in a setting of tropical beauty. Since so many islanders have left Pitcairn for destinations in the western Pacific, only twenty-five of the houses are in use, while forty-five are empty and dilapidated.

As expected, the houses are unlocked, and most of them even have the doors wide open. The whole scene is reminiscent of a lumber camp both from the outside and because housekeeping is not the forte of the Pitcairn natives. The few houses in which I peeked had separate kitchens (with dirt floors) and toilet facilities. The bedrooms have mattresses and, in lieu of built-in closets, there are upright cases (wardrobes) for storing clothes.

During my few hours on Pitcairn, most of the residents were on the ship meeting the passengers and selling beautiful handicrafts and stamps. Thus, I more or less had the village and surrounding lush valley landscape to myself and, clad in a sarong from Bali and a guayavera shirt from Yucatan, I raced to cover as much of the territory as I could. The 20th century has come to Pitcairn in that some houses have small refrigerators and washing machines. In one house I saw in the living room a VCR unit for watching movies and, a few feet away on the wall, a risque pin-up calendar next to a sign saying, "Jesus Saves." Not only is a lack of residents a serious problem on Pitcairn, but so are the trappings of modern times. With VCR units, the outside world has rapidly arrived, and just how much outside influence of this nature the island can tolerate and still keep its quaint ways is difficult to determine.

Only remoteness has kept the Pitcairn islanders from being invaded by geneticists, medical experts, and the like. The natives looked either Polynesian or Caucasian—rarely an equal blend of the two—and the skin colors varied from light to quite dark. The children are beautiful and the adults all hearty and healthy. Genetically, the situation on Pitcairn is unique, for originally there was "outbreeding" which then became inbreeding. By outbreeding it is meant that two entirely different races intermarried, and this was the case right from the start, as none of the original male and female Tahitian settlers had any children with each other. Inbreeding began almost immediately as, out of necessity, they married first cousins. This process initially had a beneficial effect because of the two races mixing, and the result was a healthy, vigorous, and fertile people. (In fact, the first child born—Fletcher Christian's son named Thursday October—stood at over six feet.)

Today, with intense inbreeding for several generations, the height of the average islander is down, and while each is physically strong, I noticed that many have very poorly formed teeth. Mentally, there are a few who are "slow" and who would be endearingly called village idiots. Whereas before ten children to a family was not uncommon, today there is a decline in fertility due to inbreeding.

Some of the bloodlines have been improved by twenty or so visitors who have stayed and married the islanders during the course of the last two centuries. Historically, children born out of wedlock have not been unusual, nor has been voyeurism (there is a local law against it which prescribes a fine). With no movie theatres, bars, shopping malls, or other places for varied social activities, such behavior is not difficult to explain. One native volunteered, "When it comes to sex, we are Polynesians first and Adventists second."

Since 1877, the Seventh Day Adventists have been prominent, but when bottles of liquor were off-loaded on Pitcairn from the *Rotterdam*, the local pastor winked. I found out that some Pitcairners classify scotch as a medicine rather than a beverage. So, while the Adventist sect is a stern one, it is not taken so seriously on the island, although the weekly church services are well attended. The church is at the main public square and it contains the Bible that was from Fletcher Christian's sea chest.

Also at the main square is the Court House, and this building may be considered the capitol of Pitcairn; it is used for meetings, as an actual court session has not been held since 1962. In the building are photos of Prince Philip and Queen Elizabeth II, who are greatly loved in the colony. The former visited the island in 1971.

In front of the Court House is one of the original anchors from the *Bounty*, and nearby is the post office. Since 1940, Pitcairn has issued her own stamps, and, as one would expect, this venture has brought in some important revenue.

The island, however, is basically a cashless society; communal living with subsistence farming and bartering with a few ships that pass through. (There is only one store on the island, a cooperative that is open just a couple of hours a week.) There is also access to Henderson Island for wood. This is an uninhabited isle that is part of the Pitcairn group 100 miles away and which is a fairly taxing trip by one longboat.

With the brief arrival of the *Rotterdam*, the islanders traded lots of bananas for eggs and chickens, and the ship's staff also gave mattresses, robes, and small carpets. Bananas and coconuts grow aplenty on Pitcairn, and many other crops are raised in individual plots in front of the islanders' houses. As has been the case for generations, when a ship arrives, the main bell outside the Court House is rung five times; when there is to be a public sharing of goods from a ship, the bell is rung four times. (Three bells means a time for public work for able-bodied natives aged fifteen to sixty-five; two bells calls a village meeting; one bell is for religious services.)

These bell calls are only one of many traditions that have persisted to the present day, and the isolation of the island favors that such ways will continue, as will the various idioms and expressions that one would find in any closed society. The language is a lilted British English with a liberal peppering of Tahitian words and archaic expressions. For example, a "musket" is any kind of gun, and a "ship" is any vessel from a banana boat to ocean liner. A question, such as "How often do ships call?" would be rendered in local patois as "Hummuch shep corl ya?" Finally, toilet paper is called "fa'hilo" because for years it came by boat from "far away in Hilo" (capital of Hawaii Island).

The person with whom I spent most of my time on Pitcairn was the island's oldest resident, ironically named Andrew Young, and I did have difficulty understanding what he said. The Englishman Tony Wilson had a better time of it and gladly translated. Young is a fifth-generation descendant and a charming old man right out of central casting, if you will. He had a sparkle in his eye and with a bit of fanfare gave me some Seventh Day Adventist literature.

Dressed shabbily, at eighty-seven he was genuinely delighted to have a few visitors ashore. Above all, he was proud to be a native of Pitcairn, and I noticed this characteristic in all of the islanders with whom I talked. They are happy to be living there, even though it is a hard and isolated life. When I asked one lady if she would ever like to live somewhere else, she replied, "Where would I go?"

The isolation and hard physical life, then, are not negatives, but positives in keeping the Pitcairn natives at Pitcairn. It is a joyful, communal society where everyone shares and toils unselfishly in a spirit of cooperation; the unique history and ancestry that virtually all the islanders share bind the people together. While Pitcairn today lacks the creature comforts, shops, and entertainment facilities that are associated with the modern life, it makes up for these "deficiencies" with attributes that enable its residents to live a natural and fruitful life. The volcanic soil, adequate rainfall, and plentiful sea life make for an abundant food supply, and the pleasant subtropical climate contributes to easy, carefree living and general contentment.

While teenagers are eager to leave to pursue higher education and a modern life in New Zealand or elsewhere, the rest wish to stay, and the island life that has existed for eight generations should continue as long as

the population does not go below a critical number—perhaps forty-five—
and as long as too many creature comforts do not invade the island. Twice
in the 1800s, there was mass migration from Pitcairn to Norfolk Island at the
extreme other end of the Pacific. If the descendants of the Pitcairners who
went to Norfolk can be lured back, the chances of the society surviving and
thriving will be greatly enhanced.

—*THE EXPLORERS JOURNAL, SEPTEMBER* 1989

*Prince Joli Kansil has studied village life in Mexico, Guatemala, Indonesia,
and Cambodia. He participated in the 1988 Zancubo Cocha Expedition in
Ecuador led by Dr. William J. Jahoda. A widely known game inventor, author,
and part-time teacher, he resides in Honolulu.*

Rowing Across the Pacific: One Stroke at a Time

BY CURTIS AND KATHLEEN SAVILLE

t was a Fourth of July we'll never forget. On that day in 1984 we stepped into a rowboat at Callao, Peru, on the west coast of South America. Our goal: to row all the way across the South Pacific Ocean to Australia. If successful, it would be the first continent-to-continent crossing in a rowboat of the world's broadest ocean.

On this voyage we were privileged to carry The Explorers Club Flag No. 152. It brought us luck and inspired us in the oceanographic research projects we conducted on the Pacific. We expanded upon programs in bioluminescence and pollution begun on our Atlantic rowing voyage in 1981. We made observations of bioluminescence and took measurements of pollution at sea and on the beaches of the islands where we stopped. Pollution in the form of plastic presents a significant threat to the ocean and coastal environment. Results of these studies will be the subject of another article.

Briefly, a neuston net with a 10cm opening was floated on the surface with a wood framework, and towed behind the boat to catch samples of surface plankton and possible pollution. Beaches are the natural collectors of pelagic pollution, and we made systematic counts of plastic debris along the high-tide lines on islands as well as the Australian coast. Samples were collected, labeled and, where possible, sent back to the U.S. from the islands.

What made us think we could row across the Pacific? A Swede by the name of Anders made two attempts in the early '70s. Beaten back onto the South American coast by adverse currents, it took several months to repair his rowboat and replace broken oars. Anders then rowed to Samoa where he had to end his voyage 3300 miles short of Australia due to intestinal problems.

A British couple, Fairfax and Cook, rowed from California to Australia, landing at an island on the Australian coast. Peter Bird, another Britisher, made two attempts from California. On the first, he lost his boat on a reef in Hawaii. On the second he made it to the Great Barrier Reef, where his boat was wrecked and he had to be rescued by the Australian Navy. We wanted to row an even greater distance: 10,000 miles from South America to Australia.

We thought we could make it because we had experience in ocean rowing and a special boat. Designed by Ed Montesi, we had built the 25-foot *Excalibur* ourselves using foam and fiberglass. She is only five feet wide and has a tiny cabin in the bow where we can squeeze in to get out of bad weather. In the stern is an even smaller cabin for storage. In the middle of the boat is an open deck area with two rowing stations complete with sliding seats. Oars are the only means of propulsion; there are no sails or motors.

We rowed her across the Atlantic in 1981 from Africa to the West Indies in 83 days (see *Smithsonian Magazine*, October 1981, and *The Explorers Journal*, March 1982). That 3600-mile voyage was as far as we could go without stopping to resupply. There simply wasn't space on such a small boat to stock enough food and water for two people to go further.

On the Pacific we would have to stop periodically at islands to buy food and fill our water jugs. That is how we planned to row the Pacific in a boat designed for the Atlantic. We looked forward to the chance to see and experience firsthand the paradise of the South Pacific islands. A few changes were made in the boat for the Pacific voyage: tinted window ports for the bright tropical sun, extra ventilation for the heat, a brighter orange color for better visibility. The rowboat was renamed *Excalibur Pacific*.

Ocean rowing is an endurance sport. It is also exploration, adventure, and survival in a very limited space for a long time at sea. Training and preparations must be taken seriously. In the summer of 1983 we took a long marathon rowing trip of 2400 miles down the entire length of the Mississippi River. The 67-day journey told us we still had the right stuff to row oceans.

Through the winter we ran the roads and mountain trails near where we lived in Vermont and sometimes carried iron bars in our hands: stamina, endurance, and conditioning were important; our survival would depend on it. In the sport of competitive rowing, we have never been very fast over the standard 2000m courses. Our best strength was in longer events, and the rougher the conditions, the better we did. For us ocean rowing is a logical extension of years of experience in racing shells.

The search for sponsorship took over a year. In all, 25 companies provided the necessary support. They sent us everything from financial support to transportation to and from the Pacific, food, medical supplies, oars, navigation equipment, paint, rope, an anchor, film, and videotape. The supplies kept coming in and we wondered how we would find space for it all on the rowboat. We needed camping equipment, such as sleeping bags, foam pads to sleep on, stoves, and a ham radio to keep in touch with civilization while out on the ocean. We couldn't forget lip balm, sun screen, sunglasses, books to read, cassette tape player and tapes, charts, navigation tables, and a sextant.

Had we forgotten anything? Hopefully everything was in the boat as we pulled it on a trailer from Vermont to Philadelphia. There we boarded the *Santa Paula* on her final voyage as a passenger-carrying freighter. *Excalibur Pacific* rode below in a 40-foot steel shipping container.

After a transit of the Panama Canal we were deposited on the dock with the rowboat at Guayaquil, Ecuador. Here we were told we would not be able to start the rowing voyage from Ecuador as originally planned. Pirates along the coast of Ecuador posed too great a threat. Highly organized, they move quickly in open motorized boats and carry modern weapons. We decided to go on to Peru and begin the voyage there, where the problem of piracy was said not to exist.

We found a small container ship, the *Strider Fearless*, that took us, together with the rowboat, south to Callao, Peru.

Callao is the port from which the Kon Tiki raft departed on its memorable voyage to French Polynesia. Times have changed since 1949. Peru was in a state of emergency when we arrived in June 1984. Terrorist bombs were blowing up power-line towers and the Russian fleet looked like it was there to stay awhile. The customs officials were on strike, so the boat was locked in a compound guarded by soldiers. It took 12 days of hassles and negotiations to get the boat released. Thanks to the lawyers and diplomats at the United States Embassy in Lima, the boat was finally released on July 4th.

Part of the agreement was for us to leave immediately in order to alleviate the fears of the Peruvian officials who thought we might try to sell the rowboat on the black market. As soon as the *Excalibur Pacific* was put in the water, we said goodbye to new Peruvian friends, officials, reporters, and soldiers who crowded along the wharf and shore to see us leave. We shoved off and started rowing. It was 5:00 P.M.

By dark we had cleared the breakwater and reached the last sea buoy. On into the night we rowed, assisted by the outflowing tide. By morning, we were far enough out and the weather was overcast and hazy, so that the coast could not be seen. We never saw the coast of South America after that first day, though we came close to it at night.

On July 6th we were asleep in the bow cabin, letting the boat drift. The night was made darker by overcast skies and a heavy mist. Every couple of hours one of us would look out to check for ships. At 1:00 A.M. I saw a light close to our starboard beam. Around us were towering rock mounds; we had drifted to the Peruvian coast.

There was an incredible amount of bioluminescence around the rocks. The water was full of shimmering green light. The waves and the direction they were going in were outlined by light streaks. Pinpoints of bioluminescence were scattered all around us. Tunnels of diffuse light were created by large schools of fish. Everywhere we looked there was light beneath the boat.

The oars went out and each of us would take turns rowing while the other steered by the light in the waves. Though the danger was immediate, the eerie light of the breaking waves gave us a true sense of direction. By 4:00 A.M. the rowboat was safely away from the coast and in open ocean again.

Marine and bird life was abundant during the first part of the South Pacific row. When we left Callao, Peru, we rowed into the Humboldt Current, rowing through it until the Galapagos Islands. The Humboldt is a cold-water current, and it supports a very active marine life.

On July 8th, four days after leaving Callao, we saw a bewhiskered sea lion swimming off our stern. He stayed with us the whole day, sometimes coming up to the side of the boat. A few days later he was replaced by a pod of huge baleen whales. It was our first experience in the rowboat with such enormous creatures. I watched with a mixture of fascination and horror as they surfaced close to the boat so that I could almost touch them.

Every day we were visited by birds, mostly blue- and red-footed boobies. For company on the boat we had a hen named Callao. She had been given to us by Peruvian friends. Callao didn't know what to make of the sea birds as they swooped down out of the sky. Sometimes she'd duck her head as if to avoid being hit by them!

Almost every boat at sea has the delightful experience of dolphins swimming beside the boat. The *Excalibur Pacific* was no exception. Black Pacific dolphins and grey spotted dolphins joined us as we rowed. An occasional brown sea turtle would bring up the rear.

We entered into a world very different from life on land. Surrounding the rowboat was a wilderness of ocean, sky and creatures few people have ever experienced in such intimate detail. In the Humboldt Current, once we cleared the Peruvian coast, we saw only two ships, and they were too far away to see us.

Late one night, long after we had taken the oars in and squeezed into the bow cabin to sleep, we had a strange visitor. An odd rasping noise on the hull woke us. I went out and saw, with the aid of a hand-held spotlight, that a 9- to 10-foot shark was rubbing against the hull. There was a remora on his back; perhaps he was trying to get it off. The shark—I think it was a blue shark— followed us for several days. At night we would stay awake talking or listening to music as long as possible to keep the shark away. But without fail, when the boat was quiet and we were asleep, he would return.

On the second night his behavior was more aggressive. He banged into the boat and pushed at the hull with his snout. It was hard to sleep with these goings-on less than an inch from our heads. By now we had noticed that whenever we heard the clicks or the blow spouts of a pair of 30-foot whales, the shark would pay us a visit.

On the third night we heard the whales right outside the boat. Then the shark made the most violent attack. He banged into the daggerboards we use to stabilize the boat. They run through two slots in the deck, and I was afraid the hull could be damaged by the repeated blows from the shark. The rudder was next and ran through a similar slot in the back cabin. It was essential to control the course and we had no spare. The shark bent the shaft of the rudder.

I finally had to kill the shark. I shot him with a small automatic that fired .22 long rifle shells. The bullet left a luminescent trail in the water that led to the middle of the shark's body. Then he got mad and banged the boat violently, nearly throwing me off balance. When he came to the surface next to the boat, I leaned over and shot him in the head at point-blank range. Blood and salt water splashed, and the shark went limp and sank slowly under the boat. It didn't bother us again.

Twenty-eight days after leaving Callao we sighted land. It was Española Island in the Galapagos. The entire day was spent rowing towards it, 12 miles away. But ten hours later we had gained only 4½ miles and were slipping westward all the time. The Galapagos Islands are known for their notorious unexact (fickle) currents. In a rowboat we were especially susceptible to them.

When at 5:00 P.M. on the 1st of August we determined the boat's course to be northwest, we decided to take advantage of the drift and slip in between Española and Floreana Islands and attempt to make it to Santa Cruz. Our chances were good that with constant pressure on the oars, Academy Bay within Santa Cruz Island could be reached.

Thirty-six hours later, after rowing constantly with sea lions and albatrosses for company, we arrived in Academy Bay at 2:00 A.M. local time. There were a few frights along the way when a shoal wave sounded off the starboard beam and just as we started into the Bay the village and navigational lights went off. (Kathleen steered by the lights from an Ecuadorian supply ship anchored in the middle of the Bay while Curtis rowed.) We dropped anchor in Academy Bay for two weeks before heading on for the Marquesas. The trip had taken 30 days, a distance of 1200 miles from Peru to the Galapagos.

The Galapagos Islands are the summits of volcanic mountains. A rugged archipelago, they are best known for their unique wildlife and many endemic species. We joined a group of students from Loma Linda University and explored caves in the mountains of Santa Cruz Island, where we found skeletons of giant tortoises, now extinct in that part of the island.

In the little village of Puerto Aroyo we built a spare rudder with the help of an Ecuadorian Indian carpenter. At the local restaurants we viewed examples of the native iguanas, which would crawl up under the tables. Darwin finches landed by our plates and would help themselves if not shooed away. Protected by the Ecuadorian government, the wildlife has become tame and survives in peaceful co-existence with the multinational human inhabitants of the little village at Academy Bay.

When we left after a two-week stay and re-supply period, we again entered the strange area between the islands—we called it the Galapagos Sea—so influenced were the currents by the island land masses. It took 30 hours of continuous rowing to make it out of the islands. We beat the current that wanted to pull us up the Canal Pinzon and made it past Isla Isabella in time for a late breakfast.

How well we ate on the voyage depended on the food available at the island re-supply points. Much of the food in the Galapagos was imported from the mainland and wasn't too fresh. Jam, noodles and cheese, candy, and fruit drink we'd brought from the States supplemented the supplies we bought locally.

Log entry: "August 29, 1984, Galapagos to Marquesas: 75 sucre bananas are going yellow like crazy. We are eating them as banana milk, banana and peanut butter snacks, and next—banana sour dough fruit drink bread. We decided to make the big meal of the day in the afternoon and eat more. . . ."

The currents in the South Pacific seem to be in a state of change or disruption. Contrary to the information on the latest Pilot Charts, we experienced considerable current from the south and even southwest. Visible on the surface, these often converging currents appeared in the form of waves coming from various directions. They presented a problem for us with lumpy seas and over 500 miles of south to make in the 3500-mile voyage to the Marquesas.

Rough conditions made us feel very tired by the time we'd been at sea for three weeks. On September 13th, while shooting stars with the sextant before dawn, Curtis was hit by a wave and knocked overboard. Though he was attached to the boat with a safety harness and line, the sextant was not and it was lost. We had no spare. To save space we'd left the extra one at home. We had a watch, ephemeris, compass, and radio.

With the help of amateur and professional navigators via the radio and a lot of experimentation we built a makeshift astrolabe to measure the sun's shadow at noon for latitude. When it was clear, we took the time of sunrise and/or sunset and compared it with the almanac times on our latitude at the Greenwich meridian for an approximation of longitude (+/- 20 miles, depending on conditions).

Marvin Cremer, just back from a circumnavigation without instruments, sent us information via radio on the ancient Polynesian methods of celestial navigation. We used all of these techniques to navigate the last 2,000 miles to the Marquesas. The U.S. Coast Guard and Navy coordinated an attempt to determine our position by using huge "ears" to home in on our radio signal. It proved impossible to determine more than an approximate position.

When we arrived where the islands should have been, no land could be seen. Finally we smelled land, and rowed north for 48 hours to find Ua Pou Island.

After the eventful 66-day trip from the Galapagos to the Marquesas we decided to drop anchor in the Marquesas for the hurricane season. It was a five-month period we would use to work on the boat, restock the food supply and rest. We also used that time from October to March to travel in French Polynesia and purchase the bulk of our boat repair material and foodstuff in the well-supplied capital of Papeete, Tahiti.

In December we left the boat in Ua Pou in the village doctor's garden and traveled south on board a sailboat to the Tuamotu Archipelago. The Tuamotus are atolls. They are coral formations, rings surrounding calm water lagoons. We visited five or six of the atolls during the weeks we were there. A few days before Christmas we caught an inter-island copra boat to Tahiti. In Papeete we renewed acquaintances with sailboat friends made in the Galapagos and Marquesas.

Some of the pressures of modern civilization have not reached this South Sea island paradise. But the beaches are natural collectors of floating pollution from the ocean. Unfortunately, plastic debris was more plentiful than pretty shells.

Supplies were plentiful in Tahiti, and the island was beautiful. Loaded with boxes of canned foods, fiberglass resin, and shells found on the beaches, we returned to Ua Pou in mid-February on the passenger freighter *Aranui*.

In the doctor's garden on Ua Pou we applied fiberglass to punctures in the hull's outer skin, repaired a broken oar shaft, inventoried all boat equipment, and spent our time replacing and cleaning up. A week before departure in March the boat bottom was painted with a fresh coat of anti-fouling paint and we were ready to leave Ua Pou.

We left Ua Pou Island on March 23, and began the 2000-mile row to the Samoa Islands. This was the finest passage in the row across the South Pacific. It was warm, it was balmy, and the seas were generally calm.

There were exceptions. Rain squalls were sometimes built up by the heat. The relatively calm sea conditions caused the clouds to rise to a great height. Squalls came through with tremendous winds that could last an hour or several hours. The fear of lightning and the sound of thunder at sea are horrible things. Following these low-pressure troughs, there would be a day or so of calm conditions.

These calms brought out the whales. Here we saw the biggest whales of the row across the South Pacific. Sixty feet in length, these baleen-type whales swam right up and nudged the boat. Curtis put on mask and fins, grabbed the underwater camera and went swimming with them. Under water the clicking sounds of their communication could be heard clearly. I never swam right up and touched the whales; I wish I had, but at the time I was too scared.

In the water with the whales I developed the feeling that they meant us no harm. They could have destroyed the boat, but these whales were only curious. When they went into a slow dive I knew they were leaving. They simply inclined their bodies steeply and then, all in formation, they sank into the depths of the sea. The wind built up and the sea built and we were rowing on towards Samoa.

The first rowing session of the new day began before sunup. Cool air, the deck wet with dew, and here and there a tiny flying fish was found on deck from a one-way flight the night before. The rowing seats were taken from the back cabin and put on the bow and stern rowing tracks, and carbon fibre oars were untied. Sometimes it seemed that putting out the oars involved a combination of moves only Curt and I knew.

Oars in place, safety harnesses out of the way, we each took two oars in hand and began rowing. The first strokes were short ones to get the feel of the boat's motion, which differed depending upon the weather. Gradually we lengthened the stroke and fell into an easy rhythm. The boat moved best when all four oars pulled through the water at the same time with even strokes. On the voyage across the Pacific we each averaged about six hours of rowing per day. Usually we rowed alone, but fairly often (nearly every day) we put in a session rowing together.

We have always found long rowing sessions (minimum one hour) a good time to think. A good imagination is especially useful. The mind never stops as the oars continue their work. We saved certain subjects to think about only when rowing. Boat designs, past trips, or high school friends. Time would fly by, the sun would be up and breakfast wasn't far off. All the aches and pains of the night before would be gone and the muscles would be working smoothly.

Forty days after leaving Ua Pou we arrived at Pago Pago, American Samoa. We stayed a total of four weeks in Pago Pago. We hadn't intended to stay so long, but there were a few problems. The rowing seats on the axles had broken and the wheels popped off. We were hammering them with nails towards the end of the last passage. We had to do repairs on them. It was a pleasure to rest and enjoy American culture for the first time in nearly a year.

We left Tutuila on May 30th ready to row for Australia. We had planned not to stop, to go straight, as it were. With the outgoing tide in the evening at six we rowed out of Pago Pago. The weather bureau on the island gave us a good weather report, but it seems every time we were given long-range weather, something unforeseen happened. About 10 P.M., the wind turned around and we had a northwest gale on our hands. We were only half a mile off the coast. It went on for several hours and by early morning we found ourselves close to the coast. It took a lot of effort to get away from the islands of Samoa.

It wasn't until a week later that we were 100 miles away from the Samoa Islands. That seemed to characterize the rest of the trip. It was a 27-day row, eventually, because we had taken on so much water during heavy weather. The hatches were constantly flooded, the food cans were rusting badly and we were exhausted from the violent motions of the seas.

The temperatures were much cooler than we were accustomed to after a year in the tropics. Most of the time we experienced 60–70°F temperatures when we were used to 90°F. All the sweatshirts and pants along with foul-weather gear came out of the stern cabin for daily use. We had sold our sleeping bags in the Marquesas, and now all we had were native pareus, a two-meter cloth apiece.

One of the most frightening things at sea between Samoa and Vanuatu was to see many pieces of volcanic pumice floating on the surface of the sea. These pieces of pumice had been released by submarine volcanic action. It was frightening to think that beneath us there could be an erupting volcano. We realized that the release of energy from the earth's core from vents on the ocean floor could contribute to shifts in Pacific Ocean currents.

Twenty-seven days after leaving Samoa an emergency stop was called for. The weather had been horrendous the entire time. The previously water-tight hatches took in water daily, food cans rusted, and supplies went moldy. The sea anchors were damaged in heavy seas and a new one was needed. Most of all, we needed a break.

Port Vila in Vanuatu turned out to be one of the best stops we ever made. Yachtsmen and local people were friendly and as helpful as could be. Fresh food supplies were plentiful and prices reasonable. We stayed a week, but the time was well used.

On July 4th, 1985, one year after leaving Peru, we rowed out of Port Vila for the very last leg of the voyage. We were nervous about the crossing of the Coral Sea. By now we knew it would be impossible to row into the wind and reach Brisbane as originally planned. Instead, armed with detailed charts and two sextants that had been sent to us in the Marquesas, we headed straight for the Great Barrier Reef.

To get there we had to control the course of the boat in changeable current conditions. Usually we had to row at an angle to the waves. The weather came from the south or southeast mostly, and we had to go west, passing through a corridor between outlying reefs.

Electronic self-steering helped a lot, though one day we were surprised to see the course had somehow changed itself. Soon we discovered the reason: A booby bird landed on the self-steering compass control and with its foot altered the course setting. After that we checked the course more often.

A tremendous gale came out of the south just as we were between the last of the outlying reefs, about 120 miles from the Australian coast. We later learned that two sailing yachts had been lost in that storm. For us it meant three days of conditions too rough to row in. First we rode on a sea anchor, then as the waves built to 35 feet with steep faces and conflicting rebound waves echoing off the Great Barrier Reef, we had to pull in the sea anchor to roll with the punches better. Under those conditions, sun lines of position (LOPs) through breaks in the clouds could only give us a rough estimate of our position.

That night we were trying to sleep in the bow cabin when a wave hit the boat in such a way as to roll her over completely. We were knocked on top of each other. Everything was in a state of disorder. Strangely, after that night the seas began to calm down and we could put out the oars and row in the direction of the Great Barrier Reef.

With the skies steadily clearing we determined our position to be such that we could make a direct course for Noggin Passage. The weather in the

Coral Sea was unstable, to say the least, and we were anxious to be within the Great Barrier Reef as soon as possible. We rowed towards Noggin Passage, approaching from the south. With the boat's shallow draft we were able to drift over submerged reefs, although we had not really planned on it.

Diurnal tides pulled us into the Great Barrier Reef sooner than we expected. Night had fallen and by moonlight we could see the coral reef beneath the boat. Rather than risk running aground during the night, we dropped a metal anchor and 300 feet of line. Squalls at dawn prevented star-sights, but a series of sun LOPs showed us to be close by Noggin Passage. Unable to retrieve the anchor, we had to cut the line, knowing there was no stopping until we reached the coast.

By nightfall we had rowed 15 miles through Noggin Passage to the inner edge of the Great Barrier Reef. Fourteen miles of open water separated us from the precipitous coast of Australia 25 miles south of Cairns. We drifted in unsettled weather, taking compass bearings every hour or so off the lights on Russell and Fitzroy Islands.

We slept through a couple of alarms on the wrist watch and awoke at dawn to find we were very close indeed to the Australian continent, about two miles. We were being pushed in by waves and rain squalls that came in with strong gusting winds. It seemed unsafe to try to row past the rock promontory of Cape Grafton under these conditions, which is what we would have to do to reach Cairns.

The storms were quickly pushing us at the coast. With no anchor we had no choice but to land. We rowed along the coast, picked a likely spot on the beach and surfed the *Excalibur Pacific* in, breaking an oar in the process. We'd made it! Ten thousand miles of rowboat voyaging from South America to Australia in just 391 days, 189 of which were spent at sea in the rowboat.

There was nobody on that beach to welcome us. There were no roads, just wild Australian outback. It was here on this remote beach that the largest concentration of plastic waste was found. The farther west we'd gone in the west-flowing currents, the more pollution we'd noticed. Along the high-tide line a 100-yard section of this beach contained no fewer than 286 individual pieces of plastic on the surface. That night the weather cleared and the super high tide came back in. By the full moon we rowed out through the surf and rounded Cape Grafton.

Shortly after noon on July 31st, we rowed into Cairns for an official welcome. So make that 190 days at sea, but it was worth it to see the marlin fishing capital of the world. Since we were kids we've always wanted to go to Australia, but at the time we never dreamed we'd arrive in a rowboat.

—THE EXPLORERS JOURNAL, DECEMBER 1985

PART NINE

United Kingdom

Biscay Gales

BY LEONARD OUTHWAITE

W e had a slight feeling of uneasiness as we slipped our moor-
ing at Falmouth early on October 4. The captain who had
brought us over from America had died, and we had had
difficulty in replacing him. We had had to organize a new
crew and bend a suit of winter canvas, which was delayed in delivery. Only
such accidents kept us on the English coast in October; only the fact that we
had to sail our ship south or abandon her thousands of miles from home justified a Biscay crossing at this late season.

But there was little visible justification for this uneasy feeling. The new
captain was beside me on deck, the weather fine and clear, and the barometer hanging quite steadily around 30 as we stood out. We brought the
Manacles abeam at ten o'clock, and here we set our log and took our departure. There was an easy swell and a light wind out of the west as we ran past
the Lizard and Wolf's Rock and dropped the English coast behind. We hoped
that the week of gales we had encountered in the Channel had now blown
itself out. I had determined to make our westing early in the passage, so that
we should have sea room in case of bad weather and an opportunity to keep
clear of the dangerous cliffs and currents of Finisterre.

As the day wore on, however, it was clear that this was not going to be an
easy matter. By evening the wind out of the southwest had already reached
force 4 on the Beaufort scale and was freshening. The short chop of the
Channel had given place to a succession of long, sweeping Atlantic gray-
backs. The barometer was dropping.

Climbing the companionway to a midnight watch, I passed the barometer and saw that it had moved down two-tenths. On deck, one quick glance
showed me that we were carrying all working canvas and charging westward,
but the going was heavy. Overside, the first impression was that of a rather

heavy sea, broken waves sending a lop of spray aboard. Gradually I was aware that something else, something fundamental, was giving us our peculiar uneasy motion. The waves we saw were just surface waves. They were simply riding over the top of great even, mountainous swells that came piling up out of the southwest. Such swells are created by storms at a distance; they travel faster than the storm; they are sometimes the precursors of bad weather.

I remember thinking this as I turned to take the watch from the Captain. We stood looking overhead, where hung a high, gray pall against which dense, dark masses of clouds were moving rapidly. As these dark clouds swept over us, squalls of wind hit us. *Kinkajou* bent to them and shook and leaped ahead, climbing for long moments up a gray slope and then sliding, sliding, down an interminably sinking hill.

"Captain, it looks as though we are in for some bad weather."

"I don't like the look of it much. But the worst of it may be blown out before it reaches us."

"Need we shorten sail before you turn in?"

"I don't think so. It's only the squalls that are heavy and they don't seem to have the weight in them that they did an hour or so ago."

"All right, Captain, I'll call you if it gets worse."

It did get worse, and by morning we were under shortened canvas, making a few painful miles to the westward whenever the gale let us, and finding ourselves all but hove to when it was blowing its worst. There was a dull, gray surface over the whole of the sky, and the even, unearthly light fell on fantastic moving mountains of water.

Yachtsmen talk about their vessels being dry in a storm—going through a blow without taking a drop of water. I'm sure that this is just a relative term which seamen use. In a full gale or in a hurricane, dryness is impossible. I know that, once the gale was well established, *Kinkajou* was wet, though at that time we had taken no solid water aboard. The force of the wind was now such that it seemed to flatten out the crests of the waves. It shaved the tops off them and sent a horizontal volley of drops over our decks that stung like bullets. High above our deck our sails were soaked with spray, and runnels of water blew out of the leeches. All about the ship vision was obscured by spindrift and gray water fumes.

The air was full of sound. At first the sound is impossible to analyze. You are simply conscious that many noises are blended in one great uproar. This uproar accompanies you wherever you go. The wind, of course, has already choked up all ordinary utterances. Even shouted orders are taken out of your mouth as they are formed and carried aloft with the spindrift. Your voice is painfully weak, lost in this vast symphony. It is only later, crouched in the lee of a deckhouse, waiting your trick at the wheel, that you have opportunity to observe the components of chaos.

There is, of course, the howl and scream of the wind about the rigging and the hull, something like the sounds about a house during a high winter storm. But, in addition to this, there are the special noises of the sea, the low, heavy thrumming noise, set up by the vibration of the rigging. Our taut-set backstay runner had an insistent ominous note of its own. All during the gale it kept up a low moaning, and when the worst of the squalls hit us, its pitch would rise into a weird chant.

From the sea itself there come two sorts of sound—the slap and thunder of the waves that strike along her side, and behind these the continuous roaring undertone of the waves that break about us without reaching us.

Then it's your watch below. You must shove back the hatch slide, duck down, and close it again as rapidly as possible. At first you feel that you have come into peace and quietness, but you have merely exchanged one order of clamor for another. The tumult of wind and waves is dimmer, and the whistling and shrieking winds sound distant as in inner rooms of a house. But the thrumming of the masts and rigging is carried down into the hull and reverberates there as the sound of the strings echoes in the body of a violin. There is some noise from the motor turning slowly to improve our steerageway. But its rhythm varies in speed as the vessel labors up the side of a wave or plunges rapidly and distressingly into a valley. There is added also all the noise from the body of the ship herself. For no vessel, no matter how well built, can stand this buffeting without speaking her mind about it. There is a great, dull boom forward, sensed as a concussion rather than as a sound, as an unusually heavy wave strikes her on the weatherbow. There's a momentary shock, and the vessel shakes herself as she gathers headway again and begins nosing over the crest. "That shook me up, but we'll go on," she says. Just after you think she has come dry through that attack, there is a drumming of heavy drops on the cabin top, a thunder of falling water on the deck, a sloshing about as she clears through the freeing ports.

We took some that time!

We had reckoned on storms but nothing of this magnitude.

"I'm all right," said my wife, "but this seems more than we bargained for. Can't we get out of it for a while? Isn't there a port we can run into?"

"There isn't, I'm afraid. We're beyond the British Isles. We've made a good deal of our westing and we're two hundred miles from Falmouth, but I'll call the Captain and we'll take stock of the situation."

In oilskins and dripping sou'wester, Captain Carter came and sat on the companionway steps. He was quiet and slow of speech and relatively cheerful.

"Captain," I said, "these are your home waters. What do you think of the weather? Should we run for a port?"

And the Captain replied: "There is no telling about the weather. It may hang on, it might billow out even before we can run back to port. There is nothing good in the Scillys and they are almost as far as Falmouth. I don't like the French ports; there are dangers off them, and the tides are terrible, particularly in bad weather. And then you're worse there, for there's more westing to make when you start again."

Georgia asked: "Is the ship all right? Shall we get through this?"

"Oh, the ship's all right. She can stand it. How about you, madam? We'd be easier running."

Georgia looked at me and shook her head. "No, Captain, we don't want to do it all over again, and it may blow out soon."

So that was settled. Even while we were talking, sunlight began to come through the cabin ports. I went back on deck with the Captain. Unexpectedly the sky had cleared now, but the wind was still blowing with great fury. We entered the wind in our log as Force 8, for both the Captain and I had a feeling that the tendency in a small ship was to exaggerate our estimates of wind and sea. Later we learned that another ship near at hand gave a conservative estimate of Force 10, and that the English and Irish coasts close by us recorded full storms and wind speeds varying between 70 and 90 miles an hour.

Do you know what wind speeds of even 60 miles an hour mean at sea? They choke the breath in your nostrils. You have to turn your head or shelter your face to breathe freely and deeply. In heavy clothes and oilskins you make a great target for the blast. Even at 40 miles an hour you can fairly lean against the wind. Every movement is an exertion, yet has to be made with precision and caution, for the deck is heaving, and a misstep may send you lurching toward the lee rail. A bit of canvas or rope not made fast becomes a lashing menace, and a solid bit of gear like a block takes charge and goes bulleting about the deck till it breaks somebody's shins or is mercifully washed overboard.

For some hours that day it stayed clear, and the sea and sky made a monstrous spectacle. The sky was a deep, hard, vivid, intense blue, and the sudden sunlight was dazzling after so many gray days. But all this seemed unreal and incongruous with this fury about us. The changing blues and greens of the waves were translucent. Behind their outlines you could discern other moving, mysterious shapes. The great mountains of water went marching by the ship like warriors in white plumes.

I suppose we all intellectually knew that the blue of the sky was too deep and too intense to presage real clearing and milder weather. Yet we all irrationally took heart. It was a game that was worth playing. Though many of us aboard were periodically sick and often uneasy, we turned up promptly for our watches and carried on. The fo'c's'le was wet, the galley a roaring, rattling confusion of pots and pans. Though the cook was sick and the fire failed and no water for dish washing would stay in place and though even the pot of coffee had to be held on the stove, we still managed to get irregular bites to eat. Little Henry, the steward, was white-faced and wobbly-kneed but he smiled wanly and managed somehow to distribute rations. We all caught something from the determination and the fury of the weather and turned this spirit to our own account in going about our duties.

But it was my watch below. No matter how much beauty or wonder was to be gathered from the scene on deck, sleep was better. I lumbered down the companionway steps, and as I passed the barometer noticed with a start that our glass stood at 29.5". That wasn't too cheering. Still . . .

"Look here, dear, it's bright and clear on deck. There's probably still some wind coming, but it looks a little better. I've got to get some rest but I want to watch the barometer. I'll lie down here and if I don't wake up you call me every hour and I'll take a reading."

I thought that we might be encouraged by a mounting-glass.

We were on the starboard tack, and my bunk was to windward. It seemed too much of an effort to crawl way up there. Anyway I had to get up each hour, so there was no good shedding clothes. I pulled together a few deck cushions, braced my feet against the drawers of the leeward bunk, and wedged my back against the entry to the wash room. "Let 'er pitch and roll."

Pitch and roll she did, and I tried faintly to sleep. First a suitcase that had been stowed behind the companionway steps escaped and came charging down on top of me. Then a square wooden box with a spare four-inch compass in it jumped out of its cuddy and struck in the middle of my back. The catch of a door sprang and the door went fanning back and forth, creating a terrific uproar with each roll of the ship. I got it locked and had just settled down again when a drawer in my bunk broke from its retaining catch and shot across the cabin. It made a dent in the woodwork just an inch or so above my head. Before I knew it the hour was up. The barometer had fallen a tenth. Then I did some fitful sleeping.

Every hour for the next four hours it had dropped a corresponding tenth.

"Shall we run for it now?" I would ask Georgia.

And she would say, "No, we might as well stick it through."

She was right in this, for it was now our only course. *It was too late to run.* Our safety lay in working off to the westward and southward and heaving to when we had to.

My memory of the sequence of events through the succeeding days is vague. The whole orderly routine of ship life was cluttered with extra duties and fractured by emergences. I was too sick and harassed to keep a record of what happened other than the notes that went into the log. There was a lot of work, and of course we must have taken food and done some sleeping, but the order of these events is difficult to follow. We went through them mechanically, and my memory is hazed with the tumult and fatigue.

Even the familiar ship took on a fantastic, sodden, bedraggled air that was hard to associate with the orderly vessel she had once been. Yet certain scenes and details come to mind with great vividness and I set them down here as I recall them.

It's midnight of the 5th. I am coming down the companionway from a trick at the wheel. We have been under way with a slow motor and a foresail set for steadiness. We have been making slow progress to the west and south, and my back and arms are numb from the labor of holding the wheel steady against the bucking seas. My hands are cold and it's almost impossible to open them. My fingers feel as though they still gripped the spokes of the wheel. The barometer is rising now as rapidly and steadily as it dropped. It goes back to 29.5" and hangs there. The gale is blowing colder now out of the northwest. I grope my way into the cabin and fling my short oilskin coat in a corner. My clothes beneath it are soaking wet. I am conscious that my toes are squinching water out of the heavy socks in my sea boots. The effort of struggling out of those boots is more than my tired will can cope with and I just drop into a dull sleep on the floor in the cabin.

An explosion rings in my ears. It carries even above the noise of the storm and is succeeded by rolls of thunder. As my eyes come open I can see by the cabin clock that it is 1:30. Without being told, I know that I am wanted on deck and must somehow get up there. As I come on deck the man at the wheel jams his body against the spokes and gropes about at his feet. He comes up with a curved bar of metal. It's a bit of the fore-sheet traveler that has carried away. This ring of metal holds the sheet block to the boom and thus keeps the whole foresail under control. It's gone now, and the foresail with its boom and gaff are swung outward and are crashing about in the fury of the storm. That confusion must be subdued or the sail will tear itself to pieces and the gaff and boom shake loose from the mast.

I take the wheel while the seaman and the Captain wrestle with that task. As the men are grouped forward, the lop of a great wave sweeps across the deck, and their forms disappear in a welter of water and spray and foam. There is a little flat following a great comber like that, and I take this opportunity to bring the ship up into the wind. Her deck rises steeply as the next wave comes up under her but she takes no more water, and the water on deck clears rapidly out of the scuppers aft. Twice the sailors throw a bight of rope around the boom and twice it breaks away from them before they can get a turn. Once two of them get catapulted across the deck and nearly go overboard. I rush forward and grab one of the men and push him toward the wheel, and we re-order our attack. Two of us go to the peak and throat halyards and slack away a good bit. For a while the flapping and confusion seems increased but we make fast and creep back to the waist of the ship. Then we watch our chance and jump simultaneously for the leech of the sail as it bellies over our heads. We smother it and can hold fast just long enough to get a hold of a reef-cringle. We heave this down, and the wild waving of the boom is damped. Now it, too, can be lashed amidships. Now we can lower away smartly and smother the canvas as it comes down. It seems a long, slow job getting everything made up and secure. Then there's the forestaysail to set. I find myself swinging to a halyard beside the old Norwegian. He has always been saying that we haven't seen real heavy weather yet. I shout in his ear, "Blowing now?"

"Ya! Plenty."

I have just taken an amazed look around before dropping below. It's a wonder to me that we are still all sound and all aboard. The gale from the northwest has been running for some hours now, and a new sea is working up from that quarter against the undercurrent of the old one. The waves have changed their shape. They are no longer orderly successions of crests and hollows, but confused pyramidal structures that tower up and collapse suddenly, so that you are conscious of the solidity, the weight, and the impact of great masses of water. The ship is behaving beautifully, but we can't dodge all of them, and every once in a while part of a crest comes aboard and sweeps the deck. This seems to me more dangerous than anything we have had yet. The exhilaration is gone out of us now and we just face dull, hard work. I'm too tired even to worry. I just drop to sleep again.

I see in the log that during his watch the Captain reports "continued gale and heavy hail squalls." One or two large stones are still melting in our scuppers in the morning and a heavy oilskin has been cut by their impact. . . .

I think it's the morning of the 6th that the Captain has a weak moment. He comes to ask if we don't want to try running off, taking a chance of working our way out of the Bay in more favorable weather. We shake our heads. Our decision seems justified. It moderates in the afternoon. The wind entries for successive two-hour periods run 6–5–4–3. There's still a terrific sea running. The cook has pulled himself together and got the rudiments of a hot meal, and Georgia and I are wedged together in the lee bunk eating in celebration of our respite.

But the 7th is just a long, bad day, the storm resuming. We take in everything and set a storm trysail on our foremast. Instead of swinging around to the north and east and blowing clear, the wind is back into the southwest, and we seem to be starting all over again. We are close hauled on the port tack. Somebody is pounding on my hatch cover. Even in my dull weariness I know this is my signal to turn out. By a glance at the clock I see that my watch below is but half up. "My God! What is it this time?" At least I don't have to struggle into clothes, but my legs in my heavy sea boots are leaden, and it seems an effort even to raise my arms. "Why do things always happen when I'm below? Can't those fools on deck take care of the ship?" I'm too tired even to swear. These curses just shape themselves in my mind, and even as they shape I know that they are unjust, for all hands have been called repeatedly. Something, maybe fear, has even galvanized our laziest sailor into willing action. After all it's my responsibility and I've got to get up that companionway. After a roll and a lurch the ship steadies for a moment. Now for it. As I step over the companionway doors and combing, my boots splash into a surge of water. The Captain is at the wheel. He is yelling something in my ear and waving his arm at the darkness, where the light from the engine room fore ports just shows some of the men huddled in the waist of the ship.

"Sea . . . broke aboard. Fo'c's'le hatch carried away . . . washed out below."

I shout back. "Have to run off."

He just nods. "Watch chance . . . ease foresheet."

We are into the wind, but the trouble is that the wind and the sea aren't coming from the same quarter. Even as Captain Carter is working his way forward, a great wall of water rises on our starboard bow. With water still on our deck it seems to me that we shall never rise before that wall collapses on us. And the hatch cover off! Won't our bow ever come up? In my anxiety I stamp on the deck, "You've got to come *up!* UP! UP!" The base of the wave is under us now, and I can feel the whole hull heaving. Then the stem begins to rise, and forward I can see the crest curling mast-high, its foam a spectral green, like witches' fire. It's toppling toward us, but our bow is rising wildly now. The crest is sweeping rapidly aft toward us, but it breaks short, and only the boiling of its collapse comes aboard amidships.

Another giant goes by harmlessly. There seems a momentary lull in the wind and just a vague, confused heaving of waves about us. Now is the time!

I turn around sideways to the wheel to get a better grip, and tug on the spokes to bring her about. At first she responds slowly and then comes around nicely. Amidships I can see the vague shapes of the men, their oilskins glistening. The foresheet is eased and now it is filling. There's a strain on the mast, and the ship gives a lurch as she feels the sudden impact, but it's only for a moment. She eases as we gather headway and now we are off before it, tramping white water under foot.

It suddenly seems quiet. Where has the sea gone? Our motion is easier and our deck is dry. The engineer has rigged our gangway light that we use in port, so that it sweeps the foredeck. The men have gathered most of the hatch from about the scuppers. They are fitting it together, improvising other board coverings, lashing down, covering all with spare canvas. At last the weary job is done, our ride is over, and we must come about to the seas again.

It's the morning of the 8th, and our gale is still holding. The fo'c's'le is washed out. I have just been up and have moved the men all back into the saloon. It's pathetic to see their efforts to find bits of half-dry clothing. And to see their cherished mementos of brief trips ashore floating around on the wash that is still slopping about across the floor. The galley, too, has taken its share of salt water, and the fire has been put out and rekindled half a dozen times this morning. The men are spread around the saloon floor now, wrapped in extra blankets. Some of the wash forward has swept under the doors, the carpets are soaked, and with each lurch of the ship little puddles of water are chasing themselves across the floor. The men have wedged themselves between overturned chairs to prop them against the rolling. They are too tired out to notice the noise and the discomfort. They are sprawled in awkward attitudes, mouths open, while the runnels of water slop back and forth about them.

We haven't had a clear shot of the sun since our bright hours, days before. We have changed canvas and course so much that we have no particular confidence in our dead reckoning. The Captain is for a direct southerly course, and I am still for keeping up to westward. After all this to run down and find that we were still inside the line of the Cape and caught in Rennell's current, which sweeps into the lower end of the Bay, would be too discouraging. All morning we have been waiting with sextants ready, hoping for a shot of the sun, however murky. Georgia knows that we badly want our position and when we don't get it this seems to her the last straw.

"You know, Len, I'm just miserable. I don't think I can stand any more of this. If we ever come to port, I think we'll have to lay up the ship and take the steamer home." Then after a little pause, "Do you think we shall get to port?"

It is pitiful to see her weariness. I must whisper her something encouraging. But how can you whisper when even a raised voice becomes lost in the insistent roar of the gale and when you have to jam yourself in a door frame to keep yourself from being pitched across the cabin? How can you be encouraging when you have just come from looking at that appalling ocean? There is no beauty in it now; it is gigantic, gray, sickening. I must say something. I grip the lee board of her bunk and kneel down beside it.

"Of course we'll make port, and this northern weather will be all behind us. Now, look here, dear, I know this is tough, but we've got to stick it. There is no other way. We've had as bad a time as comes to people even on a small ship, but it's going to be better. We figure we have good sea room around Finisterre. Even if the gale holds, we shall be edging around to the southward tomorrow. Now, let's forget it for a while!"

I grope my way forward and in a succession of trips carry aft some fresh biscuits in a sealed tin, a can of salted nuts, and a bottle of champagne. It's impossible to bring glasses, but we share the drink out of a thick, china cup and, though we eat literally hand to mouth, things begin to look a little more cheerful. We fall to reminiscences of the summer and to speculations as to what is going on at home. By the time it's my turn on deck again Georgia is ready for an easier sleep.

It's the night of the 8th. The barometer is rising now and for some hours the wind has been gradually shifting. It is blowing now from the northeast, and we are plowing along through a heavy, confused sea. It's still mean going, but we'll clear the Cape and how glad we'll be to see the high cliffs of the Spanish coast!

It's the afternoon of the 9th and we have been driving south by east. There is still a fresh gale, Force 8, blowing out of the northeast. We have had no sun and, on the chance that we were on soundings, I have let go the lead—130 fathoms and no bottom. We are all feeling that things are going easier and that we'll come in now and pick up the coast, but chance still holds a trump against us.

With a weight of water in our hold, the engineer suddenly reports that the electric bilge pump has stopped working. We had taken a good deal of water forward during the time that the fo'c's'le hatch had been off. This must be got rid of. We man the hand bilge pump on deck, only to find that the suction pipe is somehow obstructed. This suction pump is now deeply submerged in icy water, but hurried search reveals that the shipyard that had this matter in charge had never provided a proper strainer, nor had they removed all of the wood chips after fitting our new engine bed. It is these that are now making trouble for us.

We dismantle the hand bilge pump and clear its upper section, then we pour buckets of water back down the pipe. We break into laughter! It seems a mad thing to do, standing there in the driving rain with the wild sea about us and the wash slopping about our feet—pouring water back into our ship. But the mad thing works. The head of water washes away the obstructions from the pipe and for a time, pumping furiously, we throw a good stream. Then it clogs again and the operation has to be repeated, until finally the bilge begins to clear.

In the gray morning of the 10th we sound—100 fathoms, no bottom. Wind still from the northeast and strong, though possibly diminishing a little. The Captain reports that we have passed shipping in the night. We must be near the coast. I insist on getting a definite position before we come in on it. The early morning light is gray and cheerless, but the sky has a kindlier look. Then on our port hand and up to windward of us we spy two black dots, tramps bound south, and beyond them a gray shape on the horizon. Can that be land? And those ships—can we come near enough to exchange signals? At least we must try. We select one of them and then make up to cross her path with all the speed that motor and sail can give us. I haul out the signal flags and begin to arrange our hoist. We watch carefully how the bearing of the freighter alters and how she increases in size. She's a big fellow and coming down rapidly with the force of the wind behind her. She's going by us! No! We're closing on her. Up goes our ensign at the main peak and our code flag beneath it. She's moving fast now and, to save time, at our port main spreader we run up the number of our ship:

M F N W

Bracing myself against the wheelbox, I hold the binoculars to my eyes and wait for the flutter of flags from her rigging. The hoist of our message is already laid out on our deck:

Q I B

What is your latitude brought up to the moment?

It's a wonderful thing, this international code that cries the needs and the news of a ship in a universal tongue.

But does it? We've closed with the other vessel now and we're running along beside each other in clear sight. She looks very solid and efficient plodding along. On her deck we can see a few deckhands moving slowly about the last duties of the morning watch. Probably putting in time until they can flog eight bells. But she flies no ensign. Nobody is running toward the signal halyards, and there is no sign that she recognizes our existence. Thinking we may be misunderstood, we lower our ensign and code pennant and hoist them again. There's no sign from the other vessel. Then the door of her chart room opens, and an officer in blue coat and white cap steps out on the wing of the bridge. Now he sees us. He has raised his glasses and is looking our way. We wave but draw no response. For a little while he stands in the wing, quiet, casual, and all the time his vessel is drawing away from us. Then he moves in from the wing, in a leisurely fashion and, leaning on the high rail, he looks down on his own foredeck. And that is all. The ship has drawn well away from us now and we can just make out a name that seems to be *Santa Therese*, but the port beneath it is a blur.

We're quiet, stunned. So this is all there is to the code of mutual assistance at sea. I look around the horizon again and see that in the meantime the second vessel, farther on our port hand, has also drawn ahead of us. There's nothing further to do so I go below.

Now the Captain is calling, "Please come up here, sir. The other ship, she's put about and is coming back."

I rush on deck and sure enough it is true. The other ship is growing now every minute in our sight. And though she is a heavy work-a-day tramp, the sight of her is good. In great haste we run up the hoists we have previously set and immediately add the

Q I B

in our port fore-spreader. We know time is valuable to her and this is no occasion to hang on formalities. She is quite close now, and already the flags are fluttering from her halyards.

B S

The Captain calls the letters off, Georgia, now sitting in the companionway, writes them down, and I dig into the international code book.

B S	D D	P G
latitude 41°	*longitude 9°*	30'

Then I run for the chart and prick off the position, 25 miles off the Portuguese coast; Leixoes, the harbor of Oporto, lies some thirty miles to the north and east of us.

Hurrah! I rush for the deck. There's another hoist of flags now, but there's no need to dig it out for she's come around and we're running along together, the *Kinkajou* hanging close aboard her starboard quarter. Somebody with a megaphone is standing in the wings of the bridge. At first we don't hear and then the voice comes louder and clearer:

"Are you all right? Can we help you?"

She is gaining a little distance on us now but catches our answer: "All right. No, thanks."

Men are crowding along the after-rail in nondescript costumes, some from the deck, some from the engine room, and even the steward's department is represented. They are waving as they draw away from us. There's her name now:

M A R G A R I T A

LONDON

Nice ship that, and good fellows! We hoist a final signal.

X O R

Thank You

As she draws slowly away from us in the growing light there's no doubt that the wind is moderating. Could that be a touch of sun showing on the water down there?

Then I bring the chart aft. "There we are, dear. It's a day's run to Lisbon but it's only a few hours north and east to Oporto." Georgia thinks for a moment, but only a moment.

"Oh, if we're all right let's go on. I don't like to turn back even a little bit."

— *EXPLORERS CLUB TALES* (1936)

Leonard Outhwaite is an anthropologist and social scientist of parts. He has led archeological and ethnological expeditions, nowadays is an expert on museum design and education. Here he spins the yarn of a holiday that sometimes reads like a saga. The log of the Kinkajou *is a saga. Since Outhwaite had to relinquish her, she has been on many notable voyages, sunk, and raised, and now in commission. You would have to talk with Outhwaite to know the true qualities of the* Kinkajou. *This is a vacation jaunt he tells about, though only the true seaman and adventurer might so regard it.*

Wings in the Storm

BY HUGH DUNCAN GRANT

S trange as it may seem, few authentic incidents are on record of aircraft coming to grief through being struck by lightning. Not a few
instances of trouble attributable to other causes have been unjust-
ly charged to lightning. And these erroneous allegations have been
magnified in the public eye because, compared with many everyday risks, the
hazard to balloons, dirigibles, or airplanes, although very small, receives
much attention.

Nevertheless, in combat with the elements, one of my greatest thrills has
been flying in the wake of a thunderstorm in summer.

It is characteristic of heavy thunderclouds that they mushroom out like
a vast spreading umbrella. On rare occasions, after the passing of a thunderstorm, the rain ceases and a lightning bolt descends without warning.
Accompanied by a blinding flash, even in bright sunlight, and a deafening
crash, such a bolt may demolish a large tree and kill persons under it, or perform curious tricks of nature. A lady, for example, saw a lightning bolt strike
her bed, leap over her, play havoc on her dresser top, and disappear. Ill in
bed, she escaped injury but, oddly enough, her mattress was set afire.

When in an airplane, however, and imagining the core of the storm to
be many miles out of your path, such a terrifying experience may seem like
a bolt from the blue. It is nerve-racking and awe-inspiring.

The scene was the mouth of the English Channel, and the time of day,
the late afternoon. Accompanying the passage of what meteorologists call a
"V"-shaped cyclone, there was the usual rolling of thunder and a vivid display
of lightning, brilliantly illuminating the outer cloud edges.

We had circumnavigated one great towering mass of thundercloud, and
believed the storm had moved to the North-northeast of us. The course followed by the airplane was from Southwest to Northeast, or, as the crow flies,

from Brest to Dover. In other words, we flew apparently in the wake of the central path of the distant, if fiery, storm. Our height was around 4,500 feet.

Suddenly, within what we calculated to have been 600 yards abreast of us, there was a solitary, downward bolt of solid fire, accompanied by a terrific, crackling roar, a stifling, burnt-up, sulphurous atmosphere, and a backwash current of air which rocked the plane, reverberating again and again on the wings, as if we had encountered a tidal wave in mid-ocean. For several minutes, as if on a billowy sea, the plane heaved upward and downward, to and fro.

It seemed to us that several flashes of lightning—enveloped in a rose-colored mass, some forty feet in diameter—were rolled into one in a great bolt of fire, coming from the rear-portion of a storm, which, subsequently, proved to be one of marked intensity. It left in its wake a trail of damage to coastal shipping and inland property.

It seemed, too, as if the lightning had been whipped up into a final and massive discharge by the squall ahead of us, at the front of the quick-moving and erratic cyclone; and as if, in bold defiance, nature's great electrical machine had exploded, mysteriously, in a climax of fury.

Such "V"-shaped storms occur frequently in the British Isles and, pursuing as they do the line of least resistance, are the offshoots of a peculiar pressure and temperature distribution, when an irregularly shaped, Atlantic storm meets a settled, or fairly quiescent, continental atmosphere. One theory, that ball lightning is a little electric tornado of the glowing gases from the path of a lightning stroke, has been authoritatively proposed.

Fortunately there was no damage done to our plane, beyond disconnecting the radio; but what might have been our fate, had we been within closer reach of the lightning bolt, was a matter of easy conjecture. Upon regaining our equilibrium in the air, we later considered ourselves more than lucky to land in "Merrie Old England" with a whole skin, to tell the tale.

Lifted in almost no time, from 2,000 to 7,000 feet, many aviators have been caught in the fore-front of a thunderstorm. On the other hand, the air which goes down in such a storm is supplied by a return flow above the frontal squall. Aviators, so caught, agree that the turbulence within a thunderstorm is "awful" to experience. Turning over and over, like a rotary brush revolving around a horizontal axis, a squall cloud has an uncanny way of turning forward at the bottom, and upward in front. One daring pilot flew into just such a storm cloud, to see if it really rotated; and promptly his doubts were whirled out of him.

As a rule, a thunderstorm does not circle around and take a second "crack" at the same neighborhood. When this seems to occur, it is the product of a new and entirely independent cyclone. In a way, a cyclone is comparable to a rhinoceros; if it does not get you the first time it keeps on going.

But lightning *does* sometimes strike twice in the same place and a lightning bolt may come as an apparent aftermath of the main cyclonic disturbance. Occasionally, after the black thunderstorm has passed, the last drops have stopped falling, the sun comes out and everything seems serene again — then out of the blue sky comes one last, terrific stroke of levin. This is likely to be unusually destructive and comes from the tip of a long, thin, and invisible tail which sometimes drags along a mile or two behind the main cloud body.

In ancient times, ball lightning passed for the devil! A familiar tale is that of the devil coming down somebody's chimney in a shining cloud, only to vanish, presently, with a loud noise, and leaving a sulphurous smell. The shining clouds were lightning balls; the loud noises were their explosions, and the devil a figment of the observer's imagination.

Nevertheless, however destructive severe occurrences of lightning may prove to be, there is a wild beauty in the great massing of clouds, the rolling of thunder, the lighting bolts and the crashing, the tearing wind and deluge of rain, followed, perhaps, by a rainbow spanning the vaulted blue.

— *EXPLORERS CLUB TALES* (1936)

Hugh Duncan Grant possessed a record infrequently mentioned. He was a native Celt of the Scottish Highlands. Out of Skerry's and Leith Nautical Colleges, and Edinburgh University, he served in the British Navy as Ordinary Sailor and

British Seaman. He was commissioned in the British Naval Volunteer Reserve as meterologist with the Royal Naval Air Service. As Superintendent of the Meteorological Department of the British Navy, he represented the Empire at the International Meteorological Conference in Paris, 1919–20. During the war, as weather-expert of the British Admiralty he was responsible for official, secret, weather forecasts. And he had a lot to do with the naval raid on Zeebrugge. And with the Dover Patrol. He was an expert on cyclones over the North American flying routes, on the pathology of hurricanes in the Caribbean and Gulf of Mexico; contrasting hurricane conditions with those in the North Atlantic, and the North Sea. An associate of the Transoceanic Aerial Control System, New York and London, a member of the Institute of Aeronautical Sciences of America; in two words, Hugh Grant was weatherwise.

PART TEN

United States
of America,
Lower Forty-Eight

Bullwhacking Across the Plains

BY W. H. JACKSON

"Bullwhack" as defined by standard dictionaries, is "a long heavy whip with short handle" and "bullwacker" is a "driver of oxen." (Colloquial, western U. S.)

In the vernacular of the Old West all oxen are "bulls." The bullwhacker was found at his best in large commercial or military freighting outfits. The characteristic of his profession was a skillful use of the "long heavy whip with short handle."

Years ago I bullwhacked my way across plains and over mountains into the Far West. It was an experience that turned out to be well worth the hardships encountered, for it led first to my becoming an itinerant photographer, reproducing the scenes of my recent travels, and then quite naturally into the service of the U. S. Geological Survey (Dr. Hayden). For nearly ten years, with a pack-mule load of wet-plate equipment, I explored the wilds of the Rocky Mountains for pictures in places that had hitherto known only the Indian, the trapper, or the prospector.

It all came about in an unpremeditated way, my going West. In April, 1866, I was getting on fairly well in Burlington, Vermont, and was engaged to be married in June. The engagement was broken, and I took the matter so seriously that from that moment I was possessed with the one purpose of going away from that place as quickly and as far as I could.

With only the money I happened to have in my pocket, I took the first train out of town and the next day landed in New York City. There I unexpectedly ran across a comrade of Civil War days, who happened to be out of work, broke, and as ready as I for any enterprise, if far enough away from all former associations. The prominence given at that time to reports of the gold stampede to Montana decided the matter and there we would go, perhaps to gain much wealth!

With small means for such an undertaking, we left New York on April twenty-first, and two months later arrived at St. Jo, Missouri, then the end of railway transportation westward. During those two months we worked at odd jobs going from one city to another, frequently separated but coming together again by arrangement, each time a little farther on our way, until finally, at the Missouri River, we were on the threshold of our adventure.

We had been advised by mining companies in New York before leaving that at the Missouri River landings we would find trains leaving daily for the Far West, among which it would not be difficult to get employment or passage to our destination. Sure enough, St. Jo was alive with the activities of forwarding companies sending out long trains of horse, mule, and "bull" outfits into the Rocky Mountain region. In the city were also many young men thrown upon the country after the disbanding of the northern and southern armies, and various others seeking employment like ourselves.

We arrived at St. Jo with barely enough money to pay for a breakfast. A job must be had at once. An advertisement in the morning's paper caught our eyes — 100 *Teamsters Wanted for the Plains. Apply at the Intelligence Office on Francis Street bet. 2nd and 3rd.* An immediate application revealed that "bull-whackers" were wanted to drive from Nebraska City, Nebraska, to Virginia City, Montana, at $20 a month — fee for the job, $1.50 each.

That was just what we were looking for, except that the fee business stumped us for the time being and we retired to see what could be done about it. First, we made the rounds of the corrals and other places where trains were outfitted, looking for other opportunities. We were dressed about the same as when we left New York, which included stovepipe hats — then customary headgear in the East. This, with our obvious "tenderfoot" appearance, failed to impress favorably the hardboiled wagon bosses and teamsters we interviewed. We soon realized that there was no chance whatever for us with the horse-and-mule outfits, where some degree of experience was required. Not so, however, for bullwhackers, as was indicated by the low scale of wages as compared with more than double the amount for "mule skinners."

But how to raise those three dollars? Each of us went about it in his own way, my comrade Rock to scrape acquaintance with other boys applying for the same job, who might possibly be "touched" for a small loan, and I to sell or pawn something. The only thing I had of any value for that purpose was a box of colors, which was worth three or four times what I asked for it. In an all-day canvass among those having use for such colors, I failed—most fortunately, as it turned out—to get a raise of any amount, and rejoined my comrade discouraged with the prospect.

But my discouragement was changed to joy when Rock waved a five-dollar bill in my face in proof that our money troubles were over, at least for the time being. He had won the confidence of one of the boys who said he was as hard up as we, but finally dug up a little roll that he had hidden away, almost from himself. That evening all who had signed up, about two dozen, went aboard a river packet leaving at sunrise next morning for Nebraska City.

Provided only with deck passage, we found our prospective quarters occupied by and overflowing with some three hundred Mormon immigrants on their way to the new Zion in Utah. In this dilemma, we were assigned the upper, or hurricane, deck, with an injunction not to intrude on the sacred precincts of the cabin deck. During the forty-eight hours of chugging up the "Big Muddy," we found the open deck delightfully cool and pleasant for sleeping, but a very inferno when the sun beat down on its unprotected surface in daytime.

The overseas immigrants, however, as observed from above, engaged most of our attention. If we did not care, or were not allowed, to go down among them, there was no hesitation on their part, young or old, in coming up to our deck in the cool of the evening. Among them were some pretty young girls, proselytes of the Church, who were the objects of much rivalry among the adventurous youths of our party in pressing their attentions, which in some cases were carried on to a degree where vigilant *duennas* unceremoniously packed off their charges to the lower deck again.

Aside from interesting conversations with the older immigrants about their former life and the hopes and aspirations which had brought them to

America, we made acquaintance with members of our own party, with whom we were to be associated during the next few months. There were, of course, all kinds and conditions, from the professional of "Pike County, Missouri," to the "tenderfoot" from the East like ourselves; but among them were some fine young fellows of natural refinement and good education.

One of those boys, of a good Philadelphia family, who went out with a train following ours, came West well supplied with money, bought a wagon and a team of mules, and intended to make the trip independently. He was persuaded, however, for safety as well as economy, to sell his outfit and go bullwhacking. Two months later he was killed, not by Indians, but by a stroke of lightning, and was buried out on the Sweetwater under the shadow of the Devil's Gate. Accidents were much more frequent than killings.

We arrived at Nebraska City at two o'clock in the morning, the Mormons going a few miles farther up river to another landing. The town was dark and silent; no one met us, but, walking up into the business section, we slept away the rest of the night on sidewalks and porches. An agent then appeared, and, after a good breakfast, we were taken to an outfitting house and permitted to purchase, as a charge against wages, whatever we wished in the way of personal equipment for the journey. Besides necessary clothing, arms and ammunition were of most concern, for it was predicted that troublesome times were to be expected out on the plains and it was wise to be "well heeled." With these preliminaries cared for, we were marched out some three or four miles to the outskirts of the city, where our train, the wagons corralled in a great circle, was already loaded and awaiting only the arrival of its drivers to pull out.

Nebraska City at that time was the chief point of departure for the West, particularly for freighting outfits, as it was the most direct route, with fewer river crossings than those usually associated with the trail to Oregon. With its outfitting activities, it was a busy place. Only recently I found in an ancient file of The Nebraska News, of the date of our departure, that "a total of 184 wagons, each drawn by six yoke of oxen, left Nebraska City in one day." It was the last year of overland travel from the "River" by wagons, as the transcontinental railroad was then well under way in a feverish rush to beat its rival from the Pacific Coast into the Salt Lake Valley.

Our outfit, one of the many engaged in this freighting business, consisted of twenty-five wagons with trailers, drawn by six yoke of oxen, with from seven to eight thousand pounds of general groceries as the average load, all consigned to Virginia City, Montana. The personnel of the train was composed of two wagon masters (invariably called wagon bosses), a clerk, night herders, one or two extras, and the twenty-five drivers. After being assigned to our wagons, with the yokes, whips, chains, and other requisites for driving, we retired to our wagons to rest up for the ordeal of the next day.

Before it was quite daylight we were roused from our sleep by the night watchman persistently pounding the wagon sheets and shouting, "Roll Out! Roll Out! The bulls are coming!" My first sight of them as they were driven in was not reassuring. Fresh from the freedom of the range for a long season, they came in bellowing, pawing the earth, and raising a big dust generally. But there was no time to think about it, one way or another. No time, either, for breakfast. The business of yoking up began at once. The wagon boss, perched on a wheel, pointed out the ox each one was to take (which must thereafter be recognized out of its three hundred fellows for the same place in his team), and the liveliest experience I ever had was under way.

A six-yoke team was made up of leaders, three yoke in the swing, pointers, and wheelers. The procedure was first to yoke the wheelers and hitch them temporarily to a wagon wheel; then, beginning with the leaders and hitching them to another wheel, the four other yoke were added in order, connected by chains running from yoke to yoke. The wagons being parked facing outward, the wheelers were first taken out and put on the tongue; then the long string of five yoke followed and were hitched on ahead of the wheelers.

It would make a long story if I should tell all that happened in that first yoking-up. Most of those engaged in it had never seen an ox yoked, much less driven one. The corral was crowded to the limit, many of the oxen were unbroken, others had forgotten all about it in running the range, and some of the more refractory ones had to be lariated and drawn up to a wagon wheel to be yoked. The wagon bosses helped as much as possible and occasionally an old-timer lent a hand. But about all that could be done in individual cases was to have the ox pointed out to the prospective bullwhacker, and then let him go about it as best he could.

The wheelers were little trouble, for they were selected from the well broken standbys; but with the swing it was a merry scrimmage all the way through. The most difficult part of it came in the attempt to drive out this long string of five yoke to be hitched to the tongue. The contradictory "gees" and "haws" and the natural cussedness in the cattle themselves, bolting this way and that and getting into snarls with other teams, to the exasperation of their drivers, brought about a situation only straightened out by the bosses and others taking a hand in it. It was nearly high noon when all were hitched up and the bosses began starting out the teams for us, one after another.

Trailing each other closely, we went along fairly well for awhile. Our wagons, however, were not provided with brakes and at each considerable descent in the road, the team of oxen had to be stopped and a chain-lock thrown around one of the wheels. Coming to the brow of a rather steep hill, I attempted to stop my team. The wheelers held back all right, but the others pressed on and, overcoming the wheelers, raced down the hill to keep ahead of the heavily loaded wagon, which I expected to see tumbling over them in a wreck. But by good luck more than anything else the bottom was reached without a smash-up and we went on to camp and breakfast without further incident.

So much for the first day. Two weeks later and some two hundred miles on our way, we were at Fort Kearny. Matters had improved greatly in the meantime, as shown by the progress made. Our wagon boss had been wonderfully patient with his lot of green drivers, who by this time had become fairly efficient bullwhackers. The daily program was to be routed out of our wagons at daybreak, yoke up and pull out by sunrise, drive until 10 o'clock, and then corral for breakfast. The noon lay-over lasted until about three o'clock, when the cattle were again driven in and the morning's work repeated. The afternoon drive continued until a good camping-place was reached, which meant water and grass, usually about sundown, but often much later.

We were divided into three messes, from which one was chosen or volunteered as cook, in consideration of being excused from other camp duties, such as greasing up and day herding. The other members of the mess took turns in providing fuel and water. Fuel was the greater problem, as over a large part of the way there was no wood of any kind and the only substitute was "buffalo chips," the dried and hard manure of the plains. The driver providing fuel for the day usually hung a gunny sack on his wagon and during the day's drive picked up enough chips along the road to meet all requirements. The fare, ample in quantity but not always of the best quality, was flour, bacon, and coffee, occasionally diversified with beans and dried apples.

At Fort Kearny we came under military inspection as to our preparedness against Indian attacks, and it was shown that, besides individual equipment, the train itself was provided with a number of carbines. There also had to be not less than thirty wagons in each train permitted to pass farther up the Platte Valley route. A small train that had been held up a Fort Kearny now joined us, and we traveled together throughout most of the trip. Reports and rumors of uprising were continually coming in. All along the road were frequent evidences of the raids of 1865, the most serious on the Plains, when stations and ranches were destroyed and travel entirely suspended for a time.

The prevailing rumor was that the Indians intended making a clean sweep of the whole Platte Valley within the next ten days. We had seen nothing of them, except a small band of Oto Indians, who exacted a tobacco tribute from some of the drivers. It was said that this was a bad sign and that plenty of them were back in the hills watching the road, and meant mischief.

Passing through Old Julesburg, rebuilt since its burning by Indians the year before, we soon came to the Upper California crossing of the South Fork of the Platte. The river at that time was more than a half-mile wide, and running swiftly over a shifting, sandy bottom. The greatest depth at the ford was about four feet, but with many shallows and sandbars in mid-stream.

Other trains besides ours were engaged in crossing at the same time. I can hardly do justice to the scene that was being enacted before my eyes. The Platte was filled from bank to bank with moving wagons, one to two dozen oxen to each, passing back and forth. Removing most of their clothing, the drivers were in the water up to their shoulders, lined up alongside their teams. The first plunge from off the bank was the most exciting moment.

The cattle were nervous and reluctant to enter the water and, when in, it was hard work to make them string out for a steady pull. As I have said, the river bed was a shifty quicksand and, unless the wagon was kept moving, it quickly settled down and became almost unmovable. When this was about to happen, there ensued a pandemonium of shouting, with snapping of whips and beating with sticks in urging the floundering oxen back into line, so that there would be no pause or slackening.

And so it goes, all the way over. The current is swift and strong in the deeper channels, sometimes taking the smaller cattle off their feet, until pulled back into line by the others. It took about two hours to make one trip and, as there were many recrossings, we were a day and a half getting our fifty separate wagons over.

Into this hurly-burly came a band of some fifty Indians returning from a great pow-wow at Fort Laramie. They began crossing at the same time—big braves on little ponies, squaws leading the packs, dogs and papooses perched on top, with other juveniles wading through in nature's garments only. Among them, coming through on foot, was a proud old man, whose only raiment except his breech-clout was a brass-buttoned officer's coat and cocked hat, both of which had probably seen service in the Mexican War. Both sides of the river were lined with corralled wagons, while groups of bullwhackers, soldiers from the near-by post, and Indians were engaged in what was going on, or stood as onlookers along its banks.

From there on to Fort Laramie the driving became more arduous, and the landscape changed. Instead of level plains, we encountered steep hills, deep gulches, and clogging sands, which drew heavily on the endurance of men and beasts in the hard grind of each day's drive. On the way we passed groups of Indians returning from the recently disbanded treaty conference at the fort, from which Red Cloud and his affiliated bands had withdrawn in protest against the building and occupation of army posts in their last hunting grounds by an expedition that had just preceded us from Fort Kearny. But at the fort all was quiet enough.

Winding our way over the rugged foot-hills of the Laramie range, then called the Black Hills, we halted for a time at the "Junction" of the new Powder River cut-off for Virginia City, Montana, by which the distance was some five hundred miles shorter than along the old route by way of South Pass. It was optional with our wagon boss which road to take and we started out with the expectation of going over the cut-off; but, in view of the disturbed condition of the country and the massing of hostiles in the Powder River region, it was decided to keep to the longer route. Of the few outfits venturing the other way, none got through without loss, and some did not get through at all.

It was along here that we again encountered our Mormon companions of the boat ride from St. Jo to Nebraska City. The composition of their train was novel and interesting in its variety of equipment. There was nearly every kind of vehicle that ever rolled on wheels, from a single ox, drawing a cart, to the prairie schooner with its six- or seven-yoke team, with the same diversity in horse and mule outfits. They strung out on the road in a long procession, a few of the more hardy or adventurous ones a long way in advance, but the larger number walking along with the wagons.

Passing one of their encampments after nightfall, we first saw numerous little campfires, inside and outside of the corralled wagons, glimmering out of the dusk, from a distance resembling a military bivouac. Passing nearer, the aroma from coffee pots and frying-pans greeted the senses; and when the weather was favorable, the strains of music from violin and banjo could be heard, with much frolicking and dancing among the younger "Saints."

The region about Fort Caspar and from there to the Sweetwater was said to be the most dangerous on the road. Just after pulling out from Deer Creek for the Platte Bridge crossing at Fort Caspar, we were overtaken by the telegraph operator and mail carrier, flinging back word, as they dashed by on horseback, that the station had been attacked and burned, and some of the employees killed. Later we met three six-mule teams, the wagon boxes filled with soldiers and line repairers, tearing down the road like mad, bound for the scene of action. Keeping on our way, we never heard what really happened.

Soldiers at Fort Caspar gave alarming accounts of the Indian situation, but we saw nothing more of it as we traveled up the Sweetwater, over South Pass and down to the parting of the ways on Ham's Fork, where the road to Salt Lake branched off to the Southwest. At one of the Sweetwater stations I lost my new York comrade, who left the train to join the telegraph line service. I never afterward heard from him. In the meantime I lost all interest in Montana and decided that Salt Lake held greater attractions than a mining camp.

Here, at the parting of the ways, the matter had to be decided. Half a dozen others were of the same mind, but all backed out except Bill Maddern, who joined me in notifying the wagon boss of our intention to quit. Then there was the devil to pay at once. Both wagon bosses took a hand in threatening to have us arrested and sent to Fort Bridger. Despite further threats that they would see that we never got to Salt Lake or any other place, we stuck to our purpose and were allowed to depart, surrendering of course all wages due, and leaving the train as poor as when we joined it.

No trains for Salt Lake coming along just then, we were offered a job by a Mormon who had a contract to supply the Overland State Line with hay. From the hayfields five or six miles up Ham's fork, we hauled it with ox teams, first to Granger, where we put up sixty tons, and then another stack of the same amount at South Bend station. We were at it three weeks for a dollar a day and an understanding that we were to be taken into the city at the end of the job. But the Mormon was a canny old codger.

When the day of settlement came, he said he had no money with him, and would pay when we got to the city, but, if we didn't care to wait, he would give us "store pay" on the little trading ranch at the ferry. Not caring for their goods, we preferred waiting, although, as my boots were about worn out, I did get a pair of moccasins. A train coming along just then, bound for Salt Lake City with two drivers short, our old employer interested himself in getting the job for us, suggesting that we would thereby be that much better off and, as he was going in at the same time, we could easily find him at his home address. We never did find him, however, and again had only experience for our pains.

Our new train consisted of fourteen wagons, but large ones, without trailers, and the usual six-yoke teams. We were twenty-three days en route, much of the way over mountainous roads. Fortunately, good weather prevailed until almost within sight of Salt Lake Valley, when we ran into the very worst weather and road conditions of the whole season.

On October twelfth we began climbing the Wasatch Mountains, the eastern boundary of Salt Lake Valley. Next day in Parley Park, near the summit, we lay over a day on account of rain. The following day was still dark and gloomy, but the train pulled out for the summit, everyone anxious to get over before conditions became worse. The road, however, could not have been worse. It was a new grade, hardly finished, and the long soaking of the day before had made the surface as treacherous as wet clay can be.

With our tremendously big, heavily laden wagons, we had little control. On downgrades all went with a rush, the wagons skidding dangerously over the banks, with drivers and cattle floundering around in the deep mud. The steeper upgrades were made only by the last ounce of effort on the part of men and cattle. By doubling teams, one wing of the train was pulled up to near the summit and left there.

The other half of the train remained at Ferguson's. During the night, snow began falling, and by morning was several inches deep. It was freezing cold when I was called early to go out on day herd until we pulled out, the night herder coming in at daylight. My only footwear at the time was the moccasins I had bought at Granger, already well used up and of little use in running around through snow and sagebrush.

After breakfast we took the remaining wing of the train right through to the summit, but not without a tremendous amount of hard work. At first the mud was frozen quite hard, but with the passing of cattle and wagons it was soon cut deeper than ever, some of the wagons sinking in to the hubs. The amount of punishment those poor bulls had to endure was something awful; some were so exhausted as to be hardly able to stand on their feet.

In the worst places half a dozen drivers, with the bosses lined up on each side of a team and with snapping of whips, shouting, and pounding, urged the poor brutes on until they were ready to drop in their tracks. With twenty-four oxen to a team, it was nip and tuck all the way. My wagon, one of the largest and most heavily laden, became so deeply stalled that it was left behind. The last quarter-mile was the hardest, but one by one the wagons crept up, until at nightfall only mine and another remained.

My thin moccasins, of course, did not hold out long under those conditions and, before the day was over, I was running around practically on bare feet. I was still on day herd duty and with another driver had to take the cattle, as soon as unyoked, some two or three miles below, where there was better feed and shelter for them, until the night herder came out—and he was in no hurry about it. I got back to our wagons about nine o'clock, finding the campfires all out, and only the remains of bread, bacon, and coffee for a late, cold supper. Bunking in at once, I did not get out of that wagon again for three days, my feet being so sore and swollen that I could not possibly stand on them.

Next day the two remaining wagons were extricated from the frozen mud, after being entirely unloaded, and then hauled up with the rest. For two days more, in descending Parley Canyon, I was bumped around in my wagon like corn in a popper, but on the last day was able to get out at the mouth of the canyon and drive into Salt Lake City, ending my bullwhacking experiences for all time by being docked for the time I had been laid up.

—TOLD AT THE EXPLORERS CLUB (1931)

It is doubtful if anyone has done more than W. H. Jackson to preserve a pictorial record, with camera, brush, and pencil, of pioneer times in the West.

Reaching Salt Lake City in 1866 in the manner he so graphically describes in this story, he made his way through to California as a mule-team driver and then back to Omaha with a herd of broncos for the eastern market.

Here he began many years of work as a landscape photographer, first along the route of the Union Pacific until its completion and later on other railway lines from the Atlantic to the Pacific and down into Mexico. For ten years he was photographer for the famous "Hayden Survey."

In 1894–1896 he carried his camera over portions of North Africa, Asia, and Australia and crossed Siberia in winter by sledge, photographing scenes for Harper's Weekly.

He cooperated in the work of the Oregon Trail Memorial Association and took an active interest in any movement to perpetuate the story of the Old West.

In addition to numerous reports, he was the author of The Pioneer Photographer, written in conjunction with Howard R. Driggs.

Buried Alive

BY WARREN KING MOOREHEAD

During the summer of 1888 I was exploring Indian tumuli in Ross County, Ohio. In my college days I was a long-distance runner and very strong. In fact, in 1885 I ran what would now be called a Marathon—from the college buildings (Denison University, Granville, Ohio) down a long hill, through the valley, up high hills southward, to the Baltimore and Ohio Railroad tracks, up the track to East Newark and back over the same route, a distance of more than twenty-two miles. These strenuous runnings put me in excellent physical condition and my survival of the adventure about to be described is probably due to this training.

We were excavating a mound eleven feet in height, located near Austin. Our pit extended to the base line. As the men continued their trench, they threw the earth back of them. The wall in front was high, the side walls somewhat lower. Naturally, the loose earth to the rear sloped upward, there being the usual cleared space of five or six feet between the edge of this earth and the front wall. In these early days of mound exploration it was customary to undermine slightly the face of the trench, then the men would go on top, insert their shovels, and throw down a large section of mound wall. Today different and more pretentious methods are employed.

The workmen, having accomplished their task, were sent to the top of the mound and, as they prepared to cave off a section, I observed a small bone protruding at the base line and jumped down into the pit with my hand trowel. I was in a crouching position; above me towered eleven feet of wall. Suddenly, without warning, a mass of earth extending from the floor to the summit and probably eighteen or twenty inches in thickness fell. It started with a slight noise sufficient to warn me. I leaped backwards and landed on soft earth to the rear in such a position that my head and shoulders were rather higher than the rest of my body.

Had I had but another second, I might have escaped, being very athletic, as I have stated, but the mass of falling earth caught me in an instant. The first sensation was of darkness and then came intense pressure. Even to this day I can recall vividly the cold earth against my face and body and the never-ending pressure. My arms were extended, legs somewhat apart. I had fallen on a heavy clod of burnt earth and this pressed against the lumbar vertebrae, pushing two of them out of line, so that I was paralyzed from the waist down for five or six weeks.

My mouth opened and I remember the unpleasant sensation of trying to dislodge earth. I was held absolutely. I recall that it was impossible to move even a finger, although I tried. I wore a very light field costume, with a watch in the left pocket of my thin shirt. Two ribs under this watch were broken, as was the crystal. The watch chain was fastened across from left to right side. It was pressed into the flesh and left a red mark across my chest. A straw hat was jammed down over my forehead and for several days afterwards I bore a stamped pattern of the braided straw.

Clinton Cowen, a college classmate, who afterwards became an engineer, was in charge of the workmen and his testimony is that I was buried about a minute—some of the men thought a little longer. Our laborers threw earth aside frantically with their shovels and dug down nearly three feet before they reached my head. I recall a slight movement of earth above me, then a shovel struck my scalp, which under other circumstances would have been rather painful, but was a most welcome blow! At once they uncovered me down to the chest. One of the first things I observed was that the men were panting and streaming with perspiration. Cowen was wont to comment on a rather uncanny sight, that black head protruding from the earth! He also said that, having exposed the head and shoulders, they stopped for a moment and he observed that earth pressure on the body was forcing the blood up, the veins standing out prominently on my neck and head. I could not breathe, the air having been forced out of my lungs, and Cowen pressed with his hands on each side of my chest. I remember that this sudden intake of air was very painful.

They carried me out and laid me on a mass of oat sheaves, which furnished a very soft bed. I recall a small, wild canary perched on a high thistle which sang a sweet song and flitted away as the men approached, also that the sky seemed unusually blue and bright. Some farmers came, one brought a farm wagon, numbers of oat sheaves were thrown in, and the team proceeded to the residence of Strawder James. Mr. and Mrs. James kindly gave me their own room, located on the first floor of their residence, and I was put to bed for several weeks until I could be transported on a cot in a baggage car, to my home in Xenia, Ohio.

Mr. James was a very kind-hearted man. In Cincinnati he had purchased a small music box which played three tunes. He used to set this on a table near the head of my bed each morning and wind it up before he departed for his work. At noon he would repeat the process and also in the evening. Mr. Cowen, years afterwards, one evening when we were in camp at Cahokia, declared that, after a month of this musical entertainment, I was able to whistle the three tunes backwards as well as forwards!

In later years my work necessitated entering caverns and rock shelters, but I could never bring myself to explore with any degree of satisfaction underground. There always seemed to be impending danger.

The vertebrae have probably adjusted themselves, but doctors in subsequent years, examining me for life insurance, paid particular attention to that portion of the spine and reported adversely on my application.

In 1897 pulmonary tuberculosis began to develop and my physician sent me to Arizona. There a specialist, observing the condition, told Mrs. Moorehead that she should take me to Dr. G____, spinal expert, New York City. He thought that I had tuberculosis of the spine and added the cheerful information that I might not live more than a year. He placed me in a straightjacket to throw the weight of the upper body on the hips and thus relieve the spine. This aggravated the pulmonary tuberculosis and I went to the Adirondacks where I remained two years and ten months under Dr. E. L. Trudeau's care.

An interesting correspondence ensued between Trudeau and G____, both savants in their respective callings, Trudeau maintaining that, since I was suffering from severe hemorrhages of the lungs and breathing was hampered by the straightjacket, I would die from pulmonary tuberculosis unless "said jacket was removed." G____, true to his training, retorted that I would die of spinal trouble unless the jacket treatment was continued! According to the diagnosis of these two eminent authorities there was no hope— absolutely none. They finally compromised by taking the jacket off and putting me on a cot for many months.

There is a grim humor in this entire incident. Both Trudeau and G____ have gone to their rewards. They were wonderful men and I have no criticism to offer. Two skillful examiners from two of the largest life insurance companies of this country turned me down as a doubly bad risk because of "spine and lungs" and have "gone West" while I, rejected by the experts and condemned by the physicians, am still alive and able to carry on!

— *TOLD AT THE EXPLORERS CLUB* (1931)

Director of the Department of American Archaeology at Phillips Academy, Andover, Mass., Dr. Moorehead devoted many years to archeological exploration in New England, the Ohio Valley, the southern states, and the Southwest.

He was a member of the U. S. Board of Indian commissioners, an authority on the mound-builders of America, and published many scientific books and papers.

The Death of Sitting Bull

BY E. W. DEMING

Introduction by Seyward S. Cramer, Editor, *Through Hell and High Water*, 1941

When I was a kid I used to read every blood-curdling Indian story I could lay hands on. I knew the history of all the famous ones and could call them by name. Sitting Bull was a favorite and I really don't know whether it was because of his name (which appealed to me strongly) or because of the many romantic tales that had been embroidered about him. Whichever it was, I gave old Sitting Bull a fair share of hero worship.

As I grew older I became more interested in the true facts about the Indians and I noticed that the name Deming appeared on articles and books and was signed to paintings and sculptures. This man Deming became, to me, an authority on the Indian because he had lived there, with them and in their own territory. He lived in the West with the Indians in the eighties and nineties, studying and sketching them.

There has been much misinformation about the manner in which my old hero, Sitting Bull, was killed. Captain Deming was at the agency in North Dakota at the time and I should like him to tell you the true facts of the death of Sitting Bull—not an eyewitness account but from the best corroborated statements of the time.

But before he starts I want to say just another word. If I were going into dangerous country today—country where my life might depend upon my ability to shoot it out—I'd choose Captain Deming as my companion. In spite of his eighty-odd years, he is still the quickest man on the draw that I have ever seen. Ask some of the members of the New York Police Department—he taught them how to pass their tests. He also taught a number of our soldiers how to shoot in World War Number One. Yes, he is a good man to know.

I quote from Major James McLoughlan's book, "My Friend the Indian":

"Crafty, avaricious, mendacious, and ambitious, Sitting Bull possessed all of the faults of an Indian and none of the nobler attributes which have gone far to redeem some of his people from their deeds of guilt. He had no single quality that would serve to draw his people to him, yet he was by far the most influential man of his nation for many years, neither Gall, Spotted Tail, nor Red Cloud, all greater men in every sense, exercising the power he did."

During those troublesome days of 1889 and 1890, I was a guest of Major McLoughlan, then agent for the Dakotas, at the Standing Rock Agency in North Dakota. My object was to study and sketch the primitive Indians in their varying ceremonies and modes of life. It was during my stay at the agency that Sitting Bull was killed by the Indian police. He had started the Ghost Dance to incite the Indians against the white man.

In 1890, Kicking Bear, a half-crazed member of the Minniconjou band from the Cheyenne River Reservation, visited Sitting Bull at his camp on the Grand River and told him the secrets of a new religion. It would return the buffalo to the plains, drive the white man from their country, and bring back the spirits of their forefathers. Sitting Bull, knowing how the mysterious rites would affect his people, accepted the new belief, hoping he could re-establish himself as their leader.

Sitting Bull was a troublemaker. He gathered many of the discontented young braves, harangued them, told them of the "new religion," and started the Ghost Dance. He instructed them to make shirts of white cotton cloth, decorated with various mystic symbols, which he said would render them proof against the white man's bullet. As time went on, the Indians grew more and more interested in the "new religion." Their excitement was intense. They became fanatic. They danced until exhausted. Some fainted and Sitting Bull explained to his people that, during the trance, the ghost of the man had left his body to communicate with the ghosts of their ancestors.

During this time, Major McLoughlan held his Indian scouts at Sitting Bull's camp to watch the ceremonies. Their duty was to report everything that happened. He feared that Sitting Bull, with the help of the Ghost Dance, would incite the Indians to war.

To prevent this, Major McLoughlan decided upon the removal of the ringleaders, Sitting Bull and his lieutenants. Hoping to prevent bloodshed, Major McLoughlan ordered the arrest of Sitting Bull to be made by the Indian police. A company of soldiers from the fort would be near the camp should the Indian police need help.

Hawkman, an Indian scout, brought word to Major McLoughlan that Sitting Bull was preparing to leave the reservation and start for the Bad Lands. The Major sent him back immediately with an order to Lieutenant Bull Head, and to Shave Head and Red Tomahawk, for the arrest of Sitting Bull before daybreak the next morning. Meanwhile, two troops of the 8th Cavalry, about a hundred men commanded by Captain Ferchet, rode to Oak Creek, a few miles from Sitting Bull's camp.

Before daylight the next morning, thirty-nine regular Indian police and four specials, under the command of Lieutenant Bull Head and Shave Head, rode into Sitting Bull's camp. Their entrance awakened the camp but the two men did not know this. The police dismounted quietly between Sitting Bull's two houses and Bull Head, Shave Head, and ten policemen entered. Sitting Bull was awake and up. With him were his two wives and his son, Crow Foot, a boy of seventeen. Bull Head told Sitting Bull he was under arrest and must go with them to the Agency. The old Indian showed no concern and said he would go.

When they came out of the house they were surprised to see a great number of Ghost Dancers, nearly all of them armed, surrounding the Indian police. Sitting Bull was walking quietly toward his horse when Crow Foot taunted his father. He called him a coward for surrendering to the Indians in their blue uniforms, without making any resistance.

The taunts of his son shamed the old man. He looked around at the excited faces of one hundred and sixty of his warriors close about him. He talked to them in a loud, shrill voice. He knew this arrest would mean the end of his power. Seeing so many friends gave him courage, and Sitting Bull shouted the order for an attack on the Indian police. The Ghost Dancers fired, mortally wounding Bull Head and Shave Head and wounding six others of the police. Bull Head, dying on his feet, wheeled quickly and shot Sitting Bull through the body. Red Tomahawk shot him through the right cheek, killing him immediately. Bull Head and Sitting Bull fell at the same moment.

A bloody fight followed. Thirty-nine Indian police and some of their friends fought off a hundred and sixty Ghost Dancers. Red Tomahawk took command, and drove the Indians into the timber. Sitting Bull's medicine had failed and his death put a stop to the Ghost Dancing among the Dakotas of the Standing Rock Agency.

Two days later, the bodies of Bull Head, Shave Head, and four others of the Indian police were buried in the cemetery at Standing Rock with full military honors.

— *THROUGH HELL AND HIGH WATER* (1941)

A Leap in the Dark

BY CHARLES A. LINDBERGH

I took off from Lambert (St. Louis) Field, September 16, 1926, at 4:25 P.M. and, after an uneventful trip, arrived at Springfield, Ill., at 5:10 P.M. and Peoria at 5:55 P.M. I took off from the Peoria Field at 6:10 P.M. there was a light ground haze, but the sky was practically clear, containing only scattered cumulus clouds.

Darkness set in about twenty-five miles northeast of Peoria and I took up a compass course, checking on the lights of the town below, until a low fog rolled in under me a few miles northeast of Marseilles and the Illinois River. The fog extended from the ground up to about six hundred feet and, as I was unable to fly under it, I turned back and attempted to drop a flare and land, but the flare did not function and I again headed for Maywood, hoping to find a break in the fog over the field. Upon examination I discovered that the cause of the flare failure was the short length of the release lever and that the flare might still be used by pulling out the release cable.

I continued on a compass course of fifty degrees until 7:15 P.M., when I saw a dull glow on top of the fog, indicating a town below. There were several of these light patches on the fog, visible only when looking away from the moon, and I knew them to be the towns bordering the Maywood Field. At no time, however, was I able to locate the exact position of the field, although I understand that the searchlights were directed upward and two barrels of gasoline were burned in an endeavor to attract my attention.

Several times I descended to the top of the fog, which was eight to nine hundred feet high according to my altimeter. The sky above was clear, with the exception of scattered clouds, and the moon and stars were shining brightly.

After circling around for thirty-five minutes, I headed west, to be sure of clearing Lake Michigan and in an attempt to pick up one of the lights on the transcontinental line. After flying west for fifteen minutes and seeing no break in the fog, I turned southwest, hoping to strike the edge of the fog south of the Illinois River.

My motor cut out at 8:20 P.M. and I cut in the reserve. I was at that time only one thousand five hundred feet high and, as the motor did not pick up as soon as I expected, I shoved the flashlight in my belt and was about to release the parachute flare and jump when the engine finally took hold again. A second trial showed the main tank to be dry and accordingly a maximum of twenty minutes' flying-time left.

There were no openings in the fog and I decided to leave the ship as soon as the reserve tank was exhausted. I tried to get the mail pit open, with the idea of throwing out the mail sacks and then jumping, but was unable to open the front buckle.

I knew that the risk of fire, with no gasoline in the tanks, was very slight and began to climb for altitude when I saw a light on the ground for several seconds. This was the first light I had seen for nearly two hours and, as almost enough gasoline for fifteen minutes' flying remained in the reserve, I glided down to twelve hundred feet and pulled out the flare-release cable, as nearly as I could judge over the spot where the light had appeared. This time the flare functioned, but only to illuminate the top of a solid bank of fog, into which it soon disappeared without showing any trace of the ground.

Seven minutes' gasoline remained in the gravity tank. Seeing the glow of a town through the fog, I turned towards open country and nosed the plane up. At five thousand feet the motor sputtered and died. I stepped up on the cowling and out over the right side of the cockpit, pulling the rip-cord after about a hundred-foot fall. The parachute, an Irvin seat-service type, functioned perfectly; I was falling head downward when the risers jerked me into an upright position and the chute opened. This time I saved the rip-cord.

I pulled the flashlight from my belt and was playing it down towards the top of the fog when I heard the plane's motor pick up. When I jumped, the motor had practically stopped dead and I had neglected to cut the switches. Apparently, when the ship nosed down, an additional supply of gasoline drained down into the carburetor. Soon the ship came into sight, about a quarter-mile away and headed in the general direction of my parachute. I put the flashlight in a pocket of my flying suit, preparatory to slipping the parachute out of the way, if necessary. The plane was making a left spiral of about a mile diameter and passed approximately three hundred yards away from my chute, leaving me on the outside of the circle.

I was undecided as to whether the plane or I was descending more rapidly and glided my chute away from the spiral path of the ship as rapidly as I could.

The ship passed completely out of sight, but reappeared again in a few seconds, its rate of descent being about the same as that of the parachute. I counted five spirals, each one a little further away than the last, before reaching the top of the fog-bank.

When I settled into the fog-bank, I knew that the ground was within one thousand feet and I reached for the flashlight but found it to be missing. I could see neither earth nor stars and had no idea what kind of territory was below. I crossed my legs to keep from straddling a branch or wire, guarded my face with my hands and waited.

Presently I saw the outline of the ground and a moment later was down in a cornfield. The corn was over my head and the chute was lying on top of the cornstalks. I hurriedly packed it and started down a corn row. The ground visibility was about one hundred yards.

In a few minutes I came to a stubble field and some wagon tracks, which I followed to a farmyard a quarter-mile away. After reaching the farmyard, I noticed auto headlights and a spotlight playing over the roadside. Thinking that someone might have located the wreck of the place, I walked over to the car. The occupants asked whether I had heard an airplane crash and it required some time to explain to them that I had been piloting the plane and was searching for it myself. I had to display the parachute as evidence before they were thoroughly convinced. The farmer was sure, as were most others in a three-mile radius, that the ship had just missed his house and crashed near by. In fact, he could locate within a few rods the spot where he heard it hit the ground, and we spent an unsuccessful quarter-hour hunting for the

wreck in that vicinity before going to the farmhouse to arrange for a searching party and telephone St. Louis and Chicago.

I had just put in the long-distance calls when the phone rang and we were
notified that the plane had been found in a cornfield over two miles away.

It took several minutes to reach the site of the crash, due to the necessity of slow driving through the fog. A small crowd had already assembled when
we arrived.

The plane was wound up in a ball-shaped mass. It had narrowly missed
one farmhouse and had hooked its left wing in a grain shock a quarter-mile
beyond. The ship had landed on the left wing and wheel and had skidded
along the ground for eighty yards, going through one fence before coming to
rest in the edge of a cornfield, about a hundred yards short of a barn. The
mail pit was laid open and one sack of mail was on the ground. The mail
however, was uninjured. The sheriff from Ottawa arrived and we took the
mail to the Ottawa post office, to be entrained at 3:30 A.M. for Chicago.

— TOLD AT THE EXPLORERS CLUB (1931)

*To Colonel Lindbergh's world-renowned achievements in practical aviation
need merely be added here the mention of his aerial survey of the Maya territory in Mexico and Central America, which was one of the earliest applications
of the airplane to archeological exploration.*

He was made an Honorary Member of The Explorers Club.

Lost Inside the Earth

BY HORACE ASHTON

Introduction by Seyward S. Cramer, Editor, *Through Hell and High Water*, 1941

We had a grand week-end at Endless Caverns, Chief, and everybody asked about you. I think that they want you to come down and prove that a Scotsman in kilts can actually be a speleologist—I like that word "speleologist," it's a two-dollar word for "cave man."

But we did have a good time and Captain Cowling is going to remember it for a long time to come. Cowling isn't so slim as he used to be and he hates to admit it. We found a new lateral passage onto a lower level and we all went down to see what new wonders we could find. There was one point where the opening was pretty tight but as we were going down, gravity helped. We looked around for a while and then came back up.

Those of us who are svelte struggled a bit at the narrow part but we made it easily. Cowling came to that portion and stuck. He huffed and he puffed and he squeezed and squirmed but no progress. He really struggled! He was so intent on making some progress that he didn't realize there was a terrific strain on that part of his trousers resting on his hip bones. Something had to give: the rocks had been there for eons and were averse to giving way; Cowling's bones were pretty strong and didn't want to give; the only thing left was a product of the tailor's craft—and Captain Cowling's trousers gave.

He had been exerting a lot of force trying to get out of that hole and just that thickness of cloth held him back. Once the retarding factor was gone, Cowling shot out of there as though projected from a cannon. His head came smack up against a stalactite—fortunately his helmet was still on and took the blow. But he knew he had struck something and automatically ducked.

That ducking reversed that process and he went back through the hole like the recoil of the cannon. Then came an agonized cry. Of all places Cowling could have chosen for a resting place, he would not have selected a stalagmite *for a cushioned seat. But that is where he landed, right on top of a good-sized stalagmite. He got off rather gingerly and crawled up through the hole, dragging his trousers behind him. As he was getting dressed he suddenly realized that he'd had a fair amount of change in one of the pockets. Counting the money in the pocket he calculated that he had left $2.42 scattered around the bottom of that hole but nothing in the world could induce him to go back for it. But somebody evidently did because we were all smoking cigars the next day. Confidentially, it was only $1.69 that was found.*

While I was down there I found that the Club once sponsored as expedition into the Endless Caverns just after they were opened to the public. Horace Ashton was on that expedition and he had an experience I wanted you to hear, so I brought him along this afternoon. Horace, tell about that first expedition, please.

Browsing through the treasures of The Explorers Club Library back in 1925, and making notes for a future expedition into the unknown, I was interrupted by a call on the telephone asking me to represent The Explorers Club in a joint expedition with the American Museum of Natural History to attempt to find the end of Endless Caverns near Newmarket, Virginia. This sounded all right. As I had just returned from the air voyage on the *Los Angeles* to Puerto Rico and the Virgin Islands, a little trip underground offered the sort of variety we all crave, so I accepted and joined the party.

At Newmarket, in the Shenandoah Valley, we were met by cars which took us first to a delightful old farmhouse owned by Colonel Edward T. Brown, proprietor of the Caverns, and after a real southern welcome our plan of action was laid out. In one party were Dr. Chester A. Reeds, Geologist of the American Museum, and E.J. Foyles, his assistant; Henry Collins Walsh, founder of The Explorers Club; Merle LaVoy and myself; Miss Betty Larrimore of the Boston *Post*, Garrick Mallery, and Gordon Brown.

Coarse canvas coveralls similar to the early flying suits and hip rubber boots, electric flash lamps, together with several lengths of stout rope, completed our outfits. These were all placed together and laid out that night in readiness for an early morning start.

Then we went up to the caves for a walk through the explored part which has been open for visitors since 1920. Fortunately these caverns were not developed until after the perfection of electric illumination, so they have been spared the smoking up of the torches of thousands of visiting parties which has so dimmed the splendors of the formations in other American caverns.

Although they were discovered more than fifty years ago, when two boys chasing a rabbit followed it into a hole behind a rock and there espied the opening, the original owner never made any attempt to develop them for tourists. Now large parties are conducted, several times a day and every day in the year, for more than a mile along its marvelously beautiful passageways through a succession of fantastic chambers whose ceilings and floors are draped with crystal stalactites and stalagmites, the work of millions of years of the slowly dripping water through the limestone of the mountains, into passages formed by prehistoric underground rivers which have long since sunk to lower and lower levels.

All that portion which has been opened up to the public is artistically illuminated by indirect lighting skillfully placed so as to show off to the best possible advantage the marvelous natural coloring of the weirdly beautiful formations.

In one of these long chambers, known as King Solomon's Temple, Colonel Brown pointed out far below us, just visible through a tiny opening, the rippling surface of the shallow underground river. We all agreed that to trace its unknown course would make an excellent preliminary trip and accustom us to the most trying conditions of cavern exploration.

When we returned to the lodge, just before turning in, I suggested that an empty bottle containing a note and record of our trip be placed as far up and another as far down the underground river as we could go—and challenge anyone to find it and move it along. Bottles were produced, and this note placed in each:

This bottle is placed at the farthest point penetrated by members of the expedition of The American Museum of Natural History and The Explorers Club of New York, May 1925. If anyone finds it and can carry it still farther, please report to the American Museum of Natural History.

(Signed by all members of the party)

I felt that this would make an interesting game of the search for the end of Endless Caverns and as Miss Larrimore remarked after our trip, "If any one ever finds those bottles and carries them on, they deserve more than an empty bottle."

We were all up and ready at an early hour the next morning.

Reaching King Solomon's Temple, a stout rope was made fast to one of the largest stalagmites and we made our way straight down, hand over hand, for 90 feet to the river below. The water was shallow and the ceiling so low that it was necessary at first to crawl upstream on hands and knees. Sometimes the ceiling was as low as 18 inches and the only way we could progress at all was to lie flat in the water face-up and squirm along. Occasionally we came out into fairly large chambers where we could stand up and stretch. As we went along, Foyles and I mapped the river's course. In one hour and a half we had covered about 200 yards — cavern exploration is slow work.

Here the ceiling abruptly descended until it would have been necessary for us to go underwater to proceed.

In turning back we discovered a small side passage just above our heads which we had missed before, and into this we made our way. A short distance beyond, this passage, too, was completely blocked by huge stalactites and stalagmites, the first we had found on the course of this underground river.

Here Foyles discovered, and we sketched for our records, the tracks of two small animals, one of which might have been a raccoon and the other a groundhog. Then we laboriously retraced our steps, or rather crawls, to the point of entry. Half a day had been consumed in that trip, but we decided to work our way downstream in the hope of finding a possible outlet. This part of the trip proved far more interesting, as the chambers were larger and the formations more striking. Twice we reached places where it was impossible to follow the actual stream bed, but in both instances we found passages just above which led over and to the water beyond. About half a mile downstream, I discovered a long formation which I called "The Fairies' Font" and beside it was a perfect elephant's head. Here I waited for the rest of the party. We found that beyond this point there was a 15-foot silent waterfall down which we might have gone if we had brought our ropes with us, but they were attached far back for our return to the upper levels, so we had to halt. Here we placed the first of the bottles and turned back.

Two hours later we reached the hanging rope whose 90 feet we had to ascend hand over hand into the main passage, and when we emerged from our first trip into the caverns it was four-thirty in the afternoon. We had been underground seven and a half hours.

We were so stiff and sore the following day that we decided to put off our next trip to that evening, so we spent a quiet day in preparation for the greater effort.

At seven-thirty in the evening, after a light dinner, we went to the farthest end of that portion of the Caverns which is now opened, a little more than a mile from the entrance.

Here we started to crawl, and after a while were skirting the edge of a deep chasm where most of the party had to resort to a hand rope. I was ahead, and as I crawled along another narrow ledge, my hand in the darkness went over the edge of another precipice into which our feeble light could not penetrate. I dropped a rock, and after what seemed seconds I heard the faint splash as it hit the water. This assured me that we were following the course of the river upstream, crawling on one of its higher and more ancient levels, so we kept on. Some of the way proved hard going because the stalagmites which covered the floor made crawling very painful, and because some of the openings between the rocks were extremely narrow. But after we had been on the way about four hours we came upon a huge chamber, the ceiling of which was beyond the reach of our lights and the floor, the bed of the river, was far below, for we could hear the rushing water in the darkness. A long rope was rigged up and three of us determined to go down for a further exploration of the underground river, leaving the others to hold the upper end of the rope and send relief in case we did not return. This descent into the unknown more than a mile farther than any other person had ever been—was thrilling, to say the least. At the bottom we separated—two going upstream and I down. I went as far as possible, reaching another point, several hundred yards beyond the point of descent where the ceiling again descended to the water. Not being sure how far underwater I would have to go before I could come up, I turned back, sketching raccoon tracks and collecting specimens of microscopic animal life for the Museum. The others went a like distance upstream and placed the second bottle.

Unlike a recent expedition into this cavern, we were not equipped with miners' electric hat lights, depending entirely upon the ordinary pocket flashlights common at that time. Therefore, when we commenced to retrace our steps for the long and arduous return to the main cavern, we found that our lights had become much the worse for wear and only three of them would be of any real service.

We decided to keep close together on this account, but somehow, being farther behind than I realized and with a poor light, I managed to make a wrong turning somewhere along the route and did not realize that I was lost until it was too late for the sound of my voice to reach the others. At first I thought it might be wiser to remain where I was and await a rescue party, but believing that I had been proceeding all the time in the general direction desired, I decided to press on as best I could in the hope that the passage I was following might again join that followed by my companions.

In a little while, the ceiling narrowed down until I was compelled to crawl, then the floor assumed a steep incline toward my right so that I had to brace myself to keep myself from sliding down into—I did not know what.

Perhaps an hour passed while I struggled along through this steeply sloping crevasse, then it leveled off again into a long broad shelf, almost obstructed by small needlelike stalactites and stalagmites and conjoined columns the diameter of a lead pencil or a little larger. I searched all around by my rapidly dimming flashlight for an opening through which I could crawl but was forced to plow ahead, shearing off the formations as I crawled, until my progress was halted by the increasing size of the stalagmites over which I had to work my way. By this time my hands and knees were raw—in fact, my whole body— from collision with these sharp objects. Because of the lowering ceiling, it was no longer possible to crawl, I had to lie flat on my stomach and merely wriggle along as best I could.

Soon after, my flashlight died a natural death and I was left alone in the bowels of the earth in the darkest of darkness and the most silent silence imaginable. I had never before realized how dark a cave could be or how silent the inside of the earth, shut in from the myriad sounds of nature to which our ears have become so accustomed that we never notice them in ordinary life. Here for the first time in my life I actually experienced the sensations of total blindness and deafness and realized what the loss of sight and hearing might mean.

After making futile attempts to turn back, a disheartening thought at best, for I knew in the darkness I'd never be able to follow even my own trail, I lay still for what seemed a long time and put into practice a mental process I had acquired to rid myself of all fear and panic. At the same time, by a relaxation of body and mind I regained some of the strength I had lost by the fatiguing efforts of my crawl.

Many times I shouted as loud as I could and listened for a possible answer, but only the hollow echo of my own call came back to my waiting ears.

Now, somewhat rested, I came to the conclusion that I must make a final effort to get out of this particular place for it was one in which no party of searchers would think of looking. Return being out of the question, I pushed forward, redoubling my efforts to break through the ever-stronger formations. The ceiling was now not more than eighteen or twenty inches from the uneven floor but by feeling on all sides I managed to make some progress. For some time I pushed on painfully, then the going became a little easier as the ceiling lifted slightly.

Encouraged by this, I went more rapidly and soon was able almost to get up on my knees and really crawl. Then the ceiling came down again to about twenty inches and I had to sprawl and wriggle along as before.

The sound of the breaking formations tinkled on the floor like so much broken glass and I was really sorry for the damage I was doing to those jewels which nature had been building for ages.

After one of my short periods of rest, I put out my hand ahead of me to feel the way and it went over the edge of what appeared to be a sharp precipice!

What was I to do now?

How deep was it?

Where would it lead me?

Was it a crevasse, and how wide was the rift?

Was this the end? Would I have to turn and try to make my way back in this utter darkness?

These thoughts stumbled over one another in my mind. There was no panic but I realized that I was getting the thought of blackness mixed up in those other thoughts. I lay still, with my hand on the edge of the precipice.

After a few minutes I worked my way nearer the edge and reached over to feel around in the hope of discovering something about this new barrier. My hand suddenly touched what felt like a piece of wood. Petrified wood? I thought. That would be a great discovery and one which my companions would envy. But this wood couldn't be petrified because it had splinters. I felt along this board, and soon my hand came to a round metallic object, apparently coming out of one end of it. Right in the middle of this was a key.

I started to laugh — not hysteria — but I don't to this day know whether it was a laugh of relief or of the incongruity of being lost in the bowels of the earth far away from civilization and suddenly coming upon — of all things — an electric switch! I turned it and the lights that flashed on were so bright and startling that for a second I was blinded.

Believe me when I saw that I was glad to see those lights and to know that I had actually followed a new passage that ran parallel to the one the rest of the party were following. I had come out on a low shelf that marked one of the tourist paths. Then I turned around to see what I could of the way I had come. My heart sank because I realized that I had actually plowed my way through one of the scenic gems of the Caverns—

"Fairyland"—and that I had broken countless of the small formations that made the setting so beautiful.

Now that I was in the lighted section I knew my way about and hurried to the entrance. I forgot all about the darkness and the bodily discomforts and realized only that I was hungry. There I met the rescue party that had been sent back to search for me. I turned them around and together we went on a new and important search—for food.

Black may be black but it surely is blacker than that when you get right down inside the earth where there has *never* been any natural light. Believe me, because I know.

—THROUGH HELL AND HIGH WATER (1941)

Youthful Adventure

BY WILFRED H. OSGOOD

Introduction by Seyward S. Cramer, Editor, *Through Hell and High Water*, 1941

Gentlemen, I feel that I have won a great battle. I have at last heard Dr. Wilfred Osgood admit that it is possible for an explorer to have an adventure without proving his incompetence. To be sure, he does hedge a bit and say that incompetence is indicated where there are too many adventures, that is, too many in proportion to opportunity.

Dr. Osgood has had forty years of active exploration and I am more than willing to take his word. Even now, he is about to leave on an expedition with Leon Mandel and Rudyerd Boulton to the Galapagos Islands to make collections for the Field Museum. He was Chief Curator of Zoology in the museum for many years and a few months ago was made Curator Emeritus.

Doctor, won't you tell us of some of your adventures? Though we'll call them "experiences" if you prefer.

If adventure means risking one's life, it is probable that one of my greatest adventures happened when I was only sixteen years of age. Another boy had found a golden eagle's nest in a tall tree in the mountains of California, near where I lived at that time. He was afraid to climb up to it and, being a sort of Tom Sawyer, he came to me and proposed that I do the job, and get the eggs for him for a consideration. This consideration was a lot of other birds' eggs, which I coveted; in addition, there was the implied flattery of my prowess as a climber. Without even seeing the tree, I agreed, and an expedition was planned immediately.

When we reached the spot and I saw what I had to do, my heart sank. The tree was an enormous Digger pine, half dead, bare of branches practically to the top, and with patches of loose bark on its otherwise smooth and weather-hardened trunk. The nest formed a huge crown at its very tip. Stories of the fury of mother eagles in defending their homes passed through my mind, but the great tree and the rocky canyon below it were even more disturbing.

I was too young to have the courage to turn back at this stage; it seemed that I must do or die. So, while the other boy stood by, I strapped on a pair of old, rusty, and very dull climbing irons and started up. My arms reached only part way around the trunk but fortunately the tree inclined slightly. Halfway up, when I ventured to look back, I realized that this slight incline had brought me out directly over the canyon, which meant that a fall would be not the height of the tree which was only 70 feet, but several hundred feet into the canyon.

Finally my head butted into the bottom of the nest, and I stopped for a long rest on some stubs of branches just below. The nest spread out for several feet on all sides and it seemed practically impossible to get over the edge. I tried burrowing through it, but it had been rebuilt from year to year, and the sticks of its foundation were too large and too firmly meshed together.

Here again I might have given up if I had been alone, or if I had been older and more cautious, but boylike I couldn't quit while another was looking on. I had to be reckless and, finding no other way, I accepted the dubious support of one of the rotten stubs and executed a twisting sort of flip that threw my body outward and then quickly inward, landing me sprawling in the nest—and almost breaking the two large chocolate-spotted eggs that lay there.

From the comparative safety of the grass-lined center of the great nest, the eggs were placed in a sock and carefully lowered to my waiting companion, who had scrambled down the canyon to a position directly below me, and so far away that his shouts were scarcely audible. After a long rest, but with my heart still beating at a terrific rate and my hands trembling, I gradually tore away one side of the nest sufficiently to let me through and the descent was successfully accomplished.

Perhaps it wasn't really so very difficult, but looking at it in a retrospect of more than forty years it seems to me I'd rather stand on my head on the wing of a moving airplane than repeat the dizzying performance of getting over the edge of that eagle's nest.

Several years ago I drove up that same canyon in California, over a smooth motor road and, although the old pine has passed out, I recognized the spot where it stood, and realized that my memory had not exaggerated the conditions. Later years have seen many experiences much farther away from home, but I'm sure I never more deliberately risked my life. For years it gave me the shivers whenever I thought of it. The incident may not qualify for some as a real adventure, but it does for me!

A few years later, when I was twenty-three years old and, from my present standpoint, still only a youngster, I had another experience. Every detail of it is clearer to me now than many things that have happened since. After only a brief experience of collecting museum specimens in California, that paradise for the camper, I was given command of a government (Biological Survey) expedition to descend the Yukon River, in Canada and Alaska, from its source to its mouth.

This was in 1899, shortly after the great Klondike rush, when the White Pass and Yukon Railroad had only just been begun and travel conditions were rough and ready. With two other young naturalists, I built a boat on Lake Bennett, stocked it with flour, bacon, and beans, and started down the river. The dangerous White Horse Rapids and other bad waters in the upper river were successfully passed and for some two months we floated along, stopping from time to time to collect specimens of mammals and birds.

It wasn't so easy as California, but at times it seemed to be. Our boat was a sort of bateau, square-ended, flat-bottomed, roomy, and exceedingly steady. We even had a small deck forward, with a little combing tacked down to hold an inch or two of gravel, on which we placed a small sheet-iron stove so that we could cook meals while traveling. There was little to do but steer, for the old Yukon provides a current that never fails. There's scarcely a mile of slack water in its whole course, while the current probably averages four to five miles per hour.

At Circle City our boat was exchanged for a smaller and lighter one, not just what we wanted but the only thing available. It was pointed at both ends and, as compared with the other, definitely "cranky." One member of the party took steamer here and the outfit was reduced, but still the boat was over-loaded. Confidence was born of our success on the upper river, however, and two of us set out gaily in the small boat, determined to make great speed and get through before the cold weather set in.

The first day we made over a hundred miles and were much pleased with ourselves. The following day was cold, raw, and windy. After traveling six or seven hours, we were tired and hungry; above all, we wanted to get out of the raw wind for a while. No suitable stopping place appeared, and finally, when we swung out of the wind under the lee of a high cut bank, we suddenly decided to stop in the stream by tying up to a snag or pro-truding branch of a submerged tree, as we had sometimes done with the larger boat.

Unfortunately the current was swifter than we thought, the snag refused to stay put, and as soon as the fastening had been made, the end of the boat was drawn up into the current, careening, and approaching the level of the water. I reached frantically for my knife to cut the rope, but it was too late. In a few seconds the water was rushing over the side, the boat was completely swamped, and we were floundering in the cold water. I remember that I had on two pairs of trousers, heavy shoes, a sweater, and a hunting coat, and my immediate sensation was one of buoyancy. For the first few minutes—or per-haps only seconds—before we became waterlogged, there was no difficulty in keeping afloat. But the water was both cold and deep, and we were fifty yards from shore, at the mercy of a strong current that raced along at six to eight miles an hour.

Our wreckage was all about us. A wooden chest of specimens was riding high and I seized it, mentally resolving to hang on till the last gasp. We were undoubtedly in great danger of drowning, but we didn't seem to think so, and the prospect of getting ashore without food was uppermost in our minds. By great good fortune, the strong current almost immediately tore the boat loose from its fastening and we had gone only a few yards when it came bobbing along, bottom side up. Exerting all our strength, we managed to swim across the current just in time to catch it and swing an arm over it, one of us on each end. This was comparative safety, but our clothes were now soaked. Further swimming was out of the question, the icy water was beginning to numb our legs, and we knew that, wherever the current chose to take the boat, there we would go also.

Our predicament may be better understood when it is sensed that we were right on the Arctic Circle at a point where the mighty Yukon spreads to a width of seven miles and is filled with innumerable islands, around which the water passes and makes a dozen or more rivers in one. It was late in the season and, although a few steamers might go by before the freeze-up, there was no telling which channel they would take. The nearest settlement downstream was several hundred miles away.

We floated on with the upturned boat for a half mile or more, and then came to a sudden and abrupt stop against a great jam of drift logs, on the point of a small island. As we hit this, I jumped and scrambled out on the logs, giving the boat a kick as I did so, thinking only of myself, and expecting my companion to do the same. When I turned around I was horrified to find nothing in sight but the churning water. We had struck in a vortex of boiling eddies, where the current divided to pass on each side of the island, and both the boat and my comrade were drawn under in the strong suction beneath the tangle of logs. I had a moment of excruciating, paralyzing fear. Up to that time I had seemed to feel that somehow or other we would get out alive. The idea of being left alone, or with a crippled partner, was distinctly unpleasant. It was only a matter of seconds, however, before the missing man came up, spluttering and blowing, and badly scared. I reached a hand to him and soon we were both on shore and with us was the chest of specimens.

The island wasn't large enough for much playing of Robinson Crusoe. It as about half a mile long and two or three hundred feet wide, with a few spruce trees at one end and light alder and willow brush at the other. We followed our first impulse — to race down the shore on the chance that some of our duffel might have drifted in and lodged somewhere, but nothing was found. Returning to the log jam where we had landed, we noticed something very interesting. This was a mallard duck which I had shot that morning and which had been lying loose in the boat. Its head was firmly wedged in the crotch of a "sweeper" or branch, of a submerged tree which was swishing rhythmically back and forth in a swift current only some thirty feet offshore. We looked at it longingly, but the current bore toward midstream. Although we were now deeply conscious that our upset had occurred before, instead of after, a somewhat postponed luncheon, we decided it was too dangerous to try to get the duck.

The small growth on the sandy island included quantities of wild roses, the "hips," or fruit of which were fully ripe and quite fleshy. Although not very nourishing, these were edible and filling, so we stuffed ourselves with them. Obviously, however, we'd soon starve if we remained on the island, so we decided to build a raft and at least make an effort to get to the mainland, wherever that might be. So far as we could judge more islands were on all sides of us.

Boy Scouts hadn't been invented at that time, and neither of us had more than hazy ideas of making fire. We rubbed sticks together until they smoked and until we were almost exhausted, but we never got a spark. Finally, we gave it up, to play with our wet matches, one of which to our great joy sputtered for an instant and ignited a bit of dry cotton I had found in my pocket. Halfway down the shore we found dry drift logs; these we burned into lengths and from them put together a rough raft. My extra pair of canvas trousers we cut into strips and braided into rope with which the logs were rather insecurely bound together. It was a flimsy affair, and probably would have come to grief, but it wasn't finished until well into the night and we decided to get some sleep before launching it.

Our supper that night was a half cupful of oatmeal that, like every good mousetrapper, I had been carrying in the pocket of my coat. It was a sticky mess, but hailed with joy and divided with great pains into exactly equal halves. If it had been beans, I think they would have been counted.

The next morning we awoke stiff and chilly and with a hunger indescribably beyond anything of the day before. Neither of us said a word for a few minutes. We rolled over, poked the fire a bit, and stood up. Then, suddenly and practically in unison, we ejaculated, "We've got to get that duck!" The coincidence was so striking that we burst into laughter, for the first time. At once we went to the head of the island and stood on the little promontory looking over the log jam and the seething waters around it.

The duck was still there, but in the cold gray dawn its retrieval seemed less inviting. The only way was to swim for it and to hope for success in getting back to our own shore. We agreed it was a one-man job and were just about to draw cuts for it when my companion stepped back and fairly shouted, "Look at that! There's the boat!"

Sure enough! It was still under the jam of logs and had worked around until one of its pointed ends was visible just below the surface of the water. There was skim ice in quiet spots at the water's edge and the early morning air was wintry—but nothing mattered now. We stripped and went after our darling boat, so precious now, yet so roundly cursed the day before. It was wedged in tightly, and there was considerable danger from falling logs, but we finally got it out and afloat. Of course, it was empty, but an extra oar was wedged under the thwarts, and another was soon improvised, while we shouted, laughed and registered joy in every way we could.

The rest was easy. The duck offered some difficulty, even with the boat, but we got it and soon had it roasted.

After this magnificent breakfast, we packed up and shoved off in the boat. We hurried downstream until we came to a deserted Indian camp where there were some bits of dried salmon lying about; after whittling away the mold and maggots, enough of these were accumulated to carry us another day.

Shortly after that we heard the *chough-chough* of a steamer in the distance, and made frantically for what seemed to be the main channel of the river. We got there just ahead of her, and tried to hail her. She passed us by, perhaps because it was unsafe to stop in that particular place, but we shook our fists at her and relapsed into gloomy disappointment. Yukon steamers are very irregular, and we had small hope of ever seeing another, but only two days later, to our great surprise, a second old stern-wheeler came along to pick us up and take us to Bering Sea and St. Michael. This time we put our boat directly in front of her, where she had either to stop or run us down.

My companion in this escapade, Alfred Maddren, later became a prominent oil geologist and in this profession traveled all over the world, while I have done the same as a zoologist. However, I doubt if either of us ever had a more interesting and exciting time than when we were boy adventurers on the Yukon.

In subsequent trips to Alaska and Northwestern Canada, I've had a number of close calls, usually from drowning, and I've grown to have a wholesome respect for the dangers of water travel. I've been in several mild forms of shipwreck, in addition to difficulties with canoes and other small boats, I've had my men and mules carried downstream in making fords, and once I was caught in quicksand, so altogether I'm fairly convinced that water hazards are the greatest the wilderness traveler has to face. In later years I've made various long trips in south America, in the Andes and on the Amazon and other rivers, in Africa and in Asia, but most of my really narrow escapes were in Alaska. Probably other countries are no less dangerous but, it seems to me, I've become more careful of my skin and more experienced in avoiding catastrophe.

— *THROUGH HELL AND HIGH WATER* (1941)

PART ELEVEN

Horizons

Exploration Defined

BY ALFRED EISENPREIS

The root of the words "exploration," "explore," and "exploring" is the Latin *explorare*—to search out. That comes from *plorare*—a word found in the writings of Horace and Cicero. One of its meanings is to "utter a cry." The renowned philologist and lexicographer Eric Partridge says that it is to cry out "at the sight of land" or the enemy—hence also "to spy out." It is the cry of finding what was sought, of the split-second of discovery of something that was not known, of the pencil-thin line on the horizon that suddenly becomes a shore and then, land, at once both promising and threatening.

The noun "exploration" entered the English language in 1543 by way of medieval French. The verb "to explore" was introduced in 1585. The noun "explorer" makes its dictionary debut in 1740.

Today, definitions of "to explore" include "to investigate, study, or analyze; to look into; to become familiar with by testing or experimenting; to examine, scrutinize (a country, area, building) by going through it; to travel into new territory for adventure or discovery; to go on an excursion or exploration." An "explorer" is defined as "one who explores, especially a person who travels in search of geographical or scientific information."

I looked into a medical dictionary and found this interesting entry under "exploratory behavior": "the tendency to explore or investigate a novel environment. It is considered a motivation not clearly distinguishable from curiosity."

If that definition leaves one somewhat puzzled, it is understandable. It was taken from the *On-line Medical Dictionary*. Another entry from the *On-line Medical Dictionary* is this definition of "exploration": "The act of exploring, penetrating, or ranging over for purposes of discovery, especially of geographical discovery; examination, as, the exploration of unknown countries;

physical examination." The *On-line Medical Dictionary* provides one additional entry. Oddly enough, under the subhead, "dentistry," there is this entry: "Explorer is a hook-like fine-pointed instrument used in examining the teeth."

The *Miller-Keane Dictionary* compresses its definition into six words. Exploration is "investigation or examination for diagnostic purposes."

Well, enough for the medical detour.

Let's go back to the roots—to Latin. Beginning with the English-into-Latin section in the *Oxford Latin Dictionary*, the noun "exploration" is translated as *indagatio* and *investigatio*. Reversing the look-up, *indagatio* is translated as "the verb of diligently searching out." *Investigatio* is defined as "searching out."

The verb "explore" leads us to *exploro*; *perscrutor*; and *vestigo*. Respectively, these come back into English as: *exploro* = reconnoitre, test, try out, investigate; *perscrutor* = search high and low, study carefully; *vestigo* = track down, find out by searching, investigate.

In German, exploration is defined as *Erforschung*. That links us back to the English investigation and searching. The synonymous *Forschung* is translated as research. In the realm of nature, a *Forscher* becomes an explorer. To explore is translated as *erforschen*, or *untersuchen* (to search).

In *Four Quartets* ("Little Gidding"), T.S. Eliot wrote:

We shall not cease from exploration
And the end of all our exploring
Will be to arrive where we started
And know the place for the first time.

This is central to the concept of exploration—to come back to the point of departure, and to understand better our own world because we have searched out another.

In *On a Return from Egypt*, the poet Keith Douglas laments: "And all my endeavors are unlucky explorers, abandoning the expedition. . . ." That is the dreaded end—an expedition that fails; returning home, empty of hand, telling only stories of defeat; or worse yet, not returning at all.

In *The Ascent of Man*, Jacob Bronowski defines man as "a singular creature. He has a set of gifts that make him unique among the animals so that, unlike them, he is not a figure in a landscape—he is a shaper of the landscape. In body and in mind he is the explorer of nature, the ubiquitous animal who did not find but made his home in every continent."

Exploration is a mystic search, a voyage to a place not fully known, always pursued with the urgency to return, carrying high the victorious flag. It is an endless challenge, with no boundaries of age or time.

In another passage of *Four Quartets* ("East Coker"), Eliot says it all:

Old men ought to be explorers
Here and there does not matter
We must be still and still moving
Into another intensity

Such intensity, where "here and there does not matter," but only the dynamics of moving onward does—that is the real meaning of exploration.

—THE EXPLORERS JOURNAL, FALL 2002

Alfred Eisenpreis, Ph. D., a fellow of The Explorers Club since 1997 and currently chair of its Library Committee, studied Roman settlements at Carnuntum-Petronell in Austria. A chief marketing executive for Allied Stores Corporation and former head of New York City's Economic Development Corporation, Eisenpreis directed the Bicentennial Parade of Tall Ships.

Hunting Wildlife
with Pen and Palette

BY ROBERT MCCRACKEN PECK

W hen guests and members left The Explorers Club 1912 Annual Dinner, they carried with them some new stories, a few more pounds, and a printed dinner menu embellished with caricatures of the Club's more prominent members to remind them of the evening. Seventy-six years later, a single copy of the menu survives. It reveals both the serious endeavors and the fun that characterized the Club in its fourth year.

On the cover of this now-brittle souvenir, an anonymous but representative explorer stands atop a peak with an imaginary banner in hand. "The Whole World is our Playground," it proclaims. To the Club member who created the menu, this joyful motto was only partly accurate, for to Louis Agassiz Fuertes, the world was a work-ground as well. The most talented and accomplished wildlife artist of his day (some say of all time), Fuertes had traveled the world in pursuit of his subjects. He left behind a tangible legacy of achievement that records both his far-flung travels and his unique gift for capturing the very essence of wild nature in pencil and pigment.

The youngest of six children, Louis Fuertes was born in 1874 in Ithaca, New York, where his father taught engineering at Cornell University. As a child, Fuertes developed an intense interest in natural science. He spent much of his free time observing, collecting, and sketching wildlife in the countryside around his home. Though he received no formal art training until after graduating from college, he taught himself to paint at an early age and worked prodigiously during his teenage years perfecting the craft. His inspiration came from the large, hand-colored plates of John James Audubon's *Birds of America*, a book that Fuertes labored over in the Ithaca Public Library.

The impact of those plates, which Fuertes once described as his "daily bread" during adolescence, can be seen in the meticulous style of his earliest paintings. Working from field observations of live animals and dead specimens, young Fuertes drew outlines of his subjects in ink, then filled them in with watercolor wash.

As his painting technique matured, Fuertes eliminated the confining ink outlines that he had seen in Audubon's engravings. His watercolors took on a looser, livelier appearance. He began experimenting with new compositions, abandoning Audubon's formal poses and opting for the natural bird postures he had seen in the field.

While a college undergraduate at Cornell, Fuertes was introduced to Elliott Coues, who was one of America's leading authorities on birds at the time. Coues immediately recognized the artist's genius. In an 1897 issue of *The Osprey*, a popular birding magazine of the period, Coues wrote: "There is now no one who can draw and paint birds as well as Mr. Fuertes, and I do not forget Audubon himself. . . ." Fuertes was then 23 years old.

The secret of his success, Fuertes once noted, was the methodical observations of his subjects in the wild. While most earlier painters had worked primarily from dead birds or museum skins, Fuertes spent countless hours sketching the creatures alive, in the field. Carefully, he noted each bird's appearance, attitude and behavior, transferring its subtleties to paper with pencil, brush, and watercolor.

Fuertes' intensity when working often amazed his colleagues. His friend and fellow Explorers Club member, Frank Chapman, a noted scientist at the American Museum of Natural History in New York, observed that the artist had an uncanny ability to recall what he had seen. "His concentration annihilates his surroundings," said Chapman. "Color, pattern, form, contour, minute details of structure, are all absorbed and assimilated so completely by Fuertes that they become part of himself, and they can be reproduced at any future time with remarkable accuracy."

Fortunately for Fuertes, his conspicuous talent and genial personality resulted in a seemingly endless string of invitations to participate in scientific expeditions around the world. The first of these came in 1899 when Fuertes traveled to Alaska as part of a 126-person expedition, privately sponsored by the New York financier Edward Henry Harriman. The expedition, deemed "remarkable for the number of noted men participating" and the "completeness of [its] equipment" by one west coast newspaper, was by far the most luxurious of the many trips Fuertes would take during his career. Besides a crew of 65 officers and men, and an additional force of 11 hunters, packers and campers to assist the landing parties, the Harrimans took physicians, stenographers, a chaplain, a nurse, and four family servants. The scientific staff of 30 comprised many of the country's leading botanists, geologists and photographers, including: the influential naturalist John Burroughs, the most popular natural history writer of his day; John Muir, America's leading conservationist; George Bird Grinnell, editor of *Forest and Stream* and one of the founders of the National Audubon Society; William H. Dall, the Alaskan explorer for whom the Dall's sheep is named; Robert Ridgway, curator of birds at the National Museum of Natural History and president of the American Ornithologists Union; Edward S. Curtis, the highly acclaimed Indian photographer; and a host of other important and influential figures. Like Fuertes, many of the expedition's participants would later play an active roll in the nascent Explorers Club.

This assembled group of dignitaries, described by Fuertes as "a big happy family," left Seattle on May 30, 1899, and cruised north and west, visiting Sitka, Glacier Bay, the Aleutian Islands, and Siberia. The primary geographic discoveries of the trip were a large, unknown fjord (subsequently named for Harriman) and its five live glaciers. Among the thousands of biological specimens collected on the expedition were more than 13 genera and 600 species new to science. These consisted primarily of plants, insects and small mammals. Although all of the western birds were new to Fuertes, they had been previously recorded by other ornithologists and could not be counted among the expedition's discoveries.

Fuertes returned from the 4,327-mile journey with over 100 bird skins, a portfolio full of pencil sketches and watercolors, and a host of new friends, many of whom he would keep for the rest of his life. The official report of the expedition, written by John Burroughs, contained color reproductions of 16 of Fuertes' bird paintings.

Subsequent field trips took Fuertes to Texas' "Big Bend" country (1901); the Bahamas (1902); Nevada, Colorado, New Mexico, and California (1903); Jamaica (1904); Saskatchewan and Alberta (1907); Florida (1908); Magdalen Islands in the Gulf of St. Lawrence (1909); Yucatan (1910); Colombia (1911 and 1913); the Bahamas (1920); Florida (1921); and Abyssinia (Ethiopia) (1926).

Fuertes relished these field experiences and the exotic places to which they took him. "You know that I was born with an itching foot," he once wrote Frank Chapman in response to an invitation to join an expedition to Colombia. "The sight of a map—or even a time-table—is enough to stir me all up inside." But while he loved the adventurous aspects of field research, he rejected "the gratuitous search for adventure" as "the bane of a working expedition." As his trip journals and copious letters from the field indicate, Fuertes had no need for such a search; the nature, time, and location of the expeditions he joined guaranteed adventure. His many exhilarating, and at times harrowing, experiences in the field were anything but gratuitous. On one occasion he was held prisoner by a group of African tribesmen hoping for lucrative ransom in the form of whiskey and tobacco. On another, the artist narrowly escaped serious injury or death when he was bitten by a black mamba, one of the most poisonous snakes in the world. Such dangers were of little concern to Fuertes, however, and he seemed to thrive on the adversity he encountered in the field.

During the 30 years of his professional career, Fuertes prepared illustrations for more than 35 books and approximately 50 educational leaflets, handbooks, and bulletins. He was a tireless worker and contributed regularly to more than a dozen popular and scholarly journals.

Fuertes occasionally accepted advertising projects too. The most successful, and perhaps best known, was for the Church and Dwight Company, distributors of Arm and Hammer Baking Soda. In the 1920s, for his friend and fellow conservationist Charles T. Church, Fuertes painted 120 bird portraits.

The plan was to include a reproduction in each package of baking soda. There were four series of 30 studies each: song birds (two different sets), game birds, and birds of prey (the last not published until 1976). These small reproductions were collected as avidly as baseball cards, especially by children, and did much to increase public knowledge of ornithology.

Despite the unparalleled success of his scientific illustrations, in the mid-1920s Fuertes began to experiment with more inventive compositions. He indicated to his friends and family that when his current commissions were completed he intended to devote more time to painting for its own sake.

Unfortunately, he was never to have that opportunity. Following his participation in a seven-month expedition in Abyssinia, during which he created "the best lot of field studies I ever did on one trip," Fuertes was killed in an automobile accident at a grade crossing near Unadilla, New York. His wife was slightly injured in the accident. Miraculously, the Abyssinian paintings that were with him were thrown clear of the wreck.

During a memorial service for Fuertes a few months later, Frank Chapman stated: "If the birds of the world had met to select a human being who could best express to mankind the beauty and charm of their forms, their songs, their rhythmic flight, their manners for the heart's delight, they would unquestionably have chosen Louis Fuertes."

Fuertes himself could not have asked for a finer tribute.

— *THE EXPLORERS JOURNAL*, DECEMBER 1988

Robert McCracken Peck is a Fellow of the Academy of Natural Sciences of Philadelphia and author of the books A Celebration of Birds; The Life and Art of Louis Agassiz Fuertes *and* Headhunters and Hummingbirds; An Expedition into Ecuador. *He has also written articles for* American Art Review, Arts Magazine, Audubon, National Wildlife, *and other publications. An active member (and former vice chairman) of the Philadelphia Chapter of The Explorers Club, Mr. Peck has carried The Explorers Club flag on expeditions in Ecuador and Venezuela.*

Lowell Thomas Milestones

BY HOWELL L. JOINER

I t has been my good fortune to be present at several events in the history of The Explorers Club intertwined with the life and times of Lowell Thomas.

In the summer of 1968, the Club commissioned a life-size bronze bust of Lowell for prominent display in the Center for World Exploration that he helped establish. The sculptor chosen was Philip Kraczkowski of Attleboro, Massachusetts. His credentials were impressive and his work was unveiled at our Annual Dinner in the Waldorf-Astoria the following year.

Both the artist and his subject posed for their picture with the bust. Lowell was pleased with the result and requested a print, which I gladly sent to him. The photograph was later included in a small booklet on the bust.

The present clubhouse was acquired through the efforts of Lowell and several other members. When the indebtedness on the building had been reduced to $165,000, Lowell sprang a pleasant surprise at a breakfast in honor of his birthday on April 6, 1968. Thirty-three members, including myself, were present in the Carpenter Suite of the Waldorf when he wiped out the debt with a check for the amount we owed. Our headquarters were now free and clear and we could "burn the mortgage." Maynard Miller, chairman of our World Center for Exploration project, made a favorable progress report.

On April 16, 1977, The Explorers Club headquarters was dedicated and designated the Lowell Thomas Building. The photograph was set up by the wife of Ernest F. Schmidt. The personna are, from the left: the author, Lowell Thomas, and Carl Von Hoffman.

Our Annual Dinners were always something special to members and friends. Many times Lowell was our Master of Ceremonies. He could always be depended upon to come up with something special and unexpected. His resplendent dinner jacket, if memory serves me, was a gift from the King of Nepal. Once the tables were turned on him.

During the Annual Dinner on April 11, 1981, Jim Fowler, who was seated at the table with Lowell and his lovely wife Marianna Munn Thomas, rose to his feet. It was a signal for the entry of a huge lighted cake and the singing of the happy birthday song. With his usual aplomb, Lowell acknowledged the tribute to his 89th birthday. It was actually five days earlier, when his last letter to me was written.

Lowell's favorite charity, a preference I shared with him, was the American Colony Charities Association, now known as the Help for Children in the Holy Land. It was there that I first met Marianna, when she was executive director of that organization. This was in support of our late dear friend Bertha Spafford Vester, who spent 85 of her 90 years in Jerusalem helping others.

One of Lowell's closest friends was Sir Hubert Wilkins. In 1961 he wrote a biography of him. When I was unable to find a copy, Lowell sent me one inscribed with a note. Lady (Suzanne) Wilkins painted an excellent portrait of her husband in an unlikely context, which she later presented to our Club.

Another friend of Lowell's (and mine as well) is Henry S. Evans, editor of *The Explorers Journal*. It was befitting that Henry should write the Memoriam to Lowell for the December 1981 issue, as they had been friends for 50 years. Shortly after Charles F. Brush, president, gave him The Edward C. Sweeney Medal at Lowell's last Annual Dinner in 1981, I photographed Henry with his charming and helpful wife, Elsa, and his personable son, Jeff. Jeffrey had recently received his Ph.D. in clinical psychology.

To most of the world and especially to us who were fortunate enough to have known his close friendship, Lowell Thomas seemed like an ageless man, and now he is a "man of the ages."

So now we say to you, Lowell, "So long until *that* tomorrow."

Geographer and archeologist, Howell L. Joiner is a Fellow of the Royal Geographical Society, the American Geographical Society, a member of the Archaeological Institute of America, among others. He has organized or participated in five African scientific expeditions, as well as others in Cambodia, South America, and New Guinea. Joiner has also organized research studies in Egypt and Jordan. Included in his 1978 expedition in the Sahara was work done in anthropological pre-history. He continues to do research in vertebrate and invertebrate paleontology and is a Contributing Editor of The Explorers Journal.

On Exploration

BY MILBRY C. POLK

The Future of Wildlife: In Conversation with Alan Rabinowitz

For two decades, Alan Rabinowitz, director of the Science and Exploration Program at the Wildlife Conservation Society (WCS), has led numerous expeditions that have yielded important scientific discoveries about rare, large predators. He has also been instrumental in the establishment of nature preserves. He is currently working to explore and create preserves in remote areas of northern Burma.

EJ: *You have led a fantastic life of scientific exploration centered on the study of rare, wild animals. How did you begin? Did you grow up with animals?*

AR: Most people in my field talk about growing up with animals. I grew up in New York City. I never saw a living cow until I went to college in Maryland. I suffered from a severe stutter, so it was painful for me to be around people. My problem was so extreme that I was put in special classes in school with retarded and other "problem" children. It was horrible. But I discovered that I didn't stutter when I talked to animals. Animals had no expectations. So I had lots of pets, the kind you buy at pet stores like gerbils and snakes. They were my instruments of expression. Even then I saw that many of the animals I owned should not be sold in pet stores. They were exotic and not expected to live long away from their wild environment. But animals helped me to survive my childhood and so eventually I felt that I wanted to somehow help them survive as well.

EJ: *What were your other early influences?*

AR: I consumed books on adventure; Richard Burton and Jim Corbett in particular. I dreamed of being in places where they spoke different languages so that I wouldn't have to talk. I craved immersing myself in the wildest of places. Places where people were not judgmental and where the animals were making their last stand.

EJ: *What launched you into scientific exploration?*

AR: In college I was introduced to camping. For a city boy this was at first terrifying—there were too many places for people to hide! But soon I just loved it. In the dark by the fire all my tension melted away. I wanted a career that merged my love of animals with my desire for physical challenges. But I also wanted to make a difference in a substantive way through science. Ecology was then an emerging science and it offered everything I wanted. But there were only four graduate schools in the country at that time offering a Ph.D. in this new field. I eventually chose the University of Tennessee.

EJ: *How did you begin your explorations?*

AR: It started with my first encounter with George Schaller. He came to Tennessee to review the research we were doing on black bears in the Smoky Mountains. He was studying pandas in China at the time and wanted to explore the possible relationship between the two species. During one of our hikes into the mountains he asked me what I wanted to do with my life. I said I wanted to combine adventure and exploration, yet do something meaningful, but I didn't know how to make it into a career. Two weeks later, after returning to New York, George called and asked me to go to Belize to study jaguars. I had no idea where Belize was at the time but I said yes immediately. He gave me $600 and said I had six weeks to determine the status of jaguars in the country.

EJ: *Tell us about your jaguar survey and what you accomplished.*

AR: Well I stretched the six weeks into eight weeks and had to dip into some of my own savings, but I was in heaven! At that time jaguars and other wildlife were numerous in Belize; in fact while I was there a puma wandered into the capital city. I spent those eight weeks hiking through the most remote areas in the country looking for signs of jaguars. When I got back and handed George my report, he asked me if I wanted to return to make the first ecological study of jaguars in the rainforest. I was in Belize from about 1979 to 1981, living with the Maya, learning to speak some of their language, and figuring out how to capture, collar, and study jaguars. The result was the establishment of a preserve for jaguars. I discuss those experiences in my first book, *Jaguar.*

EJ: *Where did you go next?*

AR: George Schaller and what was then called the New York Zoological Society at the Bronx Zoo hired me as a field biologist. It was an incredible opportunity. George told me I could basically go where I wanted to go as long as I could justify it scientifically. After having been so successful in Belize with jaguars, I now felt I had to try something more challenging. I looked for the hardest study, with the most elusive animal, in the most difficult terrain. I chose the clouded leopard, ranging throughout Southeast Asia. No one knew anything about this magnificent beast. Eventually, I found good populations to be studied in Borneo and Thailand.

EJ: *What made you decide to concentrate on Thailand?*

AR: Well, I was shown a huge wild forested area, some 10,000 square miles about halfway between Chiang Mai and Bangkok along the border with Burma. It had some of the best populations in the region for animals such as tigers, leopards, tapirs, and gibbons. But there was no good research on most of these species and there was a lot of pressure on the government to open up the area to logging. The Thai government asked me to stay in Thailand and conduct a study on the big cats to find out how they were really doing and how much land they needed. It was unusual to get such a request from the highest levels of government, so I agreed. Although I only planned on staying in Thailand two years, I ended up staying nearly ten years, studying the big cats and other wildlife. There was just so much to do.

EJ: *What was the result of your Thai study?*

AR: I discovered that tigers were facing a desperate situation in Thailand. I estimated no more than 200 to 250 left in the country, less than half of what the Thai government thought there were. I also discovered that much of the beautiful forested areas in the country suffered the empty forest syndrome — no large animals left. We did manage however to keep the huge area of protected forest where I first worked intact. It was eventually declared an International Biosphere Reserve and we started programs to help the local people understand how to care for this extraordinary place. The years I spent there I wrote about in my second book, *Chasing the Dragon's Tail.*

EJ: *And you had an added plus in that you met your wife during this time.*

AR: Yes, she was in medical school in Bangkok, doing genetic research on malaria. She went with me on a number of expeditions including later ones to Burma.

EJ: *Where did you go next?*

AR: The two places I most wanted to go after Thailand were Burma and Laos. I managed to get into Laos just after it opened up to Westerners in 1990. I led the first survey team into the Annamite Mountain Range along the Vietnam border. After that first trip, WCS teams returned and discovered five new mammal species in those mountains, three of which were thought to be long extinct. The area turned out to be something called a Pleistocene refuge — another world really. It is an extremely rugged and wild area. It eventually became known as an "ecological hotspot" and an area of great scientific interest. But I was already looking at maps dreaming of another region — the remote Himalayan region in northern Burma and southwest China that gave birth to this mountain range long ago.

EJ: *Burma or Myanmar has to be one of the more difficult yet exciting places to work. Your latest book,* Beyond the Last Village, *is a marvelous chronicle of your years there.*

AR: After Laos I knew I absolutely had to get into northeast Burma—it was potentially the mother lode for wildlife discovery and it was an area that was relatively unexplored and unknown to science. Yet it was also a no-man's land, a place that even on the maps had a landscape that looked like a piece of crumpled up paper. All the great rivers of Asia originate there. It is the water faucet for much of the Indo-Pacific region. My latest book, *Beyond the Last Village*, describes how I managed to get into this region and what we were able to do. It was so remote that many of the villagers we met had never even met a Burmese before, let alone a foreigner. Along the way, we discovered a new deer species to science and documented the last stand of the world's only Mongoloid pygmies.

EJ: *What is the situation in this remote region now?*

AR: Because of the relationship I'd established between WCS and the Burmese government, we were able to set up two large parks in this unique northern zone with a combined area of more than 5000 square miles. Now we are in the process of implementing a program that helps the local people with what they need; things like salt, medicine, and tea, while encouraging them to decrease their hunting of the wildlife. This can work because most of their hunting was to get the animal's body parts to trade for salt to Chinese traders who then sold the parts for Chinese traditional medicine.

EJ: *What is next?*

AR: I have lots of plans. In June I am conducting a jaguar survey in a remote region of Bolivia. I am also considering a trip to Turkey to look at the status of the Anatolian leopard and investigate rumors of the Caspian tiger, which is believed to be extinct.

EJ: *Tell us about the program you and George Schaller have established at WCS.*

AR: The purpose of the Science and Exploration Program is to search out the world's last wild areas and, through good science, get these areas and the wildlife they contain known and protected for the future. However, we also want to encourage young people in scientific exploration through a small grant program focused on ecological research. I am deeply concerned that the message young people are getting is that the world has been fully explored already. This is not true. Exploration is not dead, and biologically, there is no end to the mysteries that need to be probed. There is so much left to do. In northern Burma alone there are literally scores of remote valleys that have never been explored, much less studied.

EJ: *Can The Explorers Club and its members become involved?*

AR: I welcome Explorers Club involvement in my program. To find out more you can contact kconforti@wcs.org or write Kathy Conforti, Science and Exploration, Bronx Zoo, 105th Street, Bronx, NY 10460. It is important that The Explorers Club be involved in this important work studying and preserving the remaining wildness of the world.

— *THE EXPLORERS JOURNAL,* SPRING 2002

Milbry Polk is book editor for The Explorers Journal *and author of the book* Women of Discovery. *She has journeyed through Greece, Turkey, Persia, Pakistan, and Japan, surveyed Arthurian sites in Wales, traveled with Bedouin tribesmen in Jordan and Egypt, and kayaked throughout Alaska's Prince William Sound.*

Remembering Lowell Thomas

WITH WALTER CRONKITE

"Remembering Lowell Thomas" with Walter Cronkite was broadcast as a special report over the CBS television network on August 31, 1981. Lowell Thomas's own words from his past broadcasts were incorporated into the production. Copyright © 1981 by CBS, Inc. Transcript obtained for publication in 'The Explorers Journal and the Club archives by George E. Duck.

L owell Thomas (audio over still photo montage): I did my first broadcasting fifty-one years ago. So when I first started broadcasting, Eric Sevareid was thirteen years old, Walter Cronkite was nine, Mike Wallace was seven years old, David Brinkley five, Harry Reasoner two, Bob Pierpoint, John Chancellor, Barbara Walters, Roger Mudd, Marvin Kalb, Dan Rather and nearly all the others, they were not even born. And what does that mean? Well, it doesn't mean a darn thing. It simply means that, of course, I was very lucky and the Almighty has been kind to me.

From the North Pacific, from The Hague, and from Philadelphia comes today's news. Good evening, everybody. This is Lowell Thomas. Vice President Rockefeller today made the charge. . . .

Walter Cronkite: That was the famous greeting of Lowell Thomas, the most famous broadcaster of his era. His almost forty-six years of reporting the news nightly set a record for longevity. His total audience was once estimated at 125 billion people. But he himself said he was more entertainer than journalist. He was an explorer, an entrepreneur, a newsreel voice, the author of more than fifty books, the biographer who made Lawrence of Arabia famous, a believer with the poet that it is "Sweet to ride forth at evening from the wells along the golden road to Samarkand."

He was that man-about-the-world that every adventurous boy wants to be when he grows up. Tonight, we'll look at the life and astounding times of the man called "fate's pet child."

Announcer: This is a CBS News Special Report: "Remembering Lowell Thomas." Here again is Walter Cronkite.

Cronkite: Good evening.

Lowell Thomas was eighty-nine years old when he died of a heart attack in his sleep at his home in Pawling, New York, Saturday morning. He crammed a couple of centuries of living into those four-score years and nine. And the way you remember him will likely depend on how old you are yourself. If you were around in the 1920s, your first memory of Lowell Thomas might be his celebrated film and lecture tours. If you grew up with radio, certainly part of that memory involves Lowell Thomas. And for years he was a newsreel voice when the newsreel was how people saw history. More recently, he was associated with the three-dimensional film process called Cinerama. And through it all, there were his books, with titles like *Beyond Khyber Pass, Count Luckner: The Sea Devil,* and *India: Land of the Black Pagoda.* He lived one of those rare lives which is a joy to consider. Charles Collingwood has prepared a report on that life, and it begins in the town where Thomas grew up, the town to which he returned just two weeks ago.

Thomas (August 17, 1981): I'm standing on one of the most unusual corners in the world, I suppose. This is the corner of Victor Avenue and Fourth Street in Victor, Colorado. When I lived in this particular area, this was said to be the number-one gold mining camp in North America, turning out more gold than any other mining camp.

Charles Collingwood: Only about 300 people live in Victor now, but when young Lowell Thomas lived there around the turn of the century, the population was close to 15,000 and was home to the men who worked the mines of the Cripple Creek Mining District.

He was born April 6th, 1892, in Woodington, Ohio, the son of school-teachers. But his father, who Thomas called "the most persistent scholar I ever knew," became a doctor. He moved the family first to Iowa, then back here to Colorado, to Cripple Creek, where a mining-town boyhood prepared Thomas for anything. He returned to Victor earlier this month and recalled his childhood years.

Thomas: There's the old railway station. There's the house where I used to live at the head of it. See that one up there, the white one? Marianna?

Marianna (Thomas's wife): Yes.

Thomas: We lived there at one time. Beautiful house. Yeah, it's been remod-eled. And the post office on the left, my father at one time had his office on the second floor there. And on our right was the Monarch Saloon. The town was full of saloons in those days, patronized by too many people. I've forgot-ten the names of many of these places. They've all been changed now. Where it says cafe, that used to be a saloon; where it says grocery, that used to be a saloon. And so on and so on.

Collingwood: Thomas came to believe that every town had more saloons and gambling halls than stores, with a red-light district only a few blocks away. But he remembered, "Hardly a day passed without Dad reading aloud to us from Shakespeare and the English poets, from the Bible and Kipling and Mark Twain." And if the bloody ten-month strike of the miners was part of his boy-hood, the no-questions-asked frontier town set Thomas along his own golden road to Samarkand, to fortune and fame. He spoke about that to Mike Wallace in 1970.

Mike Wallace: Why is it that you keep on working?

Thomas: Well, the only answer that I could give you—and this is not a very intelligent one—is that I've been working since I was a small child. I started selling papers in gambling halls and saloons when I was, oh, nine or ten years old.

Wallace: Out in Colorado?

Thomas: In Colorado in a mining camp. And I've been working that way all my life. It's second nature. I don't know what else to do but work and have fun. I also play games.

Wallace: I guess it was your dad who started you into the reporting business, though, wasn't it?

Thomas: No, my father was a mining surgeon. But he also had a rather odd idea. He thought that ability to speak in public was one of the most useful things that a human being could have, and he went to work on me trying to train me from the time I was four or five years old. But when I got to the usual age of rebellion—that's high-school age—I would have nothing to do with it at all.

Wallace: With public speaking?

Thomas: No, I didn't want anything to do with it. But then one day, by accident, I was called upon to speak in another part of America, in a high school where I was unknown. And as a result of my speaking before the student body that day—which was sheer accident and a long story and I won't tell it to you—as a result of that, everyone in the school spoke to me from then on. And I thought, "Well, this is extraordinary." And two weeks later I was elected captain of the football team, and I really wasn't the man for it, but I thought, "Well, perhaps my father had something." And from that time on I began to make more and more use of that.

Collingwood: Talking all the time, one can be sure, as he had learned at his father's knee, Lowell Thomas then embarked on his educational career. The family moved back to Ohio when he was fifteen. He won prizes in high school for elocution; attended Valparaiso University, where he got a B.S. degree in two years; then went back to Colorado to become a reporter and editor of the Cripple Creek newspaper. From there, he got his Master's degree at the University of Denver, then went to Chicago to study law. But his interest in news kept intervening, as he told Walter Cronkite at last year's Republican convention, where he had seconded the nomination of George Bush.

Cronkite: We haven't done many conventions that you and I haven't— haven't been able to exchange a few words since 1952, and you go back a little bit further than that, don't you?

Thomas: 1912.

Cronkite: 1912, by golly!

Thomas: The Bull Moose Convention.

Cronkite: Were you a correspondent at that convention?

Thomas: Well, I had been editing a newspaper in Colorado and I came East to study law, and it happened to be right at that time, so I attended the convention. And William Jennings Bryan was working for Hearst as a reporter, and I tried to arrange for Bryan and Teddy Roosevelt to have a picture together with Bryan interviewing TR. TR refused. He wouldn't do it. So I faked something on them. I had Bryan sit in a chair and got him, then the next day I got Teddy Roosevelt in the opposite chair, and then I made a composite picture. (Laughs)

Cronkite: Lowell Thomas, you're not telling me that! You're confessing that now, but—

Thomas (laughing): I know. Well, I got over that a little later on.

Collingwood: When the United States entered the First World War, that was a place he wanted to go, and he was sent there by, of all agencies, the Department of the Interior. His job was to film the war to bring it home to Americans. That he did, covering battle fronts from the North Sea to the Mediterranean. He got as far as Palestine, where occurred the turning point of his career.

Thomas: In the First World War, there were not very many cameramen and I took a cameraman along with me. There wasn't so much known about film-ing wars in those days. I happened to be one of only three covering the Near East campaign, the Palestine campaign. And how—how fortunate can you be to—to be only one of three covering one of the most important campaigns of all time? And then in addition to that I had the fantastic good luck of hav-ing one war entirely to myself, covering it all alone. That was the Arabian campaign. Just by chance—

Man: That's where you met T. E. Lawrence.

Thomas: I was with Lawrence for a time in the Arabian campaign and was the only observer with him, which, of course, was a fantastic opportunity.

Collingwood: Lowell Thomas made the most of that opportunity. He created a living legend of T. E. Lawrence and the beginnings of a fortune for him-self. The book that evolved from all this, *With Lawrence in Arabia*, went through 30 printings.

All this led to another opportunity. In 1930, William S. Paley, then, as now, chairman of CBS, impressed with Thomas's public-speaking ability and growing fame, thought he would be a natural for broadcasting, and Thomas joined CBS.

Thomas: I had the first regular network news broadcast in history, and that's fantastic good luck. I did the first broadcast from an airplane, I did the first from down in the mine, the first from a ship at sea.

Collingwood: He left CBS in 1932 for NBC, where he stayed 15 years. But all the while he was traveling, seeing new places, meeting new people. Naturally gregarious and a substantial public personality himself, he came to know everyone who counted, interviewing them, picking their brains and having his picked by them. He was often asked which of those world leaders had impressed him most. His answer surprised some reporters.

Thomas: I don't think I've ever really seriously and intentionally looked for a wise man, but I've often thought and often wondered if there was a wise man in the world anywhere. And I—I sometimes think that perhaps the wisest human being I ever knew was a man who was belittled for a time by his own countrymen and who was pushed aside. That was Mr. Hoover. I think he was one of the wisest human beings I ever knew. He was—he was a colossus. You know, we don't always elect our ablest people to high office, and in his case, just by chance, we—I think we had selected one of the giants of all time.

Collingwood: For 17 years, besides his travels and his radio broadcasting, Thomas was also the voice of Movietone News.

Thomas: Lowell Thomas speaking, flashing to you the news of the world pictured by Fox-Movietone.

Collingwood: Week by week, between the halves of a double-feature movie, his voice would be the accompaniment to the pictorial history of our times.

Thomas (Movietone News): Stirring days in Japan. The Emperor Hirohito attends a gala military review. Crisis in China as Tokyo advances the prestige of Nippon in the five northern provinces. Japan faces imperial destiny.

Collingwood: Somehow or other—one wonders how—Lowell Thomas continued to fit into all this what would be a full schedule of travel for someone who had nothing else to do: Tibet, Nepal, India, Africa. Wherever he had not been was where he wanted to go next, and eventually he would, usually to the most out-of-the-way places.

Thomas: My name is Sinbad—Sinbad the sailor. Here in the Persian Gulf, we are surrounded by magic names that fair tingle with romance. There's Trebizond and Far Yarkand, Rangoon and Singapore. There's Kermanshah and Kalimpong, Bombay and Bangalore. There's Timbuktu and Samarkand, Baghdad and Teheran, Potala, Lhasa, and Mombasa, Shiraz and Isfahan.

Collingwood: The pictures he'd brought back became material for a series called *High Adventure with Lowell Thomas,* which appeared on CBS in the late '50s. His trips verged on exploration, and he became not only a member of The Explorers Club of New York but, along with Admiral Peary, the first man to reach the North Pole, he was one of four honorary lifetime presidents of the club.

Henry Evans of The Explorers Club talked with Chris Kelley about Lowell Thomas as explorer.

Chris Kelley: Do you think he was more of an adventurer as opposed to explorer?

Henry Evans: I don't think so. I think one of the reasons why he never came to grief in his travels is because he was so well prepared and took these things in account, so that his time would be well spent and that he would come back with what he went to find. But adventure is something that happens to people, when a thing is unexpected. And his endurance has a great deal to do with his preparation and his knowledge of the fitness of things.

Kelley: How best do you remember Lowell Thomas?

Evans: As a very genial person, dynamic and, at the same time, knowing. He never did anything that he hadn't had any preparation for, so far as I know. It always seemed that way. Not calculating, but knowing.

Kelley: Have we seen the last of that sort of breed with the passing of Lowell Thomas?

Evans: Take it from me, it'll probably be a long time before another emerges. That's what I think.

Thomas: Good evening, everybody. This is Lowell Thomas. . .

Collingwood: In 1947, Lowell Thomas returned to CBS to do a 15-minute Monday-through-Friday broadcast. Part of the deal was that he could broadcast from his beloved estate in Pawling, New York, which he had bought in 1926.

After his retirement from regular broadcasting in 1976, he undertook a series for public broadcasting—*Lowell Thomas Remembers.*

Thomas (Lowell Thomas Remembers): They called him "Blackjack" because, as a young officer, he was in command of a crack negro outfit. He served his country in style for many, many years, and he was regarded as a classic soldier.

Hello, everybody. This is Lowell Thomas remembering with you the life of General John J. Pershing—a West Pointer, a guerrilla fighter among the Indians. Then he went through the Spanish-American War, and for a time he had a command in the Philippines. And he came to the attention of the American people mainly when he went into Mexico, chasing the bandit Pancho Villa.

Man: I used to listen to you when I was a kid back in Pennsylvania on the evening news.

Collingwood: That was in Victor, Colorado, early this month. Lowell was there to inaugurate a museum partly devoted to him and his exploits. He had come full circle—from a boy selling newspapers in Victor's saloons to a returning hero, one who had chronicled nearly 70 years of history. He'd come a long way from Victor, but he was still at home there, as he was wherever he went. And he went to a lot of places.

Thomas: This is Lowell Thomas, inviting you to join me in a return to the land of Shangri-La here at the top of the world. Not long ago, this was a forbidden country. Very few travelers ever journeyed to this mysterious, sealed-off mountain kingdom. But we're going to make that journey. We're going to climb up into the world of the fabled Sherpa mountaineers.

Collingwood: He sought adventure all his life and, hence, Lowell Thomas's life became a constant adventure. No mean epitaph, that.

Cronkite: Some of Lowell Thomas's friends and colleagues are here tonight to recall the man and his work. Eric Sevareid is in our Washington studio, and here with me in New York are Charles Collingwood and Dallas Townsend.

Eric, what's your most vivid memory of Lowell Thomas?

Eric Sevareid: Well, I think it was the night of the Dewey defeat in '48. Dewey was his neighbor and his great friend. Let me say first, Walter, that I realize it's almost hard to feel grief at Lowell's death, because he won, you know. He accomplished life in such an absolutely full and joyous and complete way. And I think we all envied that quality in that man.

But the scene that I do remember so much was when we were broadcasting returns of the Truman-Dewey election in a little radio station in New York. I was there, Ed Murrow, I think Charley Daly and some others, and we had some guests. That started the tradition of a few guests, distinguished people—one was Irene Dunn, the actress, I remember—sitting down in front of us in little seats. And Lowell was there wearing that white Stetson of his, which he kept on all evening, absolutely certain that his close friend and neighbor, Tom Dewey, was going to be the next President.

I think he had taught Dewey how to speak, because when you listened to Dewey's speeches and closed your eyes you heard Lowell Thomas and that very distinctive way.

But anyway, as the returns went on, Lowell's smile slowly faded and his head slowly drooped and that hat went down over his eyes. And late, late in the evening, when it was clear that Dewey wasn't going to make it, I think he fell either into a deep sleep or into a depression, but he was immobile. And that I never forgot.

Cronkite: Dallas, when did you first meet Lowell Thomas?

Dallas Townsend: Well, Walter, I met Lowell for the first time more than 40 years ago, in November, 1940. I was studying at Columbia then, and I was taking tickets at Baker Field for some of the Columbia football games, and I saw Lowell coming toward me. I recognized him, of course, so I said, "Hello, Mr. Thomas." And he reached out his hand and grabbed mine in that powerful grip of his, and he said, "Hello, young fellow. How are you?" And a couple of years ago, I reminded him of that at a Dutch Treat dinner, at which I had the pleasure of giving him the Dutch Treat Club's annual award for outstanding service. And Lowell said, "How can you remember a thing like that?" And I said, "Lowell, how could I forget?"

Cronkite (laughing): He had a way with people in exactly that style. Everybody he met, as far as I know, he made a friend of. And he had a million of them around the world.

Townsend: More than anybody I ever met.

Cronkite: All walks of life, because of that very thing. If you spoke to Lowell Thomas, he spoke back, grabbed your hand, and you were one of his followers from that point on.

Charles, you had a long acquaintance with him. You substituted for him, as Dallas did, as I did.

Collingwood: Well, I substituted for him in 1949, when he went on that famous expedition to Tibet, on which he broke his leg, and so, instead of six weeks, it stretched on to longer. So I (was) doing his show for a long time.

But you know what I remember best? It was when, a couple of years ago, maybe three, I was in Denver doing something, a broadcast—a series of broadcasts that you and I did on education in the United States, and I was in Denver doing it. And I was staying at Brown's Hotel, and I guess the desk told him I was there. And anyway, he had slipped a note under my door saying, "Just passing through. Heard you were here. Would you like to have breakfast at eight or eight-thirty in the morning?" Well, it turned out I had a breakfast with the president of the board of education or whatever, and so I palmed him off on somebody and sat with Lowell and his wife. Now here he was, 86 or 87 by then, and he looked at his watch and he said, "Well, I've got to go off because we're going skiing at 15,000 feet altitude." And when I looked back and thought back and I thought of the enormous energy, vitality which still flowed, as it had flowed throughout his entire life—

Cronkite: The biggest problem I had with Lowell Thomas was this problem of skiing. I remember when he first met Art Devlin and decided that skiing was the thing. And he was in his 60s then. And he and Art Devlin developed—I'm sure it was Art Devlin . . . I don't think I've got the person wrong . . . I'm sure it was Art—developed the short skis, the shortie skis. And he built a ski run up at Pawling, at Quaker Hill, at his house, so that he could ski every morning, and at the age of 60 with these short skis, and even jumping. He was doing little jumps at the time. And he—every time you saw him, or I saw him thereafter, he said, "You ought to be on skis. You're the kind of guy that'd really love skiing." Well, I tried to pacify Lowell by saying I tried it, but I was really lying quite a lot. I didn't try it very hard. But there he was in his 60s doing this thing. . . .

Townsend: You know, Charles, you mentioned his breaking his leg in Tibet—

Collingwood: Yeah.

Townsend: —which was a very painful and arduous experience—

Collingwood: Yes, it was.

Townsend: —just getting him back to New York for the operation. And afterwards the doctor told him that he would walk with a permanent limp and would never ski again. And Lowell said, "Nonsense, I'll be skiing by Christmas!" And he was.

Collingwood: He was absolutely indestructible. And this, I think, is one of the things he'll be remembered for. I don't think he made very many particularly memorable broadcasts. That wasn't his stock in trade, as it was Ed Murrow's, Eric's, yours, Dallas's, others. He'll be remembered for the life that he led—a life full of incident, adventure, everything.

Cronkite: I think one of the really remarkable things about the man was he was a producer. The precision with which he did everything. He was thinking it through. He lived a life of adventure, but he knew what he was up to when he was doing it.

Collingwood: Yes, indeed.

Cronkite: Eric, when was the last time you saw him?

Sevareid: Well, I think the last time was when he made a speech here at the (Overseas) Press Club—I don't know, three, four, or five years ago—and he talked for an hour and a half. He held that audience absolutely in his grip. See, Lowell was a storyteller. As a journalist, he was a kind of a wandering

minstrel in prose. He didn't care who took care of the country's macroeco-
nomics or geopolitics as long as he could tell its stories. He just loved the face
of the earth. I suppose he would have agreed with Macaulay, you know, who
wrote somewhere that there are two things that endure through the ages. One
is the great features of nature and the other is the human heart. And Lowell
loved the seas and the deserts and the mountains and he loved stories about
people, and that's almost a kind of journalism that's gone, I'm afraid. We're
all too damn serious.

Cronkite: Yeah. I think that the fact that he loved stories about people made
him love people. He was always seeking out anybody who had a story to tell
or had anything of vitality to express. And I saw him just three or four weeks
ago and he was still up to his old game. He was climbing up and down the
hills of California, visiting various friends in those hills and having a ball. And
I think he went the way we all would like to go—after a full life, as Eric said
a little earlier, and with no regrets.

Sevareid: Yes.

Cronkite: And whether or not he considered himself a journalist, Lowell
Thomas enjoyed enormous success bringing people the news over four
decades. And we didn't get around to talking about it here, but how do you
account for that? One analyst said that it was because Thomas had a voice
like an organ. But that wasn't the whole thing, of course, at all. Another
argued that Thomas and radio were invented for each other, and since
Thomas was invented first, he could make the medium do his bidding. A
columnist believed that Thomas gave the impression of saying, "Now
here's the news with some human slants on it and you can interpret it to
suit yourself."

Well, Thomas himself recalled, "Over the years, I have had only two
absolute rules on the air. The first is not to confuse opinions with hard news
or to be drawn into taking sides. My second rule has been to remember

always that the disembodied voice behind the dial comes from a human being." That's not a bad legacy for a newsman to leave.

But the final words tonight should come, once again, from Lowell Thomas. He somewhat altered his famous sign-off on the occasion of his final nightly news broadcast in 1976.

Thomas: Instead of my usual "So long until tomorrow"—or until Monday, since this is Friday—tonight it will simply be: "Here's to all of you. So long."

—*THE EXPLORERS JOURNAL*, DECEMBER 1987

Permissions Acknowledgments

Jørgen Bitsch, "Woman, You Are A Beast", previously unpublished; published with permission of the author, 1970s.

Steven Eisenpreis, son of Alfred Eisenpreis, "Exploration Defined" from *The Explorers Journal*, Fall 2002.

Estate of L. Ron Hubbard, "It Bears Telling" from *Through Hell and High Water* (1941).

Howard Joiner, "Lowell Thomas Milestones" from *The Explorers Journal*, December 1987.

Prince Joli Kansil, "Pitcairn Island After 200 Years" from *The Explorers Journal*, September 1989.

Reeve Lindbergh, son of Charles Lindbergh, "A Leap in the Dark" from *Told at The Explorers Club* (1931).

Stanley Olsen, "The Elephant-Headed Deity Ganesh" from *The Explorers Journal*, June 1990.

Robert M. Peck, "Hunting Wildlife with Pen and Palette" from *The Explorers Journal*, December 1988.

Milbry Polk, "On Exploration" from *The Explorers Journal*, Spring 2002.

Glenn Porzak, "1990 American Everest-Lhotse Expedition" from *The Explorers Journal*, Summer 1991.

Kathleen Saville, "Rowing Across the Atlantic" and "Rowing Across the Pacific Ocean One Stroke at a Time" from *The Explorers Journal*, March 1982, and December 1985.

Lowell Thomas, Jr., son of Lowell Thomas, "Memories of the Last Crusade," from *Explorers Club Tales* (1936) and "Over the Khyber to Kabul," from *Through Hell and High Water* (1941).

A good faith effort has been made by both The Explorers Club and The Lyons Press to locate all authors, their heirs, or their estates, for the purpose of obtaining permission to use material in this compendium. In those few cases where we were unable to locate an author, his heirs, or his estate, the Lyons Press will offer due compensation, should a permissions claim be made.